D0217008

An Introduction to Criminal Evidence

A CASEBOOK APPROACH

R. ALAN THOMPSON, Ph.D.
The University of Southern Mississippi

LISA S. NORED, J.D., Ph.D.
The University of Southern Mississippi

JOHN L. WORRALL, Ph.D.
The University of Texas-Dallas

CRAIG HEMMENS, J.D., Ph.D.
Boise State University

New York   Oxford
OXFORD UNIVERSITY PRESS
2008

OXFORD
UNIVERSITY PRESS

Oxford University Press, Inc., publishes works that further
Oxford University's objective of excellence
in research, scholarship, and education.

Oxford New York
Auckland Cape Town Dar es Salaam Hong Kong Karachi
Kuala Lumpur Madrid Melbourne Mexico City Nairobi
New Delhi Shanghai Taipei Toronto

With offices in
Argentina Austria Brazil Chile Czech Republic France Greece
Guatemala Hungary Italy Japan Poland Portugal Singapore
South Korea Switzerland Thailand Turkey Ukraine Vietnam

Copyright © 2008 by Oxford University Press, Inc.

Published by Oxford University Press, Inc.
198 Madison Avenue, New York, New York 10016
www.oup.com

Oxford is a registered trademark of Oxford University Press.

All rights reserved. No part of this publication may be reproduced,
stored in a retrieval system, or transmitted, in any form or by any means,
electronic, mechanical, photocopying, recording, or otherwise,
without the prior permission of Oxford University Press.

Library of Congress Cataloging-in-Publication Data

An introduction to criminal evidence : a casebook approach / R. Alan
Thompson ... [et al.].
p. cm.
Includes bibliographical references.
ISBN 978-0-19-533256-8 (alk. paper)
1. Evidence, Criminal—United States—Cases.   I. Thompson, R. Alan.
KF9660.A7T49 2009
345.73'06—dc22
2007043148

9 8 7 6 5 4 3 2 1

Printed in the United States of America on acid-free paper

CONTENTS

ACKNOWLEDGMENTS

THE AUTHORS ARE APPRECIATIVE OF THE SUPPORT RECEIVED from the editorial staff at Oxford University Press who masterfully guided this project through to completion once acquired from Roxbury. In particular, Sherith Pankratz has been a thoughtful editor as has her assistant, Leigh-Ann Todd-Enyame. The task of production would not have gone as smoothly as it did without the watchful eye and dedicated patience of Marianne Paul. The authors would also like to thank Claude Teweles for his support of our individual and collective projects over the years. Claude has been an exceptional editor, responsible for introducing many unique and valuable texts to the discipline of criminal justice. His presence, and that of Roxbury, will be long remembered and appreciated by many. The authors would also like to thank two members of Claude's staff—Scott Carter and Carla Plucknett—for their administrative assistance and production support.

R. Alan Thompson would like to thank his co-authors for their enduring friendship as well as the opportunity to work alongside such highly respected peers. He would also like to recognize his wife, Leslie, for her courage and love.

Lisa S. Nored would like to acknowledge her dear mother, Camille, her husband, Deron and her dear children, Hunter, Holden, and Hayden.

John L. Worrall would like to thank his co-authors and family for their continued support.

Craig Hemmens would like to thank his co-authors for making life much easier. He would also like to thank Mary and Emily for making his life wonderful.

ABOUT THE AUTHORS

R. Alan Thompson is an Associate Professor in Administration of Justice at The University of Southern Mississippi. He received his Ph.D. in criminal justice from Sam Houston State University in 2001 and previously co-authored *Significant Cases in Criminal Procedure* with Hemmens and Worrall (Roxbury, 2004). He is also the author of *Career Experiences of African American Police Executives: Black in Blue Revisited* (LFB Scholarly, 2003). His other publications have appeared in *International Journal of Police Science and Management*, *Policing: An International Journal of Police Strategies & Management*, *American Journal of Criminal Justice*, and *Journal of Police and Criminal Psychology*. Dr. Thompson is a former police officer and current editor of *Journal of Police and Criminal Psy*chology.

Lisa S. Nored is an Associate Professor of Administration of Justice at the The University of Southern Mississippi, where she serves as Department Chair. She holds a law degree from Mississippi College School of Law and Ph.D. in Public Administration from Mississippi State University. Her teaching and research interests include criminal law and procedure, juvenile justice, and child welfare. Her publications include various journal articles and books, most recently including *Child Advocacy in Mississippi* (Thomson/West, 2005).

John L. Worrall is an Associate Professor of Criminology at the University of Texas at Dallas. He received his Ph.D. in political science from Washington State University in 1999. He is the author of several books, the most recent of which are *Criminal Procedure: From First Contact to Appeal* (Allyn and Bacon, 2007) and *Crime Control in America: An Assessment of the Evidence* (Allyn and Bacon, 2006). His work has appeared in a number of journals, including *Criminology, Evaluation Review,* and *Justice Quarterly.*

Craig Hemmens holds a J.D. from North Carolina Central University School of Law and a Ph.D. in criminal justice from Sam Houston State University. He is a professor in the Department of Criminal Justice at Boise State University, where he has taught since 1996. Professor Hemmens has published ten books and more than a hundred articles on a variety of criminal justice-related topics. His primary research interests are criminal law and procedure and corrections. He has served as the editor of the *Journal of Criminal Justice Education*. His articles have appeared in *Justice Quarterly*, the *Journal of Criminal Justice*, *Crime and Delinquency*, the *Criminal Law Bulletin*, and the *Prison Journal*.

FOREWORD

MARVIN ZALMAN

Jerome Hall's classic essay, "Police and Law in a Democratic Society,"[1] written just eight years after the Allies defeated Germany's Nazi dictatorship in World War II and while the Soviet gulag state was in full bloom in Russia, contrasted policing in a dictatorship with policing in a democracy. Police in dictator-states owe their entire loyalty to the ruler and "are the chief physical instrument of political domination." Democracies are not controlled from the top but are essentially self-governing. Because "police reflect the general culture of the society they represent," in a democratic society they are "trained specialized helpers in a type of law enforcement that is compatible with democratic values." The rule of law, an essential democratic value, means that the "sovereignty of law is opposed to the unfettered power of officials."

Some view law, including criminal evidence, as a dry and narrowly technical subject consisting of a bunch of arbitrary rules. Nothing is further from the truth. Democratic government rests on the rule of law, which in large measure depends on democratic policing. These ends are not achieved by overripe political rhetoric or empty appeals to morality. Democratic policing under the rule of law is achieved by continuing efforts to operate under and through the rules of specific laws. As "trained specialized helpers" who can bring about the kind of order required by a democratic society, today's professional police officers must become experts in substantive criminal law, constitutional criminal procedure, and the law of evidence. This is no easy task. As Jerome Hall noted, "Rules of law are certain standards and commands, expressed in thousands of statutes, decisions, regulations, and in constitutions. It is important to note the interconnectedness of the entire body of legal rules. They are arrangeable in a

[1] *Indiana Law Journal*, 28:133–177 (1953).

harmonious order extending from the very general propositions of constitutional law through the middle range of statutes and decisions, down to the very specific concrete applications of them by police officers."[2]

This admirable text by Alan Thompson, Lisa Nored, John Worrall, and Craig Hemmens helps to fulfil the ideals of democratic policing and the rule of law by placing the subject of criminal evidence in an historical context, a context of constitutional rights, and a context of our judicial system. This context is essential for the higher education of police professionals who will help to ensure a proper balance of order and liberty. This text does not portray evidence law as a series of sterile rules. The chapter on privileges, for example, explores the evolution of legal doctrines. Throughout the text doctrines of substantive criminal law like intoxication and insanity are explored in tandem with the evidentiary rules that guide their admission or exclusion in the trial. These links help students understand how the rules apply in policing and trial practice. This expertly paced text contributes to the general education of university students by honing students' skills in critical thinking, as for example, in the chapter on presumptions and inferences.

Law, of course, is both a grand subject and a technical subject, and the authors do not shirk from explicating the specifics of thorny areas, such as the American law of hearsay. Many would argue that these rules unnecessarily interfere with the search for the truth, in contrast to the more open approach to presenting the facts of a case in the courts of democratic European nations. This may be true, but the hearsay rule, and the entire apparatus of trial by jury, is an inextricable part of *our* system of law and criminal justice, and cannot be avoided. Again, the authors help students understand how the hearsay rule is embedded in our notions of constitutional trial rights including the right to confront adverse witnesses. A great value of the study of criminal evidence is that it conveys to students that the work of policing is not autonomous. It is aimed at the proof of guilt in courts of law, where the efforts of police will be tested by the cross-examination of defense attorneys. Democratic policing is thus part of a group effort in which prosecutors, defense attorneys, juries, and judges play roles, guided by constitutional principles, in upholding not an autocratic but a democratic order.

By absorbing the specific legal rules of evidence law, and by developing skills in legal reasoning, students who will become police officers, prosecutors, defense attorneys and judges gain the intellectual foundations for becoming, in Hall's words, "the living expression[s] of democratic law with all its values, meanings, and potentialities." A text that demonstrates

[2] Hall, Police and Law, p. 144.

the specific ways in which the police function becomes law-abiding as well as law-enforcing, and thereby becomes a democratic police function, is valuable to all citizens, not just to future police officers and lawyers. Democratic policing is vital to a just society because it makes democratic law possible, and democratic law is ethical law that represents self-rule. "[W]e find in democratic law standards of fairness, reasonableness, and human decency. Democratic law expresses and encourages equality and human dignity. It allows free play for value experience and consequent progress. It disciplines officials who otherwise lack definite standards to apply regularly and consistently."[3] The text thus helps to steer educated citizens away from the dangerous assumption that because a society is *labeled* democratic that everything it does *is* democratic. The arduous legal process, with its evolving legislative rules generated by political conflict and its court rulings generated by clashing ideas of right, becomes a discipline in which police officers play important roles as they apply the law in individual cases.

I wish to add that it is gratifying to know that the authors of this text are not only lawyers, but are also social scientists whose ongoing empirical research contributes to the understanding of criminal justice as it grows out of its infancy as an academic discipline. It is unfortunate that too many criminologists and criminal justice scholars view law as a marginal and intellectually unsatisfying subject. In truth, the size, scope, and policy influence of legal writing, both as sources of law (legislation and case law) and as legal scholarship, far outweighs that produced by criminal justice scholars, and at its best is remarkably sophisticated and wide-ranging. It is unfortunate that criminal justice lags behind the discipline of political science in the study of legal institutions, even as the empirical study of courts is not as prominent a part of political science as it was a few years ago. In universities what is taught is properly related to the research interests of faculty members. An unfortunate effect of this salutary relationship is that the relative paucity of court and legal process research in criminal justice tends to devalue the teaching of legal subjects in criminal justice departments. This is a perilous matter because our graduates will go to work in a legal environment, and it is the tenor of that legal environment that will determine whether criminal justice practices will continue toward democratic governance or turn in an autocratic direction.

[3] Ibid., p. 145.

SECTION ONE

Preliminary Matters/
Setting the Stage

CHAPTER 1
INTRODUCTION: A BRIEF HISTORY OF EVIDENCE LAW

Key Terms & Concepts

Administrative regulations

American Law Institute (ALI)

Assistance of counsel

Bill of Rights

Bills of attainder

Code of Hammurabi

Common law

Competent evidence

Constitution

Constitutionalism

Cruel and unusual punishment

Double jeopardy

Dual sovereignty doctrine

Due process

Eighth Amendment

Equal protection

Establishment clause

Evidence

Evidence code

Evidence law

Ex post facto law

Excessive bail

Federal Rules of Evidence (FRE)

Federalism

Fifth Amendment

First Amendment

Fourteenth Amendment

Fourth Amendment

Fundamental rights

Habeas corpus

Impartial jury

Incorporation

Individual rights

Intermediate scrutiny

Judicial review

Legislation

Model Code of Evidence

Ninth Amendment

Particularity requirement

Penal code

Precedent

Probable cause

Public trial

Rational basis review

Relevant evidence

Roman Twelve Tables

Second Amendment

Selective incorporation

Seventh Amendment

Sixth Amendment

Speedy trial

Standards of review

Stare decisis

Statutes

Strict scrutiny

Suspect classifications

Tenth Amendment

Third Amendment

Thirteenth Amendment

Total incorporation

Total incorporation plus

Chapter Learning Objectives

By the end of this chapter, the student should be able to:

- Trace the development of law
- Explain the concepts of precedent and stare decisis
- Identify various sources of law in contemporary society

- Identify various sources of individual rights
- Explain the content of the first fourteen amendments to the Constitution
- Distinguish between the multiple standards of review applied to equal protection claims
- Understand the mechanism by which certain rights have been applied to the states through the process of incorporation
- Identify and explain what is meant by the phrase "fundamental right"
- Relate the history and authority of judicial review
- Understand the purpose and need for evidence law
- Trace the historical development of evidence law

Introduction

The law exists in good measure because people need a mechanism for enforcing order and resolving disputes peacefully. All societies have developed methods of resolving disputes. Laws provide rules to guide conduct, as well as a means of resolving disputes and maintaining order. The court system of today is simply one form of conflict resolution. Laws are created by legislatures; the courts are the mechanism whereby laws are enforced.

In this text we focus on the rules of evidence and the legal decisions that interpret those rules. Collectively these are referred to as the law of evidence, or the set of rules that govern how trials are conducted. The law of evidence applies to both civil and criminal trials, although some significant and important differences exist between civil and criminal law. This book focuses on the application of evidence law to criminal trials. Evidence law is (or at least should be) an exciting subject of study, as it governs the conduct of trials and plays a major role in the criminal justice process. Although much of evidence law may seem peculiar at first, there are very good reasons for (virtually) every rule of evidence. It is our hope that this book will help you, the student, understand the significance of this important subject.

In this chapter we discuss the historical development of the law, focusing on the Anglo-American concepts of the common law, precedent, and stare decisis. We also examine the sources of law as well as the sources of evidence law in particular.

Development of the Law

The earliest examples of conflict resolution can be found in pre-industrial societies, which had informal rules for how individuals were to act and relate to each other. Disputes arose and were settled by the tribal leadership, which usually consisted of a king/chief and his deputies, or councilors. The tribal leader was expected to act on behalf of the entire tribe and not be an advocate for one side against the other.

The Western legal tradition may be traced to the **Code of Hammurabi**, the first known written legal code, which expressed a retribution-oriented "eye for an eye" philosophy. Roman law, the next major codified set of legal principles, was heavily influenced by Babylonian legal principles. The **Roman Twelve Tables** (450 B.C.) was the first entirely secular written legal code. Around this time, crimes came to be seen as offenses against not just the victim but society as well. However, trials as we understand them today still did not exist.

http://www.fordham.edu/halsall/ancient/12tables.html

The spread of the Roman Empire brought Roman law to Western Europe. The Norman Conquest (1066) brought feudal law to the British Isles. During the following several hundred years, England developed what came to be known as the common law system.

Common Law

After the Norman Conquest, the new rulers established new forms of government, including courts of law. By the reign of Henry II (1154–1189), a body of law had been developed that was applied not just in local courts, but nationally. Decisions began to be written down, circulated, and summarized. The result was a more unified body of law, which came to be known as the **common law** because it was in force throughout the country; it was literally the law in common throughout England. The common law system was well developed in England by the thirteenth century.

The common law was judge-made law. That is, it was law created by judges as they heard cases and settled disputes. Judges wrote down their decisions and in doing so attempted to justify the decision by reference to custom, tradition, history, and prior judicial decisions. As judges began to rely on previous judgments, they developed the concepts of stare decisis and precedent. Of course, for there to be precedent there must be prior decisions. At first, judges made decisions without referring to other cases or courts. They simply heard a case and decided the appropriate outcome, based on their understanding of the law as they had learned it through the reading of legal treatises and encyclopedias. But as time went by, judges came to rely on prior decisions as a means of justifying their decision in a particular case. From this came the reliance on precedent and the concept of stare decisis.

Precedent and Stare Decisis

Under the common law system, every final decision by a court creates **precedent**. Precedent governs the court issuing the decision as well as any lower, or inferior, courts. The common law system was brought to America by the early colonists. Many of the principles of the common law, including precedent and the concept of stare decisis, remain in force today in American courts. Thus, all courts within a particular state are bound to follow the decisions of the highest court in the state, usually known as the state supreme court. All courts in the federal court system are bound to follow the decisions of the United States Supreme Court. This is the notion of precedent.

However, precedent is binding only on those courts within the jurisdiction of the court issuing the opinion. Thus, for example, a decision of the Idaho Supreme Court is not binding on Wyoming courts. Wyoming courts are not subject to the jurisdiction or control of Idaho courts, and thus are free to interpret the law differently from Idaho courts if they see fit to do so. Decisions from courts in other jurisdictions, while not binding, may be persuasive, however. This simply means that another court may give consideration and weight to the opinion of other courts. Thus, a Wyoming court may, if it chooses, consider the judgment of an Idaho court. Courts may do so when faced with an issue they have not dealt with before but that other courts have examined.

Stare decisis means "let the decision stand." Under the principle of **stare decisis**, if a prior decision on a legal issue applies to a current case, the court will be guided by that prior decision and apply the same legal principles in the current case. Stare decisis is thus a means of establishing the value of prior decisions, or precedent. In other words, if an issue has been decided one way, it will continue to be decided that way in future cases. Through reliance on precedent and the principle of stare decisis, common law courts are able to provide litigants with some degree of predictability regarding the courts' decisions.

Precedent is not necessarily unchangeable. Judge-made law may be set aside or overruled by a legislative act if the constitution permits the legislature to do so. Additionally, the court that issued the precedent may overrule it, or a higher court may reverse the decision of a lower court.

If an intermediate-level appeals court decides an issue one way and the losing party appeals to a higher appeals court (such as the state supreme court), that higher court may reverse the decision of the lower court. Higher-level appeals courts are not bound by the judgments of lower courts; they are bound only by the decisions of courts above them. Stare decisis, then, involves a respect for, and belief in, the validity of precedent. Precedent is simply the influence of prior cases on current cases.

Courts are understandably reluctant to reverse previously rendered decisions, because doing so is a tacit admission of error. Courts do make reversals, however, when presented with a compelling justification. Thus, stare decisis is not an inflexible doctrine but rather the general rule—there are always exceptions, as with most areas of the law! Alternatively, rather than expressly overrule a prior decision, a court may instead seek to distinguish the prior case from the present case on the ground that the facts are slightly different. By doing so, the court can avoid overruling a prior decision while coming to what it considers the proper result in the present case. Until a decision is expressly overruled, it stands as an accurate statement of legal principles, or "good law."

Sources of Law

The two main sources of law are judge-made law (the common law) and legislative law (which includes the Constitution, statutes, ordinances, and administrative regulations). There are others, but these are the most common. In addition, it should be remembered that there are other sources for what constitutes appropriate conduct, such as religion and ethics.

Legislation may be enacted by a legislature under the authority granted it by a constitution. A **constitution** creates a government; it literally *constitutes* the government. Legislatures are given the authority to act in certain areas. Legislative enactments, or bills, are often referred to as **statutes,** and statutes are collected into codes. Statutory law includes civil and criminal law. The criminal law is sometimes referred to as the **penal code**.

Legislators are sometimes referred to as *lawmakers* because they quite literally make law. Acts of the legislature are not, however, per se lawful. In other words, just because a legislature passes a bill does not mean the bill is a lawful exercise of the legislature's authority. Acts of the legislature may not limit the constitution under which the legislature was created. Thus, for instance, the United States Congress may not lawfully pass legislation that abolishes the First Amendment. The Constitution may be changed only by a constitutional amendment, which can be passed only by following certain procedures set forth in the Constitution itself.

Who decides when the legislature has acted beyond the scope of its authority? In the United States, it is the Supreme Court that has the final say as to the legality of statutes passed by either state or federal legislatures. This concept, known as the power of **judicial review**, is discussed in greater detail later in this chapter.

Administrative regulations are another form of legislation that may, under certain circumstances, have the force of law. That is, they will be enforced by the courts just like statutes. Administrative regulations are issued either by agencies of the executive branch, which derive their authority from a delegation of power by the executive, or by independent agencies created through a delegation of power from the legislature. Examples include regulations affecting food and drugs and occupational safety requirements. Both the federal and state governments have administrative regulations.

Statutes are frequently written broadly, leaving administrative agencies with the task of filling in the blanks. Agencies are empowered to do so through the delegation of authority to them by the executive or legislative branch. Common examples include the Department of Health and Human Services and the Department of Veterans Affairs. Violation of an administrative regulation is generally treated not as a crime but as a civil violation.

Just as statutes are often written broadly, leaving much room for interpretation, so too is the U.S. Constitution. For example, the Fourth Amendment prohibits "unreasonable searches and seizures." So what is unreasonable? For that matter, what constitutes a search or a seizure? There are no easy answers to these questions, and the U.S. Supreme Court has struggled to define the terms.

Why, then, are statutes ambiguous? Why don't the legislatures write more clearly and explain exactly what they mean? There are several reasons. First is the difficulty in defining, in a few sentences, something involving human conduct—there is an almost infinite range of possible actions by individuals. Second, legislators are politicians, and politics involves compromise. Thus, a statute may be written so that it appeals to the greatest possible number of legislators, but as a result the language of the statute may be watered down and made less precise rather than more precise. This situation is particularly likely to happen with controversial issues. Politicians may simply decide to leave it to the courts to more clearly define the terms of a statute. While judges in some jurisdictions hold office for life and cannot be removed simply for declaring legislation void, in many states judges are elected and thus are subject to removal if the electorate does not approve of their interpretation of legislation.

Sources of Individual Rights

There are several sources of *individual rights* in the United States: federal and state constitutions, case law, court rules, and legislation. **Individual rights** are those rights that are possessed by the individual and that protect him or her from others as well as from the government. Examples include the freedom of speech, freedom of religion, and the right to counsel. The Constitution, particularly the Bill of Rights, is the primary source of individual rights. Although states are free to provide more individual rights than the Constitution does, neither Congress nor a state may enact a law that abridges a federal constitutional right. This is because the Constitution is paramount—it is the supreme law of the United States.

The Constitution

In 1787 delegates from 12 of the 13 original states met in Philadelphia, at the request of the Continental Congress, to write a new Constitution. The Continental Congress was hampered by lack of power vis-à-vis the states, so the delegates realized a new nation would need a stronger central government. Supporters of a strong centralized government were called Federalists. Supporters of a weak central government, with power left almost entirely in the hands of the states, were what today are called states' rights supporters.

The Continental Congress was formed through the adoption of the Articles of Confederation in 1781. This first attempt at creating a unified United States was a failure, in large part because the federal government created by the articles was virtually without power. It lacked the authority to tax, to raise an army, and to force the states to comply with any mandates.

http://www.yale.edu/lawweb/avalon/artconf.htm

The result of the convention in Philadelphia was the creation of the *United States Constitution*. The Constitution differs from ordinary legislation in that it is primarily concerned with establishing the powers and limitations of the government, both between the branches of government and between the government and the individual citizen. The Constitution itself contains few protections of individual rights. The only individual rights mentioned in the Constitution proper are the right to seek a writ of **habeas corpus** (request for release from unlawful detention or imprisonment), the prohibition on **bills of attainder** (legislation imposing punishment without trial), and the prohibition on **ex post facto laws** (legislation making prior conduct criminal).

When the Constitution was submitted to the states for ratification, several states were reluctant to ratify it without more clear-cut protections of individual rights. In response to these concerns, the Bill of Rights was added. These provisions were initially drawn up by James Madison as additions to the original Constitution. Madison's proposals were condensed into ten amendments, commonly referred to as the *Bill of Rights.* With the addition of these amendments, the Constitution was ratified in 1788.

http://www.archives.gov/national-archives-experience/charters/constitution.html

The Bill of Rights

The first eight amendments enumerate individual rights. These rights include protections against government action of all kinds. It should be noted, however, that these rights were originally intended to apply only to actions by the federal government. The Bill of Rights was added to reduce the fears of states' rights supporters who thought a strong central government would infringe on the rights of citizens of the states (Anastaplo, 1995). It was not until the twentieth century that the provisions of the Bill of Rights were applied to actions of state governments, through a process referred to as *incorporation*. We will discuss incorporation later, after reviewing the most significant provisions of the Bill of Rights.

First Amendment

> Congress shall make no law respecting an establishment of religion, or prohibiting the free exercise thereof; or abridging the freedom of speech, or of the press; or the right of the people peaceably to assemble, and to petition the Government for a redress of grievances.

The **First Amendment** establishes the freedom of religion, freedom of speech, freedom of the press, and freedom of assembly. It is not surprising that the very first provision of the Bill of Rights deals with these topics because religion was a primary force in the settling of America. Religion held a central position in people's lives in England in the 1500s and 1600s, and many bloody conflicts had occurred over which should be the official religion of England. Colonists sought to avoid such conflicts and to avoid further persecution for their religious beliefs. Freedom of speech and of the press and the freedom to assemble peacefully were also issues of great concern for the colonists prior to the American Revolution.

With respect to religion, there are two guarantees in the First Amendment: The government shall not establish an official, state-supported religion, nor shall it interfere with individuals' religious practices. The essence of these two clauses is that the government is not to be in the business of either promoting or destroying religion. Whereas the state was heavily involved in religion in England, the founding fathers wanted government to stay out of the business of religion entirely.

The first guarantee is often referred to as the **establishment clause**. It creates what the U.S. Supreme Court has referred to as a "wall of separation between church and state" (*Everson v. Board of Education,* 1947). This doctrine does not mean the government cannot be to some degree involved in religion, but the Supreme Court has stated that any statute affecting religion is valid only if three condition are met: The statute must have a secular (nonreligious) purpose, the primary purpose of the statute must be neither pro-nor anti-religion, and the statute must not foster "excessive" government entanglement with religion (*Lemon v. Kurtzman,* 1971).

This guarantee does not mean the freedom to worship is absolute. Valid government regulations that incidentally restrict religious practices are permitted. Thus, a state may ban polygamy under its authority to enact health and safety regulations, even though this legislation at one time imposed a restriction on the religious practices of some Mormon sects.

The freedom of speech is one of the most treasured rights possessed by Americans. This right has been accorded great, but not total, weight by the Supreme Court. The Court has held that the freedom of speech includes the right to say things that may anger others, including so-called hate speech or speech directed at minority groups. The Court has also held that the freedom of speech includes not just verbal statements but written statements and some physical acts. These physical acts, when intended to make a point, are referred to as "symbolic speech" or "expressive conduct." Examples include signs, picketing, and even the burning of the American flag (*Texas v. Johnson,* 1989).

Freedom of speech is not absolute, however. The Supreme Court has held that the government can regulate obscenity (*Miller v. California,* 1973), as well as speech that is likely to provoke a violent response, or "fighting words" (*Chaplinsky v. New Hampshire,* 1942). Commercial speech may be regulated to a greater degree than so-called "political" speech (*Virginia State Board of Pharmacy v. Virginia Citizens Consumers Council, Inc.,* 1976). In general, however, the Supreme Court looks with disfavor on attempts to curb speech. Instead, the Court has repeatedly endorsed the view of Justice Oliver Wendell Holmes that society is improved by permitting a "free marketplace of ideas."

Second Amendment

A well regulated Militia being necessary to the security of a free State, the right of the people to keep and bear Arms shall not be infringed.

The **Second Amendment** provides citizens with the right to "keep and bear arms," and states that this right shall not be "infringed." Opponents of gun control legislation seize upon this wording as support for their claim that the state may not limit the use and possession of firearms. The history of the amendment suggests this interpretation may not be completely accurate, however, and the Supreme Court has repeatedly held that states may regulate firearms, upholding legislation that prohibits the possession of certain weapons and that requires firearm registration.

The history behind the Second Amendment suggests it was intended, at least in part, not to allow individuals to possess any weapons they wanted as protection against other individuals but rather to allow the states and groups of citizens (a militia) to have weapons to protect themselves against oppression by the federal government. There was a great concern at the time of the passage of the Bill of Rights that the federal government might become oppressive, and allowing states to form militias would not be of much use if the federal government had previously outlawed weapons. At this time there were no public stores of weapons, so if the federal government were to prohibit private ownership, states would be unable to fight back because their citizens would be unarmed.

Third Amendment

No Soldier shall, in time of peace be quartered in any house, without the consent of the Owner, nor in time of war, but in a manner to be prescribed by law.

The **Third Amendment** is another amendment that was a product of its times. Prior to the Revolution, English troops were sometimes housed in the homes of private citizens, against the wishes of the owners. The Third Amendment makes such a practice unconstitutional by expressly forbidding the quartering of soldiers in private homes against the wishes of the owners at any time.

Fourth Amendment

The right of the people to be secure in their persons, houses, papers, and effects, against unreasonable searches and seizures, shall not be violated, and no Warrants shall issue, but upon probable cause, supported by Oath or affirmation, and particularly describing the place to be searched, and the persons or things to be seized.

The **Fourth Amendment** is the provision of the Constitution that stands most directly between the individual citizen and the police. This amendment forbids "unreasonable" searches and seizures and requires the existence of probable cause before warrants may be issued or a search or seizure may take place. Additionally, warrants are required to describe their subject with "particularity."

The **particularity requirement** is a response to the British practice in colonial times of issuing general warrants. General warrants allowed British customs inspectors to search for virtually anything, anywhere, at any time. The colonists found this practice most distressing, and it was one of the prime precipitating factors in the Revolution.

Requiring probable cause to search or seize was the Founding Fathers' attempt to limit the ability of the police to interfere at will in the lives of individual citizens. Instead, they must have some amount of evidence that the person is a criminal. This degree of proof is probable cause. **Probable cause** indicates a greater probability than not that a crime has occurred. It is less than proof beyond a reasonable doubt, but more than a hunch.

The Fourth Amendment does not forbid all searches and seizures but rather requires that they not be unreasonable. The obvious question, then, is what is reasonable? Courts have struggled mightily to define this phrase. Much of criminal procedure law is devoted to an explication of this phrase.

Fifth Amendment

No person shall be held to answer for a capital, or otherwise infamous crime, unless on a presentment or indictment of a Grand Jury, except in cases arising in the land or naval forces, or in the Militia, when in actual service in time of War or public danger; nor shall any person be subject for the same offence to be twice put in jeopardy of life or limb; nor shall be compelled in any criminal case to be a witness against himself, nor be deprived of life, liberty, or property, without due process of law; nor shall private property be taken for public use, without just compensation.

The **Fifth Amendment** provides a number of protections for individual citizens. They include the right to an indictment by a grand jury, freedom from double jeopardy, the right to due process and just compensation, and the privilege against self-incrimination. These rights are all associated with criminal trials. Many of the provisions of the Fifth Amendment were born out of reaction to practices in Europe during the Middle Ages. The Star Chamber and the Spanish Inquisition are examples of the sort of intrusive activities by governments during this time, when arrested individuals had few rights and torture and forced confessions were common. Such practices made their way to American shores, as evidenced by the Salem witch trials.

The Fifth Amendment requires that a person be indicted by a grand jury before he or she may be tried on a criminal charge. The purpose of the grand jury is to ensure the government does not prosecute individuals without some proof of guilt. Thus, the grand jury is meant to serve as a check on the power of the government, as a barrier standing between the individual citizen and the government.

It should be noted that the requirement of an indictment before a criminal prosecution is one of a handful of provisions of the Bill of Rights that have not been incorporated into the Fourteenth Amendment and applied to the states. In *Hurtado v. California* (1884) the Supreme Court expressly held that the right does not apply to state criminal trials, and this decision has never been overruled. Nonetheless, a number of states either require indictment by statute or state constitutional provision or provide prosecutors with the choice of seeking an indictment or proceeding via an information. An *information* is a substitute for an indictment and is filed directly with the court by the prosecutor.

The Fifth Amendment also prohibits placing someone in **double jeopardy.** This means a jurisdiction may not (1) prosecute someone again for the same crime after he or she has been acquitted, (2) prosecute someone again for the same crime after he or she has been convicted, and (3) punish someone twice for the same offense.

This provision does not mean a state may not try someone again if their first trial ends in a mistrial—in this situation there has been neither an acquittal nor a conviction. Additionally, if a conviction is overturned on appeal, the state may retry the person, as the reversal on appeal is not an acquittal.

While the double jeopardy clause bars multiple punishments for the same offense, there are exceptions. Under the **dual sovereignty doctrine** a person can be prosecuted in both federal and state courts for the same offense or in multiple state courts for the same offense. Double jeopardy does not apply in these situations because a different sovereign, or jurisdiction, is prosecuting the person. However, a person may not be tried for the same crime in both a municipal court and a state court, as these two courts derive their authority from the same source—the state constitution.

The Fifth Amendment also protects individuals from being forced to incriminate themselves. The privilege against self-incrimination, so familiar to those who have watched television shows and seen police officers read *Miranda* warnings to suspects, is a right we often take for granted today but that did not exist at early common law. The privilege allows a defendant to refuse to speak to police about the crime charged and to refuse to testify at trial. Furthermore, the prosecution is barred from commenting on a defendant's refusal to testify, as the Supreme Court has determined that doing so would limit the privilege against self-incrimination by suggesting that asserting a constitutional right was somehow evidence of something to hide (*Griffin v. California,* 1965).

The privilege is not total, however. The Supreme Court has held that the privilege protects a person from compelled testimonial communications—meaning spoken admissions (*Malloy v. Hogan,* 1964). The privilege does not apply to obtaining evidence from a suspect by other means, such as from blood samples, from fingerprints, or in a lineup.

Finally, the Fifth Amendment also provides for due process of law. Exactly what constitutes due process is highly debated. Essentially, **due process** means the state must follow certain procedures, designed to protect individual rights, before depriving an individual of his or her liberty or property.

Sixth Amendment

> In all criminal prosecutions, the accused shall enjoy the right to a speedy and public trial, by an impartial jury of the State and district wherein the crime shall have been committed, which district shall have been previously ascertained by law, and to be informed of the nature and cause of the accusation; to be confronted with the witnesses against him; to have compulsory process for obtaining witnesses in his favor, and to have the Assistance of Counsel for his defense.

The **Sixth Amendment** extends several important protections to defendants facing criminal prosecution. Notable among these is the right to confront and cross-imagine witnesses, the right to notice of charges, the right to a speedy trial, the right to a public trial, the right to an impartial jury, and the right to counsel. Historically speaking, the most-often cited reason for requiring a speedy trial is to minimize the stress and anxiety associated with a protracted trial that is otherwise placed upon the defendant when proceedings are delayed without cause. This does not mean, however, that justice should be rushed but, instead, that the prosecution must avoid unnecessary delays in bringing cases to trial rather than just allowing them to linger into the indefinite future. For this reason, most, if not all, state codes clearly spell out the maximum amount of time that may elapse between arrest, indictment, and prosecution.

Much more problematic is the Sixth Amendment's requirement that defendants be allowed to confront and cross examine witnesses, especially where confidential informants or child witnesses are concerned. As for child witnesses, who are subject to being traumatized by the testimonial experience, the Supreme Court early on rejected an approach involving the use of a semi-transparent screen to shield the child victim from actual face-to-face contact with the defendant in a child sex abuse case (*Coy v. Iowa,* 1988). In the later case of *Maryland v. Craig* (1990), the Supreme Court upheld the use of closed-circuit one-way television as a compromise between the right to confront witnesses and the public policy interest of victim/witness protection.

The right to a **speedy trial** means the defendant must be brought to trial without "unnecessary delay" (*Barker v. Wingo,* 1972). The right to a **public trial** means the defendant has a right to have the public attend the trial if they so wish. The right to notice of the charges against the defendant simply means the prosecution must inform the defendant prior to trial what he or she is accused of, so a defense may be prepared. This notification can occur through the filing of an information or the handing down of an indictment by the grand jury.

The right to a speedy trial means the defendant must be brought to trial without "unnecessary delay" (*Barker v. Wingo,* 1972). While no exact time frame conclusively establishes the existence of unnecessary delay, courts utilize the factors set forth by the U.S. Supreme Court in *Barker v. Wingo* (1972). Thus, in determining whether unnecessary delay has occurred a trial or appellate court will balance the following factors: (1) the length of delay, (2) the reason for the delay, (3) whether the defendant asserted his or her right to a speedy trial, and (4) whether the defendant was prejudiced by the delay. In addition to the constitutional right to a speedy trial, many jurisdictions have statutes that require trials to be held within a specific time period. As such, when examining the right to a speedy trial one must include both the constitutional and statutory guarantees.

The right to a trial by an **impartial jury** means the right to a jury, selected from the community where the crime occurred, that is not pre-disposed to believe the defendant is guilty. In other words, the members of the jury need not be unaware of the events that led to the trial, but they must not have formed an opinion as to the guilt (or innocence) of the accused—this right is the presumption of innocence. Trial by jury is an ancient right, mentioned in the Assize of Clarendon (1166) and affirmed in the Magna Carta (1215).

The Sixth Amendment also provides for the **assistance of counsel**. The Supreme Court has interpreted this provision to include the right to assistance of counsel not only at trial but at any proceeding deemed a "critical stage" (*Kirby v. Illinois,* 1972) in the proceedings. Precisely what constitutes a critical stage is subject to some dispute but includes the preliminary hearing, the arraignment, the trial itself, and the appeal of right.

The Supreme Court has also determined that the right to assistance of counsel means that indigent defendants who cannot afford to hire a lawyer must be provided one at the state's expense, as long as the person faces the possibility of incarceration for six months or more. Additionally, the Supreme Court has held that the right to counsel includes the right to effective assistance of counsel (*Strickland v. Washington,* 1984).

Seventh Amendment

> In suits at common law, where the value in controversy shall exceed twenty dollars, the right of trial by jury shall be preserved, and no fact tried by a jury, shall be otherwise reexamined in any Court of the United States, than according to the rules of the common law.

The **Seventh Amendment** provides for the right to a trial by jury in federal civil trials. This amendment applies only to federal trials; it has not been incorporated into the Fourteenth Amendment by the Supreme Court.

Eighth Amendment

> Excessive bail shall not be required, nor excessive fines imposed, nor cruel and unusual punishments inflicted.

The **Eighth Amendment** prohibits several things, including: (1) excessive bail, and (2) cruel and unusual punishment. Both of these prohibitions are written broadly, and the courts have struggled with interpreting them.

Regarding the prohibition on **excessive bail**, this provision does not expressly state that bail must be set in all cases—it only states that bail cannot be excessive. While the Eighth Amendment does not clearly provide for a right to bail, such a right existed as common law and has been codified in state statutes. What constitutes excessive bail, according to the Supreme Court, is bail set at a figure higher than necessary to ensure the presence of the defendant at trial (*Stack v. Boyle,* 1951). Thus, courts aim to set bail at an amount sufficient to ensure the presence of the defendant at trial yet not punitive in nature. In arriving at an appropriate amount, courts typically evaluate the following factors: the nature of the offense, the financial ability of the defendant, prior criminal history of the defendant, and risk of flight. However, in most jurisdictions if the offense is a capital offense, bail is automatically denied. Criminal defendants may contest the amount of their bail and seek a reduction in every jurisdiction.

The prohibition on **cruel and unusual punishment** limits the type and form of punishment imposed by a state after conviction of a crime. It prohibits torture, as well as punishment that is disproportionate to the offense. The cruel and unusual punishment clause does not prohibit the death penalty because it is deemed to be in accord with contemporary standards of decency (other objections notwithstanding).

Ninth Amendment

The enumeration in the Constitution, of certain rights, shall not be construed to deny or disparage others retained by the people.

The **Ninth Amendment** simply states that the listing of some rights in the Constitution should not be construed as a listing of *all* the rights retained by individual citizens. In other words, the rights provided in the Bill of Rights should not be taken as the only rights that citizens have—these are merely some of the rights retained by the people.

The obvious question, then, is if the Bill of Rights is not all-inclusive, what exactly are the other rights retained by the people? The Supreme Court has struggled to provide a framework for delineating these rights, as the discussion of incorporation (later in this chapter) indicates. In at least one case, the Supreme Court expressly mentioned the Ninth Amendment as providing a basis for giving individual citizens other unenumerated rights, such as a right to privacy (*Griswold v. Connecticut,* 1965). Generally, however, the Court has ignored the Ninth Amendment.

Tenth Amendment

The powers not delegated to the United States by the Constitution, nor prohibited by it to the States, are reserved to the States respectively, or to the people.

The **Tenth Amendment**, like the Ninth, has been largely ignored by the Supreme Court. It simply states that the rights not delegated to the federal government by the Constitution are reserved for the states or individual citizens. This codifies the principle of **federalism** and **constitutionalism** the federal government is a government of enumerated powers. That is, it has no authority unless so granted by the Constitution. And where the federal government has no authority, the states and individual citizens retain the authority.

Other Amendments

In addition to the individual rights enumerated in the Bill of Rights, several other later-enacted constitutional amendments directly implicate individual rights. These include the Reconstruction Amendments, passed shortly after the Civil War and intended to protect the recently freed slaves from abuse at the hands of state governments.

Thirteenth Amendment

> Neither slavery nor involuntary servitude, except as a punishment for crime whereof the party shall have been duly convicted, shall exist within the United States, or any place subject to their jurisdiction. Congress shall have power to enforce this article by appropriate legislation.

The **Thirteenth Amendment** prohibits slavery in the United States. Since its passage it has been used to uphold civil rights legislation passed by Congress to prevent racial discrimination by private citizens. Where other amendments prohibit discrimination by state governments, no such limiting language appears in the Thirteenth Amendment. Courts have thus interpreted it as not merely outlawing slavery but forbidding so-called badges of slavery, or practices intended to keep blacks at lower social and economic levels than whites.

Fourteenth Amendment

> All persons born or naturalized in the United States, and subject to the jurisdiction thereof, are citizens of the United States and of the State wherein they reside. No State shall make or enforce any law which shall abridge the privileges or immunities of citizens of the United States; nor shall any State deprive any person of life, liberty, or property, without due process of law; nor deny to any person within its jurisdiction the equal protection of the laws.

The **Fourteenth Amendment** is very important. It is the first amendment that specifically forbids states from mistreating their citizens. The Bill of Rights was intended to apply only to actions of the federal government. After the Civil War, congressional leaders realized that individual states were just as capable of oppressing individual citizens as the federal government was. They responded by enacting the Fourteenth Amendment, which forbids states from denying citizens due process of law or equal protection of the laws. These two clauses have dramatically altered the way states deal with citizens.

The due process clause is identical to the clause in the Fifth Amendment. It has been interpreted to incorporate the various provisions of the Bill of Rights, making them applicable to the states.

The **equal protection** clause has been interpreted to preclude states from making unequal, arbitrary distinctions between people. It does not ban reasonable classifications, but it does prohibit classifications that are either without reason or based on race or gender. These are sometimes referred to as **suspect classifications.**

Not all classifications are a violation of equal protection. States may treat people differently if they have a legitimate reason to do so. Thus, states may refuse to issue a drivers' license to a minor or may limit the age at which a person can lawfully consume alcoholic beverages. Classifications based on age are not suspect (meaning likely illegal), because (1) the state can demonstrate an interest in the health and safety of minors who are a peculiarly vulnerable segment of society, and (2) there is no history of "invidious" discrimination of minors, as there is for minorities and women. Furthermore, juveniles are seen as possessing fewer rights, or lesser rights, than adults. Thus a juvenile curfew might be upheld whereas a general curfew including adults would be struck down. To date, the Supreme Court has held that only race and religion are suspect classifications in all circumstances, although gender, illegitimacy, and poverty have occasionally been treated as suspect classifications.

Standards of Review

Often in constitutional law, the outcome of a case is determined as much by the **standard of review** the court uses as by the facts of the case. Not all of the individual protections set forth in the Bill of Rights are accorded the same respect—rather, there is a hierarchy of rights. The court uses one of three levels of review in cases where a citizen alleges an infringement on his or her constitutional rights: (1) strict scrutiny, (2) intermediate scrutiny, or (3) rational basis review. The level depends on whether the right involved has been deemed "fundamental" or whether a suspect classification is involved.

Fundamental rights are those freedoms essential to the concept of ordered liberty—rights without which neither liberty nor justice would exist (*Palko v. Connecticut,* 1937). Examples include virtually all of the rights guaranteed in the various provisions of the Bill of Rights, as well as the Fourteenth Amendment guarantees of due process and equal protection.

Under **strict scrutiny** review, the state may not enact legislation that abridges a fundamental right or that utilizes a suspect classification unless (1) it has a compelling interest that justifies restricting a fundamental right, and (2) the legislation is "narrowly tailored" so that the fundamental right is not abridged any more than absolutely necessary to effectuate the state's "compelling interest." An example of a compelling interest is the state's interest in the health and safety of its citizens. Additionally, the Supreme Court requires that for legislation to be narrowly tailored, a sufficient nexus must exist between the legislative body's stated interest and either the classification drawn or the means chosen to advance the state's compelling interest.

This standard of review is referred to as the strict scrutiny test because it requires the court to closely examine the purpose and effect of the questioned legislation rather than merely accept the claim that the it is needed or presumptively valid. The reason for using a higher standard of review when legislation affects a fundamental right or suspect classification is that closer analysis is required when individual liberties are threatened. The strict scrutiny test is the most difficult test for the state to meet. In fact, in the majority of cases requiring the application of this test, the law will be struck down by the court and deemed unconstitutional. Thus, states vigorously argue for the application of the intermediate standard or rational basis review.

In cases involving gender, illegitimacy, age, poverty and other issues that do not involve fundamental constitutional rights but where individuals are nonetheless entitled to increased protection, the court often utilizes the standard of **intermediate scrutiny**. This test requires the state to prove (1) that the law or regulation furthers an important state interest, and (2) that the law is substantially related to the achievement of that interest. Thus, the intermediate test is not as exacting as the strict scrutiny test but nonetheless poses a challenge for states to overcome.

In all other cases that do not involve fundamental rights, suspect classifications, or other issues falling within areas requiring application of the intermediate standard of review, the court will utilize rational basis review. Thus, in all other matters a state may enact legislation abridging that right or affecting a class as long as there is a rational basis for the legislation. This standard of review is generally referred to as **rational basis review** because the court will not strike down legislation that appears to have some rational basis. The court does not look closely at the effects of the legislation, unlike with the strict scrutiny test. Under this standard of review, state actions are presumptively valid. This standard of review is obviously a much easier one for states to pass. The legislature need not choose the best possible means; it must choose means that are not wholly unrelated to achievement of the legislative purpose. In other words, as long as the state can establish some rational basis for the law, the court will not strike it down. Standards of review are summarized in Table 1.1.

Table 1.1   Standards of Review

	Standard		
	Strict Scrutiny	**Intermediate Scrutiny**	**Rational Basis**
Nature of state interest	Compelling state interest	Important government interest	Reasonable government objective
Degree of relationship	Narrowly tailored	Substantial relationship	Some rational basis for law or regulation
Areas of application	Fundamental rights, suspect classification (race)	Nonfundamental rights, quasi-suspect classifications	All other cases

Incorporation of the Bill of Rights

Originally, the Bill of Rights applied only to the federal government, and state and local governments were not bound by its various provisions. This distinction arose out of a fear of a strong centralized government. State governments were viewed much more favorably, and many state constitutions contained protections of individual rights similar to those in the Bill of Rights. In 1833 the Supreme Court, in *Barron v. Baltimore,* expressly held that the Bill of Rights applied only to the federal government.

After the Civil War and the failed attempt by the Southern states to secede from the Union, federal legislators felt it was necessary to amend the Constitution to provide greater protections for individuals from the actions of state governments. In particular, there was a fear that the Southern states would attempt to limit the ability of the recently freed slaves to become equal citizens. The result was the 1868 passage of the Fourteenth Amendment.

The Fourteenth Amendment, as discussed above, contains three clauses: the privileges and immunities clause, the due process clause, and the equal protection clause. The essence of each of these clauses is that they bar states, not the federal government, from infringing on individual rights. The amendment was expressly intended to control state action, but it was unclear exactly how far the amendment went. The original spur for it was a desire to protect the rights of the freed slaves, but the language of the amendment was broad and not specifically limited to state actions infringing on the rights of blacks.

An early attempt to apply the language of the privileges and immunities clause to other persons failed in the *Slaughterhouse Cases* (1873). During the later part of the eighteenth century, however, the Supreme Court began to use the due process clause of the Fourteenth Amendment to strike down state action involving economic regulation. Under a theory known as substantive due process, the Court repeatedly held that states could not impose regulations such as minimum wage laws and child labor laws on private businesses because doing so violated due process. The violation of due process consisted of the regulatory taking of a right, such as the right to work or to enter into a contract.

During the 1930s, the use of the due process clause to protect economic interest fell into disfavor, in part because the Supreme Court used it to strike down much of President Roosevelt's New Deal legislation, which was intended to ease the burden of the Great Depression. At the same time, however, the Supreme Court began to use the due process clause of the Fourteenth Amendment to protect individual rights from state action. Beginning in the late 1930s, the Supreme Court incorporated most of the provisions of the Bill of Rights into the Fourteenth Amendment's due process clause and applied them to the states. Many of the criminal law provisions were applied to the states during the 1960s by the Supreme Court under the leadership of Chief Justice Earl Warren.

The term **incorporation** refers to the interpretation of the due process clause of the Fourteenth Amendment, which says that no state shall deprive a person of life, liberty, or property without "due process of law," as prohibiting states from abridging certain individual rights. Many of these rights are included in the Bill of Rights (which originally applied only to the federal government), hence these rights were included (or incorporated) in the definition of "due process." Several approaches to incorporation have been advocated by various Supreme Court justices during the twentieth century. These are each discussed next.

Total Incorporation

Under the **total incorporation** approach, the due process clause of the Fourteenth Amendment made the entire Bill of Rights applicable to the states. In essence, the phrase "due process of law" was interpreted to mean "all of the provisions of the Bill of Rights." However, this approach has never commanded a majority of justices on the Court. Prominent supporters of this approach have included Justice Hugo Black.

Total Incorporation Plus

As the term suggests, the **total incorporation plus** approach goes a step further than the total incorporation approach. Under total incorporation plus, the due process clause of the Fourteenth Amendment includes all of the Bill of Rights and, plus other, unspecified rights. A principal advocate of this approach was Justice William Douglas, who argued that the provisions of the Bill of Rights created the penumbras of privacy emanating from the First, Third, Fourth, and Fifth Amendments, allowing one to interpret the Ninth Amendment to include the right to privacy (*Griswold v. Connecticut,* 1965). In Douglas' view, the whole was greater than the sum of the parts—that the individual rights contained in the Bill of Rights, when examined together, created other rights. Thus, he argued that the various provisions limiting the ability of the government to intrude into a person's private life (such as the Fourth Amendment prohibition on unreasonable searches and the Third Amendment prohibition on quartering troops in private residences) created a general right to privacy.

Fundamental Rights

In *Twining v. New Jersey* (1908) the Supreme Court suggested that some of the individual rights in the Bill of Rights might also be protected from state action, not because the Bill of Rights applied to the states but because these rights "are of such a nature that they are included in the conception of due process of law." This became known as the "fundamental rights" or "ordered liberty" approach.

Under this approach, there is no necessary relationship between the due process clause of the Fourteenth Amendment and the Bill of Rights. The due process clause has an independent meaning, which prohibits state action that violates rights "implicit in the concept of ordered liberty" or those rights that are "fundamental" (*Palko v. Connecticut,* 1937). Exactly what constitutes a fundamental right is left to judicial discretion exercised in light of history and tradition of the law. However, the general standard utilized to determine whether a right is "fundamental" is noted in several landmark decisions. Essentially, the court will determine whether the right is (1) implicit in the concept of ordered liberty (2) and deeply rooted in the history and tradition of our nation. If the court answers these questions in the affirmative, the right is fundamental. Additionally, justices consider the "totality of the circumstances" (*Illinois v. Gates,* 1983) of each case in determining whether a right is fundamental. This approach provides justices with greater discretion, and they may interpret it either narrowly or broadly. This approach enjoyed strong support on the Court until the late 1960s. A principal advocate of this approach was Justice Felix Frankfurter.

Selective Incorporation

The **selective incorporation** approach combines elements of the fundamental rights and total incorporation approaches, in modified form. Selective incorporation rejects the notion that all of the rights in the Bill of Rights are automatically incorporated in the due process clause of the Fourteenth Amendment but does look to the Bill of Rights as a guide for which rights are incorporated. Selective incorporation rejects the "totality of the circumstances" component of the fundamental rights approach and instead incorporates rights deemed fundamental to the same extent and in the same manner as applied to the federal government.

As an example, under the total incorporation approach, the Fourth Amendment prohibition on unreasonable searches and the exclusionary rule, which states that evidence seized in violation of the Fourth Amendment cannot be used at trial, apply to both the federal government and the states. Under the fundamental rights approach, the Fourth Amendment was deemed fundamental and applied to the states, but the exclusionary rule was deemed nonfundamental and not applied to the states. Consequently, state law enforcement was told by the Court to obey the Fourth Amendment, but failure to do so would not result in the exclusion of the evidence sought to be obtained through a violation of the Fourth Amendment. Under selective incorporation, the Court holds both the right (freedom from unreasonable searches) and the means of enforcing the right (the exclusionary rule) to be part of the due process clause of the Fourteenth Amendment.

Selective incorporation became popular in the 1960s with the Warren Court. A principal advocate was Justice William Brennan. While selective incorporation accepts the idea that the due process clause protects only "fundamental rights" and that not every right in the Bill of Rights is necessarily fundamental, over time it has led to the incorporation of virtually everything in the Bill of Rights. The criminal protections not yet included are the right to an indictment by a grand jury and the prohibition on excessive bail.

Judicial Review

Given the varied sources of law and the ambiguous language of many statutes and constitutional provisions, it is inevitable that laws will come into conflict or that interpretations of statutes will differ. When this happens, who decides which law is paramount? In the United States, the answer to that question is the courts, through the power of judicial review.

Judicial review simply means the power of the court, specifically judges, to examine a law and determine whether it is constitutional. If a judge determines the law to be constitutional, he or she upholds the law. If the judge determines the law to not be constitutional, he or she declares it unconstitutional and therefore void. To make this determination, judges must examine the law and compare it with the Constitution. This process requires them to interpret the language of both the statute and the constitution.

For example, the Fourth Amendment prohibits "unreasonable" searches. Suppose a state legislature passes a law allowing police officers to search anyone they encounter on a public street. Is this law constitutional? Or does it violate the prohibition on unreasonable searches? To answer this question, judges must examine the history and meaning of "unreasonable" as contained in the Fourth Amendment. They do so by examining precedent.

Judicial review is not specifically provided for in the Constitution. Rather, judicial review is judge-made law. *Marbury v. Madison* (1803) established the authority of the U.S. Supreme Court to engage in judicial review of the acts of the other branches of government. The Supreme Court stated in *Marbury* that it is the duty of the judiciary to interpret the Constitution and to apply it to particular fact situations. The Court also said that it is the job of the courts to decide when other laws (acts of Congress or state laws) are in violation of the Constitution and to declare these laws null and void. This is the doctrine of judicial review.

Marbury v. Madison (1803) is perhaps the most important case ever decided, because it established the authority of the high court. Article III of the Constitution created the Supreme Court but did not discuss whether the Supreme Court could review legislation or interpret the Constitution.

At the time of the adoption of the Constitution, there was heated debate concerning which branch of government had the authority to declare an act void. Three suggestions were made as to how to handle such a situation: (1) Each branch within its sphere of authorized power has the final say; (2) the Supreme Court has the final say, but only as to the parties in cases before the Court; and (3) the Supreme Court has the final say. This controversy was finally resolved by the opinion in *Marbury*. An examination of the case provides insight into this controversy and how the Supreme Court handled the situation.

http://usinfo.state.gov/usa/infousa/facts/democrac/9.htm

President John Adams, a Federalist, appointed 42 of his fellow Federalists as justices of the peace for the District of Columbia just days before turning over the office to incoming President Thomas Jefferson, a Democrat. Adams' Secretary of State, John Marshall, delivered most of the commissions to the newly appointed justices of the peace but failed to deliver Marbury's. James Madison, the newly appointed Secretary of State, refused to deliver Marbury's commission, so Marbury applied directly to the Supreme Court for a writ of mandamus (a writ compelling a public official to perform his duty). The Supreme Court was granted original jurisdiction in such matters by the Judiciary Act of 1789. The Supreme Court agreed to hear the case but was unable to for 14 months because Congress passed a law that prohibited the Supreme Court from meeting.

In 1803 the Supreme Court reconvened, heard the case, and decided that Marbury was entitled to his commission but that the Supreme Court could not issue a writ of mandamus. Chief Justice John Marshall (formerly Adams' secretary of state!) wrote the opinion of the court.

Chief Justice Marshall opined that (1) Marbury was entitled to his commission, as he had a legal right that was not extinguished by the change in office of president, (2) a writ of mandamus was proper legal remedy for enforcing Marbury's right, but (3) the Supreme Court lacked the constitutional authority to issue such a writ. The Judiciary Act of 1789 gave the Supreme Court original jurisdiction in such cases, but this grant of authority was unconstitutional because Article III of the Constitution defined Supreme Court jurisdiction. The Judiciary Act of 1789 had the effect of changing (by enlarging) the jurisdiction of the Supreme Court, and Congress cannot pass a statute that changes the Constitution. The only way to change the Constitution is through a constitutional amendment. As stated by Chief Justice Marshall, "An act of the legislature, repugnant to the Constitution, is void." In other words, the Constitution is superior to congressional legislation.

Prior to the decision in *Marbury,* Democratic-Republicans argued the Supreme Court lacked the authority to declare acts of other branches of the federal government unconstitutional, while Federalists supported judicial review. If the Supreme Court had issued a writ of mandamus, it could not have forced Madison to honor it. The Supreme Court was thus faced with a serious challenge to its authority. Marshall's opinion saved the court's prestige while allowing the Democrats to claim a political victory (not having to appoint any more Federalists as justices of the peace). More important, the decision established as law that the Supreme Court has the authority to review the constitutionality of congressional activity (and presidential acts)—this is judicial review.

This was obviously a major victory for the Supreme Court and was not unopposed at the time, but it was accepted at least in part because the result in the case was satisfactory to opponents of a strong Supreme Court. The Supreme Court did not use power of judicial review to invalidate congressional legislation again until 1857, so Congress had little reason to complain. However, the Supreme Court did use judicial review to invalidate state legislation as violative of the Constitution.

Evidence Law

As noted at the beginning of this chapter, **evidence law** is the set of rules that govern what the jury can hear (and see) during a trial. These rules place limits on the type of testimony that may be presented as well as the forms of physical evidence that may be admitted. Evidence law may be confusing to a person who does not understand the rationale for a particular evidentiary rule. Evidence law has a long history, built in large part on past experience.

Generally speaking, **evidence** is the information presented to the jury during a trial that allows the jury to render a verdict. Jurors are not supposed to consider any information they obtain outside the courtroom, such as news reports or gossip from friends. Rather, jurors are supposed to base their verdict solely on what they learn in the courtroom, during the course of the trial.

The Purpose of Evidence Law

Persons not familiar with evidence law are often surprised to discover that information that initially appears relevant may not necessarily be admitted at trial. The variety of objections to the types and forms of evidence is at first glance bewildering. Evidence law has developed over a long period of time. It is created by judges as well as through the passage of statutes. Why a particular evidence rule exists today is not always clear; in some instances it is because the rule has an ancient origin and purpose that may not apply to the world of today.

Evidence law is intended to ensure that jurors hear or see only the information that is both relevant and competent. **Relevant evidence** is evidence that pertains to the matter at hand and has some bearing on the trial. For example, evidence about a defendant's feelings about the murder victim might be useful in explaining why the defendant killed (or did not kill) the victim. **Competent evidence** is evidence that is in a form the jury is permitted to hear or see. For example, hearsay evidence is sometimes deemed incompetent because it lacks reliability. Evidence must be both relevant and competent for it to be deemed admissible at trial. It is evidence law that helps the court sort out what evidence the jury will be allowed to see and hear.

The Development of Evidence Law

Evidence law developed over a long period of time. In medieval times, trials as we now understand them did not exist. Societies used a variety of methods for determining the "truth." For instance, in eleventh-century England, guilt was often determined through trial by battle, in which an accused would fight his accuser; if the accused won, he was determined to be innocent. Other societies appealed to God to reveal guilt or innocence. A person might be tied to a heavy stone and placed in a lake. If the person did not drown, it was seen as evidence that the person was corrupted by the devil. If the person did drown, it was assumed that he or she was innocent. Obviously this determination was of little use to the drowned person, at least in this life.

A movement toward trial by jury began in the thirteenth century in England. A person accused of crime gathered people who would swear to his innocence. These persons were known as oath helpers. Over time, oath helpers began not only to swear to the innocence of the accused but also to provide facts relevant to his guilt or innocence. This was the beginning of the use of witnesses at trial. In 1215 the Magna Carta was adopted, which provided for criminal jury trials.

http://www.bl.uk/treasures/magnacarta/translation.html

Several legal systems are in existence today. The United States follows the common law system brought over to the colonies from England. During the common law period, evidence rules developed sporadically, on a case-by-case basis. Today, evidence law in virtually every state is governed by statute, or code. The **evidence code** is a compilation of the common law evidence rules, written down (or codified) by the legislature. The best-known example is the **Federal Rules of Evidence**, or **FRE**, which apply in all federal courts; more than 40 states have also adopted the FRE in whole or part.

The FRE were enacted by Congress in 1975. While the rules have been in existence for less than 30 years, they are the product of many years of discussion, research, and deliberation by lawyers, judges, scholars, and legislators. Additionally, there were earlier attempts at evidence codes, such as the **Model Code of Evidence**, drafted by the **American Law**

Institute (ALI) in 1942 (the same body that developed the Model Penal Code, which is still in use today).

While many states have adopted the FRE, others have not. It is crucial the student know whether his or her state follows the FRE or has its own evidence law. The rules of evidence may vary widely among the states. Moreover, the FRE act in conjunction with rules of court that govern procedure in each jurisdiction.

Summary

There are many important concepts central to understanding the law, both generally and with specific regard to the rules of evidence. Among these are the various sources of law, the Bill of Rights, and the manner by which these rights have been extended to the states via selective incorporation. The importance of incorporation cannot be overemphasized—it is the mechanism by which state citizens now enjoy certain constitutional protections otherwise only available at the federal level. This process, combined with the concepts of judicial review, precedent and stare decisis play important roles in not only the development of law, but its day-to-day application through rules of criminal procedure and evidence.

Discussion Questions

1. Explain *Marbury v. Madison* (1803) and the impact of this case on the judicial system.
2. Explain the concepts of precedent and stare decisis.
3. Why is the Fourteenth Amendment among the most important concerning the rights of citizens? What are the three clauses, and why are they so important?
4. Explain the standards of equal protection review mentioned in the text.
5. What is a fundamental right? Give some examples.
6. In thirteenth-century England there were people known as "oath takers." What was their function, and what did their function evolve into?
7. What is meant by FRE?
8. Does your state follow the FRE? Cite references supporting your answer.
9. Give arguments for and against using the FRE.

10. What is a bill of attainder, and why was it prohibited by the Constitution?
11. Explain the importance of stare decisis.
12. Explain the total incorporation approach. What does the total incorporation plus approach add to total incorporation?
13. How does the selective incorporation approach differ from total incorporation?
14. Explain the importance of rules of evidence. Give examples.
15. Explain the importance of common law to our system of law today.
16. Give an example of a situation that might convince a court to overturn a previous case

Further Reading

Amar, A. R. (1998). *The Bill of Rights.* New Haven, CT: Yale University Press.

Anastaplo, G. (1989). *The Constitution of 1787: A Commentary.* Baltimore, MD: The Johns Hopkins University Press.

Anastaplo, G. (1995). *The Amendments to the Constitution: A Commentary.* Baltimore, MD: The Johns Hopkins University Press.

del Carmen, R. V. (1998). *Criminal Procedure.* Belmont, CA: Wadsworth.

Domino, J. C. (1994). *Civil Rights and Liberties.* New York: HarperCollins.

Kelly, A. H., W. A. Harbison, and H. Belz. (1983). *The American Constitution: Its Origins and Development* (6th ed.). New York: W. W. Norton.

Massey, C. R. (1995). *Silent Rights: The Ninth Amendment and the Constitution's Unenumerated Rights.* Philadelphia: Temple University Press.

Peltason, J. W. (1991). *Understanding the Constitution.* New York: Harcourt Brace.

Tribe, L. H. (1988). *American Constitutional Law.* Mineola, NY: Foundation Press.

Cases Cited

Barker v. Wingo, 407 U.S. 514 (1972)

Barron v. Baltimore, 32 U.S. (7 Pet.) 243 (1833)

Chaplinsky v. New Hampshire, 315 U.S. 568 (1942)

Coy v. Iowa, 487 U.S. 1012 (1988)

Everson v. Board of Education, 330 U.S. 1 (1947)

Griffin v. California, 380 U.S. 609 (1965)

Griswold v. Connecticut, 381 U.S. 489 (1965)

CHAPTER 2
THE AMERICAN CRIMINAL COURT SYSTEM

Key Terms & Concepts

Affadavit

Appellate jurisdiction

Appointed counsel

Arraignment

Arrest

Article Three Courts

Attorney general

Booking

Challenged for cause

Change of venue

Circuit courts

Closing arguments

Complaint

Court actors

Court of last resort

Cross examination

Defense attorneys

Direct appeal

Direct examination

Discovery period

District court

Diversity of citizenship

En banc

General jurisdiction

Geographic jurisdiction

Grand jury

Hierarchical jurisdiction

Indictment

Information

Initial appeal

Intermediate appellate courts

Judge

Judiciary Act of 1789

Jurisdiction

Jury selection

Limited jurisdiction

Magistrate judges

Methods of judicial selection

Mistrial

No bill

Opening statements

Original jurisdiction

Peremptory challenge

Personal jurisdiction

Plea

Preliminary examination

Preliminary hearing

Presentence/Investigation Report

Pretrial motions

Prosecutors

Public defenders

Retained counsel

Rule of four

Sentence

Subject matter jurisdiction

Supreme Court

Trial courts

Trial de novo

True bill

Venue

Verdict

Voir dire

Writ of certiorari

Writ of habeas corpus

Chapter Learning Objectives

By the end of this chapter, the student should be able to:

* Identify the various functions that courts perform in contemporary society

- Explain the structure of federal and state courts in American society
- Distinguish between the various forms of jurisdiction that courts exercise
- Explain the procedure by which the Supreme Court accepts or rejects cases for consideration
- Identify the roles filled by various court actors
- Relate the various methods by which judges are selected
- Trace the stages/phases of a criminal case
- Understand the types of pretrial motions
- Explain the process of jury selection
- Trace the generally established order by which evidence is presented/ rebutted by both the prosecution and defense during the trial phase
- Distinguish between the trial, sentencing and appeal phases of adjudication

Introduction

Courts perform several functions. First, courts settle disputes by providing a forum for obtaining justice and resolving disputes through the application of legal rules and principles. It is in court that injured parties may be heard and that the state may seek to punish wrongdoers. Private parties may seek redress in civil court, while the state may seek to punish violators of the criminal law in criminal court. Although the courtroom is obviously not the only place where people may go to settle disputes, Americans traditionally have turned to the courts for redress. Other countries, such as Japan, use the courts much less frequently.

Second, courts make public policy decisions. Policymaking involves the allocation of limited resources (such as money, property, and rights) to competing interests. America has a long tradition of settling difficult policy questions in the courtroom rather than the legislature. This is because politicians often avoid settling complex or difficult problems among themselves. Additionally, the rights of minorities are often unprotected by the legislature, so courts are forced to step into the breach. Finally, litigation is accepted as a tool for social change.

Third, courts serve to clarify the law through interpretation of statutes and the application of general principles to specific fact patterns. Courts are different from the other branches of government in many ways, but perhaps the most significant difference is that courts are reactive: Courts do not initiate cases but rather serve to settle controversies brought to them by others—plaintiffs and defendants, in legal parlance. This function frequently involves the interpretation of statutes written by the legislature.

In this chapter, we examine the structure of the American court system. It is a bit misleading to think of America as having just one court system—actually it has 50 state court systems and the federal court system. The court systems of the various states and the federal system share a number of characteristics but can also be quite different. First, we review some key concepts that all of the court systems share. Next, we examine the federal and state court systems. After our discussion of court structure, we discuss the trial process, focusing on the criminal trial and the appeals process.

Jurisdiction

In order to appreciate how and why court systems are set up the way they are, it is important to understand the concept of jurisdiction. **Jurisdiction** involves the legal authority of a court to hear a case. Jurisdiction is conferred by statutory or constitutional law. There are four primary types of jurisdiction: personal, subject matter, geographic, and hierarchical.

Personal jurisdiction refers to the authority of the court over the person. A court may acquire personal jurisdiction over a person if that person comes in contact with the court, either by being a citizen of the state or by committing an act (criminal or noncriminal) or series of acts within the state.

Subject matter jurisdiction involves the authority conferred on a court to hear a particular type of case. Some courts may hear only a specified type of case, such as a juvenile court or probate court. Other courts are given broad subject matter jurisdiction and may hear both civil and criminal proceedings of all kinds.

Geographic jurisdiction refers to the authority of courts to hear cases that arise within specified boundaries, such as a city, county, state, or country. Geographic jurisdiction is also sometimes referred to as **venue**. For a court to have jurisdiction over an event, that event must have taken place, in whole or part, within the geographic jurisdiction of the court. Thus, a person who kills someone in Idaho could not be prosecuted in North Carolina for that killing. The proper venue would be in Idaho. Furthermore, the proper court within Idaho would be that for the county in which the killing occurred.

Precisely where a crime occurs is not always clear-cut. For instance, a person may be kidnapped in California and taken to Texas. In this case, the kidnapping is a continuing offense—that is, each state into which the victim is taken could charge the kidnapper with a crime. Furthermore, both California and Texas may prosecute without violating the prohibition on double jeopardy, as they are each separate sovereign governments. This means each state derives its authority from a different source—its own state constitution. While two states can prosecute a person for the same offense, a state and a county in that state cannot do so, because the county derives its jurisdiction from the same source as the state (that state's constitution).

Within each state there are jurisdictions, usually defined by county boundaries. A state crime must be tried both within the proper state and the proper district within the state. Occasionally, a defendant in a criminal case may request a **change of venue**. Such a request must be based on evidence that it is impossible for the defendant to get a fair trial in the original court, perhaps because of substantial adverse publicity.

Hierarchical jurisdiction refers to the division of responsibilities and functions among the various courts. Jurisdiction can be general or limited, original or appellate.

General jurisdiction means a court has the authority to hear a variety of cases, that it is not limited to hearing only a particular type of case. An example is the state trial court, which often has the authority to hear all manner of civil and criminal cases. Civil cases involve a dispute between two private parties, such as in contract or property law. Criminal law involves a prosecution of an individual by the state for violating state criminal law.

Limited jurisdiction means that a court is limited to hearing only a particular class of cases. Examples include traffic court (traffic offenses and other misdemeanor offenses), juvenile court (delinquency, abuse, and neglect) and probate court (wills and estate matters, guardianship, trusts, and certain land matters). Smaller jurisdictions often do not have such courts; rather, they combine all the specialized courts in one court because of limited resources.

Original jurisdiction means the power of the court to hear the case initially. The court of original jurisdiction is where the trial takes place. For example, in federal court, all felony-level cases begin in the district court, while a suit between two states would start at the U.S. Supreme Court.

Appellate jurisdiction means the power of the court to review a decision of a lower court. Appellate courts may affirm (uphold) or reverse (overturn) lower-court judgments and either enter a new judgment or remand (return) the case to the lower court for reconsideration in light of its decision. Appellate courts do not conduct a retrial; rather, they are generally limited to a review of the trial record to determine whether there were any major legal errors. The court hears oral arguments by the attorneys for each side, reads legal briefs filed with the court, and bases its decision on these materials rather than new evidence.

The Federal Courts

There are essentially two court systems in the United States: the systems of the 50 states, and the federal system. The jurisdictions of the federal and state courts frequently overlap when a crime in a state may also be punishable under federal law.

The Constitution drafted at the Constitutional Convention of 1787 created a federal government with three branches: the legislative, executive, and judicial. The duties of each branch were set forth in separate articles of the Constitution. The duties of the judicial branch were listed in Article Three. This article established the Supreme Court and authorized "such inferior courts as Congress" chose to create. Neither the number of members of the Supreme Court nor the form of any potential "inferior" (meaning lower) courts were described.

At first, the idea of creating inferior federal courts met with much resistance from supporters of states' rights, who were afraid federal courts would infringe on the jurisdiction and authority of state courts. Several contributors to the Federalist Papers argued for a strong federal court system, as a bulwark against the actions of a democratically elected legislature. Additionally, these writers saw the Constitution as fundamental, paramount law and believed the job of the courts to be interpreting it and preventing the legislature from passing laws that took away fundamental rights. One of the first acts of the newly elected Congress was to pass the **Judiciary Act of 1789**. This act established Supreme Court membership at six justices and created 3 federal circuit courts and 13 district courts, one in each state. From this act an entire federal system has grown, today encompassing some 13 federal circuit courts and 94 district courts. The first set of intermediate-level appellate courts with purely appellate jurisdiction was established over a hundred years later, in 1891. Courts created under the authority of Article Three of the Constitution are sometimes referred to as **Article Three Courts**.

The federal court system today consists of three primary tiers: district courts, intermediate appellate courts, and the Supreme Court. Each of these courts has different functions.

District Courts

http://www.uscourts.gov/districtcourts.html

The **district court** is the trial court, or court of original jurisdiction, for the federal court system. There are currently over 100 federal judicial districts. Each state has at least one district court; some, such as California and Texas, have as many as four. With minor exceptions, no judicial district crosses state lines.

Each district has a United States District Court. The number of judges in each district ranges from 2 to 32, depending on the population of the individual district. While each district has more than one judge, only one judge presides over a particular trial. There are approximately 650 federal district judges.

Within each district court are subordinate judicial officers, referred to as **magistrate judges.** These judicial officers conduct preliminary proceedings in cases before the district court and issue warrants. Judgments entered by magistrates are considered judgments of the district court. Federal magistrate courts are similar to courts of limited jurisdiction in state courts.

Federal district courts have original jurisdiction over both civil matters and criminal cases involving federal statutes. Their jurisdiction is defined by both the Constitution and federal statute. District courts conduct trials for all federal criminal offenses and have jurisdiction to hear civil cases in which there is diversity of citizenship between the parties. **Diversity of citizenship** refers to situations in which the opposing parties are from different states. Until recently, much of the federal court docket was made up of civil cases, but this balance has begun to shift as Congress has greatly increased the number of federal crimes. Although the civil cases filed in federal district court still far outnumber criminal cases, criminal trials take up a significant portion of the district court's time. Some jurisdictions have been forced to postpone all civil proceedings to deal with the backlog of criminal cases. Because the Constitution requires a "speedy trial," criminal cases take precedence, and civil cases are often delayed.

Federal district courts are not courts of general jurisdiction. Rather, they have jurisdiction to hear only those types of cases specified by acts of Congress, and Congress may authorize district courts to hear only those cases and controversies specified in Article Three. The majority of cases in federal court deal with claims arising out of federal law, either civil or criminal. These may be based on federal statutes or the Constitution. The other major category of cases heard in federal courts are civil cases arising out of the court's diversity jurisdiction. District courts are authorized to hear any civil matter, even if it involves state law, if the amount in question exceeds $75,000 and the parties are citizens of different states. Federal courts were originally given diversity jurisdiction because the founding fathers feared state courts would be biased in favor of their residents when presented with a suit between a resident and a nonresident. Allowing the nonresident to shift the case to federal court was seen as a means of ensuring a fair trial.

Federal judges are appointed for life. Furthermore, their salary cannot be reduced during their term of office. This policy protects the independence of the federal judiciary and sets it apart from state court judges, most of whom are appointed or elected to a defined term of years.

Federal Courts

http://www.uscourts.gov/courtsofappeals.html

The next level in the federal system is the federal courts of appeals, also referred to as **circuit courts**. There are today 13 courts of appeals: 11 for the 50 states, 1 for the District of Columbia, and 1 for the federal circuit. Figure 2.1 illustrates the boundaries of the 11 circuits exercising jurisdiction over the 50 states and territories.

The jurisdiction of the Court of Appeals for the Federal Circuit is defined by statute to include appeals from several federal administrative agencies, patent claims, and decisions of the Claims Court and the Court of International Trade, two specialized federal trial courts. The District of Columbia has its own appeals court in part because of the large volume of cases filed in the District of Columbia. Federal judges are appointed to their positions for life.

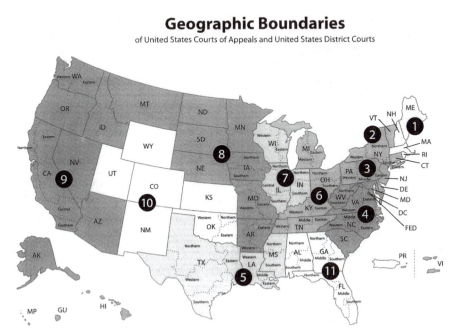

Geographic Boundaries
of United States Courts of Appeals and United States District Courts

Figure 2.1 Geographic boundaries of the United States Courts of Appeals and United States District Courts

The eleven remaining courts of appeals are organized on a territorial basis, with each covering several states. For instance, the Eleventh Circuit encompasses the states of Florida, Georgia, and Alabama, while the Ninth Circuit, the largest of the courts of appeals, includes the states of Alaska, Hawaii, California, Nevada, Arizona, Idaho, Oregon, Washington, and Montana, as well as Guam and the Northern Marianas Islands.

The number of judges on each of the courts of appeals varies from 6 in the First Circuit to 32 in the Ninth Circuit. Appeals are heard by three-judge panels. The makeup of these panels is constantly changing, so that Judge A does not repeatedly sit with Judge B. If conflicting decisions involve the same legal issue between two panels, the entire circuit may sit **en banc** (meaning as a group) and rehear the case. Doing so can obviously be a bit unwieldy in those circuits that have a large number of judges; consequently, federal law permits courts of appeals with more than 15 active judges to sit en banc with less than all of their members. The Ninth Circuit may hold en banc hearings with as few as 11 of its 32 judges. As with district court judges, courts of appeals judges are appointed for life.

The Supreme Court

http://www.uscourts.gov/supremecourt.html http://www.supremecourtus.gov/

The final and highest tier of the federal court system is the **Supreme Court**. This is the "court of last resort" for all cases arising in the federal system as well as for all cases in state courts that involve a federal constitutional issue. The Supreme Court has original jurisdiction over a very small number of situations, including suits between states, suits between the United States and a state, and suits between a state and a foreign citizen. These cases rarely occur. The bulk of the Court's docket consists of cases taken on appeal from either the federal courts of appeal or the state supreme courts.

The Supreme Court's appellate docket is almost entirely discretionary—that is, the Court may choose which cases it takes and which it refuses to hear. When a party asks the Court to accept a case, it submits a petition for a **writ of certiorari**. A writ of certiorari is an order issued by the Supreme Court to the lower court to send the record of the case up to the Supreme Court. The justices vote on whether to accept a case. If four or more justices vote to accept a case, it is placed on the Court's docket. This is known as the **rule of four**. If four votes are not obtained, the petition for a writ of certiorari is denied, and the decision of the lower court is left undisturbed. Refusal to accept an appeal is not considered a decision on the merits and has no binding precedential value. It simply means the Court has chosen not to hear the case, for whatever reason.

The Supreme Court has three main purposes: (1) to resolve disputes between states, (2) to resolve conflicting opinions of lower federal and state courts, and (3) to resolve constitutional questions. The Court uses its discretionary docket to take only those cases that fit into these categories. Thus, the Court may refuse to grant certiorari in a case because there is no difference of opinion on the issue among the circuit courts or because no federal constitutional issue is raised.

The Court is currently composed of nine justices, one of whom is designated the Chief Justice. Congress has the authority to either enlarge or reduce the number of justices on the Supreme Court and has at times done so. Congress has not changed the number of justices in over 100 years however, so it seems unlikely it would try to do so now, in the face of a longstanding tradition of having nine justices on the Court.

Although it was created as a third branch of the federal government, the Supreme Court did not immediately establish a significant presence in the affairs of the country. In fact, there was so little for the Court to do that the first Chief Justice, John Jay, resigned to take a position as an ambassador. It was not until the term of John Marshall that the Supreme Court was able to establish its role in the government. Today, the Supreme Court plays a significant role in public affairs, through the power of judicial review (discussed in Chapter 1).

The State Courts

http://www.ncsconline.org/index.html

Although the federal courts, particularly the Supreme Court, capture much of the attention of the media and the general public, the reality is that state courts are the workhorses of the American judicial system. State courts process in excess of 100 million cases a year. These cases range from the most serious of criminal cases to complex civil litigation to routine divorces and traffic violations.

The structure of state courts is much more varied than the structure of the federal court system. The 50 states have created a multiplicity of court structures. Some court systems are unified and clearly organized, while others are a jumble of overlapping jurisdiction and confusion. In this section we present a "typical" state court system, but your state court structure may differ.

The most common state court system consists of four levels, or tiers: (1) courts of limited jurisdiction, (2) courts of general jurisdiction, (3) intermediate appellate courts, and (4) a final appellate court, or court of last resort.

Courts of limited jurisdiction are those courts that deal with the less serious offenses and civil cases. These courts are referred to by a variety of names, including justice of the peace court, magistrate's court, municipal court, and county court. These lower courts handle a wide variety of matters, including minor criminal cases, traffic offenses, violations of municipal ordinances, and civil disputes under a certain amount. On the criminal side, these courts may also be responsible for issuing search and arrest warrants and conducting the preliminary stages of felony cases, such as the preliminary hearing and arraignment. On the civil side, these courts may handle a variety of matters, including juvenile delinquency, family law, and probate.

Proceedings in lower courts are often more informal than those in appellate or trial courts. There is generally no right to a jury trial provided in these courts; a losing party who wishes to appeal an adverse decision must do so through a trial de novo in the court of original jurisdiction. A **trial de novo** is not like a standard appeal in which the higher court concerns itself only with a review of the trial record and consideration of any possible legal errors; instead, it is an entirely new trial.

While courts of limited jurisdiction receive little attention, they are important for several reasons. First, they are the only experience that most citizens will have with the court system. Second, these courts process a tremendous number of cases, and there are a lot of these courts. The National Center for State Courts reports that there are almost 14,000 lower courts, and these courts process some 71 million cases each year. Third, these courts are often involved in the crucial early stages of criminal cases, in the issuance of warrants and the determination whether to set bail and to hold the suspect over for trial.

The next level in a typical state court system are the courts of general jurisdiction. These are the trial courts for civil and criminal matters. They are also courts of original jurisdiction, and it is here that trials for felonies are held. These courts are generally authorized to hear any matters not exclusively designated for courts of limited jurisdiction; in some states they may even have concurrent jurisdiction with lower courts on some matters, such as misdemeanors. They may also hear appeals, in the form of a trial de novo, from lower courts.

Trial courts are usually referred to as the district court, circuit court, or superior court, although at least one state, New York, refers to its trial court as the supreme court and its court of last resort as the court of appeals. While there is no hard evidence that New York did this with the express purpose of confusing students, the authors do have their suspicions.

The precise workload of the trial courts varies by jurisdiction. In less-populous areas, the trial court may hear all manner of cases, including civil and criminal. In more-populated areas, there may be a greater specialization, with one court handling only felony trials and another handling only civil matters.

Currently, at least 38 states have two levels of appellate courts consisting of an intermediate appellate court and a court of last resort. Intermediate appellate courts are largely a creation of the twentieth century. As jurisdictions became more crowded and court dockets increased, officials saw a need to relieve the state supreme court of the burden of hearing all appeals of right. The states that have not created an intermediate court tend to be either small or not densely populated.

The **intermediate appellate courts** are referred to by a variety of names, but by far the most common is *court of appeals*. The primary purpose of the intermediate court of appeals is to hear felony appeals of right and certain appeals from judgments in civil cases. The number of judges on intermediate appellate courts varies. Additionally, some states have more than one intermediate appellate court.

The **court of last resort** in most states is called the state supreme court. Forty-eight states have one court of last resort; two states (Oklahoma and Texas) have two (Meador 1991). These states have a court of last resort for all civil cases and a court of last resort for all criminal cases. The number of judges on the court of last resort varies by state from three to nine.

The court of last resort usually hears the majority of appeals on a discretionary basis, similar to the U.S. Supreme Court. This allows them to control their docket and focus on cases involving significant legal issues. The exceptions are those states that do not have an intermediate appellate court and, in other states, death penalty cases. In states without an intermediate appellate court (usually the smaller and less-populous states), the state supreme court is the only appellate court and thus is mandated by law to hear all appeals. Most states also require their supreme court hear all appeals in cases involving the death penalty. This requirement is provided as an extra safeguard because the punishment in these cases is obviously the most severe possible, and the states wish to be absolutely sure the defendant has received a fair trial.

For most cases, the state supreme court is the end of the line, the final arbiter of the dispute. The only option for a losing party in the state Supreme Court is to appeal directly to the U.S. Supreme Court, and to do so the party must be able to identify a legal issue that involves the United

States Constitution or a federal law. Defendants who lose in state courts also have the option of filing a writ of habeas corpus in federal district court.

Court Actors

There are three key **court actors**: judges, prosecutors, and defense attorneys. Each of these actors are attorneys trained in the law, but each performs different tasks.

Judges

The **judge** serves as a referee, responsible for enforcing court rules, instructing the jury on the law, and determining the law. Judges are expected to be completely impartial. Trial judges have tremendous power to control a case. As a whole, judges are not representative of American society. They are mostly white, male, and upper middle class; women and minorities are underrepresented throughout the judiciary. A number of commentators have argued that this under-representation results in bias, either intentionally or unintentionally. Others have suggested that even if bias does not in fact exist, there is a perception among many segments of the population that justice is not obtainable, because minorities and women are underrepresented on the bench (Slotnick 1984).

There are three common methods of judicial selection: (1) appointment, (2) election, and (3) the merit system. Different jurisdictions use different methods of selecting judges. Some jurisdictions use more than one method, while others, such as the federal system, use only one method.

http://www.moderncourts.org/Advocacy/judicial_selection/methods.html

Appointment by the chief executive of the jurisdiction (the president of the United States or the governor of an individual state) is the oldest method of selecting judges. All 13 of the original colonies used it, and it is used today in the federal system and about 20 states.

Election of judges became popular during the 1830s when Democrats under the leadership of Andrew Jackson gained control of Congress from the Federalists. Jackson and his supporters believed wholeheartedly in popular democracy and thought appointment of judges was undemocratic. Georgia was the first state to implement judicial elections in 1824. Currently, 29 states use popular elections to select judges.

These elections take one of two forms. Some states have partisan (meaning aligned with a particular party) elections, in which candidates for judicial office run in the party primary and their political affiliation is listed on ballot; 13 states use this method. In 16 other states, judges are selected in nonpartisan elections, in which no political affiliation is listed.

A third method of selecting judges is the merit system. This system is based on system originally developed by the American Judicature Society in 1909 and endorsed by the American Bar Association in 1937. It was first adopted by Missouri in 1940 and consequently is sometimes referred to as the "Missouri Plan."

The merit system has become popular only recently. In 1960 only 4 states used the system, but by 1998 about half the states were using it. The merit system has three parts. First, a nonpartisan nominating commission selects a list of potential candidates, based on the candidates' legal qualifications. Second, the governor makes a selection from this list. Finally, the person selected as a judge stands for election (this is referred to as retention) within a short time after he or she is selected, usually within one year.

Prosecutors

http://www.ndaa.org/

Under the early common law, there were no public prosecutors. Instead, private citizens were responsible for litigating their criminal cases. Private prosecution gave way to public prosecution as society came to view crime as an offense not just against the person, but against society as well. Today, private prosecution is no longer permitted in any state; in its place are prosecutor's offices. There are over 25,000 **prosecutors** today, although about half of them are part-time (primarily in small jurisdictions).

The 1789 Judiciary Act provided a United States attorney for each court district (appointed by the U.S. president). In 1870 Congress authorized the creation of the Department of Justice, with an attorney general and assistants (Meador 1991). The **attorney general**, a political appointee, is an administrator who sets prosecution priorities for deputy attorney generals. Deputy attorney generals are appointed by the president and confirmed by the Senate and serve at the pleasure of the president. Assistant United States attorneys are not political appointments.

State prosecutors are called by various names, such as district attorney, solicitor, county attorney, state's attorney, and commonwealth attorney. State prosecutors are usually elected officials, with appointed assistants who do most of the trial work. Only four states (Alaska, Connecticut, Delaware, and New Jersey) do not have an elected district attorney. The district attorney's duty is not only to prosecute cases in the name of the people but also to do justice by pursuing only those who have in fact committed crimes. District attorneys have tremendous power to decide whether to prosecute. This is often referred to as prosecutorial discretion. In most jurisdictions, this power is largely unreviewable by courts or other authorities.

Defense Attorneys

http://www.criminaljustice.org/public.nsf/freeform/publicwelcome?opendocument
http://www.afda.org/

Defense attorneys are expected to represent their client as effectively as possible while acting within the rules of court. The right to counsel existed at common law and in state constitutions; the Sixth Amendment codified this right. The Supreme Court has interpreted the Sixth Amendment right to counsel as applying at any "critical stage" of the prosecution, not just at trial. Thus, a defendant has been held to have the right to counsel at a lineup that takes place after indictment, at the preliminary hearing, and during pretrial discovery.

The role of defense counsel is primarily (1) to ensure that the defendant's rights are not violated (intentionally or in error) by the police or during a criminal trial; (2) to make sure the defendant knows all his or her options before making a decision; (3) to provide the defendant with the best possible defense, without violating ethical and legal obligations; (4) to investigate and prepare the defense; and (5) to argue for lowest possible sentence or best possible plea bargain.

There are several types of defense counsel. These include private, retained counsel; public defenders; and appointed counsel. **Retained counsel** are attorneys selected and paid by the defendant. **Public defenders** are hired by the state but work for defendants who cannot afford to hire their own lawyer. **Appointed counsel** are private attorneys who are paid by the state on a case-by-case basis to represent indigent defendants.

http://www.nlada.org/Defender

While the Supreme Court has held that the Sixth Amendment grants criminal defendants the right to counsel in criminal cases, the Court has not held that this means a right to the counsel of the defendant's choice. Rather, the Court has held that the Sixth Amendment guarantees a criminal defendant the right to competent and effective legal counsel, but not a particular attorney. (See the discussion of *Strickland v. Washington* that follows.) A person who can afford to hire a lawyer may do so; those who cannot afford a lawyer will be provided one, but there are limits on when the appointment will occur, and defendant's have little or no say in who is selected to represent them. To qualify for appointed counsel, the defendant must be able to establish that he or she is indigent or without the resources to hire an attorney. Each jurisdiction has a method of determining indigence, which typically involves an evaluation of the income, assets, and financial obligations of the defendant.In the landmark decision of *Strickland v. Washington* (1984), the U.S. Supreme Court examined the role of defense counsel in criminal trials. Since that decision was handed down, the guidelines established in *Strickland* have been the benchmark for determining whether counsel was "effective" in providing representation.

Strickland v. Washington
Supreme Court of the United States
466 U.S. 668 (1984)

During a 10-day period in September 1976, Washington planned and committed three groups of crimes, which included three brutal stabbing murders, torture, kidnapping, severe assaults, attempted murders, attempted extortion, and theft. After his two accomplices were arrested, respondent surrendered to police and voluntarily gave a lengthy statement confessing to the third of the criminal episodes. The State of Florida indicted the defendant for kidnapping and murder and appointed an experienced criminal lawyer to represent him.

Counsel actively pursued pretrial motions and discovery. He cut his efforts short, however, and he experienced a sense of hopelessness about the case, when he learned that, against his specific advice, respondent had also confessed to the first two murders. By the date set for trial, respondent was subject to indictment for three counts of first-degree murder and multiple counts of robbery, kidnapping for ransom, breaking and entering and assault, attempted murder, and conspiracy to commit robbery. Respondent waived his right to a jury trial, again acting against his attorney's advice and pled guilty to all charges, including the three capital murder charges.

(continued)

In the plea colloquy, Washington told the trial judge that he had no significant prior criminal record and that at the time of his criminal spree he was under extreme stress caused by his inability to support his family. He also stated, however, that he accepted responsibility for the crimes. The trial judge noted that he had "a great deal of respect for people who are willing to step forward and admit their responsibility" but that he was making no statement at all about his likely sentencing decision. Defense counsel advised Washington to invoke his right under Florida law to an advisory jury at his capital sentencing hearing, but Washington rejected the advice and waived the right. He chose instead to be sentenced by the trial judge without a jury recommendation.

In preparing for the sentencing hearing, the defense attorney spoke with Washington about his background. He also spoke on the telephone with respondent's wife and mother, though he did not follow up on the one unsuccessful effort to meet with them. He did not otherwise seek out character witnesses for respondent. Nor did he request a psychiatric examination since his conversations with his client gave no indication that respondent had psychological problems. Defense counsel decided not to present and hence not to look further for evidence concerning respondent's character and emotional state. That decision reflected trial counsel's sense of hopelessness about overcoming the evidentiary effect of respondent's confessions to the gruesome crimes. It also reflected the judgment that it was advisable to rely on the plea colloquy for evidence about respondent's background and about his claim of emotional stress: the plea colloquy communicated sufficient information about these subjects, and by forgoing the opportunity to present new evidence on these subjects, counsel prevented the State from cross-examining respondent on his claim and from putting on psychiatric evidence of its own.

Defense counsel excluded from the sentencing hearing other evidence he thought was potentially damaging. He successfully moved to exclude respondent's "rap sheet" because he judged that a pre-sentence report might prove more detrimental than helpful, as it would have included respondent's criminal history and thereby would have undermined the claim of no significant history of criminal activity, he did not request that one be prepared.

Following the sentencing hearing, the trial judge found numerous aggravating circumstances and no (or a single comparatively insignificant) mitigating circumstance. He therefore sentenced respondent to

(continued)

death on each of the three counts of murder and to prison terms for the other crimes. The Florida Supreme Court upheld the convictions and sentences on direct appeal.

*****

In reaching its decision, the Supreme Court provided an extensive review of the right to counsel. In a long line of cases that includes *Powell v. Alabama*, 287 U.S. 45 (1932), *Johnson v. Zerbst*, 304 U.S. 458 (1938), and *Gideon v. Wainwright*, 372 U.S. 335 (1963), this Court has recognized that the Sixth Amendment right to counsel exists, and is needed, in order to protect the fundamental right to a fair trial. The Constitution guarantees a fair trial through the Due Process Clauses, but it defines the basic elements of a fair trial largely through the several provisions of the Sixth Amendment, including the Counsel Clause. A fair trial is one in which evidence subject to adversarial testing is presented to an impartial tribunal for resolution of issues defined in advance of the proceeding. The right to counsel plays a crucial role in the adversarial system embodied in the Sixth Amendment, since access to counsel's skill and knowledge is necessary to accord defendants the "ample opportunity to meet the case of the prosecution" to which they are entitled.

*****

For that reason, the Court has recognized that "the right to counsel is the right to the effective assistance of counsel." *McMann v. Richardson*, 397 U.S. 759, 771, n. 14 (1970). However, a convicted defendant's claim that counsel's assistance was so defective as to require reversal of a conviction or death sentence has two components. First, the defendant must show that counsel's performance was deficient. This requires showing that counsel made errors so serious that counsel was not functioning as the "counsel" guaranteed the defendant by the Sixth Amendment. Second, the defendant must show that the deficient performance prejudiced the defense. This requires showing that counsel's errors were so serious as to deprive the defendant of a fair trial, a trial whose result is reliable. Unless a defendant makes both showings, it cannot be said that the conviction or death sentence resulted from a breakdown in the adversary process that renders the result unreliable. Because Washington could not establish either prong of the test, his conviction and sentencing was upheld.

Overview of the Criminal Process

This section provides a brief overview of the major stages in a typical criminal trial as illustrated in Figure 2.2. The process begins with the arrest of a suspect and ends with the verdict at trial or, potentially, an appeal. Evidentiary issues may arise at any point during the proceeding, although the bulk of evidence law deals with the conduct of the trial.

http://www.ojp.usdoj.gov/bjs/justsys.htm

Pretrial Proceedings

The criminal process begins with either the filing of a **complaint** or an **arrest**. A complaint may be filled out by a police officer, a prosecutor, or a private citizen. If an arrest is made first, a complaint will be sworn out afterward, usually by the arresting officer. The complaint serves as the charging document for the preliminary hearing.

Search and arrest warrants are obtained by police officers, who first must fill out an **affidavit** stating the facts relied on to create what is called *probable cause*. There must be probable cause to arrest or search. As noted in Chapter 1, probable cause is a legal concept referring to the amount of proof a police officer must have in order to search or arrest someone.

After someone is arrested, he or she is booked. **Booking** is an administrative procedure that involves entering of the suspect's name, arrest time, and offense charged into the police blotter and taking fingerprints and photographs.

The first court appearance is referred to as the **initial appearance**. Once a person is arrested, he or she must be brought before a magistrate "without unnecessary delay." Bail is generally set during the initial appearance. The next stage in the proceedings is the **preliminary examination**, sometimes referred to as the **preliminary hearing**. Here the magistrate determines whether there is probable cause to believe that an offense was committed and that it was defendant who committed it. In *County of Riverside v. McLaughlin* (1991), the Supreme Court held that a probable cause determination must be made within 48 hours of arrest. If probable cause is established, the defendant is "bound over" for trial. The preliminary examination is a formal adversarial proceeding conducted in open court. The Supreme Court has defined it as a "critical stage" of the prosecution, which means the defendant has a right to have a lawyer present.

There are two ways that charges may be filed against a defendant: by an **information** filed by the prosecutor or by an **indictment** issued by a grand jury. An information is adequate if it informs the defendant of the facts and the elements of the offense charged. It is a more efficient

Sequence of events in the criminal justice process

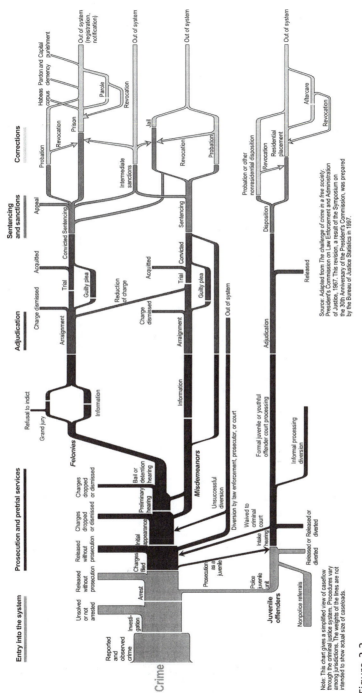

Note: This chart gives a simplified view of caseflow through the criminal justice system. Procedures vary among jurisdictions. The weights of the lines are not intended to show actual size of caseloads.

Source: Adapted from *The challenge of crime in a free society*, President's Commission on Law Enforcement and Administration of Justice, 1967. This revision, a result of the Symposium on the 30th Anniversary of the President's Commission, was prepared by the Bureau of Justice Statistics in 1997.

Figure 2.2

way to proceed than a grand jury indictment because it eliminates the need to organize a grand jury and present evidence.

On the federal level, the Fifth Amendment requires the government to proceed via an indictment handed down by a grand jury. This clause of the Fifth Amendment is one of the few that has not been applied to the states, however, so states may use an information instead. Fewer than half the states require an indictment; 12 states require indictment by a grand jury only for felonies, while three states require indictment by a grand jury only for capital offenses. Four states require indictment by a grand jury for all felonies and misdemeanors.

The typical **grand jury** is composed of 23 people, and its proceedings are not open to the public. The only persons present aside from the members of the grand jury are the district attorney and any witnesses the prosecutor calls. The rationale behind requiring indictment by a grand jury is that this body can act as a check on an overzealous prosecutor, preventing him or her from prosecuting cases for which there is not sufficient evidence. In reality the grand jury today is unlikely to refuse to indict anyone. This fact does not necessarily mean that the jury is not achieving its purpose of preventing improper prosecutions, because its very existence may prevent prosecutors from taking shaky cases to the grand jury. In this way, the grand jury does check the prosecutor's power. If the grand jury returns an indictment, it is referred to as a **true bill**. If the grand jury refuses to indict the defendant, it is referred to as a **no bill**.

At the **arraignment** the defendant enters a **plea**. Possible pleas include (1) guilty, (2) not guilty, (3) no contest, and (4) standing mute. Standing mute means refusing to plead—in these instances the court enters a "not guilty" plea for the defendant, thus preserving the defendant's constitutional right to trial. A no contest plea, also referred to as nolo contendere, means the defendant accepts whatever punishment the court would impose on a guilty defendant but refuses to admit liability. This plea is frequently used by defendants who fear being exposed to civil liability for their criminal misdeeds.

Pretrial Motions

Prior to trial, both the prosecution and defense may file motions with the court. These motions may cover a variety of issues. Common **pretrial motions** in criminal cases include (1) a motion to compel discovery, and (2) a motion to suppress evidence. These motions are usually made by the defense. The judge rules on these motions before the trial begins.

The period of time between arraignment and trial is often referred to as the **discovery period**. This is the time when both sides may seek to discover what evidence the other side has. Discovery is typically done via a pretrial motion. The defendant has a constitutional right to any *exculpatory evidence* (evidence that tends to suggest the defendant is innocent) in the possession of the prosecution.

Jury Selection

The next step in the process is the trial itself. Once a trial date is set, **jury selection** begins. The jury is chosen from the eligible members of the community who are selected at random, usually from voting records or automobile registration records. These records are used to obtain as complete a list as possible of all the residents of a community. Prospective jurors are examined by the judge or the attorneys to determine whether any bias, prejudice, or interest would prevent the potential juror from being impartial. This process of questioning the jurors is referred to as the **voir dire**.

http://www.212.net/crime/jury.htm

It should be noted that while the purpose of the voir dire is to obtain an unbiased jury, in reality each side seeks not only to excuse potential jurors who are biased against their side but also to keep on the jury those individuals who are biased toward their own side. Attorneys sometimes use the services of professional jury consultants to help them determine what type of person is more likely to favor the prosecution or defense.

Jurors may be **challenged for cause** or removed through the use of a **peremptory challenge**. A peremptory challenge is one for which no reason need be given. While challenges for cause are unlimited, peremptory challenges are usually limited to a certain number. The Supreme Court has held that peremptory challenges may not be used to exclude potential jurors on the basis of race (*Batson v. Kentucky,* 1986) or gender (*J. E. B. v. Alabama,* 1994). In *Batson v. Kentucky*, the Court examined the widespread and common use of peremptory challenges to exclude potential jurors from service based solely on their race.

The Supreme Court has also held that juries need not be composed of the traditional 12 members. Juries as small as 6 have been approved for both civil and criminal trials (*Williams v. Florida,* 1970). Furthermore, there is no constitutional requirement that the jury verdict be unanimous, even in criminal cases. The Supreme Court has approved both 9–3 and 10–2 verdicts (*Johnson v. Louisiana,* 1972; *Apodaca v. Oregon,* 1972). However, a 6-person jury must be unanimous. Finally, the requirement of a "jury of one's peers" has been interpreted simply to require that the jury be selected from the community in which the crime takes place. It does not mean the jury must share any other similarities with the defendant.

Batson v. Kentucky
Supreme Court of the United States
476 U.S. 79 (1986)

Petitioner, a black man, was indicted in Kentucky on charges of second-degree burglary and receipt of stolen goods. On the first day of trial in Jefferson Circuit Court, the judge conducted voir dire examination of the venire, excused certain jurors for cause, and permitted the parties to exercise peremptory challenges. The prosecutor used his peremptory challenges to strike all four black persons on the venire, and a jury composed only of white persons was selected. Defense counsel moved to discharge the jury before it was sworn on the ground that the prosecutor's removal of the black veniremen violated petitioner's rights under the Sixth and Fourteenth Amendments to a jury drawn from a cross section of the community, and under the Fourteenth Amendment to equal protection of the laws. Counsel requested a hearing on his motion. Without expressly ruling on the request for a hearing, the trial judge observed that the parties were entitled to use their peremptory challenges to "strike anybody they want to." The judge then denied petitioner's motion, reasoning that the cross-section requirement applies only to selection of the venire and not to selection of the petit jury itself.

Racial discrimination in selection of jurors harms not only the accused whose life or liberty they are summoned to try. Competence to serve as a juror ultimately depends on an assessment of individual qualifications and ability impartially to consider evidence presented at a trial. See *Thiel v. Southern Pacific Co.*, 328 U.S. 217, 223–224 (1946). A person's race simply "is unrelated to his fitness as a juror." Id., at 227 (Frankfurter, J., dissenting). As long ago as *Strauder*, therefore, the Court recognized that by denying a person participation in jury service on account of his race, the State unconstitutionally discriminated against the excluded juror. 100 U.S., at 308; see *Carter v. Jury Comm'n of Greene County*, supra, at 329–330; *Neal v. Delaware*, supra, at 386.

The harm from discriminatory jury selection extends beyond that inflicted on the defendant and the excluded juror to touch the entire community. Selection procedures that purposefully exclude black persons from juries undermine public confidence in the fairness of our system of justice. *See Ballard v. United States*, 329 U.S. 187, 195 (1946); *McCray v. New York*, 461 U.S. 961, 968 (1983) (Marshall, J., dissenting from denial of certiorari). Discrimination within the judicial system is most

(continued)

pernicious because it is "a stimulant to that race prejudice which is an impediment to securing to [black citizens] that equal justice which the law aims to secure to all others." *Strauder*, 100 U.S., at 308.

Accordingly, the component of the jury selection process at issue here, the State's privilege to strike individual jurors through peremptory challenges, is subject to the commands of the Equal Protection Clause. Although a prosecutor ordinarily is entitled to exercise permitted peremptory challenges "for any reason at all, as long as that reason is related to his view concerning the outcome" of the case to be tried, *United States v. Robinson*, 421 F.Supp. 467, 473 (Conn. 1976), mandamus granted sub nom. *United States v. Newman*, 549 F.2d 240 (CA2 1977), the Equal Protection Clause forbids the prosecutor to challenge potential jurors solely on account of their race or on the assumption that black jurors as a group will be unable impartially to consider the State's case against a black defendant.

To hold otherwise would be next to impossible. A perfect example is the O. J. Simpson case. If the jury should have been made up of people with similar attributes, how would we have defined them? As black men, rich people, ex-football players, or bad actors? Instead, jury members simply had to be Los Angeles County residents.

The Trial

Once the jury is selected and sworn in, the trial can begin. The first step is the making of **opening statements** first by the prosecution and then by the defense. The defense may choose to reserve its opening statement until after the prosecution has presented its evidence. This presentation is referred to as the prosecution's *case-in-chief*. During this phase, the prosecution must establish each element of crime charged beyond a reasonable doubt.

Once the prosecution has presented its evidence and called its witnesses, the defense has an opportunity to present its case-in-chief. The defense is not required to put on any case, but if the defense chooses to, it may raise several types of defenses. These include either an alibi or an affirmative defense such as insanity or self-defense.

Witnesses may be called to testify by both the prosecution and the defense. The side that calls the witness to testify conducts what is called the **direct examination**. The other side conducts the **cross examination**. There are many limitations on what a witness may testify about, such as whether a witness can give an opinion or whether the witness may mention what someone told him or her. If an attorney believes a witness is asked an improper question, the attorney may make an objection.

Next are **closing arguments,** in which each side has the opportunity to sum up its case. Here the prosecution gets to go last, since it has the burden of proof. There are, however, some states (such as Florida) where the defense gets to argue both first and last if no evidence other than the defendant's testimony has been offered. After closing arguments (or in some jurisdictions *before* them), the judge will give the jury instructions on the applicable law. These include instructions on the elements of the crime charged, the presumption of innocence, and the burden of proof—which in criminal trials is proof beyond a reasonable doubt.

Once the jury has received its instructions, it retires to the jury room to deliberate. It remains there until a **verdict** is reached. In most jurisdictions, criminal verdicts must be unanimous. Failure to achieve a unanimous jury means the case is declared a **mistrial.** If a mistrial occurs, the defendant may be retried without violating the prohibition against double jeopardy.

Sentencing

If a jury returns a verdict of "not guilty," the defendant is set free. The constitutional prohibition on double jeopardy prevents the state from prosecuting the defendant again for the same act. If the verdict is "guilty," a **sentence** must be imposed. In some states the judge imposes the sentence, while in others the jury has the power to impose sentence. The exception is death penalty cases, in which the jury traditionally imposes, or at the very least recommends, the sentence. The sentence is usually not handed down immediately after the verdict. Instead the judge orders a **presentence investigation (PSI)** and sentencing recommendation, written by officers in a probation department.

http://www.mcacp.org/issue58.htm

A number of sentences are possible, including probation, a suspended sentence, or a fine. Factors influencing sentence include the information contained in the **presentence report (PSR),** the attitude of defendant, and the defendant's prior criminal and personal history. The presentence report and investigation is critical to the judge's ability to impose an appropriate sentence. The presentence investigations are typically conducted by probation staff. The resulting report provides the court with a summary of the social, family, mental, physical, and criminal history of the defendant, often followed by a sentencing recommendation. Information contained within the presentence report cannot, however, be used as the basis for a finding of aggravating factors that enhance the sentence to be imposed. In recent years, there has been a move to increase sentence length and require incarceration. One favored method is the increased use of habitual offender and mandatory sentencing laws. Such laws diminish the discretion of the sentencing judge and typically result in a significant increase in the number of persons incarcerated.

Appeals

Once a person has been convicted and sentenced, there are two ways for him or her to challenge the trial outcome: a **direct appeal** or an indirect appeal, also known as a **writ of habeas corpus**. *Habeas corpus* translates as "you have the body," and the writ requires the person to whom it is directed to either produce the person named in the writ or release that person from custody. There is no federal constitutional right to an appeal, but every state allows a direct appeal by either statute or state constitutional provision.

The writ of habeas corpus is considered an indirect appeal because it does not directly challenge the defendant's conviction but instead challenges the authority of the state to incarcerate the defendant. The state defense to a habeas writ is based on the criminal conviction. Habeas corpus is an ancient legal remedy, dating back at least to the Magna Carta. It is often referred to as the "Great Writ."

There is no time limit for filing of habeas petitions, unlike direct appeals, which in most jurisdictions must be filed within a set period, usually several months. However, Congress has recently restricted the use of habeas corpus by imposing time limits on federal habeas petitions if there is evidence of intentional delay by the defendant that does injury to the prosecution's case. Additionally, Congress and the Supreme Court have recently restricted habeas corpus by imposing limits on how such appeals are filed and pursued, such as requiring that inmates include all their appealable issues in one writ, rather than doing separate, consecutive writs for each issue.

http://usinfo.state.gov/usa/infousa/laws/majorlaw/s735.htm

Summary

While justice may be an elusive concept, one with different meanings for different people in the United States, it is clear that the court system is intended to provide a forum for doing justice. There are many types of courts, but all share this common feature. Courts serve as a forum for

settling disputes between private parties, as a means of prosecuting individuals who break the law, and as a place where public policy is sometimes
made. The common refrains "I'll sue you" and "I'll take it all the way to
the Supreme Court" are evidence that courts are a popular forum. This
chapter has examined the structure of the federal and state courts. Both the
federal and state court systems typically have three levels, the trial court,
an intermediate appellate court, and a supreme court. The U.S. Supreme
Court is the court of last resort, the final arbiter of legal disputes.

The courtroom is populated with a number of actors, all of whom
are crucial to its operation. For our purposes, the three most important
courtroom actors are the judge, the prosecutor, and the defense attorney.
These are the individuals who will organize the presentation of evidence
and conduct the examination of witnesses. The jury hears the evidence and
makes a determination of whether the defendant is guilty as charged.

There are a number of steps in the trial process, which begins with an
arrest or the filing of a complaint and the issuance of an arrest warrant.
Each of these stages requires different actions by the courtroom actors.
Evidence law is most prominently displayed during trial, but evidentiary
issues may also arise and be dealt with in pretrial proceedings.

Discussion Questions

1. Explain the concept of jurisdiction and give four examples of the types of jurisdiction.
2. How does a case get to the Supreme Court? What is the basis for acceptance of an appeal?
3. What are the three main purposes of the Supreme Court?
4. Who are the three key actors in court? What are the duties of each?
5. When a trial begins, which side presents its case first and why?
6. Briefly explain the types of appeals.
7. What is voir dire? What are the different challenges available during voir dire? Have any of them been abused in the past?
8. What is the Judiciary Act of 1789, and what did it do?
9. What does the phrase "court of last resort" mean, and which courts does it apply to?
10. Who is the current chief justice of the Supreme Court, and how long has he or she been chief justice? Who are the other eight members of the Supreme Court?
11. What are the methods of selecting judges?
12. List the process involved in pretrial proceedings in the order that they occur after arrest.

Further Reading

Abraham, H. J. (1987). *The Judiciary: The Supreme Court in the Governmental Process* (7th ed.). Boston: Allyn and Bacon.

Blumberg, L. (1967). "The Practice of Law as Confidence Game: Organizational Co-optation of a Profession." *Law and Society Review* 15(1):18–21.

Brigham, J. (1987). *The Cult of the Court.* Philadelphia: Temple University Press.

Graham, B. L. (1990). "Judicial Recruitment and Racial Diversity on State Courts." *Judicature* 74(1):28–34.

Harris, D. A. (1992). "Justice Rationed in the Pursuit of Efficiency: De Novo Trials in the Criminal Courts." *Connecticut Law Review* 24:382–431.

Horwitz, M. J. (1977). *The Transformation of American Law 1780–1860.* Cambridge, MA: Harvard University Press.

Kelly, A. H., W. A. Harbison, and H. Belz. (1983). *The American Constitution: Its Origins and Development* (6th ed.). New York: W. W. Norton.

Meador, D. J. (1991). *American Courts.* St. Paul, MN: West Group.

Shreve, G. R., and P. Raven-Hansen. (1994). *Understanding Civil Procedure* (2nd ed.). New York: Matthew Bender.

Slotnick, E. E. (1984). "The Paths to the Federal Bench: Gender, Race, and Judicial Recruitment Variation." *Judicature* 67(8):370–388.

Smith, C. E. (1992). "From U.S. Magistrates to U.S. Magistrate Judges: Developments Affecting the Federal District Courts' Lower Tier of Judicial Officers." *Judicature* 75(4):210–215.

Uphoff, R. J. (1992). "The Criminal Defense Lawyer: Zealous Advocate, Double Agent, or Beleaguered Dealer?" *Criminal Law Bulletin* 28(5):419–456.

Wasby, S. L. (1993). *The Supreme Court in the Federal Judicial System.* Chicago: Nelson-Hall.

Cases Cited

Apodaca v. Oregon, 406 U.S. 404 (1972)

Batson v. Kentucky, 476 U.S. 79 (1986)

County of Riverside v. McLaughlin, 500 U.S. 44 (1991)

J. E. B. v. Alabama ex rel T.B., 511 U.S. 127 (1994)

Johnson v. Louisiana, 406 U.S. 356 (1972)

Strickland v. Washington, 466 U.S. 668 (1984)

Williams v. Florida, 399 U.S. 78 (1970)

CHAPTER 3
IMPORTANT CONCEPTS UNDERLYING EVIDENCE LAW

Key Terms & Concepts

Affirmative defenses

Battered Child Syndrome (BCS)

Battered Woman Syndrome (BWS)

Burden of production

Burden of proof

Castle doctrine

Clear and convincing evidence

Consent

Defense of others

Defense of property

Duress

Durham test

Excuse defense

Execution of public duties

Fleeing felon doctrine

Insanity

Insanity Defense Reform Act of 1984

Intoxication

Irresistible impulse test

Justification defense

M'Naghten test

Mens rea

Mistake of fact

Mistake of law

Parens patriae doctrine

Preponderance of the evidence

Prima facie showing

Proof beyond a reasonable doubt

Reasonable doubt

Retreat doctrine

Right or wrong test

Self-defense

Substantial capacity test

True man doctrine

Chapter Learning Objectives

By the end of this chapter, the student should be able to:

- Explain the difference between burden of production and burden of proof
- Identify the various levels of proof
- Explain what is meant by an affirmative defense
- Explain what is meant by a justification defense
- Explain what is meant by an excuse defense
- Identify the various standards used to establish insanity as a defense
- Explain how Battered Child Syndrome and Battered Woman Syndrome are utilized in criminal trials

Introduction

While Chapter 2 introduced the background and structure of American courts, Chapter 3 expands on that foundation by examining basic elements of the criminal trial process. These basic elements center upon concepts such as burden of proof, burden of production, defenses to prosecution, and the insanity defense. Within this context, we explain which side bears the burden of proving guilt and the standard that must be met in doing so. We also provide a workable definition of "proof beyond a reasonable doubt." The chapter gives detailed consideration to and explanation of various affirmative defenses to prosecution including self-defense, defense of others, and consent. The notion of diminished culpability/legal responsibility through the use of various "excuse" defenses is also addressed. For example, the claim of duress asserts that one had no choice but to commit a given crime in the face of an impending threat or other source of harm. The issue of intoxication as a mitigating factor in the evaluation of criminal culpability is discussed, as well as other excuse defenses such as age and mistake of fact/mistake of law. The chapter concludes with an overview of the insanity defense along with the different standards that have been adopted and relied on over the years to determine whether or not a defendant is not guilty by reason of insanity.

Burdens of Production and Proof

In the United States, the criminal courts use the adversary system to establish the guilt of a criminal defendant. Both the prosecution and the defense are expected to do everything they can to win their case yet play by the rules established to ensure that the proceedings are fair. In theory, this adversary system is intended to ensure that all relevant evidence will be brought out and that each side will have an opportunity to fully and adequately present its case. In criminal trials, the prosecution has both the burden of production and the burden of persuasion.

The Burden of Production

The **burden of production** refers to the obligation placed on one side in a trial to produce evidence to make a prima facie showing on a particular issue. A **prima facie showing** means having enough evidence to justify submission of the matter to the jury if unchallenged by the other side. It is also called burden of going forward.

In a criminal case, the prosecution has the burden of production. Placing the burden of production on the prosecution means a criminal defendant cannot be found guilty unless the prosecution introduces sufficient evidence to prove that the defendant committed the crime. The defendant is under no obligation to introduce evidence that he or she is innocent and, in fact, may elect not to call any witnesses or introduce evidence during the trial. The failure by the prosecution to introduce evidence of each element of the crime charged will result in a directed verdict for the defendant, without any requirement that the defense introduce evidence or call any witnesses.

The Burden of Proof

The **burden of proof** is placed on the prosecution to convince a judge or jury regarding a particular issue. By comparison, the burden of production merely requires the prosecution to provide some evidence. Of the two, the burden of proof is a more demanding standard because it requires the prosecution to provide evidence sufficient enough to justify a conviction.

There are different levels of the burden of proof depending on the type of trial. Generally, in civil matters the burden of proof is typically proof by a **preponderance of the evidence.** This burden requires that the party with the burden of proof must establish that the facts asserted are more probably true than false. This standard is a relatively easy one to meet. For some, it often helps to quantify the discussion on burdens of proof. For example, in a garden-variety civil case, the plaintiff must "tip the scales" in his or her favor. In other words, using 100 percent as the total, the plaintiff must prove his or her case by 51 percent. If a tie results at trial and the proof is essentially equal (e.g., 50/50) the plaintiff will lose the case. In certain civil cases, a higher standard is utilized. This burden requires proof by **clear and convincing evidence.** In other words, the plaintiff must establish that the facts supporting their case are quite likely true. This standard lies somewhere between proof by a preponderance of the evidence and proof beyond a reasonable doubt. In essence, the difference is largely one of quantity. Again, thinking in terms of percentages, the clear and convincing standard would require the plaintiff to tip scales but in much greater proportion. Generally, legal scholars suggest that the stricter standard requires the plaintiff to establish his or her case by approximately 75 percent. In other words, the plaintiff must produce evidence that is both clear and convincing on the issues they must establish at trial. Thus, in these civil cases it is no longer sufficient to simply tip the scales. Civil cases that may require a higher burden of proof include paternity cases, will contests, civil commitment proceedings, deportation hearings, and termination of parental rights. Essentially, the legal system demands much greater proof where the stakes are higher.

The Reasonable Doubt Standard

The burden of proof in a criminal trial is **proof beyond a reasonable doubt.** This means that the facts asserted are highly probable. Because the liberty or life, in cases where the death penalty is sought, of a criminal defendant is at stake, this burden is a difficult one to meet. Every state has a statutory provision, usually found in the penal code, requiring that no defendant shall be found guilty in a criminal case unless guilt is established "beyond a reasonable doubt." Determining that the prosecution has failed to meet its burden of proof is different from determining that the defendant is innocent. That is why the verdict delivered is "not guilty" rather than "innocent." "Not guilty" is a legal finding that the prosecution has failed to meet its burden of proof, not necessarily a factual description of reality or an indication that the defendant is innocent.

The requirement that the prosecution prove the guilt of the defendant "beyond a reasonable doubt" is derived from the common law, and the Supreme Court has held that it is required by the due process clause of the Constitution (*In re Winship*, 1970). However, precisely what constitutes "reasonable doubt" is less clear. Many courts have attempted to define it for the jury with varying degrees of success.

The **reasonable doubt** standard traces its roots as far back as the twelfth century. The phrase "moral certainty" was equated with "reasonable doubt" at that time. Achieving "moral certainty" meant that a juror was virtually certain of the defendant's guilt. The standard of persuasion at this time was often referred to as the "satisfied conscience test," meaning that jurors were to convict only if in their conscience they were sure that the defendant was guilty. While the language is different, the "satisfied conscience" standard is similar to the concept of "reasonable doubt" in that jurors were instructed that a guilty verdict should be delivered only if the evidence supporting it was very strong.

By the early eighteenth century, American courts commonly required proof of guilt beyond a reasonable doubt in criminal trials. Yet, there were few attempts to define the term. The most famous attempt occurred in *Commonwealth v. Webster* (1850). Most current definitions of reasonable doubt are derived from Chief Justice Shaw's oft-cited opinion, which states:

> [W]hat is reasonable doubt? It is a term often used, probably pretty well understood, but not easily defined. It is not mere possible

doubt; because everything relating to human affairs, and depending on moral evidence, is open to some possible or imaginary doubt. It is that state of the case, which, after the entire comparison and consideration of all the evidence, leaves the minds of jurors in that condition that they cannot say they feel an abiding conviction, to a moral certainty, of the truth of the charge.

Most states today have case law that provides some definition of reasonable doubt. While some states adhere to only one definition, other states accept multiple definitions. There are a number of commonly used definitions of reasonable doubt. They include "a doubt that would cause one to hesitate to act" (used in some form in at least 20 states), "a doubt based on reason" (used in 17 states), and "an actual and substantial doubt" (used in 10 states). Other, less-popular definitions include "a doubt that can be articulated" and "moral certainty" (Hemmens, Scarborough, and del Carmen, 1997). While no universal rule regarding reasonable doubt exists, it is clear, that a conviction may be obtained despite the existence of some doubt. Thus, jurors are not required to be able to set aside all doubt in order to return a guilty verdict but rather must labor to ensure that there is no reasonable doubt regarding the guilt of the defendant.

The U.S. Supreme Court has upheld several definitions of reasonable doubt. In *Leland v. Oregon* (1952), the Court recommended that courts define reasonable doubt using the "hesitate to act" formulation. In 1970, the Court in *In re Winship* applied the reasonable doubt standard to juvenile adjudications and stated that the reasonable doubt standard is a constitutionally required protection for a criminal defendant. Justice O'Connor acknowledged in a more recent case (*Victor v. Nebraska,* 1994) that while the requirement of proof beyond a reasonable doubt "is an ancient and honored aspect of our criminal justice system, it defies easy explication." She noted, however, in upholding the jury instruction used in this case, that the Constitution does not require that any particular definition of reasonable doubt be used.

The Supreme Court has reason for concern over the definition of reasonable doubt. Researchers have conducted a number of studies of the abilities of juries to understand jury instructions. These studies have found that juror misunderstanding is created by the instruction's terminology, phrasing, and manner of presentation and by the general unfamiliarity of the jurors with legal terminology (Kassin and Wrightsman, 1979; Severance and Loftus, 1982). A study of Florida jurors found that half of the jurors who were given an instruction on the burden of proof erroneously believed a defendant was required to prove his innocence (Strawn and Buchanan, 1976).

Several studies have attempted to determine how jurors quantify "reasonable doubt." One early study found that jurors quantified it as 87 percent sure of guilt (Simon and Mahan, 1971), while a later study found jurors quantified it as 86 percent sure of guilt (Kassin and Wrightsman, 1979). Interestingly, this result compares with an estimate of 90 percent or more by judges (McCauliff, 1982). While these findings suggest that jurors understand the phrase "reasonable doubt" to mean something close to absolute certainty, it is unclear how different definitions of reasonable doubt might affect the quantification of the concept.

Other Standards

While the general rule is that the state has the burden of production and the burden of proof in a criminal trial, there are exceptions to the rule. If a defendant wishes to raise an affirmative defense, such as alibi, self-defense, or insanity, he or she must introduce evidence to support that defense. Thus, the burden of production may shift to the defense.

In most states, the burden of proof is also shifted to the defendant when an affirmative defense is raised. However, the general rule is that the burden of proof is by "a preponderance of the evidence" rather than "beyond a reasonable doubt." As stated earlier, proof by a preponderance of the evidence is the burden of proof used in civil trials and is often quantified as 51 percent sure, or if the jury believes it is more likely than not. This is a relatively easy burden of persuasion to meet. A few states do not switch the burden of proof to the defense but instead still require the state to disprove the affirmative defense beyond a reasonable doubt.

Recently, a few states and the federal courts have changed the burden of proof for the affirmative defense of insanity, requiring the defense to prove it by "clear and convincing evidence." Recall that this quantum of proof lies somewhere between "a preponderance of the evidence" and "proof beyond a reasonable doubt." This shift in the level of the burden of proof was in response to several "not guilty by reason of insanity" verdicts in high-profile cases, such as the trial of John Hinckley Jr., for the attempted assassination of President Ronald Reagan. There was a feeling that defendants in such cases were finding it too easy to escape criminal liability for their actions.

Affirmative Defenses

A defense is a response made by the defendant to a charge in a criminal trial. It is raised after the prosecution has established its case and permits the defendant to avoid liability even when the government has met its burden of proof on the elements of the offense. The general defenses of justification and excuse are referred to as **affirmative defenses** because the defendant must raise them for the jury to consider them (this is an example of the burden of production).

http://www.law.cornell.edu/wex/index.php/Affirmative_defense

Generally, the defendant must also meet the burden of persuasion on an affirmative defense by a "preponderance of the evidence," although some states impose a greater burden of persuasion on the defendant for certain defenses such as the insanity defense, while other states require the prosecution to disprove an affirmative defense beyond a reasonable doubt.

Justification Defenses

A **justification defense** is raised when the defendant admits he or she is responsible for the act but claims that under the circumstances the act was not criminal that it was lawful. Justified behavior precludes punishment because the conduct lacks blameworthiness. Examples of common justification defenses include (1) self-defense, (2) defense of others, (3) defense of property, (4) consent, and (5) the execution of public duties.

Self-Defense

Self-defense may be successfully claimed if the defendant can demonstrate that he or she used force to repel an imminent, unprovoked attack that would have caused him or her serious physical injury or death. In such situations, the defendant may use only as much force as he or she honestly and reasonably believes is necessary to repel the attack the defendant cannot use excessive force. Additionally, force may only be used against unprovoked attacks. This means the defendant cannot provoke the attack; or, if he or she did, he or she must have withdrawn completely from the fight before asserting a right to self-defense. Force may be used only when the victim honestly and reasonably believes he or she is about to be killed or seriously injured. Threats that cannot be taken seriously do not justify the use of force. Force may be used only when an attack is either in progress or "imminent" meaning it will occur immediately. It cannot be used to prevent a future attack. One cannot claim self-defense against someone who is justified in using force; self-defense may be asserted only against an aggressor using unlawful force. In addition, the law of self-defense applies to both deadly and nondeadly uses of force. One may use deadly force only if faced with it. Less-than-deadly attacks authorize less-than-deadly responses.

There are a number of limitations and exceptions to the general rules of self-defense. The **retreat doctrine** requires that a person must retreat rather than use deadly force if it is possible to do so without endangering the retreating party. This doctrine places a premium on human life and discourages the use of deadly force unless absolutely necessary and is endorsed by the majority of states. The **true man doctrine**, conversely, states that the victim of an attack need not retreat and may use whatever force is necessary to repel an attack, even if a safe retreat was possible. It is based on the idea that the criminal law should not force a victim to take a cowardly/humiliating position. Few states follow this doctrine today. The **castle doctrine** states that a person attacked in the home does not have to retreat, even if retreat is possible. This exception to the retreat doctrine is based on the idea that a home is one's castle and that one should never be forced by the criminal law to abandon it.

While it is generally agreed upon that one may use self-defense in situations where the threat of serious bodily injury or death is imminent, jurisdictions differ with regard to the standard that must be used to determine the state of mind of the defendant regarding the threat. For example, the majority of jurisdictions use an objective approach, which requires the defendant to establish that a reasonable person would have believed that the threat of serious bodily harm or death was imminent. Thus, the jury is to view the evidence from the perspective of a reasonable person. In other words, would a reasonable person who was in the position of the defendant believe an attack was imminent? The second approach or standard is the subjective approach, which allows the jury to consider the facts and circumstances from the perspective of this particular defendant. Thus, the jury may consider any unusual or individual characteristics of the defendant that may have contributed to or altered the person's perceptions and his or her belief that force was necessary. In such jurisdictions, the jury is not limited to the perspective of a hypothetical reasonable person.

Gradually, the legal system has begun to recognize the existence of the **Battered Woman's Syndrome (BWS)** and the **Battered Child Syndrome (BCS)**. Each syndrome suggests that there are certain characteristics of victims in these cases that alter their perceptions and ability to control their response to a threatened or perceived violent attack. In other words, the perceptions of victims who have been repeatedly beaten are different than those of an average person who has not endured long-term abuse. These syndromes are typically raised in cases where the "victim" is on trial for the murder of the "abuser" and are typically raised where the killing is not in direct response to an attack. Rather, in many cases, the victim kills the abuser when the abuser is sleeping or walking away.

Traditionally, these cases would result in murder convictions because there was not an imminent threat of death or serious bodily injury. However, evidence regarding the syndrome and its effects on the person is admitted for purposes of understanding the perception of the defendant regarding an imminent threat of death or injury. Expert testimony is required in order to establish that the defendant does, in fact, suffer from the syndrome and to inform the jury about the syndrome and its effects. The jury is then asked to determine whether, in light of the circumstances, whether the defendant is responsible for the killing or may have been acting in self-defense. Interestingly, in many cases, juries are not persuaded by the existence of the syndrome or its effect on abuse victims. Rather, juries tend to be reluctant to excuse the killing of a person, especially in cases where they do not believe there was an imminent threat to the killer. This, of course, goes to the essence of these syndromes—the altered perception of an imminent threat and the availability of alternatives.

One of the most notorious cases involving the admission of evidence regarding battered child syndrome was the case against Lyle and Erik Menendez. There, the brothers, on trial for the murder of their parents, argued that they were acting in self-defense following years of sexual and physical abuse. Following months of testimony (both expert and otherwise) and a second trial, the jury was not persuaded that the Menendez brothers acted in self-defense and returned convictions of murder. They were sentenced to life in prison.

Defense of Others and Defense of Property

Self-defense may also apply to **defense of others** and, in very limited circumstances, to the **defense of property**. Historically, defense of others was allowed only for family members. Most states have expanded this restriction to include other special relationships, such as lovers and friends, while other states have abandoned the special relationship requirement altogether. However, to use the defense of others, the defendant must establish that the "other" person would have had the right to defend herself or himself. Thus, if A provokes an attack by B, C could not use force against B and claim defense of A. Most states restrict the use of deadly force to defense of the person or the home and allow only non-deadly force for defense of property. Some states, such as Texas, go further in allowing deadly force to protect land or certain types of property, such as natural gas.

Consent

Consent is a defense to some crimes. Most jurisdictions provide that persons may consent to suffer what would otherwise be considered a legal harm. The acts a person can consent to suffer are quite limited, however, and it must be demonstrated that the consent was voluntary, knowing, and intelligent. There can be no duress, trickery, or incompetence involved in the obtaining of consent. Additionally, one cannot consent after the fact to injuries already received.

Most jurisdictions allow consent only for minor injuries or for activities that society widely recognizes have a high potential for injury. An example of consent is professional athletes who choose to engage in activity in which injury similar to an assault may occur, as in a boxer punching another boxer. One cannot consent to serious injury as to do so is assumed irrational. Thus, one cannot claim consent as a defense in mercy killing/euthanasia cases.

Moreover, when raising consent as a defense to a criminal charge, the defendant must establish that the victim was competent to consent to the conduct. For example, in statutory rape cases, the consent of the victim is irrelevant because the female is under the age of consent. Thus, the age of the victim renders her leally unable to consent. In other words, the law has determined that children under a certain age (generally between 14 and 16) are legally incompetent to give consent to sexual conduct. In addition to minority, other factors may vitiate the ability of a victim to give consent, including intoxication, mental incapacity, unconsciousness, and senility. Moreover, the mere acquiescence in the conduct by the victim is not the equivalent of consent.

Execution of Public Duties

The common law allowed public officials to use reasonable force in the **execution of public duties.** This defense recognizes the value society places on obeying the law and in permitting those charged with official duties with the necessary authority to carry out those duties. Today an agent of the state, such as a police officer or soldier, is permitted to use reasonable force in the lawful execution of his or her duties. This defense allows the use of deadly force under the proper circumstances and also allows police to engage in activities that would otherwise be deemed criminal if committed by an ordinary citizen. However, public officials may only engage in such conduct if they are doing so as part of their law enforcement efforts, such as posing as a drug dealer.

At common law, police could use deadly force to apprehend any fleeing felon. At this time, felonies were capital offenses, and it was particularly difficult to apprehend fleeing criminals. This was known as the **fleeing felon doctrine.** The U.S. Supreme Court, in *Tennessee v. Garner* (1985), held that police use of deadly force to apprehend fleeing criminal suspects was limited by the Fourth Amendment, which requires that all seizures be conducted in a reasonable manner. Thus, post-*Garner*, police officers must reasonably believe that the suspect is armed and dangerous and poses an imminent threat to the life of the officer or others. It is no longer sufficient to use deadly force against a suspect merely because he or she is suspected of a felony.

Excuse Defenses

The second type of affirmative defense is the **excuse defense**. With an excuse defense the defendant admits that what he or she did was wrong but argues that under the circumstances should not be held responsible for the improper conduct. Examples of excuse defenses include duress, intoxication, mistake, age, and insanity.

Duress

Duress may be raised as a defense in a limited number of situations. For example, suppose A is forced by B to rob a store, who holds a gun to A's head and threatens to kill A unless A does as instructed. In this instance, A commits a serious crime, the robbery, but does so only to avoid a more serious crime, being murdered by B. Duress is allowed as a defense under the rationale that those forced to commit a crime in such circumstances do not act voluntarily, and the criminal law, as a practical matter, cannot force people to act irrationally against their own self-interest.

At common law, the defense of duress was permitted only when the defendant was threatened with both imminent and serious harm and when the act committed under duress resulted in less harm than the threatened harm. Most states now allow the defense for all crimes except murder (which is never excused), while some still limit the defense to minor crimes. Some states allow the duress defense only under fear of "instant harm," but most still follow the common law "imminent harm" rule. In most jurisdictions, threats to harm a third person or property do not constitute duress. However, in some jurisdictions, threats to harm a child or close family will constitute duress.

Intoxication

The effect of alcohol or drug **intoxication** on criminal liability differs according to whether it was voluntary or involuntary. Involuntary intoxication will serve as a defense provided the defendant is able to establish that the intoxication was involuntary; that due to the intoxication, the defendant was unable to appreciate the difference between right and wrong; and finally, that the crime was a result of the intoxication. Voluntary intoxication never provides a complete defense, but it may be used to mitigate the punishment. Involuntary intoxication may provide a defense if it can be shown that the actor was unaware that he or she was being drugged. In such cases, the actor is excused because he or she is not responsible for becoming intoxicated; consequently, it would be unfair to hold him or her liable for the resulting uncontrollable and unintended action. Interestingly, the Supreme Court has held that due process does not require that states allow the defense of intoxication (*Montana v. Egelhoff*, 1996). Obviously, intoxication is also never recognized as a defense in situations where intoxication is an element of the crime, such as drunk driving or public intoxication.

Montana v. Egelhoff
Supreme Court of the United States
518 U.S. 37 (1996)

In July 1992, while camping out in the Yaak region of northwestern Montana to pick mushrooms, respondent made friends with Roberta Pavola and John Christenson, who were doing the same. On Sunday, July 12, the three sold the mushrooms they had collected and spent the rest of the day and evening drinking, in bars and at a private party in Troy, Montana. Some time after 9 p.m., they left the party in Christenson's 1974 Ford Galaxy station wagon. At about midnight that night, officers of the Lincoln County, Montana, sheriff's department, responding to reports of a possible drunk driver, discovered Christenson's station wagon stuck in a ditch along U.S. Highway 2. In the front seat were Pavola and Christenson, each dead from a single gunshot to the head. In the rear of the car lay respondent, alive and yelling obscenities. His blood-alcohol content measured .36 percent over one hour later. On the floor of the car, near the brake pedal, lay respondent's .38 caliber handgun, with four loaded rounds and two empty casings; respondent had gunshot residue on his hands.

Respondent was charged with two counts of deliberate homicide, a crime defined by Montana law as "purposely" or "knowingly" causing the death of another human being. A portion of the jury instruction, uncontested here, instructed that "[a] person acts purposely when it is his conscious object to engage in conduct of that nature or to cause

(continued)

such a result," and that "[a] person acts knowingly when he is aware of his conduct or when he is aware under the circumstances his conduct constitutes a crime; or, when he is aware there exists the high probability that his conduct will cause a specific result." Respondent's defense at trial was that an unidentified fourth person must have committed the murders; his own extreme intoxication, he claimed, had rendered him physically incapable of committing the murders, and accounted for his inability to recall the events of the night of July 12. Although respondent was allowed to make this use of the evidence that he was intoxicated, the jury was instructed that it could not consider respondent's "intoxicated condition . . . in determining the existence of a mental state which is an element of the offense." The jury found respondent guilty on both counts, and the court sentenced him to 84 years' imprisonment.

Following review by the United States Supreme Court, the Court upheld Egelhoff's convictions and held that it is not surprising that many States have held fast to or resurrected the common-law rule prohibiting consideration of voluntary intoxication in the determination of mens rea, because that rule has considerable justification, which alone casts doubt upon the proposition that the opposite rule is a "fundamental principle." A large number of crimes, especially violent crimes, are committed by intoxicated offenders; modern studies put the numbers as high as half of all homicides, for example. See, e.g., *Third Special Report to the U.S. Congress on Alcohol and Health from the Secretary of Health, Education, and Welfare* 64 (1978); Note, Alcohol Abuse and the Law, 94 *Harv. L. Rev.* 1660, 16811682 (1981). Disallowing consideration of voluntary intoxication has the effect of increasing the punishment for all unlawful acts committed in that state, and thereby deters drunkenness or irresponsible behavior while drunk. The rule also serves as a specific deterrent, ensuring that those who prove incapable of controlling violent impulses while voluntarily intoxicated go to prison. And finally, the rule comports with and implements society's moral perception that one who has voluntarily impaired his own faculties should be responsible for the consequences. See, e.g., *McDaniel v. State*, 356 So. 2d 1151, 11601161 (Miss. 1978).

There is, in modern times, even more justification for such laws. Some recent studies suggest that the connection between drunkenness and crime is as much cultural as pharmacological, that is, that drunks are violent not simply because alcohol makes them that way, but because they are behaving in accord with their learned belief that drunks are

(continued)

violent. See, e.g., Collins, Suggested Explanatory Frameworks to Clarify the Alcohol Use/Violence Relationship, 15 *Contemp. Drug Prob.* 107, 115 (1988); Critchlow, The Powers of John Barleycorn, 41 *Am. Psychologist* 751, 754–755 (July 1986). This not only adds additional support to the traditional view that an intoxicated criminal is not deserving of exoneration, but it suggests that juries who possess the same learned belief as the intoxicated offender will be too quick to accept the claim that the defendant was biologically incapable of forming the requisite mens rea. Treating the matter as one of excluding misleading evidence therefore makes some sense.

Mistake

There are two types of mistake defenses: mistake of law and mistake of fact. The cliché "ignorance of the law is no excuse" is actually a misstatement. **Mistake of law** has always excused some (but very little) criminal responsibility. Ignorance is an excuse if the defendant undertakes reasonable efforts to learn the law but is still unaware that he or she has violated some obscure, unusual law. The constitutional prohibition on vague laws means persons must be provided with reasonable notice of what constitutes criminal conduct before they are punished for such conduct. For example, in *Miller v. Commonwealth* (1997), the Court concluded that the defendant could prevail on his defense of "mistake of law" to the charge of possession of a firearm by a convicted felon. In *Miller,* the defendant argued that he relied on the assurance by his probation officer that he could possess a muzzle-loading rifle but not other types of firearms. As such, the defendant established that he was mistaken regarding the type of weapon that he was prohibited from possessing following his conviction.

Mistake of fact excuses criminal liability only when the mistake negates a material element of the crime. The mistake must be both reasonable and honest. An example would be if a student took another student's notebook in class by mistake, thinking it was his or hers. While he or she has taken the property of another, as in larceny, he or she lacks the requisite intent to deprive another of his or her property.

Age

Historically, youth has been treated as a defense to criminal liability on the ground that persons below a certain age lack the requisite mental capability to form **mens rea**, or criminal intent. At common law there was an irrebuttable presumption that children under the age of 7 years were incompetent. Children between the ages of 7 and 14 were presumed incapable, but this presumption could be rebutted by the prosecution. Children over the age of 14 were presumed to have mental capacity to form mens rea, but the defense could rebut this presumption. Today the various jurisdictions define the age of majority at different ages, ranging from 16 to 21.

Those classified as juveniles are dealt with not in the criminal justice system but rather in the juvenile justice system. The juvenile court was established as an alternate, more forgiving, approach to juvenile offenders and was based on the *parens patriae* **doctrine**, which holds that the state should act in the best interests of a child. Today the *parens patriae* doctrine of the juvenile court is slowly giving way to an increased desire to treat juveniles similarly to adult offenders; hence, a number of states have removed juvenile court jurisdiction for serious crimes or repeat offenders or have lowered the age at which a juvenile can be transferred to adult criminal court (Fritsch and Hemmens, 1996).

Insanity

http://www.lawandpsychiatry.com/html/landmark.html#landmark

Insanity is a legal term that describes mental illness. Contrary to popular belief, it is not a medical term. Criminal liability is excused because insanity results in impaired *mens rea* (state of mind) of the defendant. Thus, if a defendant is determined insane, he or she is not blameworthy or culpable. Several legal tests for insanity have developed over time, usually in response to a particularly egregious crime. These tests focus on the reason and willpower of the defendant. These tests include the right-or-wrong test (also called the M'Naghten rule), the irresistible impulse test, the Durham test, and the substantial capacity test. Each of the tests to determine insanity is slightly different.

http://www.law.cornell.edu/wex/index.php/Insanity_defense

The **M'Naghten test** for insanity focuses on the defendant's intellectual capacity to know what he or she is doing and to distinguish right from wrong. It is a two-prong test: (1) the defendant must suffer from a disease or defect of the mind, and (2) this disease must cause the defendant either to not know the nature and quality of the criminal act or to not know right from wrong. Questions about this definition include the following: (1) What constitutes a "disease of the mind"? Is it any mental problem, or just a severe psychosis? (2) What does "know" mean? Most courts have held that it means intellectual awareness, which nearly everyone has. Other courts say it means being able to grasp an act's true significance.

(3) What is "wrong"? Does it refer to what is defined as wrong by the law, or to what is considered immoral?

The **irresistible impulse test** for insanity is used when a defendant is unable to control his or her conduct because he or she suffers from a mental disease. This test holds that the defendant is not responsible if a mental disease keeps him or her from controlling his or her conduct, even if the person knows the conduct is wrong. This test is broader than the right-wrong test, but critics have argued that it ignores mental illnesses that involve reflection. Consider the case of Andrea Yates. She suffered from postpartum depression and psychosis and was convicted of murder for the drowning deaths of her five young children. Although Yates was initially convicted by the state of Texas under the M'Naghten rule, she was later found not guilty by reason of insanity upon retrial. As such, whether Yates knew her acts were wrong was a critical issue in her defense and ultimately defeated her insanity defense. However, if Yates were tried in a jurisdiction that used the irresistible impulse test, the outcome of her first trial may have been different. In such a jurisdiction, Yates could have argued that although she understood the act of drowning her children was morally and legally wrong and illegal, her mental disease prohibited her from conforming her conduct to those standards.

The **Durham test** for insanity states that the defendant is not criminally responsible if his act was "the product of mental disease or defect." This is also called the *product rule*. It is an attempt to go beyond the right-wrong test's emphasis on intellectual cognition and the irresistible impulse test's emphasis on volition. This test has been widely criticized as too imprecise and has fallen out of favor.

The **substantial capacity test**, drafted by the American Law Institute, defines insanity as existing when the defendant lacks substantial capacity to either control his or her conduct *or* appreciate the wrongfulness of his or her conduct. This test became popular during 1970s as a modified version of the right-or-wrong and irresistible impulse tests. This test states that a defendant is not responsible if he or she lacks "substantial capacity to appreciate criminality of an act or to conform his conduct." This test requires that the defendant lack substantial as opposed to total capacity to conform. The right-wrong and irresistible impulse tests are ambiguous on this point. The substantial capacity test also uses "appreciate" instead of "know." Thus a defendant who intellectually knows right from wrong but doesn't appreciate (understand and perceive consequences) the difference may be excused unlike with the M'Naghten rule.

http://www.law.umkc.edu/faculty/projects/ftrials/hinckley/hinckleytrial.html

All of these tests have been criticized as either too difficult or too lenient. Several states and the federal courts have recently limited the use of the insanity defense or have altered the burden of proof in establishing the defense. This movement stems from a fear that insane defendants will not be adequately punished or will be released too soon. An example is the **Insanity Defense Reform Act of 1984**, passed shortly after John Hinckley, Jr. was found not guilty by reason of insanity for attempting to assassinate President Ronald Reagan. This legislation shifted the burden of proof from requiring the government having to prove sanity beyond a reasonable doubt to requiring the defense to prove insanity by clear and convincing evidence (a tougher standard than the preponderance of the evidence standard usually applied to affirmative defenses). The Model Penal Code rejects this approach and requires the state to prove sanity beyond a reasonable doubt. Some states allow a verdict of "guilty but mentally ill." Such a verdict requires the state to treat the defendant in a hospital instead of putting him or her in prison. However, once the defendant is deemed well, he or she may be transferred to a correctional facility. Critics contend that this approach undermines effective therapeutic intervention because patients who face transfer have no incentive to get well. Some states have abolished the insanity defense altogether.

Summary

This chapter examined several concepts important for understanding how American courts operate. For example, it is important to define exactly what is meant by use of the term "proof beyond a reasonable doubt." This concept can be compared against other standards of proof, such as a preponderance of the evidence and clear/convincing proof. A related concept, the burden of production, refers to determining which side bears the responsibility of producing evidence at trial.

Affirmative defenses include the justification defenses of self-defense, defense of others and/or property, and consent. These justification defenses are contrasted with excuse defenses, which include duress, intoxication, age, mistake of fact, and mistake of law. The insanity defense is a controversial one, judged by several differing standards.

These concepts, which are frequently bantered about within pop culture by the mass media, are oftentimes difficult to operationally define, given their lengthy legal histories. Combined with changing public attitudes regarding individual responsibility and the degree to which mentally ill individuals should be held accountable, this situation makes the various affirmative and excuse defenses sometimes difficult to apply. Nonetheless, they are important elements of the law and, as such, provide an important basis for understanding much of the information regarding evidence law to be presented in later chapters.

Discussion Questions

1. Define and give three examples of a justification defense.
2. Define and give three examples of an excuse defense.
3. What is an affirmative defense?
4. Name and explain the different standards for the burden of proof.
5. Although there is no clear definition of "reasonable doubt," we do have many interpretations of meaning. Why is there concern over having a definition?
6. What are the various definitions that have been used for the term "reasonable doubt"?
7. Explain the reasonable doubt standard. What cases has the Supreme Court used to define this standard?
8. Give examples of what you believe to be the difference between a preponderance of the evidence and proof beyond a reasonable doubt.
9. Explain the M'Naughten rule.
10. What is the Durham test for insanity? What is the argument against this test?
11. What is the substantial capacity test?

Further Reading

Amar, A. R. (1997). *The Constitution and Criminal Procedure*. New Haven, CT: Yale University Press.

Brown, R. M. (1991). *No Duty to Retreat: Violence and Values in American History and Society*. New York: Oxford University Press.

Bugliosi, V. (1981). "Not Guilty and Innocent: The Problem Children of Reasonable Doubt." *Court Review* 20:16–25.

DeLoggio, L. (1986). "Beyond a Reasonable Doubt—A Historic Analysis." *New York State Bar Journal* 58(3):19–25.

Dressler, J. (1995). *Understanding Criminal Law*. New York: Matthew Bender.

Fletcher, G. (1978). *Rethinking Criminal Law*. Boston: Little Brown.

Fritsch, E. and C. Hemmens. (1996). *Juvenile Waiver in the U.S. 1977–1993: A Juvenile and Family Court Journal* 46:3.

Gardner, M. R. (1993). "The Mens Rea Enigma: Observations on the Role of Motive in the Criminal Law Past and Present." *Utah Law Review* 1993: 635.

Hart, H. M. (1958). "The Aims of the Criminal Law." *Law and Contemporary Problems* 23:401.

Hemmens, C. and D. Levin. (2000). "Resistance Is Futile: The Right to Resist Unlawful Arrest in an Era of Aggressive Policing." *Crime and Delinquency* 46:472.

Hemmens, C., K. Scarborough, and R. V. del Carmen. (1997). "Grave Doubts About Reasonable Doubt: Confusion in State and Federal Courts." *Journal of Criminal Justice* 25:231–254.

Kadish, S. (1987). "Excusing Crime." *California Law Review* 75:257.

Kassin, S. and L. Wrightsman. (1979). "On the Requirements of Proof: The Timing of Judicial Instruction and Mock Juror Verdicts." *Journal of Personality and Social Psychology* 37:1877–1887.

Katz, L., M. S. Moore, and S. J. Morse. (1999). *Foundations of Criminal Law.* New York: Foundation Press.

Kerr, N., R. Atkin, G. Stasser, D. Meek, R. Holt, and J. Davis. (1976). "Guilt Beyond a Reasonable Doubt: Effects of Concept Definition and Assigned Decision Rule on the Judgments of Mock Jurors." *Journal of Personality and Social Psychology* 34:282–294.

McCauliff, C. (1982). "Burden of Proof: Degrees of Belief, Quanta of Evidence, or Constitutional Guarantees?" *Vanderbilt Law Review* 35:1293–1335.

Morano, A. (1975). "A Reexamination of the Development of the Reasonable Doubt Rule." *Boston University Law Review* 55:507–528.

Morris, N. (1982). *Madness and the Criminal Law.* New York: Oxford University Press.

Morse, S. J. (1985). "Excusing the Crazy: The Insanity Defense Reconsidered." *Southern California Law Review* 58:777.

Schulhofer, S. J. (1974). "Harm and Punishment: A Critique of Emphasis on the Results of Conduct in the Criminal Law." *University of Pennsylvania Law Review* 122:1497.

Severance, L. and E. Loftus. (1982). "Improving the Ability of Jurors to Comprehend and Apply Criminal Jury Instructions." *Law and Society Review* 17:153–197.

Shapiro, B. (1991). *Beyond Reasonable Doubt and Probable Cause: Historical Perspectives on the Anglo-American Law of Evidence.* Berkeley: University of California Press.

Simon, R. and L. Mahan. (1971). "Quantifying Burdens of Proof: A View From the Bench, the Jury, and the Classroom." *Law and Society Review* 5:319–330.

Strawn, D. and R. Buchanan. (1976). "Jury Confusion: A Threat to Justice." *Judicature* 59:478–483.

Ward, P. (1997). "Judicial Activism in the Law of Criminal Responsibility: Alcohol, Drugs and Criminal Responsibility." *Georgetown Law Journal* 63:69.

Cases Cited

Commonwealth v. Webster, 59 Mass. 295 (1850)

In Re Winship, 397 U.S. 357 (1970)

Leland v. Oregon, 343 U.S. 790 (1952)

Miller v. Commonwealth, 492 S.E.2d 482 (1997)

Montana v. Egelhoff, 518 U.S. 37 (1996)

Tennessee v. Garner, 471 U.S. 1 (1985)

Victor v. Nebraska, 511 U.S. 1 (1994)

CHAPTER 4

REAL, DEMONSTRATIVE, AND TESTIMONIAL EVIDENCE

Key Terms & Concepts

Ability

Ascertainable fact

Blank pad rule

Circumstantial evidence

Common knowledge

Demonstrative evidence

Direct evidence

Habits of guilt

Indisputable fact

Informed individual

Intent

Judicial notice

Judicial notice of adjudicative facts

Judicial notice of law

Judicial notice of legislative facts

Modus operandi

Motive

Real evidence

Rule 201

Tacit judicial notice

Tenor

Testimonial evidence

Uniform Judicial Notice of Foreign Law Act

Chapter Learning Objectives

By the end of this chapter, the student should be able to:

- Distinguish between real, demonstrative, and testimonial forms of evidence
- Explain the difference between direct and circumstantial evidence
- Understand the concept of judicial notice by comparison to the blank pad rule
- Identify the varieties of judicial notice
- Explain the relative benefits and criticisms of judicial notice

Introduction

In this chapter we turn our attention to the various "forms" of evidence. We begin by distinguishing between real and testimonial evidence. We then draw distinctions between direct and circumstantial evidence and examine the concept of judicial notice.

The various topics covered throughout this chapter are all interrelated. For example, real evidence can be direct and circumstantial. Jurors can draw inferences based on testimonial evidence. Judicial notice can be taken with reference to real evidence. In short, a great deal of overlap exists between the various evidentiary topics covered within this chapter.

Other important topics addressed in the chapter include the defendant's intent or motive was the act in question committed by accident or with malice? A closely related topic is whether the defendant demonstrates consciousness of guilt, as manifested by an attempt to conceal or destroy evidence, for example. The chapter also describes certain circumstantial forms of evidence, such as the character of a victim or suspect, and introduces the concept of judicial notice, varieties of notice, and the procedures for its application along with notable criticisms and the practical necessity for such measures.

Types of Evidence

Two types of evidence are repeatedly referred to throughout this text: real evidence and testimonial evidence. **Real evidence** refers broadly to any tangible item that can be perceived with the five senses. Real evidence can consist of physical items, such as articles of clothing, weapons, and drugs, or of documents, such as contracts, letters, newspaper articles, and so on. Photographs, videos, and the like are also considered real evidence.

One particularly important type of real evidence is known as **demonstrative evidence**. Demonstrative evidence is, as the term suggests, evidence intended to "demonstrate" a certain point. Examples of demonstrative evidence are drawings and diagrams, displays and demonstrations, computer simulations, and many others. What sets demonstrative evidence apart from other forms of real evidence is its ability to help jurors sort through a complex matter. For example, a diagram may show how several pieces of real evidence are linked together.

The second type of evidence, **testimonial evidence**, refers to what someone says. However, not just anything that is said can be considered testimonial evidence. Testimonial evidence is evidence given by a competent witness who is testifying in court and under oath. Other types of testimonial evidence include affidavits and depositions taken out of court. The key to testimonial evidence is that it be given under oath. If a statement is not made under oath, it may not be admissible as evidence. Certain exceptions to this rule exist. Some hearsay statements, for example, are

Table 4.1   **Types of Evidence**

	Real Evidence	**Testimonial Evidence**
Definition	Tangible items	Things people say
Types	Demonstrations, Physical evidence	In-court testimony, Validly obtained confessions

admissible in court as evidence (see Chapters 12 and 13). Table 4.1 shows the relationships between the types of evidence covered in this book.

Direct and Circumstantial Evidence

There are two varieties of real and testimonial evidence: direct and circumstantial. It is possible for real evidence to be either direct or circumstantial, and it is also possible for testimonial evidence to be either direct or circumstantial.

Direct evidence is evidence that proves a fact without the need for the juror to infer or presume anything from it. It is evidence that speaks for itself that directly proves a certain fact. By contrast, **circumstantial evidence** is evidence that indirectly proves a fact. Circumstantial evidence requires jurors to draw their own conclusions concerning whether the evidence in question should be taken as proof of the defendant's guilt (or lack thereof). Circumstantial evidence does not speak directly to the defendant's involvement in a crime; it shows involvement in a roundabout way.

An example of direct evidence is testimony by a witness that the accused committed the crime. Assuming the witness can be believed, his or her statements in court do not require that jurors infer the defendant's guilt. More specifically, if a witness testifies that she saw the defendant shoot the victim, jurors need not make much of an intellectual leap between the witness's testimony and the defendant's guilt. Again, this assumes that the witness is to be believed.

Another example of direct evidence could be a convenience store videotape clearly showing the defendant robbing the teller. If the video is properly authenticated (see Chapter 9), the jurors will not have to infer the defendant's guilt. In other words, the video speaks for itself. Unfortunately, direct evidence is not very common. By far the most common type of evidence is circumstantial. Thus, we will devote attention here to examples of and rules surrounding the admissibility of circumstantial evidence.

We have already described circumstantial evidence as being "indirect" in nature. Return to our example of the witness who saw the accused shoot the victim. If, instead, the witness testified that she overheard, rather than observed, the accused and the victim fighting and, further, that she heard a gunshot, jurors could only infer that the victim was shot by the accused.

Circumstantial evidence does not require that an inference be drawn. That is, once circumstantial evidence is presented to the jury, it is up to individual jurors to decide on the merits of the evidence in question. Some circumstantial evidence is highly convincing and nearly direct. Other types require a substantial leap between the evidence and the conclusion. Given the many types of circumstantial evidence (some strong, others weak), we frequently say that jurors "may" infer the defendant's guilt.

The most common methods by which jurors can infer guilt include circumstantial evidence (1) of the defendant's ability to commit the crime, (2) of the defendant's intent or motive, (3) the defendant's consciousness of guilt, (4) involving the victim, or (5) involving the character of the suspect or victim. Let us consider each type of circumstantial evidence in more detail.

Ability to Commit the Crime

Sometimes it is clear that the defendant possessed the **ability** to commit the crime. This information can assist jurors in concluding that the defendant is guilty. For example, assume that the defendant is on trial for bombing a government embassy. If the prosecution can show that the defendant had the technical knowledge to construct a bomb, the jury may able to infer guilt. By contrast, if the defense can show that the accused lacked the technical knowledge to build the bomb, jurors may infer that the accused is not guilty.

Another method by which the accused can be shown to have the ability to commit the crime is to demonstrate that he or she has the means to offend. For example, if the prosecution shows that the defendant owns a gun that it is of the same type and caliber as that used in the killing of the victim, the jury may infer the defendant's guilt. Or, if a youth is arrested and found to have sparkplug porcelain (a burglary tool) in his possession, and this evidence is introduced at trial, the jury may be able to conclude that the youth is guilty of burglary.

A defendant's physical capacity can also be considered evidence of an ability to commit a crime. If the facts of the case show that only a person with a certain body makeup could commit the crime, jurors may infer guilt. More specifically, if a victim was killed by being crushed with a

500-pound barbell, jurors may be able to infer the defendant's guilt if he is big enough to complete such a feat.

Finally, a defendant's mental capacity may be enough to constitute circumstantial evidence of guilt. If it can be shown that the defendant possessed the knowledge and intelligence to engage in a sophisticated insider trading scheme, the jury may infer the defendant's guilt. If, by contrast, someone of subnormal intelligence with no understanding of the stock market is put on trial for the same offense, it would be difficult for the jury to infer guilt. The defense would capitalize on this fact and strive to show that the defendant could not possibly have been involved in such a sophisticated crime.

Usually, the defendant's mental capacity is not treated as circumstantial evidence. Indeed, most of the time the defendant's mental status is irrelevant. This is because most crimes are not highly sophisticated and most are committed by people of "normal" intelligence. Mental capacity usually only "matters" when the defendant claims insanity, when perhaps a juvenile is involved, or when, as we have seen, the crime requires a level of sophisticated knowledge that the ordinary person probably does not possess.

Intent or Motive

Three types of circumstantial evidence are relied on in order to show **intent** or motive. The first is **modus operandi**, which literally means "the method of operation." The second is motive, and the third is threats. If it can be shown that one of these three is present, jurors may be able to infer guilt.

If the prosecutor points out that the defendant has committed past crimes that are similar to the present one, this is circumstantial evidence. For example, if a homicide defendant has been twice convicted of murdering his victims by decapitation, jurors may be able to infer guilt if the same method was used in the homicide for which the defendant is currently being tried. It is not enough for the prosecution to show that the defendant was convicted of similar crimes in the past; rather, it must show that the method of operation was the same. Because evidence of prior crimes is not usually admissible, the prosecutor will need to convince the judge before circumstantial evidence of modus operandi will be allowed.

Motive can also provide circumstantial evidence of guilt. Motive rarely needs to be proven by the prosecution, unless it is an element of the underlying offense, but it can still help convince jurors that the defendant is guilty. For example, if the prosecution shows that a husband took out a $1 million life insurance policy on his wife before her murder, it may also seek to convince the jury that the defendant sought to profit from his wife's death. Motive can also come from a need for revenge or retaliation, and it can come from hate and prejudice. Countless other forms of motive can be identified, depending on the nature of the offense.

Finally, if it is clear that a defendant has threatened the victim of a crime on several occasions, the jury may infer that he or she is guilty. For example, if in a trial for aggravated assault, the prosecution shows that the defendant repeatedly threatened to "beat up" the victim, jurors may be inclined to infer guilt from this pattern of activity. Again, the decision on whether to assign value to such evidence is the jury's. It could be that the defendant has a pattern of making empty threats and never carrying them through to fruition. If the defense shows that this is the case, the jurors would probably downplay this form of circumstantial evidence. The prosecution would then need to introduce other evidence and make a more convincing case that the defendant is guilty of aggravated assault.

Consciousness of Guilt

If the prosecution can show that the defendant is demonstrating the **habits of a guilt**, jurors may be inclined to infer guilt from such evidence. Guilt can be demonstrated in several ways, including fleeing, concealing or destroying evidence, possessing the fruits of crime, showing sudden wealth, and making threats against witnesses. Let us briefly elaborate on each.

First, if a person flees to avoid punishment, guilt can sometimes be inferred. Why else would someone who is about to be tried for a crime flee? Flight from the police, after being released on bail and at other stages of the criminal process, can be used to infer guilt. For example, if a securities fraud defendant flees the country following his release on bail and assuming he doesn't seek refuge in a non-extradition country and is brought back to the United States for trial, the prosecution will probably point out to the jury that the defendant fled and that he should be considered guilty of the crime for doing so.

Next, if the prosecution can show that the defendant took steps to conceal evidence, jurors may again be inclined to infer guilt. Also, if it can be shown that the defendant consciously destroyed evidence, guilt may be inferred. Even falsifying or tampering with evidence can provide circumstantial evidence of guilt. For example, if the police find a discarded pistol with the defendant's fingerprints on it, the jury may conclude that his decision to throw the gun away is evidence of some criminal act; why else would someone throw away a perfectly good gun? Likewise, if the prosecution shows that the defendant attempted to flush illegal narcotics down the toilet, the jury may conclude that he or she is guilty.

Clearly, if the defendant is caught with the fruits of a criminal act, it may be tempting to infer guilt. Say, for example, that a burglary defendant is caught with stolen stereo equipment. If the prosecution introduces evidence of this possession at trial, the jury may conclude that the defendant is guilty of the crime. What about someone who possesses the fruits of crime but honestly does not know that the material was illegally obtained? Rarely is ignorance a defense, and it is still a criminal act in most jurisdictions to be caught in possession of stolen property. Either way, when a defendant possesses material that he or she did not legally acquire, juries can easily infer a certain measure of guilt.

Circumstantial evidence of guilt also exists when the defendant appears to amass sudden wealth. For example, if the defendant in a narcotics trial recently bought a $2 million mansion and does not appear to be engaged in any legitimate business activities the jury may conclude that such sudden wealth is indicative of guilt. Indeed, in many such situations the government will seek forfeiture of the defendant's property either civilly or criminally. All states as well as the federal government have laws that provide for the forfeiture of property that is used to facilitate a crime or is derived from criminal activity. Forfeiture applies to many offenses other than narcotics violations.

Finally, let us consider a hypothetical trial of a mafia kingpin. If the prosecution can show that the defendant repeatedly threatened to kill witnesses who would testify against him (perhaps through their own testimony), jurors may conclude that the defendant is guilty. The very fact that he would not want witnesses to say anything at trial suggests that he has something incriminating to hide.

Evidence Involving the Victim

Most circumstantial evidence directly involves the defendant: Something about the defendant, such as his or her habits, life changes, experiences, and so on, points to guilt. However, circumstantial evidence can also involve other parties to a criminal case. In particular, something that has happened to a victim can provide circumstantial evidence of the defendant's guilt. Let us consider some examples.

First, assume a defendant is on trial for rape. His defense attorney claims that the victim consented to intercourse. However, the prosecution introduces expert medical testimony to the effect that the injuries suffered by the victim were not indicative of a consensual sexual encounter. In this instance, the victim's injuries help provide circumstantial evidence of the defendant's involvement in the crime.

As another example, let us assume that a man is on trial for first-degree murder. He is accused of forcing the victim to get on his knees and of shooting the victim in the back of the head, execution style. Assume further that the defense argues that the victim's injuries were self-inflicted and that the defendant could not have been involved in the crime because he was at the movies with friends. However, the prosecution introduces expert testimony to the effect that the victim's injuries were not consistent with suicide. That is, the prosecution argues that the injuries suffered by the victim were a result of an intentional shooting. With this information, the jury may be inclined to conclude that the defendant is guilty. And with additional evidence by the prosecution, such as evidence pointing to a gap in the defendant's alibi and perhaps gunshot residue on the defendant's hands, its case would be substantially more persuasive.

Evidence Involving the Character of the Suspect or Victim

In Chapters 6 and 7 we will discuss the important topics of witness competency, credibility, and impeachment. Of these topics, credibility is important to our current discussion. Credibility refers to the veracity of the witness whether he or she should be believed. Credibility is basically synonymous with character. If a person is of questionable character, he or she may not be credible. Evidence concerning a person's character is not direct evidence. Rather, it requires that an inference be drawn, which means that character evidence is circumstantial evidence.

Issues of character can be brought into a criminal trial in one of two ways. First, the defendant's character may be questioned. However, before a defendant's character can be attacked by the prosecution, the defense must first present testimony to the effect that the defendant is of solid moral character. Only when the defendant plays the character card can the prosecution attack his or her character. Whether the defense or prosecution is more convincing does not matter here; either way, the jury will be forced to infer that the defendant is of good character or not.

The character of victims is also called into question from time to time. For example, if the defendant in a criminal trial argues that he killed the victim in self-defense, he or she may attempt to show that the victim lacked character and was, perhaps, prone to violent outbursts. The character of rape victims has also been questioned in some criminal trials, but rape shield laws curtail this practice to a certain extent. Regardless of how victim character is called into question, jurors again must weigh this form of circumstantial evidence and reach their own conclusions concerning the defendant's involvement in the criminal act at issue.

Judicial Notice

http://www.law.indiana.edu/instruction/tanford/b723/jnotice.html

Judicial notice is a procedure that courts use to determine the truth or falsity of a matter *without* having to follow the normal rules of evidence. Another common definition of judicial notice is any use of a fact that has not been proved by ordinary evidentiary means. The normal rules of evidence are the main topic of this book. We turn later to specific rules for determining what types of evidence are admissible and when. Judicial notice, by contrast, does not require attention to any of these guidelines.

Why judicial notice? Without it, courts would be bound to the **blank pad rule**. This rule provides that the court and jury in a criminal case know nothing about the dispute between the two parties involved. The only way that the court and the jury come to know about the dispute is through evidence properly introduced. However, if *every* shred of information relevant to the case had to be introduced in accordance with the formal rules of evidentiary procedure, trials would take years.

Another way to understand the need for judicial notice is to put yourself in the shoes of a person with absolutely no knowledge or awareness of anything, except the English language. Without judicial notice, judges and jurors would have to be educated on every minute detail relevant to the case, from proving the sun rises every day to showing where Idaho is located, showing that gravity causes objects to fall to the earth, and so on.

Judicial notice is therefore best understood as a method for saving time. In this vein, judicial notice is something of a substitute for evidence; it gives all parties involved in any case jurors, judges, and the attorneys a means of agreeing on a particular fact without undue delay and debate. Understood in yet another way, judicial notice is legalese for preexisting or common knowledge.

Who Is Responsible for Judicial Notice?

Judicial notice is always taken by the judge in a case. That is, the judge gives judicial notice of certain facts. The term *judicial notice* itself suggests that a judge gives notice of something. The "something" that notice refers to is, again, anything that is common knowledge and that does not need to be presented to the court in accordance with the formal rules of evidence.

Varieties of Judicial Notice

There are several varieties of judicial notice. One is **tacit judicial notice**, which occurs when the judge does not make any statements to the effect that judicial notice is being given with regard to a certain fact. It is unspoken judicial notice. An example of tacit judicial notice could occur when jurors hear from a witness to a vehicle accident that the victim died in the crash. The court will give tacit judicial notice by allowing the jurors to infer that the term "vehicle" refers to some sort of automobile with four or so wheels. In such an instance, the judge will not interrupt the witness and explain to the jury what a vehicle is; every potential juror already knows.

Tacit judicial notice probably accounts for almost all facts that the court takes notice of. Rarely is it actually the case that a judge will pause to give judicial notice to a certain fact. Common knowledge is what it is knowledge that almost everyone has. There seems little need to stop or otherwise interrupt a trial to reinforce common knowledge. Thus, it is not totally inaccurate to state that judicial notice is an academic exercise. It is hardly ever explicitly mentioned outside the pages of textbooks such as this.

The second type of judicial notice is **judicial notice of law**, which occurs when courts accept what is written in statutes, constitutional provisions, and court cases. A court could be given judicial notice that the penal code contains two elements for the crime of second-degree murder: (1) intentional (2) killing of another. It would be a significant distraction if the parties were required to stop and convince the court that the penal code is authentic as well as written and enacted by the legislature.

http://www.law.cornell.edu/rules/frcp/ACRule44_1.htm

What about the laws and rules of other jurisdictions? Judicial notice of law must be taken in the area that law covers. The very purpose of the laws of a particular state, for example, is that they be used and enforced by the courts. Many states have also adopted the **Uniform Judicial Notice of Foreign Law Act**, which requires that every court in a specific state give notice of the common law or statutes of every other jurisdiction in the United States. Next, because federal law is to quote Article VI of the U.S. Constitution "the supreme law of the land," all federal and state courts must given judicial notice of its provisions. Judicial notice can also be taken of municipal ordinances and administrative regulations, but it is typically limited to the courts that enforce them. Finally, judicial notice of foreign laws is hardly ever taken.

Closely connected to judicial notice of law is **judicial notice of legislative facts**. Legislative facts are the facts that courts rely on when interpreting statutes, constitutional provisions, and the like. Think of legislative facts as those bits of information legislators assume to be true when passing laws. For example, federal guidelines requiring that firearm retailers be licensed implicitly assume that guns are dangerous and can kill people. Accordingly, a court may give judicial notice that firearms are inherently dangerous.

Judicial Notice of Adjudicative Facts

The next type of judicial notice is **judicial notice of adjudicative facts**. Adjudicative facts constitute a catchall category. They are matters of general knowledge not otherwise connected to statutes, constitutions, administrative rules, or other sources of law. Given that there are so many types of adjudicative facts, we explain them in a separate subsection.

According to **Rule 201** of the Federal Rules of Evidence, a court can only take judicial notice of an adjudicative fact if it is (1) indisputable, (2) common knowledge, and (3) an ascertainable fact. Let us consider each of these criteria in some detail.

The "Indisputable" Component

An **indisputable fact** is one that speaks for itself and requires virtually no interpretation or debate as to its truthfulness (FRE 201[b]). We have included the terms "reasonably" and "virtually" in this definition because there are certain facts that can be disputed, however far-fetched the argument. For example, most educated people know that the earth is round, but some people still believe it is flat. Likewise, some organized groups steadfastly believe that humans were put on earth by aliens, even though there is no publicly available evidence other than blind faith to support such an outlandish claim.

The Common Knowledge Component

The component of common knowledge seems simple enough, but it can be fairly difficult to define with precision (see FRE 201[b]). A fact is considered **common knowledge** if it is (1) generally known, (2) by informed individuals (3) within the jurisdiction of the trial court. These three elements are discussed in the next three paragraphs.

The notion of an **informed individual** is somewhat abstract. For example, informed individuals know that the Supreme Court is made up by nine justices, even though many Americans are ignorant of this fact. Likewise, it is well known that exceeding the posted speed limit in one's car by 30 miles an hour is risky, but it can be quite a feat to convince young drivers that this is true.

Next, the phrase "within the jurisdiction of the trial court" refers to the district, county, or state within which the court sits. This limitation on judicial notice is important because there are certain bits of common knowledge in one area but not another. For instance, it would be common knowledge to Seattle residents that the Redhook Brewery originated in Ballard, Washington. Jurors in other cities or states may not know this.

What, then, are facts that are "generally known"? Perhaps some specific examples from actual court cases will prove illustrative. Courts have considered it general knowledge that pistols are deadly weapons (*State v. Taylor,* 1916) and that full-choke shotguns scatter more than open-bore shotguns (*Sanders v. Allen,* 1911). Courts have also taken notice that automobiles cause extensive injury and loss of life (*State v. Przybyl,* 1937).

Generally known facts can have a historical dimension as well. For example, that the stock market crash of 1929 actually occurred is considered generally known. In fact, almost any documented historical event with a date attached to it can be considered general knowledge, even though many jurors' understanding of history is sketchy. Similarly, geographical facts can be considered general knowledge. Courts take judicial notice of the location of prominent geographic features, the division of the country into states, the division of states into counties, distances between certain points, and the like. It would be a waste of the court's time for the parties to prove such matters.

Other types of generally known facts include facts relating to nature and science as well as facts connected to language, symbols, and abbreviations. Certain natural events and varieties of scientific knowledge even if not known to the layperson can be considered generally known. Examples of such knowledge can be found in the laws of physics. With regard to language and symbols, courts usually take judicial notice of words defined in the dictionary. It would be a distraction to say the least if the parties to a case had to debate the meaning of certain words. They also take notice of symbols such as road signs; a red octagon with the word STOP in the middle is noticed as a stop sign. Similarly, courts take judicial notice of certain abbreviations provided they are generally known. An example is the abbreviation Ph.D. after someone's name. Most people know that Ph.D. is an advanced degree known as a doctorate of philosophy in some subject (such as criminal justice).

The Ascertainable Fact

Finally, getting back to our definition of an adjudicative fact, an **ascertainable fact** is one that can be determined by looking it up in some source (such as a dictionary), the accuracy of which cannot be easily disputed (FRE 201[b]). An example of an ascertainable fact is the distance in miles between Seattle and Los Angeles. The mileage can easily be determined by consulting a popular road atlas.

A fact cannot be considered ascertainable if it is exceedingly difficult to locate a source to back it up. Some facts are ascertainable only by experts trained to identify the information in question. For example, the periodic table of elements is a source whose accuracy cannot be easily disputed, but most laypeople cannot understand most of what it contains.

Obviously, certain sources cannot be trusted. A source is considered accurate if its accuracy cannot reasonably be questioned. Thus, a claim that someone's destiny is based on the day's horoscope is not a fact that courts will take judicial notice of; the accuracy of astrology can easily be questioned. Finally, with regard to the nature of the source, courts generally prefer to consult written documents when taking judicial notice of certain facts that need to be "looked up." Sometimes, however, people can serve as the source for factual information, provided their knowledge cannot reasonably be disputed.

Rule 201. Judicial Notice of Adjudicative Facts

(a) Scope of rule.

This rule governs only judicial notice of adjudicative facts.

(b) Kinds of facts.

A judicially noticed fact must be one not subject to reasonable dispute in that it is either (1) generally known within the territorial jurisdiction of the trial court or (2) capable of accurate and ready determination by resort to sources whose accuracy cannot reasonably be questioned.

(c) When discretionary.

A court may take judicial notice, whether requested or not.

(d) When mandatory.

A court shall take judicial notice if requested by a party and supplied with the necessary information.

(e) Opportunity to be heard.

A party is entitled upon timely request to an opportunity to be heard as to the propriety of taking judicial notice and the tenor of the matter noticed. In the absence of prior notification, the request may be made after judicial notice has been taken.

(f) Time of taking notice.

Judicial notice may be taken at any stage of the proceeding.

(g) Instructing jury.

In a civil action or proceeding, the court shall instruct the jury to accept as conclusive any fact judicially noticed. In a criminal case, the court shall instruct the jury that it may, but is not required to, accept as conclusive any fact judicially noticed.

Procedure for Judicial Notice

As indicated already, judicial notice will sometimes go without mention. The court and the parties to the case will automatically assume, without reflection, that certain facts are true. However, when the court opts to take formal judicial notice of a certain fact, it is required to follow a certain procedure according to the Federal Rules of Evidence (notably Rules 201[c]–[f]).

First, a court may take judicial notice of a certain fact without anyone requesting that the court do so. That is, neither attorney in the case has asked the court to take notice of a fact. Rather, the judge informs the parties to the case that the court has noticed, or intends to notice, a certain fact. This allows both parties an opportunity to contest the court's decision to take notice of the fact.

Both parties to a case can also formally request that the court take judicial notice of some fact. There are two components to such a request. First, the party seeking judicial notice of some fact must formally request notice. Second, the party must also provide the source of the fact and prove that the source is accurate. This method of securing judicial notice is also open to contest. For example, one party may succeed in securing judicial notice but the other may disagree.

What if one of the parties disputes the court's decision to take judicial notice on some fact? Usually, both parties and the judge will confer on the matter outside the hearing range of the jury on the judge's decision. There are two methods of contesting judicial notice. First, one or more parties can challenge the "propriety" of taking notice by showing that the fact is not generally known. Alternatively, one or more parties can challenge the **tenor** of the fact noticed. Tenor refers not to whether the fact is generally known but rather to whether the fact, as the court has interpreted it, is wrong.

It is conceivable that, even with a persuasive argument to the contrary, a court could wrongfully take judicial notice of a certain fact. If this situation occurs, the issue can be resolved at the appellate level. That is, appellate courts can decide whether the lower court's decision to take judicial notice was valid. Appellate courts can also take judicial notice of facts themselves say, in the event that the lower court failed to do so. Parties cannot, however, request judicial notice at the appellate level; it is entirely within the discretion of appellate courts to do so.

More Benefits of Judicial Notice

As we have seen, judicial notice is something of an efficiency mechanism; it speeds events up. How precisely does it do so? First, judicial notice bars

Table 4.2   Arguments for and Against Judicial Notice

Arguments for Judicial Notice	Arguments Against Judicial Notice
1. Speeds events up, prevents delay	1. May violate Sixth Amendment protections
2. Bars contrary evidence	2. May threaten confrontation
3. Makes the job of jury members easier	

contrary evidence. That is, it prohibits the opposing party (if one party contests notice) from introducing evidence to contradict the fact. Second, judicial notice makes jury members' duties easier. The court instructs the jury that it is to assume that a fact is true, which avoids time-consuming deliberations on its truthfulness (see Table 4.2).

Criticisms of Judicial Notice

Although judicial notice has advantages, haste can make waste. In particular, some critics of judicial notice have argued that it violates the Constitution. The Sixth Amendment guarantees the right to a jury trial, but when courts take judicial notice of facts, they essentially circumvent this provision. Similarly, when a court takes notice of a certain fact, it threatens the right of confrontation. Defendants are given the constitutional right to confront witnesses against them, but judicial notice even if both parties to a case agree on the court's decision essentially bars argument to the contrary.

Despite criticisms, judicial notice is a fixture of the American judicial system. Without it, court cases would drag on indefinitely. Judicial notice is actually much like plea bargaining in this way. Both save the court's time. If every criminal defendant asserted his or her right to trial, or if every fact were subject to dispute, the wheels of justice would grind to a screeching halt; little, if anything, would ever be accomplished in our nation's courts.

Summary

There are two general types of evidence, real and testimonial. Real evidence is any tangible item and can also consist of demonstrative evidence. The latter refers to the use of demonstrations to prove a point. A computer simulation is demonstrative evidence, as would be the use of a diagram to outline a suspect's presumed patterns of movement. Testimonial evidence refers to what people say under oath.

Real or testimonial evidence can be either direct or circumstantial. Direct evidence is evidence that proves a fact without the need for the juror to infer or presume anything from it. It is evidence that speaks for itself. A knife with the victim's blood on it is direct evidence. Circumstantial evidence requires an inference that a certain assertion is true. For instance, it would be reasonable to conclude that a defendant is guilty if he or she had the ability and opportunity to commit the crime, along with intent to do so, motive, and consciousness of guilt. Other types of circumstantial evidence exist.

Judicial notice is best understood as a substitute for evidence. When a court takes judicial notice of something, it is concluding that something is true and need not be debated by the opposing parties in open court. It is a procedure that courts use to determine the truth or falsity of a matter *without* having to follow the normal rules of evidence. Without judicial notice, judges and jurors would have to be educated on every minute detail relevant to every case.

Discussion Questions

1. What is the difference between real evidence and testimonial evidence?
2. What is the difference between direct and circumstantial evidence?
3. What are the three types of circumstantial evidence relied upon in order to establish intent or motive?
4. What are the two ways that issues regarding the character of the defendant or victim can be brought into trial?
5. Explain three types of judicial notice.
6. What are the criticisms of judicial notice? Do you agree or disagree? Why?

Further Reading

Fishman, C. S. (1992). *Jones on Evidence, Civil and Criminal* (7th ed.). Eagan, MN: West Group.

Graham, M. H. (1992). *Federal Practice and Procedure: Evidence* (interim ed.). Eagan, MN: West Group.

Lilly, G. C. (1996). *An Introduction to the Law of Evidence* (3rd ed.). Eagan, MN: West Group.

Mueller, C. B. and L. C. Kirkpatrick. (1999). *Evidence* (2nd ed.). Gaithersburg, MD: Aspen Publishers.

Strong, J. W. (1992). *McCormick on Evidence* (4th ed.). Eagan, MN: West Group.

Weinstein, J. B., J. H. Mansfield, N. Abrams, and M. A Berger. (1997). *Evidence: Cases and Materials* (9th ed.). Westbury, NY: Foundation Press.

Cases Cited

Sanders v. Allen, 65 U.S. 220 (1911)

State v. Przybyl, 6 N.E.2d 848 (1937)

State v. Taylor, 182 S.W. 159 (1916)

CHAPTER 5

PRESUMPTIONS, INFERENCES, AND STIPULATIONS

Key Terms & Concepts

Actus reus

Conclusive presumption

Inference

Mens rea

Presumption

Presumption against suicide

Presumption of a guilty mind following possession of fruits of the crime

Presumption of death upon unexplained absence

Presumption of fact

Presumption of innocence

Presumption of intended consequences resulting from voluntary actions

Presumption of knowledge of the law

Presumption of law

Presumption of regularity of official acts

Presumption of sanity

Presumption that young people are not capable of crime

Rebuttable presumption

Rule 301

Stipulations

Chapter Learning Objectives

By the end of this chapter, the student should be able to:

*   Distinguish between presumptions and inferences, explaining the practical need for both
*   Compare conclusive and rebuttable presumptions
*   Compare presumptions of law versus presumptions of fact
*   Identify the most common legal presumptions
*   Explain what is meant by a stipulation
*   Explain the use of stipulations in trials

Introduction

This chapter continues our examination of the various forms of evidence—real, demonstrative, and testimonial. Chapter 4 provided a preliminary overview of real and testimonial evidence and discussed the differences between direct and circumstantial evidence. It also outlined the concept of judicial notice and its role as a practical necessity in criminal proceedings.

Having established this backdrop, this chapter examines the use of presumptions, inferences, and stipulations. Like plea bargaining and judicial discretion, these are necessary elements of our court system without them criminal trials would most certainly come to a screeching halt. In this chapter, these "substitutes" for evidence are introduced and reviewed in detail. For example, we distinguish between presumptions and inferences. Additionally, we contrast conclusive presumptions against those of a rebuttable nature. Also of note are the differences between presumptions of law and of fact. We review various presumptions, including those of innocence, sanity, and knowledge of the law (among others), as common examples of this legal concept.

Presumptions and Inferences

Jurors rarely have occasion to witness the acts that call them to service. For example, jurors who have to decide the fate of a murder defendant rarely, in fact probably never, witness the murder firsthand. If an individual juror *did* happen to witness the murder firsthand, he or she would probably be a witness rather than a juror in the case. What happens in the real world is that jurors are presented evidence by both parties and must make their own decisions as to whether the defendant actually committed the crime. Two methods of doing so are making presumptions and inferences.

Distinguishing Between Presumptions and Inferences

With a **presumption,** a person draws a conclusion from one or more facts presented during a case. Understood differently, a presumption is a legal practice whereby a court accepts the existence of one fact from the existence of another fact that has already been proven. A presumption can also be understood as a substitute for evidence; it is a logical decision based on human knowledge, a decision that connects two or more important facts together in some fashion. Presumptions are covered in **Rule 301** of the Federal Rules of Evidence:

Rule 301. Presumptions in General Civil Actions and Proceedings

In all civil actions and proceedings not otherwise provided for by Act of Congress or by these rules, a presumption imposes on the party against whom it is directed the burden of going forward with evidence to rebut or meet the presumption, but does not shift to such party the burden of proof in the sense of the risk of nonpersuasion, which remains throughout the trial upon the party on whom it was originally cast.

http://www.lectlaw.com/def2/p149.htm

Inferences are often confused with presumptions, but there is a subtle distinction between the two. Presumptions are typically mandatory, meaning that the jury is *required* to draw some conclusion. **Inferences**, by contrast, are not mandatory. It is up to each jury member to draw inferences. As one court has put the matter:

> [An] inference is merely a logical tool which permits the trier of fact to proceed from one fact to another, whereas a "presumption" is a procedural device which not only permits an inference of the "presumed" fact, but also shifts to the opposing party the burden of producing evidence to disprove the presumed fact. (*Commonwealth v. DiFrancesco*, 1974)

Another court has drawn a distinction between inferences and presumptions in this way:

> Presumptions are one thing; inferences another. Presumptions are assumptions of fact which the law requires to be made from another fact or group of facts; inferences are logical deductions or conclusions from an established fact. Presumptions deal with legal processes, whereas inferences deal with mental processes. (*State v. Jackson*, 1989)

Because it is up to each individual juror to draw inferences, the rules of evidence make it difficult to restrict inferences. Presumptions, by contrast, are subject to several important restrictions. We therefore devote more attention to presumptions in the following sections.

Conclusive Versus Rebuttable Presumptions

Two types of presumptions can be identified. The first is a **conclusive presumption**, which requires that all parties in the case accept as true the presumed fact. Further, conclusive presumptions are presumptions that cannot be challenged by either the prosecution or the defense. Finally, conclusive presumptions are used where the law demands that the presumption be drawn. These are sometimes called irrebuttable presumptions.

The second type of presumption is a **rebuttable presumption,** in which the party against whom the presumption operates may introduce evidence to disprove the presumption. For example, it is reasonable to conclude that a letter that was stamped, addressed, and mailed arrived at the addressee. This is a *rebuttable presumption* because one party could argue that the letter never arrived. Another example of a rubuttable presumption would be asking the jury to infer that a person's disappearance for five years means that the person is dead. The party who would be harmed by this presumption, say, a murder defendant would vehemently attempt to rebut such a presumption because people can disappear for five years and not be dead.

Presumptions of Law Versus Presumptions of Fact

Presumptions can also be divided into presumptions of law and presumptions of fact. With a **presumption of law,** the law requires that an inference or deduction be drawn. An example of one such presumption is the **presumption of innocence:** Our criminal justice system requires that accused persons be presumed innocent until proven guilty.

Presumptions of law do not require that members of the jury draw some conclusion in all cases and at all times. Rather, juries must assume the presumption is factual until evidence is introduced to the contrary. Thus, when the prosecution introduces evidence suggesting that the defendant is guilty, the jury can change its mind and declare that the accused is guilty. Another way to understand presumptions of law is to think of them as applying at the outset of a criminal case.

Presumptions of fact are not required by law. Instead, they deal with facts, issues, and circumstances as they arise. Presumptions of fact cannot be made at the outset of a criminal case, like presumptions of law can. The need for presumptions of fact arises once both parties to a case begin to present evidence. The presumption that a stamped, addressed, and mailed letter reached its addressee is a presumption of fact and is not necessary until such evidence is brought to light at trial.

The Effect of Presumptions

The effect of presumptions varies depending on whether the case is civil or criminal. We focus here on the effect of presumptions in criminal cases because the rules of civil procedure would make the discussion unnecessarily complex. There are two important effects of presumptions in criminal cases: (1) the effect on the jury and (2) the effect on the burden of proof.

First, presumptions have the effect of causing the jury to draw some inference. Returning to our example of the mailed letter, if the opposing party does not claim that the letter was not received, the judge will instruct the members of the jury to conclude that the letter indeed reached its recipient. That is, the judge will instruct the jury that it must conclude that the letter arrived.

The second effect of presumptions is on the burden of proof. First, however, it is important to remember that the burden of proof in a criminal case almost always falls on the prosecution; it is proof beyond a reasonable doubt that the accused committed the crime (see *In re Winship*, 1970). This means that the state cannot put the burden of proof of any elements of the crime on the defense (see *Sandstrom v. Montana*, 1979). However, when a rebuttable presumption is offered by the prosecution, the burden of proof is shifted to the defense. In such an instance the presumption effectively "disappears," and the jury will be instructed by the judge to decide whether the presumption is factual.

A Sixth Amendment violation occurs when a conclusive presumption is required by law. This issue arose in the case of *Leary v. United States* (1969). In that case, Timothy Leary was convicted of "possession of marijuana knowing it was imported into the United States." The statute under which he was convicted required the presumption that people who possess marijuana know it was imported illegally. The Supreme Court held that the statute was unconstitutional because it did not leave it up to the jury to decide whether knowledge of illegal importation existed.

The Need for Presumptions and Inferences

Presumptions, like judicial notice, serve important purposes. First, since presumptions especially conclusive presumptions are substitutes for evidence, they speed up proceedings. Without certain presumptions, juries would be required to weigh every shred of evidence introduced by either side in the case. This process would be time-consuming and distracting.

Second, presumptions can serve important purposes for public policy outside the courtroom. As an example, it is commonly assumed that a child born in wedlock by two parents who live together (and by parents who are capable of having children) is legitimate. To assume otherwise would open a Pandora's box requiring that every child's parents be identified by DNA analysis. As another example, it is presumed that all people in the United States know criminal law (*Bakody Homes v. City of Omaha*, 1994). To assume otherwise would mean that every criminal defendant could claim ignorance as a defense.

Finally, presumptions are necessary for the normal functioning of governments and public organizations. For example, it is necessary to presume that public organizations and governments keep adequate records. Without such a presumption, the accuracy of records at all levels of government and in all public organizations could easily be disputed, causing unnecessary delay in daily functioning. If, for instance, a student could claim that her grade point average is really a 4.0, and not the 2.8 listed in her transcript, because a new person is working in the records office, universities would be an awkward predicament (and everyone would graduate with highest honors).

Types of Presumptions

Rebuttable presumptions are much more common than conclusive presumptions. Also, because conclusive presumptions are mandated by law, a complete review of such presumptions would require an extensive search of each state's statutes. We devote most of our attention in the rest of this chapter to rebuttable presumptions. Such presumptions pop up in courts throughout the country and do not require knowledge of each state's statutory provisions.

Examples of rebuttable presumptions include (1) the presumption of innocence, (2) the presumption of sanity, (3) the presumption against suicide, (4) the presumption of a guilty mind following possession of fruits of the crime, (5) the presumption of the regularity of official acts, (6) the presumption that young children are not capable of committing crime, (7) the presumption that people intend the consequences of their voluntary actions, and (8) the presumption of death following a lengthy unexplained absence. An example of a conclusive presumption is the presumption of knowledge of the law.

The presumption of innocence

As indicated earlier, because the presumption of innocence can be refuted, it is a type of rebuttable presumption. As we also indicated, the presumption of innocence is required by law and exists until evidence is offered (by the prosecution) to the contrary. The rebuttable presumption of innocence requires that the prosecution prove beyond a reasonable doubt that the accused is guilty. One court has pointed out that the presumption of innocence:

is not a mere belief at the beginning of the trial that the accused is probably innocent. It is not a will-o'-the-wisp, which appears and disappears as the trial progresses. It is a legal presumption which the jurors must consider along with the evidence and the inferences arising from the evidence, when they come finally to pass upon the case. In this sense, the presumption of innocence does accompany the accused through every stage of the trial. (Dodson v. United States, 1928)

The presumption of innocence is not one that jurors are expected to know coming into the trial. It is the judge's responsibility to instruct the jury members that the accused should be presumed innocent until it is proven otherwise. Here is an example of such instructions that were upheld by the U.S. Court of Appeals for the Fifth Circuit:

> I remind you that the indictment is merely the formal charge against the defendants; it is not evidence of guilt. Indeed, the defendants are presumed to be innocent. The law does not require a defendant to prove innocence or produce any evidence at all, and no inference whatever may be drawn from the election of a defendant not to testify . . . The government has the burden of proving a defendant's guilt beyond a reasonable doubt, and if it fails to do that, you must acquit the defendant. (*United States v. Castro,* 1989)

The Presumption of Sanity

Another common presumption is the **presumption of sanity**, which means that every person tried for a criminal offense is assumed to be of sound mind absent evidence to the contrary. You may be asking, what about defendants who are clearly insane? Nothing prohibits defendants from raising defenses such as sanity, but the salient point is that, going into the trial, the defendant is presumed sane. Also, if the defense attorney cannot show that the defendant is insane, the jury must *continue to presume* that the defendant is sane. Remember that the prosecution does not need to show that the defendant is sane; only the burden of proving guilt falls on the prosecution.

The presumption of sanity can more easily be understood with reference to the Fifth Circuit's decision in *United States v. Lyons* (1983). In that case the defendant sought to show that he was not guilty by reason of insanity. Specifically, the defendant tried show that he was involuntarily addicted to drugs. With regard to the presumption of sanity, the court stated:

> It is equally well established that the defendant is presumed sane, and where no evidence to the contrary is presented, that presumption

is wholly sufficient to satisfy the required proof that the defendant
is sane, and hence responsible for his actions . . . however, should
the defendant produce even slight evidence tending to prove his
insanity at the time of the alleged offense, the government has the
burden of proving the defendant's sanity beyond a reasonable doubt.
(*United States v. Lyons,* 1983)

What is necessary to overcome the presumption of sanity? The answer
depends on the state. Several different tests are used, and you will need
to consult a criminal law text for the answer. Also, some states require
that once the defendant has presented evidence to overcome the presumption of sanity, the prosecution must then show that the defendant was
sane at the time the alleged offense was committed. Again, you should
familiarize yourself with your state's requirements as necessary.

The Presumption Against Suicide

When a person dies, it is presumed that the person did not die by his or her
own hand. That is, it is assumed that all people have an inherent respect
for their own lives (and themselves) and, as such, are unlikely to contribute
directly to their own mortality. Clearly this assumption is wrong some of
the time, but the **presumption against suicide** like the presumption of
sanity operates in such a way that someone is presumed to die by causes
other than suicide unless evidence is offered to the contrary.

The presumption against suicide rarely arises in criminal cases. The
reason should be quite obvious: One who has committed suicide cannot
be charged for engaging in that act (suicide is a criminal act in most
states). Rather, the presumption against suicide often arises in cases where
a person's death may result in a life insurance payment. Under normal
circumstances, the deceased will be presumed to have died of natural
causes. The burden will then fall on the insurance company to show
otherwise. In other words, the insurance company will be required to
show that the deceased killed himself or herself.

The Presumption of a Guilty Mind Following Possession of the Fruits of Crime

Another important presumption is that of a guilty mind where the
accused is found to be in possession of stolen property, also referred to
as the "fruits of crime." As one court explained:

> Possession of recently stolen property, if not satisfactorily explained,
> is ordinarily a circumstance from which you may reasonably draw

the inference and find, in light of the surrounding circumstances shown by the evidence in the case, that the person in possession knew the property had been stolen. (*Barnes v. United States,* 1973)

Without this presumption it would be exceedingly difficult to convict criminal defendants in the absence of full confessions. Let us consider an example. If a person were to be caught driving a stolen automobile and tried for grand theft auto, and the presumption we are referring to did not exist, the suspect would probably be acquitted. The only way to secure a conviction absent the presumption that he who possesses the fruits of the crime is guilty would be for the police to obtain a confession.

This presumption operates in the same way as the others we have already discussed. In particular, if the defense introduces evidence to the contrary, the presumption can be overcome. This is the very essence of a rebuttable presumption; the defense can try, and succeed, to sway the jury in another direction. If in our example the defense attorney were able to show that the accused thought he was borrowing a friend's car, the presumption of his guilt would be overcome and the jury would find the defendant not guilty of grand theft auto.

The Presumption of Knowledge of the Law

It is commonly said throughout criminal law that ignorance is not a defense. This statement carries some weight with regard to evidentiary procedure as well. Specifically, it is presumed that all persons in the United States know the law. In reality, thorough knowledge of the law is beyond even the most competent lawyer, but without this presumption, guilty criminals would simply appeal to their own ignorance and escape conviction. Of course, accused persons are not presumed to know the law of other states or of other countries. This type of presumption is not rebuttable.

The Presumption of the Regularity of Official Acts

This presumption refers to the official acts engaged in by public officials. It is presumed that public officials going about their official duties do, in good faith, what is required of them. An example is the chain of custody. It is presumed that police officers who seize evidence from crime scenes do so properly. It is further presumed that the evidence is properly logged and stored until which point it is needed in court. Of course, this presumption can be overcome by evidence of tampering supplied by the defense. Without such evidence, however, the jury will be required to infer that the evidence was not tampered with or improperly handled in any way whatsoever.

The Presumption That Young Children Are Not Capable of Crime

Some states make it a conclusive presumption that children under a certain age, say, 7are not capable of committing crime. Obviously, some very young children commit serious crimes. As a result, some states have changed this presumption to a rebuttable one. That is, if the prosecution can show that the child knew that the act he or she committed was wrongful, the jury would decide that the child-defendant is guilty.

The Presumption of Intended the Consequences Resulting From Voluntary Actions

It has often been presumed that a person intends the consequences of his or her voluntary actions. To use a specific example, this presumption assumes that a person who kills another intended to do so. In at least two important cases (*Sandstrom v. Montana,* 1979; *Francis v. Franklin,* 1986) the Supreme Court considered the constitutionality of instructions to the jury that it is required to presume that persons intend what they voluntarily set out to do. In both cases, the Supreme Court held that this presumption violates the Fourteenth Amendment's due process clause.

In the former case, the Supreme Court concluded that the Fourteenth Amendment was violated with a jury instruction "that the law presumes that a person intends the ordinary consequences of his voluntary acts." In the latter case, the unconstitutional jury instructions were "the acts of a person of sound mind and discretion are presumed to be the product of the person's will, but the presumption may be rebutted." Thus, it is unconstitutional to require (or even allow) juries to presume that defendants intend the results of their voluntary actions.

Why is this presumption unconstitutional? Recall that the burden of proof in a criminal case falls on the prosecution; its responsibility is to prove beyond a reasonable doubt that the accused committed the crime. Going back to basic criminal law, this requires that the state prove both important elements of a criminal act: actus reus and mens rea. **Actus reus** refers to the criminal act itself; **mens rea** refers to intent. This means that the burden falls on the prosecution to prove that the defendant intended to commit the crime. It is a violation of due process to require the defense to show that the defendant *did not* intend to commit the crime for which he or she is charged.

The Presumption of Death Upon Unexplained Absence

Many states have so-called "presumed decedents laws." These laws permit a presumption that someone is dead after he or she has been missing for several years. Where this presumption is recognized and used, it is usually rebuttable. That is, the party against whom the presumption operates can introduce evidence to the contrary evidence that the person who has disappeared is still alive somewhere.

In general, this presumption does not apply to fugitives from justice. The reason is that fugitives from justice seek to hide from authorities for as long as possible. However, at least one court has held that a person who was a fugitive from justice could still be presumed dead for life insurance purposes (*Blodgett v. State Mutual Life Assurance Co.,* 1961). Of course, the presumption remains rebuttable.

A Quick Summary

The reader may be somewhat confused concerning the distinctions between rebuttable and conclusive presumption vis-à-vis presumptions of law and presumptions of fact. Table 5.1 attempts to sort out the distinctions, using some of the discussed presumptions as examples. Note that we have not discussed the conclusive presumption of fact (that today's date is accurate) is not listed here. Even so, it is clear that today's date cannot reasonably be disputed by an opposing party.

Constitutional Requirements for Presumptions

When legislatures mandate specific presumptions in criminal statutes, they are bound by constitutional restrictions. In particular, the due process clauses of the Fifth and Fourteenth Amendments limit legislatively mandated presumptions. Basically, for the presumption to be considered

Table 5.1   Question Asked When Distinguishing Between Open Fields and Curtilage

1. Is the area close to a house or a residence?

2. Is the area enclosed within a fence or similar enclosure?

3. To what use is the area being put?

4. What steps were taken to protect the area from observation?

constitutional, a rational connection must exist between some fact and a presumption that follows from it. Let us consider an example.

In the case of *Tot v. United States* (1943), the Supreme Court had occasion to decide on the constitutionality of a statute providing that "the possession of a firearm or ammunition by any such person shall be presumptive evidence that such firearm or ammunition was shipped or transported or received, as the case may be, by such person in violation of this Act." The Court declared that this legislatively mandated presumption was unconstitutional:

> Under our decisions a statutory presumption cannot be sustained if there be no rational connection between the fact proved and the ultimate fact presumed, if the inference of the one from proof of the other is arbitrary because of lack of connection between the two in common experience. This is not to say that a valid presumption may not be created upon a view of relation broader than that a jury might take in a specific case. But where the inference is so strained as not to have a reasonable relation to the circumstances of life as we know them, it is not competent for the legislature to create it as a rule governing the procedure of courts. (pp. 467–468)

Two important summary propositions can be gleaned from this quote. First, the presumption needs to logically follow some specific fact. If it is a stretch for the jury to presume something, the presumption will be unconstitutional. Second, legislatively mandated presumptions should not shift the burden of proof to the defense in any way whatsoever. That is, the defense should not be forced to prove the defendant's innocence. The only time the defense should be required to offer proof against some presumption is if that presumption is specifically rebuttable, not conclusive or legislatively mandated.

Stipulations

http://www.mcacp.org/issue38.htm

Stipulations are agreements between opposing attorneys about some important fact. Stipulations can also be viewed as "concessions" made by either side to a case. Stipulations are usually made with regard to facts that have little bearing on the outcome of the trial. An agreement is reached in the interest of expediency and efficiency; it would be too time-consuming to debate trivial facts.

Some stipulations are made over relatively serious facts. For example, both sides often stipulate in advance that the defendant has one or more prior convictions. The advantage of doing so is that it minimizes potential for prejudice against the defendant if the issue is raised at trial. There are, however, important restrictions on the prosecution bringing in evidence of other convictions (see Chapter 7).

There are limitations on stipulations. One is that the defense should not stipulate to the prosecution on all points. To do so would be to put on an inadequate defense. Second, if either side stipulates in error, the court is not bound to accept the stipulation. In this vein, the court is not required to accept a stipulation that would be damaging to the defendant's case (see, for example, *United States v. Grassi,* 1979). Finally, stipulations can be withdrawn if the need arises.

Summary

A presumption occurs when a person draws a conclusion from one or more facts presented during a case. Inferences are often confused with presumptions, but there is a subtle distinction between the two. Presumptions are usually mandatory, which means that the jury is required to draw some conclusion. Inferences, by contrast, are not mandatory. It is up to each jury member to draw inferences. Presumptions and inferences are also understood as substitutes for evidence, much like judicial notice.

We referred primarily to presumptions throughout this chapter, largely because they can be controlled by the courts. Individual jurors' inferences are somewhat beyond the control of the court. That said, there are two types of presumptions, conclusive and rebuttable. Conclusive presumptions are required, which means the opposing party cannot argue against the presumption. Rebuttable presumptions can be challenged by the opposing party. Presumptions are essential to the smooth operation of criminal trials. As such, they come in several varieties.

Stipulations are agreements between opposing attorneys about some important fact. They can be understood as "concessions" made by either side to a case. Stipulations can also be understood as substitutes for evidence, much like judicial notice and presumptions and inferences. They expedite trials and spare jurors the headache of having to decide inconsequential facts.

Discussion Questions

1. Explain the main differences between inferences and presumptions. What purpose is served by the use of presumptions or inferences?

2. What are the constitutional requirements for presumptions?
3. What are stipulations, and why are they used?
4. What are the three procedures that are used as substitutes for evidence in court?

Further Reading

Fishman, C. S. (1992). *Jones on Evidence, Civil and Criminal* (7th ed.). Eagan, MN: West Group.

Graham, M. H. (1992). *Federal Practice and Procedure: Evidence* (interim ed.). Eagan, MN: West Group.

Lilly, G. C. (1996). *An Introduction to the Law of Evidence* (3rd ed.). Eagan, MN: West Group.

Mueller, C. B., and L. C. Kirkpatrick. (1999). *Evidence* (2nd ed.). Gaithersburg, MD: Aspen Publishers.

Strong, J. W. (1992). *McCormick on Evidence* (4th ed.). Eagan, MN: West Group.

Weinstein, J. B., J. H. Mansfield, N. Abrams, and M. A Berger. (1997). *Evidence: Cases and Materials* (9th ed.). Westbury, NY: Foundation Press.

Cases Cited

Bakody Homes v. City of Omaha, 516 N.W.2d 244 (1994)

Barnes v. United States, 412 U.S. 837 (1973)

Blodgett v. State Mutual Life Assurance Co., 32 Ill. App. 2d 155 (1961)

Commonwealth v. DiFrancesco, 329 A.2d 203 (1974)

Dodson v. United States, 23 F.2d 401 (1928)

Francis v. Franklin, 471 U.S. 307 (1986)

In re Winship, 397 U.S. 358 (1970)

Leary v. United States, 395 U.S. 6 (1969)

Sandstrom v. Montana, 442 U.S. 510 (1979)

State v. Jackson, 112 Wash. 867 (1989)

Tot v. United States, 319 U.S. 463 (1943)

United States v. Castro, 874 F.2d 230 (1989)

United States v. Grassi, 602 F.2d 1192 (1979)

United States v. Lyons, 704 F.2d 743 (1983)

SECTION TWO

Criminal Evidence

CHAPTER 6
WITNESS COMPETENCY

Key Terms & Concepts

Actual marriage

Affirmation

Common law marriage

Competency

Corroborative evidence

Cumulative evidence

Dead man's statutes

Grounds for challenging competency

Mental incapacity

Oath

Perjury

Prior convictions

Religious beliefs

Rule 501

Rule 601

Rule 605

Rule 606

Spousal privilege

Testimony

Witness

Chapter Learning Objectives

By the end of this chapter, the student should be able to:

- Relate the important role that witness competence plays in criminal proceedings
- Explain the concept of competence
- Identify the various grounds for challenging witness competency
- Explain the practical reason that children may not be reliable witnesses
- Explain the spousal privilege and identify relevant state and federal restrictions on its invocation
- Relate the reasons that judges and jurors should not serve as witnesses
- Identify the significance of oaths/affirmations and the duty of witnesses to tell the truth
- Explain the practical and historical need for dead man's statutes
- Explain when corroboration of witness testimony is required

Introduction

A **witness** is a person who has knowledge about the facts of a case. For example, if a person witnesses a fight in a bar, he or she may have important information to supply when the case goes to trial. Similarly, if a gas station patron observes a robber flee from the station in a car, the patron-now-witness has important information that may be needed if the robber is caught, arrested, charged, and tried in court.

Witnesses are essential in criminal trials. They present evidence in the form of testimony to the judge or a jury. **Testimony** is an oral or verbal description of a person's present recollection of some past event or set of facts.

It is not the case that all witnesses supply information intended to prove guilt. Witnesses can testify on behalf of the defendant in order to absolve the defendant of guilt. For example, a witness can give testimony to confirm a defendant's alibi. If a murder defendant states that he was out with a friend on the night the murder took place and argues that his friend can confirm that he was not at the scene of the crime, the defendant's friend may testify in that regard. Thus, witnesses in the U.S. court system serve one of two purposes: They can testify for either the prosecution *or* the defense. It is a rare case indeed when a witness will testify for both the prosecution and defense in the same trial.

The Role of Witnesses

Without witnesses, it can be exceedingly difficult to prove guilt. Consider the following hypothetical situation: A motorist runs a stop sign and hits a pedestrian while she is crossing the street, killing her. The only witness to the incident is another motorist who happened to be waiting at the stop sign on the cross street. If the first motorist is charged criminally for vehicular homicide, the testimony of the second motorist might be very helpful to the prosecution. This witness would be especially important if no physical evidence was found to link the first driver to the pedestrian's death.

Not just anyone can be a witness. First and foremost, a witness must have something meaningful to contribute to the trial; the witness needs to be witness to something. Besides experts, if someone lacks personal knowledge concerning the case, he or she cannot be considered a witness. Stated differently, a witness may not testify to a matter unless evidence is introduced sufficient to support a finding that the witness has personal knowledge concerning the facts at issue in the trial. A court of appeals judge held that lay testimony that is, testimony by ordinary persons not based on personal information is useless, because a witness cannot supply information about a matter he or she knows nothing about (*United States v. Allen*, 1993).

United States v. Allen
Seventh Circuit Court of Appeals
10 F. 3d 405 (1993)

This case involved the conviction of a veteran law enforcement officer for aiding and abetting the conduct of an illegal gambling operation. At trial, the government argued that Allen provided protection to the gambling business in order to shield the operation from the attention of local law enforcement. According to the government, Allen, with his connections in the police and sheriff's departments and to local politicians, would seem like an ideal person to talk to if one was seeking protection from law enforcement officials. At trial, the main evidence against Allen consisted of video and audio tapes and the testimony of live witnesses which detailed conversations between Allen and undercover FBI agents.

On appeal, Allen raised several evidentiary challenges. In particular, Allen challenged the admission of the testimony of an FBI undercover agent wherein the Agent stated that, "I assumed...that he would continue to do favors for us, protecting our gambling spot, because he was anticipating that we could do him a favor." Allen argues that the district court should have struck this testimony because Minor's "assumptions" were irrelevant to whether Allen actually was providing protection to the club.

Following review, the appellate court held that the fact that the statement was in terms of an assumption makes it neither necessarily irrelevant nor inadmissible. Federal Rule of Evidence 701 "permits a lay witness to offer an opinion or inference that is rationally based on the witness' perceptions and that is helpful to the development of evidence at trial." Minor's assumption can be recast as either an opinion or inference the label she herself used is not determinative and is admissible under Rule 701 if it meets that rule's requirements.

The first of those requirements is that Minor's assumption had to have been rationally based on her own perceptions. In other words, did Minor have sufficient personal knowledge to form an inference about whether Allen was providing and would continue to provide protection? Allen argues that he never told Minor he was providing protection. True, Allen never used the word "protection." But Minor had dealt with Allen several times. She knew she and Joiner wanted protection; and she also knew that Allen was receiving favors from her

(continued)

and Joiner and that Allen was concerned that when somebody does a favor, the recipient should not forget that favor.

The basis for Minor's personal knowledge is not overwhelming. But Rule 701 places great reliance on a party's ability to cross-examine an opponent's witness and present any weaknesses in the witness's testimony to the trier of fact. "The trier of fact can normally be depended upon with the aid of counsel to pick up the nonverbal signals which, although absent from the record, indicate fairly clearly when the witness is describing what he saw and when he is describing what he thinks happened; the trier of fact also should generally be depended upon to give whatever weight or credibility to the witness' opinion as may be due."

Rule 701's second requirement is that the testimony be helpful to the jury's understanding of the issues at trial. At trial, Allen's attorney objected that Minor's "assumption" about Allen providing protection "is what this case is all about anyway." This sounds like an objection based on the fact that Minor was offering an opinion on an "ultimate issue." But under the federal rules, that is no longer a valid objection. Rule 704 provides that "testimony in the form of an opinion or inference otherwise admissible is not objectionable because it embraces an ultimate issue to be decided by the trier of fact."

Despite the abolition of the ultimate issue rule, the relationship of the opinion to the issues in the case is important to determine helpfulness. "The closer the subject of the opinion gets to critical issues the likelier the judge is to require the witness to be more concrete . . . because the jury is not sufficiently helped in resolving disputes by testimony which merely tells it what result to reach." "Meaningless assertions which amount to little more than choosing up sides," such as statements that a defendant is "guilty," are properly excluded by the helpfulness requirement.

Ultimately, the question of whether a lay opinion falls into the category of "meaningless assertion" or whether that opinion actually will help the jury decide an issue in the case is a judgment call for the district court. Minor's testimony was relevant, and Allen's lawyer had ample opportunity to clarify (and pick apart) her testimony on cross-examination. In any event, nothing in Allen's trial objection specifically referenced the court to Rule 701's helpfulness requirement. In these circumstances, we find no abuse of discretion in the district court's failure to strike Minor's assumption about Allen's providing protection at the club.

What this case illustrates is that witness testimony, as a form of evidence, must satisfy the criterion of relevance (introduced in Chapter 9). If a witness communicates information unrelated to the case at hand, the witness's "testimony" will be deemed irrelevant. In such a situation, the witness will probably not be permitted to testify.

This chapter focuses on who can be a witness. First, it covers the topic of witness competency. Second, it covers the various means of challenging witness competency. The next section considers witness credibility and impeachment, while the last section discusses witness rehabilitation. Additional sections of this chapter consider such topics as witness oaths, the importance of corroboration, and the duty to tell the truth and narrate events. In short, this chapter pours the foundation for discussions in subsequent chapters of expert versus lay witnesses and the privileges associated with witness communication.

Competency

Competency, as defined in *Donovan v. Sears Roebuck and Company* (1994), is the presence of particular characteristics and the absence of particular disabilities that render the witness legally qualified to testify in court. The "particular characteristics" referred to in this definition include such things as the potential witness's age, role in the trial, and relationship to the defendant. Age, for example, can be a relevant factor in determining competency. Naturally, a 3-year-old's testimony would need to be viewed cautiously when compared to that of an adult. "Disabilities" concerns a person's understanding of the duty to tell the truth. If a person cannot understand the duty to tell the truth, he or she cannot be a witness.

Judges are responsible for assessing a witness's competency. Often judges will decide on competency outside the presence of the jury so that the jury does not confuse competency with credibility. This task is usually accomplished in a separate hearing designed to determine competency. Indeed, in *United States v. Gates* (1993), the Eleventh Circuit Court of Appeals stated that courts have a *duty* to hold separate hearings to determine witness competency. The procedures for judging the competency of witnesses are found in **Rule 601** of the Federal Rules of Evidence.

Rule 601. General Rule of Competency

Every person is competent to be a witness except as otherwise provided in these rules. However, in civil actions and proceedings, with respect to an element of a claim or defense as to which State law supplies the rule of decision, the competency of a witness shall be determined in accordance with State law.

http://www.law.cornell.edu/rules/fre/ACRule601.htm

The party seeking to call a witness bears the burden of convincing the judge that the person is competent. If the prosecutor wants to call a witness, he or she bears the burden of demonstrating the witness's competency. Alternatively, if the defense attorney wants to call a witness, he or she bears the same burden. The judge then decides whether the witness can be considered competent. Note, however, that competency is assumed at the outset unless the opposition objects to the witness. For example, if the prosecution objects to a defense witness, it is at that point that the defense attorney must convince the judge that the witness is competent to testify.

We should distinguish at this point between the competency of *witnesses* and the competency of *evidence*. A witness may be competent to give testimony yet cannot because the rules of evidence preclude the witness's testimony. For example, assume a witness hears two suspects conversing about a crime they "got away with." Because of the hearsay rule, which we will discuss in Chapter 12, the witness will probably not be able to introduce what he or she heard in trial. Thus, even though this witness has something meaningful to communicate, and even though he or she is competent, the rules of evidence may preclude the witness from reporting what he or she heard when the case goes to trial.

Grounds for Challenging Witness Competency

At common law, many people were barred from testifying because they fit into specific categories. For example, people who failed to believe in God, people convicted of crimes, and children were frequently declared incompetent to be witnesses. See Table 6.1 for the so-called "Five I's" of incompetence under English Common Law.

Table 6.1   The Five "I's" of Incompetence Under English Common Law

---

Interest	Witnesses with an interest in the outcome of the case may be motivated to lie and should be disqualified.
Infants	Young children should be disqualified because of their inability to understand the obligation to tell the truth.
Insane	Insane persons are incapable of recalling events and understanding the duty to tell the truth.
Idolatry	The idolatry of adherents to nonmainstream religions make the oath nonbinding on their consciences.
Infamy	Infamous criminals are deemed civilly dead and are thereby incapable to serve as witnesses.

Today, the competency requirement has nothing to do with "categories" of persons. Rather, it focuses on a person's ability to narrate the events in question and understand the duty to tell the truth. Some of the "I's" in Table 6.1 (e.g., insanity) are therefore relevant today, because of the contemporary focus on the duty to narrate and tell the truth. An "insane" person, in other words, may be considered incompetent because of an inability to describe what he or she witnessed.

The Federal Rules of Evidence explicitly state that, "every person is competent to be a witness except as otherwise provided in these rules" (Rule 601). Similarly, California's general competency rule states that "except as otherwise provided by statute, every person, irrespective of age, is qualified to be a witness and no person is disqualified to testify to any matter" (Ca. Evidence Code, Section 700). On the other hand, Alabama's Evidence Code (Section 12–21–165) defines as incompetent "persons who have not the use of reason, such as idiots, lunatics during lunacy and children who do not understand the nature of an oath..."

It is actually more meaningful to speak in terms of witness "qualification" rather than witness competency. This is because nearly anyone can be a witness if he or she possesses the qualifications already discussed. A more appropriate question would seem to be whether the person is qualified to be a witness. Nevertheless, courts still refer to witness competency at trial and in their opinions.

At least six categories of people have been challenged on competency/qualification grounds throughout history: (1) those whose mental capacity is called into question, (2) children, (3) spouses, (4) people previously convicted of crimes, (5) people who have certain religious beliefs, and (6) judges and jury members.

Before addressing each witness category, it is critical that we point out that these six types of people are not objectionable as witnesses because of who they are. That is, they are not undesirable witnesses for reasons tied to discrimination, narrow mindedness, or bigotry. Rather, their ability to narrate events and understand the duty to tell the truth is what is generally questioned. It should also be emphasized that just because persons are mentally infirm or under age does not mean they cannot be witnesses. We are merely providing a historical overview of the categories of individuals who have proven to be the most problematic as witnesses. Keep in mind that anyone can be a witness, as long as he or she can communicate adequately and understand the duty to tell the truth.

Mental Incapacity

While mental incapacity is generally believed to be a ground on which potential witnesses must be deemed incompetent to offer testimony, in *District of*

Columbia v. Armes (1882), the Supreme Court developed an approach that focused on the unique abilities of each individual as opposed to a general rule of disqualification that excludes all who suffered from a mental defect or disease from offering testimony. In *Armes*, the Court held:

> [The general rule is that] a lunatic or a person affected with insanity is admissible as a witness if he has sufficient understanding to apprehend the obligation of an oath, and to be capable of giving a correct account of the matters which he has seen or heard in reference to the questions at issue; and whether he has that understanding is a question to be determined by the court, upon examination of the party himself, and any competent witnesses who can speak to the nature and extent of his insanity." (pp. 521–522).

Interestingly, the Supreme Court has observed that, "the existence of partial insanity does not prevent individuals so affected...from giving a perfectly accurate and lucid statement of what they have seen or heard" (p. 521). In *Armes*, the Supreme Court actually admitted the testimony of a person who was confined to an asylum and who had attempted suicide a number of times by sticking a fork into his neck.

Other courts have relied on the Supreme Court's standard set forth in *Armes*. For example, the Ninth Circuit Court of Appeals in *Shibley v. United States* (1956) ruled that the trial court was correct in admitting the testimony of a person who had previously been deemed insane. Accordingly, just because a witness is determined to be insane, even by a court of law, such a determination is generally not enough to declare the witness incompetent to give testimony in a criminal trial.

Indeed, given Rule 601 of the Federal Rules of Evidence, it is exceedingly difficult for a person to be declared incompetent solely because of a mental condition. In *United States v. Roach* (1979), the court held that the rule that "every person" can be a witness, provided he or she is competent, means that it is doubtful that a mental condition can be enough to disqualify someone as a potential witness. Similarly, one court ruled that the lower court was wrong to declare a witness incompetent "because he had been found to be criminally insane and incompetent to stand trial and was subject to hallucinations" (*United States v. Lighty*, 1982). In another case (*United States v. Bloome*, 1991) the court ruled that, even though a government witness suffered traumatic effects from a bullet wound to the head, he was competent to testify because there were no observable long-term effects or prolonged mental illness.

In a rather extreme case, the appellate court in *United States v. Gates* (1993) affirmed the decision of the trial court to deem a witness competent and allow testimony at trial.

United States v. Gates
Eleventh Circuit Court of Appeals
10 F.3d 765 (1993)

Gates was convicted of three counts of armed bank robbery and three counts of use of a firearm in connection with the robberies. Gates was acquitted on eight counts of armed robbery.

Prior to trial, Gates filed a motion asking that government witness Gary Hooper be ordered to undergo a psychiatric examination before trial. The motion cited Hooper's grand jury testimony describing how, at the request of co-defendant and James, he engaged in a "staged theft" of an automobile later used by James in the first (October 30) robbery, for which he was paid $ 1,000. James had earlier told Hooper that, "he had a partner named Charles that was going to help him." After being excused and offered an opportunity to correct his testimony, Hooper told the grand jury that Gates went with him and James to buy gloves and a ski mask, that they cased banks to rob and that Gates and James selected a bank and robbed it with Hooper at the wheel of the getaway car.

The motion also alleged that in October 1989, approximately 10 days before the first bank robbery, Hooper had been hospitalized at a Georgia state mental health institution for two days. The records of the institution indicated that Hooper had been hospitalized for mental illness in 1980; that he was a daily user of crack cocaine; he was hallucinating, suicidal and homicidal; his wife described him as hallucinating and paranoid. The records referred to psychological testing which indicated a conscious deception by Hooper to look good; that he typically had severe underlying guilt that he projected unto others; and that he brooded about real or imaginary wrongs. This institutionalization was approximately ten days before the first bank robbery.

The Court acknowledged the inherent problems in allowing psychiatric examination of a witness, such as invasion of privacy, limiting availability of witnesses, chilling testimony, and battles of experts over competency. Rule 601 allows one not mentally competent to testify, and it assumes that jurors are capable of evaluating a witness's testimony in light of the fact that he is not mentally competent. Notwithstanding Rule 601, a court has the power to rule that a witness is incapable of testifying, and in an appropriate case it has the duty to hold a hearing to determine that issue.

(continued)

Despite the allegations regarding the psychiatric background of the witness, the Court concluded that the witness was cross-examined vigorously, searchingly and over a wide range for almost 50 pages of transcript. He was examined about details of the first robbery that he described in his trial testimony but had not mentioned before the grand jury. The medical records of the institution in which he had been placed were put into evidence and he was examined about their contents. The institutionalization in question had occurred more than two years before the trial. The trial judge had before him the grand jury testimony and the medical records. Considering all the circumstances we cannot say that the judge erred in not granting an examination and in not conducting a hearing on the issue of competency.

Thus, the central question that courts should address in determining competency is if the witness is *currently* competent to testify. Just because a person was declared insane in the past, committed to a facility, or otherwise mentally challenged in some fashion does not necessarily mean the person cannot give testimony. The only time that a witness will not be competent to testify because of a mental condition is if the witness does not have the capacity to recall the events in question or does not fully understand the duty to testify truthfully during criminal trial.

Regardless of mental condition, any witness is competent to testify unless evidence is introduced to the contrary. The burden of persuading the court that a witness is incompetent because of a mental condition falls on the party alleging that the witness is incompetent. The challenging party needs to demonstrate one of three things: (1) the witness does not understand the oath and the obligation to give truthful testimony; (2) the witness does not understand the consequences of giving false testimony; or (3) the witness cannot perceive or recall enough to give an accurate account of the events for which he or she was presumably a witness.

Childhood

Another common ground for challenging witness competency is youth. The reason that people have been opposed to children giving testimony is that young children may not understand their role as witness or be able to recall important events. Just as the judge determines the competency of a witness who has a mental condition, so too is the judge responsible for determining the competency of a child. It is not essential that a child understand the full meaning of the "oath" to give truthful testimony, but the child should be able to distinguish truth from falsehood. To illustrate, consider the case of *Idaho v. Wright* (1990).

In *White v. Illinois* (1992), on the other hand, a 4-year-old child's statements to her mother and her doctor were admitted as evidence in a case

---

Idaho v. Wright
Supreme Court of the United States
497 U.S. 805 (1990)

Laura Lee Wright and Robert Giles were charged on two counts of lewd conduct with a minor under the age of 16. The victims were Wright's daughters, ages 5½ and 2½. Following an examination of the younger child, the court ruled that the younger daughter was not capable of communicating to the jury and could not serve as a witness. However, despite the finding regarding competency, the trial court admitted statements made by the younger child to a psychologist. On appeal, Wright challenged the admissibility of those hearsay statements on a variety of grounds including the prior finding regarding competency.

Following review, the Court rejected the respondent's contention that the younger daughter's out-of-court statements in this case are per se unreliable, or at least presumptively unreliable, on the ground that the trial court found the younger daughter incompetent to testify at trial. First, respondent's contention rests upon a questionable reading of the record in this case. The trial court found only that the younger daughter was "not capable of communicating to the jury." Although Idaho law provides that a child witness may not testify if he "appear[s] incapable of receiving just impressions of the facts respecting which they are examined, or of relating them truly," the trial court in this case made no such findings. Indeed, the more reasonable inference is that, by ruling that the statements were admissible under Idaho's residual hearsay exception, the trial court implicitly found that the younger daughter, at the time she made the statements, was capable of receiving just impressions of the facts and of relating them truly. In addition, we have held in any event held that the Confrontation Clause does not erect a per se rule barring the admission of prior statements

(continued)

> of a declarant who is unable to communicate to the jury at the time of trial. Although such inability might be relevant to whether the earlier hearsay statement possessed particularized guarantees of trustworthiness, a per se rule of exclusion would not only frustrate the truthseeking purpose of the Confrontation Clause, but would also hinder States in their own "enlightened development in the law of evidence."

where the defendant was accused of sexual assault against the child. The *White* case dealt with the hearsay rule for children (discussed more fully in Chapter 12), but at issue here is the child's age. Similarly, in another case the court permitted a 5-year-old rape victim and her 7-year-old sister to testify even though their competency was challenged by the defense (*Pocatello v. United States*, 1968).

Some statutes expressly prohibit children from being witnesses. For example, Ohio law provides that "children under ten years of age, who appear incapable of receiving just impressions of the facts respecting which they are examined, or of relating them truly" cannot be considered competent (Ohio R. Evid. 601A). Generally, though, there are no age restrictions. In *Wheeler v. United States* (1895), the Supreme Court offered clarification:

> That the boy was not by reason of his youth [5½ years], as a matter of law, absolutely disqualified as a witness is clear. While no one would think of calling as a witness an infant only two or three years old, there is no precise age which determines the question of competency. This depends on the capacity and intelligence of the child, his appreciation of the difference between truth and falsehood, as well as of his duty to tell the former. (p. 524)

Problems arise when a witness is of sufficient age at the time of trial but was significantly younger at the time the crime was committed. This is not an uncommon problem, given the length of time it may take for a case to come to trial. In one such case, the witness was 10 at the time of the trial but was asked to narrate events that occurred when he was 4. In light of such situations, some courts have ruled that competency should be determined at two points in time, at the time of the crime and later, at trial (*Huprich v. Paul W. Varga and Sons, Inc.*, 1965; *Cross v. Commonwealth*, 1953). In other words, the child must be able to narrate the events as they occurred in the past but also remain competent as a trial witness.

What exactly are the rules for determining the competency of a child? There are no clear answers, but the courts have offered a number of guidelines in several important cases. For example, in *Kelluem v. State* (1978, 5), the Supreme Court of Delaware ruled that four factors must be considered: (1) the child's ability to perceive accurate impressions of fact or capacity to observe the acts about which he is to testify; (2) the child's ability or capacity to recollect these impressions or observations; (3) the child's ability to recall and his capacity to communicate what was observed; and (4) the child's understanding of truth and falsity and his capacity to appreciate the moral responsibility to be truthful.

Similarly, in *State v. Cabral* (1980, 628–629), a Rhode Island court ruled that a competent child witness must possess four criteria: The child must be able to (1) observe, (2) recollect, (3) communicate, and (4) appreciate the necessity of telling the truth.

In an important study, McCord (1986) found that while adults are naturally more capable of recalling and communicating events, it is not necessarily the case that children are more vulnerable to suggestion or less capable of recalling and communicating events than adults. McCord pointed out that, "there is some intriguing evidence that young children sometimes notice potentially interesting things that older children and adults miss" (p. 48).

To ensure that child testimony is accurate, McCord offers a number of suggestions: (1) children should be able to testify out of court that is, by closed-circuit television or some other medium; (2) children should be allowed to meet courtroom officials, including the judge, before trial if they are to be required to testify in court; (3) judges should caution the prosecution or the defense if the questions asked of a child are too advanced or difficult to understand; and (4) tired and traumatized children should be allowed to rest or take a break during testimony, if it is determined that such would improve the child's ability to accurately narrate the events.

Spousal Privilege

In the past, husbands and wives were considered incompetent to testify for or against each other. The reasons were self-interest of the witness spouse and protection and preservation of marital harmony. For example, if the husband is accused of rape, the wife may wish to testify on behalf of her husband, arguing that he could not have committed the crime. Assuming that the wife believes in her husband's innocence, she has a strong self-interest in seeing that he is found not guilty. On the other hand, if the wife were to testify against her husband, consensus was that such testimony would be impermissible. The Fifth Amendment, as we have seen, prohibits self-incrimination, and it was believed that husbands and wives are "one person" in essence, so to have one partner testify against the other would violate the Fifth Amendment.

Federal Restrictions

Rule 501. General Rule

Except as otherwise required by the Constitution of the United States or provided by Act of Congress or in rules prescribed by the Supreme Court pursuant to statutory authority, the privilege of a witness, person, government, State, or political subdivision thereof shall be governed by the principles of the common law as they may be interpreted by the courts of the United States in the light of reason and experience.

http://www.law.cornell.edu/rules/fre/ACRule501.htm

As noted in *Trammel v. United States* (1980), FRE **Rule 501**, recognizes no marital privilege per se but rather, recognizes a general privilege which "shall be governed by the principles of the common law as they may be interpreted by the courts of the United States in the light of reason and experience."

Hawkins v. United States (1958) was an early case decided by the Supreme Court that addressed the spousal privilege. In *Hawkins*, the Court held that in order for a spouse to testify against another, mutual consent of the parties (both spouses) was required. This rarely occurred, as the defendant spouse in a criminal trial had a vested interest in prohibiting his or her spouse from providing valuable testimony against him or her. Moreover, the *Hawkins* Court addressed the underlying logic of spousal privilege. There, the Court observed the following:

The basic reason the law has refused to pit wife against husband or husband against wife in a trial where life or liberty is at stake was a belief that such a policy was necessary to foster family peace, not only for the benefit of husband, wife and children, but for the benefit of the public as well.... There is still a widespread belief, grounded on present conditions, that the law should not force or encourage testimony which might alienate husband and wife, or further inflame existing domestic differences. Under these circumstances we are unable to subscribe to the idea that an exclusionary rule based on the persistent instincts of several centuries should now be abandoned.... However, this decision does not foreclose whatever changes in the rule may eventually be dictated by "reason and experience".

Not surprisingly, the courts have created a number of exceptions to the rule of **spousal privilege**, which holds that wives cannot testify against their husbands and vice versa. In *Stein v. Bowman* (1837), the U.S. Supreme Court held that the rule barring spousal testimony does not apply in cases where the husband commits a crime against the wife (or, by extension, where the wife commits a crime against the husband). Other courts have subsequently reaffirmed this ruling, holding that the self-interested motives of one party should not prevent his or her testimony (*Fund v. United States*, 1933). Because defendants are permitted to testify on their own behalf, it does not make sense to prevent spouses from testifying.

As early as 1887, Congress permitted spouses to testify in prosecutions for bigamy, polygamy, and unlawful cohabitation. Congress then expanded this rule to permit spousal testimony in cases involving the importation of aliens for immoral purposes (18 U.S.C. Section 1328). The law also permits spousal testimony in cases where marriages are premised on fraud. For example, in *Lutwak v. United States* (1953), three illegal aliens married war veterans, who were prosecuted for conspiracy to defraud the United States because it was believed their marriages were designed solely for the purpose of allowing the women to obtain U.S. citizenship. The court ruled that the women were competent to testify against their "husbands" because they had no intention to live together as husband and wife once they were safely inside the U.S. border.

More recently, in 1980 the U.S. Supreme Court revisited its earlier ruling in *Hawkins v. U.S.* (1958). In *Trammel v. United States*, the Court made sweeping changes in the federal courts' endorsement of the Hawkins approach.

Trammel v. United States
Supreme Court of the United States
445 U.S. 40 (1980)

On March 10, 1976, petitioner Otis Trammel was indicted with two others, Edwin Lee Roberts and Joseph Freeman, for importing heroin into the United States from Thailand and the Philippine Islands and for conspiracy to import heroin. The indictment also named six unindicted co-conspirators, including Trammel's wife, Elizabeth Ann Trammel.

(continued)

According to the indictment, petitioner and his wife flew from the Philippines to California in August 1975, carrying with them a quantity of heroin. Freeman and Roberts assisted them in its distribution. Elizabeth Trammel then traveled to Thailand where she purchased another supply of the drug. On November 3, 1975, with four ounces of heroin on her person, she boarded a plane for the United States. During a routine customs search in Hawaii, she was searched, the heroin was discovered, and she was arrested. After discussions with Drug Enforcement Administration agents, she agreed to cooperate with the Government.

Prior to trial on this indictment, Trammel moved to sever his case from that of Roberts and Freeman. He advised the court that the Government intended to call his wife as an adverse witness and asserted his claim to a privilege to prevent her from testifying against him. At a hearing on the motion, Mrs. Trammel was called as a Government witness under a grant of use immunity. She testified that she and petitioner were married in May 1975 and that they remained married. She explained that her cooperation with the Government was based on assurances that she would be given lenient treatment. She then described, in considerable detail, her role and that of her husband in the heroin distribution conspiracy.

The trial court ruled that Mrs. Trammel could testify in support of the Government's case to any act she observed during the marriage and to any communication "made in the presence of a third person"; however, confidential communications between petitioner and his wife were held to be privileged and inadmissible. The motion to sever was denied. At trial, Elizabeth Trammel testified within the limits of the court's pretrial ruling; her testimony, as the Government concedes, constituted virtually its entire case against petitioner. He was found guilty on both the substantive and conspiracy charges.

On appeal, Trammel challenged the admission of the adverse testimony of his wife, over his objection, as a violation of the rule in *Hawkins v. United States.*

The modern justification for this privilege against adverse spousal testimony is its perceived role in fostering the harmony and sanctity of the marriage relationship. Notwithstanding this benign purpose, the rule was sharply criticized.

The Hawkins case, then, left the federal privilege for adverse spousal testimony where it found it, continuing "a rule which bars the testimony of one spouse against the other unless both consent."

(continued)

However, in so doing, the Court made clear that its decision was not meant to "foreclose whatever changes in the rule may eventually be dictated by reason and experience," 358 U.S., at 79.

The Federal Rules of Evidence acknowledge the authority of the federal courts to continue the evolutionary development of testimonial privileges in federal criminal trials "governed by the principles of the common law as they may be interpreted ... in the light of reason and experience." Fed. Rule Evid. 501. Cf. *Wolfle v. United States,* 291 U.S. 7, 12 (1934). Although Rule 501 confirms the authority of the federal courts to reconsider the continued validity of the *Hawkins* rule, the long history of the privilege suggests that it ought not to be casually cast aside. That the privilege is one affecting marriage, home, and family relationships already subject to much erosion in our day also counsels caution. At the same time, we cannot escape the reality that the law on occasion adheres to doctrinal concepts long after the reasons which gave them birth have disappeared and after experience suggests the need for change. This was recognized in *Funk* where the Court "[declined] to enforce ... ancient [rules] of the common law under conditions as they now exist," 290 U.S., at 382. For, as Mr. Justice Black admonished in another setting, "[when] precedent and precedent alone is all the argument that can be made to support a court-fashioned rule, it is time for the rule's creator to destroy it." *Francis v. Southern Pacific Co.,* 333 U.S. 445, 471 (1948) (dissenting opinion).

It is essential to remember that the *Hawkins* privilege is not needed to protect information privately disclosed between husband and wife in the confidence of the marital relationship once described by this Court as "the best solace of human existence." *Stein v. Bowman,* 13 Pet., at 223. Those confidences are privileged under the independent rule protecting confidential marital communications. *Blau v. United States,* 340 U.S. 332 (1951); see n. 5, supra. The *Hawkins* privilege is invoked, not to exclude private marital communications, but rather to exclude evidence of criminal acts and of communications made in the presence of third persons.

The ancient foundations for so sweeping a privilege have long since disappeared. Nowhere in the common-law world, indeed in any modern society, is a woman regarded as chattel or demeaned by denial of a separate legal identity and the dignity associated with recognition as a whole human being. Chip by chip, over the years those archaic notions have been cast aside so that "[no] longer is the female destined

(continued)

solely for the home and the rearing of the family, and only the male for the marketplace and the world of ideas." *Stanton v. Stanton,* 421 U.S. 7, 14–15 (1975).

The contemporary justification for affording an accused such a privilege is also unpersuasive. When one spouse is willing to testify against the other in a criminal proceeding, whatever the motivation, their relationship is almost certainly in disrepair; there is probably little in the way of marital harmony for the privilege to preserve. In these circumstances, a rule of evidence that permits an accused to prevent adverse spousal testimony seems far more likely to frustrate justice than to foster family peace. Indeed, there is reason to believe that vesting the privilege in the accused could actually undermine the marital relationship. For example, in a case such as this, the Government is unlikely to offer a wife immunity and lenient treatment if it knows that her husband can prevent her from giving adverse testimony. If the Government is dissuaded from making such an offer, the privilege can have the untoward effect of permitting one spouse to escape justice at the expense of the other. It hardly seems conducive to the preservation of the marital relation to place a wife in jeopardy solely by virtue of her husband's control over her testimony.

Our consideration of the foundations for the privilege and its history satisfy us that "reason and experience" no longer justify so sweeping a rule as that found acceptable by the Court in *Hawkins.* Accordingly, we conclude that the existing rule should be modified so that the witness-spouse alone has a privilege to refuse to testify adversely; the witness may be neither compelled to testify nor foreclosed from testifying. This modification, vesting the privilege in the witness-spouse, furthers the important public interest in marital harmony without unduly burdening legitimate law enforcement needs.

Here, petitioner's spouse chose to testify against him. That she did so after a grant of immunity and assurances of lenient treatment does not render her testimony involuntary. Cf. *Bordenkircher v. Hayes,* 434 U.S. 357 (1978). Accordingly, the District Court and the Court of Appeals were correct and are therefore affirmed.

State Restrictions on Spousal Privilege

A number of restrictions continue to govern spousal testimony, but the restrictions depend on the laws in specific states. Many states permit spouses to testify against each other, but only for certain offenses. For example, under Ohio state law spouses can testify on behalf of each other without restrictions but are only allowed to testify against each other in (1) prosecutions for personal injury in which one partner inflicts harm on the other, (2) prosecutions for bigamy, and (3) prosecutions for failure to provide for, neglect of, or cruelty to their children (Ohio Rev. Code Ann., Section 2945.42, 1994). Some states leave the decision to testify in the hands of the husband and wife. For example, Georgia law holds that spouses are competent to testify against each other, but courts cannot compel testimony by the husband or the wife (OCGA, Section 24–9–23, 1994).

California's Evidence Code (Article 4, Section 970) provides that "a married person has a privilege not to testify against his spouse in any proceeding." The rationale behind California's rule is that a requirement of spousal testimony, particularly incriminating spousal testimony, would seriously disrupt or disturb the marital relationship. California's Evidence Code also grants a privilege not to be called as a witness against a spouse (Article 4, Section 971). The only exception to this second rule is if the party calling the spouse does so in good faith without the knowledge of the marital relationships.

Interestingly, California's Evidence Code (Article 4, Section 972) outlines a number of exceptions in which a married person does not have a privilege to decline to testify or be called to testify. The exceptions are proceedings (1) brought by or on behalf of one spouse against the other; (2) to commit or place a spouse or his or the spouse's property, or both, under the control of another because of the spouse's alleged mental or physical condition; (3) brought by or on behalf of a spouse to establish his or her competence; (4) under Juvenile Court Law; and (5) in which one spouse is charged with a specific crime. California's Evidence Code refers to several "specific crimes." Examples are crimes against the person or property of the other spouse and bigamy.

An interesting issue related to spousal testimony concerns the ability of the prosecution to compel such testimony. Even though many evidence codes seem to grant a privilege to spouses who decline to testify against their partners, prosecutors can nevertheless "threaten" potential witnesses with charges if they refuse to testify. This is something of a deceptive, manipulative tactic, but one that has certainly happened from time to time.

As we have seen, the privilege of a spouse to decline to testify against his or her partner is based on the logic that such testimony would disrupt marital harmony. But what if the marriage is on shaky ground prior to the trial? Alternatively, what if the marriage is based on a whirlwind courtship and at the time of testimony the partners have known each other for less than three months? In both situations the rationale for the spousal privilege against giving adverse testimony is called into question. Unfortunately, there have not been any cases addressing such issues.

Another interesting issue concerning the spousal privilege to not testify adversely against a partner has to do with the distinction between actual and common law marriages. An **actual marriage** is one in which a formal ceremony has taken place in the presence of a judge, priest, or other person authorized to perform such events. A **common law marriage**, by comparison, is one in which a couple lives together for a long period of time and such cohabitation can be considered a marriage for all practical purposes. In one case, a couple had lived together for four years and the court ruled that the legislature should determine whether the privilege should apply to such relationships (*People v. Delph,* 1979). The lack of case law with regard to this issue is important, especially in light of the current debate over "domestic partnership." One controversial question that has yet to be answered is whether the privilege should apply to same-sex domestic partnerships.

http://www.unmarried.org/index.html

The privilege granted to a spouse to not give adverse testimony does not survive the termination of marriage. In *United States v. Bolzer* (1977) the Ninth Circuit Court of Appeals held that the privilege no longer applies, even during divorce judgments under appeal by the husband or wife (see also *United States v. Fisher,* 1975). The same rule seems to apply to some marriages that, while still intact, are no longer viable.

United States v. Cameron
Fifth Circuit Court of Appeals
556 F.2d 752 (1977)

In *United States v. Cameron* (1977) the court disallowed the privilege in a damaged marriage where both partners had no desire for reconciliation. In *Cameron,* the Court held that the exclusion of adverse testimony by a spouse is not an absolute privilege. There have been long recognized exceptions, such as exist in prosecutions for crimes committed by one spouse against the other or against the children of either; actions by one of the spouses against an outsider for an intentional injury to the marital relation; or in a criminal prosecution against one spouse in which a declaration of the other spouse made

(continued)

confidentially to the accused would tend to justify or reduce the grade of the offense. The Federal Rules of Evidence, Rule 501, recognizes no marital privilege per se, but rather recognizes a general privilege which "shall be governed by the principles of the common law as they may be interpreted by the courts of the United States in the light of reason and experience."

This reason and experience which the Supreme Court spoke of in *Wolfe, Hawkins,* and various other opinions, and which Congress refers to in Rule 501, places on the federal courts the responsibility of examining the policies behind the federal common law privileges so as to alter or amend them when reason and experience demand. If we are to fashion any exception in the case before us we must do so consistent with the rationale for the privilege. In the present case there were a number of factors, which indicate that in spite of the legal existence of the marriage, as a social fact it had expired. There was no residence at which both spouses lived; there was a great disparity between the amount of time that the couple cohabited and the time that one or the other chose not to live together; the husband had a more permanent living arrangement with another partner than with his spouse and, indeed, fathered a child with that person. All these factors cumulatively signify a marriage that was moribund. If the marital privilege is intended to preserve domestic harmony, the most substantial argument that judges and writers today advance in support of it, it is apparent that the present case is not one in which the privilege would serve any such purpose.

We fashion no broad rule with our holding today as to when the marital privilege should be disallowed. We decide narrowly on the facts as they appear before us. That is, where, as here, the spouse was called to testify only as to objective facts, with no questions allowed as to any communication between the spouses, and where the evidence supported a finding that the marriage was no longer viable and its members had little hope or desire for reconciliation, reason, experience and common sense indicate that the traditional policy reasons for the privilege are nonexistent. It was properly disallowed.

It is appropriate to mention at this juncture that the privilege discussed in this section applies only to testimonial or communicative evidence from the spousal witness. It does not include the use of the spousal witness's fingerprints where such evidence tends to incriminate the partner (*United States v. Thomann,* 1979). Handwriting samples can also be required by one partner if such samples tend to incriminate the other partner (*In re Rovner*, 1974). It also appears that the privilege is not extended to protect a spouse from being called to testify before a grand jury (*In re Lochiatto*, 1974).

Prior Convictions

The Supreme Court decided in 1918 that "the dead hand of the common law rule" disqualifying witnesses because they had previously been convicted of a crime should no longer be applied in criminal cases in federal court (*Rosen v. United States*, 1918). Many states have followed suit and have begun to permit the testimony of people previously convicted of crimes. In one federal case, for example, the court ruled that "the government cannot be expected to depend exclusively upon the virtuous in enforcing the law, and so long as a reasonable jury could believe an informant's testimony, after hearing relevant impeachment evidence regarding his or her reliability, the government may rely upon such testimony" (*United States v. Richardson*, 1985, p. 1521), even if the witness has been previously convicted. In another case involving a witness who had been treated for alcoholism and had an extensive criminal record, a Connecticut court ruled that such a background could not render the witness incompetent to testify (*State v. Valeriano*, 1983).

While prior convictions may be immaterial as far as competency is concerned, prior convictions can be of profound significance with regard to witness credibility. The general rule is that a witness's prior convictions damage the witness's credibility but do not "disqualify" or render the witness incompetent to testify. There are several exceptions to this general rule, however. We consider the credibility issue, in reference to prior convictions as well as several other issues, later in this chapter.

Religious Beliefs

Religious beliefs cannot be considered grounds to declare a witness incompetent. In other words, if a person has an objectionable religious belief or opinion, that person cannot be declared incompetent. The issue, instead, is "whether or not the individual has the ability to observe, recollect and communicate, and some sort of moral responsibility" (*State v. Phipps*, 1982, p. 131). In the past, a lack of religious background was also used to declare some witnesses incompetent. Nowadays, though, if the witness is able to understand the obligation to tell the truth, he or she can be considered competent even if he or she has no religious background (e.g., *Chapell v. State*, 1986).

There are at least two situations in which a person's religious beliefs and opinions may be brought up in court. First, religious opinions can be grounds for impeachment. It is possible for the prosecution or defense to argue that a witness cannot be considered credible because of a belief he or she holds. Second, religious beliefs can be cause for concern during the jury selection process. For example, if a potential juror is fundamentally opposed to the death penalty for capital crimes, that person will probably not serve on the jury in a capital case. Generally, religion cannot factor into the competency determination.

Judges and Jurors as Witnesses

A final, though certainly not the last, reason for challenging competency occurs when judges and jurors become witnesses. Controversy exists, in particular, over the role of judges and jurors as witnesses in their own trials. Admittedly, the occasions where judges or jurors are called to testify are rare, but they deserve some attention nonetheless.

Rule 605. Competency of Judge as Witness

The judge presiding at the trial may not testify in that trial as a witness. No objection need be made in order to preserve the point.

http://www.law.cornell.edu/rules/fre/ACRule605.htm

There has been some debate over the rule of judges as witnesses in the trials over which they preside, but **Rule 605** of the Federal Rules of Evidence now states, "The judge presiding at the trial may not testify in that trial as a witness..." Indeed, federal law requires that judges excuse themselves from cases in which they are or have been witness to the events in question (28 U.S.C. Section 455). Many states have adopted similar rules in their evidence codes. For example, Nebraska law holds that a judge presiding at a trial may not testify as a witness in that trial.

With regard to jurors, the generally accepted rule is that jurors may not testify as witnesses in the trials of which they are a part. The reasoning for this rule is clear: A juror who testifies for either the prosecution or the defense is likely to have an undue influence on the outcome of the case. For example, if a juror testifies to the effect that the defendant's friends threatened her while she was serving on the jury, her testimony would probably influence not only her decision during deliberations but also the opinions of the other members of the jury. Therefore, as **Rule 606** of the Federal Rules of Evidence dictates, "A member of the jury may not testify as a witness before that jury in the trial of the case in which the juror is sitting..."

Rule 606. Competency of Juror as Witness

(a) At trial

A member of the jury may not testify as a witness before that jury in the trial of the case in which the juror is sitting. If the juror is called so to testify, the opposing party shall be afforded an opportunity to object out of the presence of the jury.

Jurors are also granted protection from being compelled to testify about their deliberations. The federal courts have recognized (and Rule 606(b) serves as the basis for such recognition) that permitting people to attack jury verdicts would be unduly burdensome on jury members. However, Rule 606(b) does hold that jurors can be compelled to testify as to extraneous information or outside influences concerning the verdict. An example of extraneous information would be if a newspaper article that is prejudicial to the defendant finds its way into jury deliberations. An example of outside influence would be threats against a particular jury member to vote a certain way. In either case, the court would explore the extent and consequences of extraneous or outside information and attempt to decide whether such information influenced the jury's decision, calling on specific jury members only as a last resort (*Owen v. Duckworth,* 1984; *United States ex rel. Buckhaha v. Lane,* 1986).

Rule 606. Competency of Juror as Witness

(b) Inquiry into validity of verdict or indictment.

Upon an inquiry into the validity of a verdict or indictment, a juror may not testify as to any matter or statement occurring during the course of the jury's deliberations or to the effect of anything upon that or any other juror's mind or emotions as influencing the juror to assent to or dissent from the verdict or indictment or concerning the juror's mental processes in connection therewith, except that a juror may testify on the question whether extraneous prejudicial information was improperly brought to the jury's attention or whether any outside influence was improperly brought to bear upon any juror. Nor may a juror's affidavit or evidence of any statement by the juror concerning a matter about which the juror would be precluded from testifying be received for these purposes.

http://www.law.cornell.edu/rules/fre/ACRule606.htm

An interesting case with regard to juror testimony is *Fulgham v. Ford* (1988). In that case, two jurors, well after the trial, communicated to the defendant's counsel that they thought the defendant had been insane at the time of the murder but decided not to return a verdict of not guilty by reason of insanity for fear that the defendant would be released into society. The defense challenged the verdict on these grounds, but the Eleventh Circuit Court of Appeals ruled that the jurors' statements could not be used to challenge the verdict. However, in *Isaacs v. Kemp* (1985), the court held that a jury member's testimony that she attended the trials of other persons involved in the same case could be admitted, as it was considered an outside influence within the meaning of Rule 606(b).

Isaacs v. Kemp
Eleventh Circuit Court of Appeals
778 F.2d 1482 (1985)

Petitioners Carl J. Isaacs and George Elder Dungee appeal from the federal district court's denial of their habeas corpus petitions. On May 14, 1973, five members of the Alday family were shot to death in their mobile home in Donalsonville, Georgia. A sixth person, Mary Alday, was taken from the mobile home, raped and then shot to death. On September 4, 1973, Seminole County's grand jury indicted Carl Isaacs, Dungee, Billy Isaacs, and Wayne Carl Coleman on six counts of murder. Some three months later, Billy Isaacs, Carl's sixteen-year old brother, pleaded guilty to armed robbery and burglary. He was sentenced to a forty-year prison term. Shortly thereafter, the three remaining defendants were tried separately, convicted, and sentenced to death by electrocution.

*****

Moreover, there is an additional factor in Dungee's case, which provides significant support for a finding of presumed prejudice. During the supplemental evidentiary hearings held in the district court, Ms. Thelma Harrington testified that before she served as a juror in Dungee's case, she spent "most of the day" attending Carl Isaacs' trial each day that Isaacs' trial went on.

*****

It is clear that Ms. Harrington, a juror in Dungee's trial, sat through the earlier trial of Carl Isaacs and heard the cornerstone of the state's

(continued)

case, i.e., the testimony of Billy Isaacs. We need not decide whether that fact would constitute a separate and independent basis for finding a due process violation. *United States v. McIver* found that a similar factor constitutes an independent due process violation. In *McIver* and *Stratton*, it was held that a defendant's Sixth Amendment right to be tried by an impartial jury is violated where the defendant is tried by the very same jury that has convicted his co-defendants. Both cases involved a bifurcated trial procedure in which the prosecution's case against all defendants was presented to the jury, but one defendant's defense was postponed until after the jury had deliberated with respect to the codefendants. The *McIver* court specifically held that such a procedure "violates the Sixth Amendment because the jury might consider, even if inadvertently, the guilt of the defendant before it has heard the defendant's case." The *Stratton* court stated that a "clearer case of jury prejudice is difficult to imagine." After earlier finding the co-defendants guilty, the *Stratton* jury was "predisposed to find guilt" and "virtually bound to convict" the later defendant. We note the potential analogy between *McIver* and *Stratton*, where all jurors prematurely heard the government's case against the defendant, and Dungee's case in which one juror prematurely heard the cornerstone of the state's case against Dungee. We note also the similarity between juror Harrington's premature exposure to Billy Isaacs' testimony in this case, and the premature exposure of three jurors in *Rideau* to the televised confession. Because we consider juror Harrington's premature exposure to Billy Isaacs' testimony as another factor in the totality of the circumstances mandating a conclusion of presumed prejudice, we need not address the question of whether it would constitute a separate and independent basis for a due process challenge.

To summarize, we have briefly introduced six grounds for challenging witness competency. Most modern evidence codes, including the Federal Rules of Evidence, have done away with the past practice of declaring certain witnesses incompetent because they fall into a certain category (such as that they possess a strange religious belief or are of a fixed age). The rules of evidence vary a great deal across states, but the general rule concerning witness competency is (1) if a person has something relevant to say, (2) understands the obligation to tell the truth, *and* (3) is capable of narrating the events in question, the person will almost certainly be permitted to serve as a witness. (see Table 6.2 for a different way of thinking about these three requirements of witness competency.)

Table 6.2   **Essential Requirements of a Competent Witness**

Requirement	Description
Perception	The person must be capable of perceiving events (usually by seeing them).
Recollection	The person must be able to recall the events.
Narration	The person must be able to narrate/recount the events.
Sincerity	The person must be sincere in his or her testimony—sincerity is generally assumed but is nonetheless sought by administering an oath.

Witness Requirements

We give careful consideration in the following sections to the duty to tell the truth as well as to what it means to narrate the events in question, both of which are essential witness requirements. Then, before getting to our discussion of witness credibility, impeachment, and examination, we briefly comment on the so-called dead man's statutes as well as the occasional requirement that witness testimony be corroborated.

The Duty to Tell the Truth

The duty of witnesses to tell the truth is traced to the oath they are required to take before providing testimony. The most common oath administered to witnesses is one in which the person promises to "tell the truth, the whole truth, and nothing but the truth, so help me God." It is not necessary that a witness swear on the Bible or even that God be mentioned in the oath. This is because atheists and agnostics may not see any value in an oath with religious language. Sometimes, instead of an oath an "affirmation," or promise to tell the truth, will be preferred. Regardless of the actual terminology in the oath, the witness must understand the duty to tell the truth.

The purpose of an **oath** or **affirmation** is to communicate to a witness that he or she will be testifying under penalty of perjury. That is, if the witness lies on the stand, he or she can be prosecuted for **perjury**, the offense of lying under oath (or following an affirmation). The mere threat of being charged with perjury would seem to be enough to ensure that witnesses will always tell the truth, but in reality, perjury charges are rarely filed.

For illustration, let us consider California. California's Evidence Code (Section 710) provides that "Every witness before testifying shall take an oath or make an affirmation or declaration in the form provided by law," but this requirement alone does not require a moral obligation to tell the truth. It is conceivable that a would-be witness would swear or affirm to tell the truth but have no intention to do so. What, if anything, can be done to disqualify such a witness? Fortunately, Section 701(a)(2) of California's Evidence Code states that "A person is disqualified to be a witness if he or she is...incapable of understanding the duty of a witness to tell the truth." Thus, at least in California, witnesses must swear to tell the truth as well as understand the duty to do so.

The form of the oath has received some scrutiny in recent trials. Consider the case of *United States v. Ward* (1992). Ward was the president of I & O Publishing Company, a mail-order house and publisher in Boulder City, Nevada. He was prosecuted for failure to pay income taxes for the years 1983, 1984, and 1985. Ward chose to represent himself at trial, and on July 9, 1990, he filed a "Motion to Challenge the Oath." In his motion he proposed an alternative oath that replaced the word "truth" with the phrase "fully integrated honesty." He believed that the word "honesty" was preferable to "truth."

The court in the *Ward* case ruled that, "the oath or affirmation which has been administered in courts of law throughout the United States to millions of witnesses for hundreds of years should not be required to give way to the defendant's idiosyncratic distinctions between truth and honesty." The district court then overruled Ward's objections to the magistrate's ruling. As a result, Ward did not testify in his own trial and was convicted. He then appealed his case to the United States Court of Appeals for the Ninth Circuit, arguing that because the district court did not allow him to swear to an oath of his own creation, he was precluded from testifying in his own defense. The Court of Appeals reversed the lower court decision and remanded the case for a new trial. This case illustrates that the form of the oath does not matter so much as what the oath stands for. As long as witnesses swear in one form or another to tell the truth, the precise terminology they use prior to doing so would seem to be immaterial.

The situation is considerably more complicated with regard to children. Because young children may not understand the meaning of "oath," "affirmation," or "under penalty of perjury," they are often sworn in a different, somewhat simplistic fashion. Young children who serve as witnesses are often asked whether they know that it is wrong to tell a lie, or some other question that can be easily understood. It would not be fair to exclude child testimony just because a child cannot understand the meaning of the term "perjury." Instead, other methods should be taken to swear in child witnesses when it is necessary.

What of expert witnesses? We turn attention to expert witnesses in Chapter 10, but their oaths/affirmations are worthy of consideration in this section. It is well known that expert witnesses are frequently paid for testifying. Moreover, they are not called unless the calling party (a defense attorney, for instance) has good reason to believe they will testify in the party's favor. Consider a hypothetical murder case: A woman's body was dumped on a rural dirt road and the only trace of evidence left behind was a set of tire tracks. At trial an expert witness for the prosecution testifies that the tire tracks matched the tires on the defendant's vehicle. An expert witness for the defense, on the other hand, testifies that the tire tracks could not possibly match those on the defendant's vehicle. Who is telling the truth? Is it that each side honestly believes that his/her testimony is accurate? These are difficult questions, but it is certainly possible that one or the other (or both) of these hypothetical expert witnesses is not telling the truth.

In summary, witnesses are duty-bound to tell the truth. Of course, it would be naive to assume that every witness is truthful. One need only consider recent litigation involving "big tobacco." The CEOs of several leading cigarette manufacturers were lambasted for flagrant lies during the course of their testimony in civil trials and before Congress.

If the "penalty of perjury" is not enough to deter dishonesty, little recourse is available. Fortunately, most people are truthful in their testimony and legitimately fear the potential consequences they may face for being dishonest. The main message of this section is that "truth," the hopeful result of witness testimony, is what is important, not the procedure for ensuring that the witness swears to be truthful.

The Ability to Observe and Remember

To be a witness, a person must be able to communicate with the judge and jury about what happened. In other words, the witness will be required to describe the events in question. Witnesses may have trouble communicating about what happened for any number of reasons. They may not understand the question, because of a mental condition or a language barrier. Or they may not be able to remember and recall what happened, particularly if the crime was committed some time in the past. As such, there is a great deal of controversy regarding the ability of witnesses to observe, remember, and communicate, also collectively referred to as "witness capacity."

There is a great deal of controversy about witnesses' ability to observe and remember important events. There is also controversy over witnesses giving their "opinions" as to what they reportedly saw. We give more detailed treatment to the subject of opinions in the next chapter, but opinions are worth considering here as well. For example, in the case of *Gladden v. State* (1951) a police officer testified that he believed the defendant, who was charged with drunk driving, was drunk at the time of his arrest. The defendant attempted to exclude the officer's testimony but was unsuccessful, and he was ultimately convicted. On appeal, the Court of Appeals of Alabama stated:

> Where in a proper case a non-expert is permitted to give opinion evidence, and cross examination discloses that his opportunity for observation was insufficient to afford any reasonable basis for the conclusion expressed, his opinion testimony should be excluded on motion. Where however an opportunity for observation is shown, even though slight, a witness should be considered competent to testify as to what he did observe. Certainly we know of no way to measure a witness's capacity for observation, other than as it may be determined by a jury which hears the testimony tending to show its strength or weakness on the facts developed from examination of the witness. (p. 199)

The last sentence of this case excerpt is telling. The appellate court basically suggested that it is impossible to measure witness's ability to observe and remember important events. The question as to the accuracy of their testimony should be left up to the jury.

Another illustrative case is *State v. Ranieri* (1991). This case involved a prosecution for burglary and assault. Someone broke into Elsie's apartment during the night and assaulted her. Hearing the commotion in Elsie's apartment, a neighbor, Picard, entered the apartment and attempted to remove the assailant from Elsie. Picard was also assaulted while attempting to intervene. For many months after the incident Elsie said she could not identify the assailant; however, on the eve of the trial, she stated that she could identify him. Before the trial she picked the defendant's picture out of a photographic lineup and also identified him at trial. The question before the Supreme Court of Rhode Island was if Elsie had sufficient opportunity to view the defendant to be considered a competent witness. Despite her identification of the defendant during and immediately preceding the trial, the court ruled that she was incompetent as a witness because she "had an insufficient opportunity to view the assailant."

The court further stated:

> We think it unmistakenly clear that Elsie has a history of making unwarranted and unfair accusations against defendant. Elsie had absolutely no factual basis to make two prior serious allegations

against defendant and we see nothing to indicate a factual basis . . .
to consider her competent as a witness.

The message from the court was basically that witnesses, though afforded
a great deal of latitude in their testimony, must be able to communicate
a certain minimal amount of information to be considered competent and
have their testimony included at trial.

In another case (*State v. Singh*, 1979) the question of a child's ability
to recall and narrate events was raised. In that case, the Missouri Court
of Appeals heard an appeal from a defendant who was convicted in a
lower court of manslaughter of his wife. The defendant testified at trial
that in the course of an argument with his wife, which became violent,
she had gone to a closet and obtained a revolver, which the defendant
had then taken from her and put in his pocket. The defendant also
testified that the wife hit him with a stick and that a struggle then
occurred, first inside the house then outside, at which point the gun
"went off." The government offered as a witness the nearly 6-year-old
daughter, who had been present. She testified that she was awakened by
the quarrel, that she observed her mother lying down outside the house,
and that the mother had been shot. The defense moved to declare the
child witness incompetent; however, the Court of Appeals permitted the
testimony, stating that, "this child appears to have been candid, alert and
intelligent." Moreover, according to the court, "There is no fixed age at
which a child may be a competent witness." In support of its decision
the court noted that the time interval between the crime and daughter's
testimony was relatively short, which served to reinforce the belief that
her testimony was accurate and believable.

By way of contrast, another court ruled that it is wrong to find competent a girl who was 4 at the time of the incident and 11 at the time of
trial. "The evidence does not support a finding that Jane had a reasonable
ability to recall . . . , in 1991, events that occurred in 1983. She was unable
to recall even basic aspects of her life as it was in 1983 other than the
detailed description of the events of the one day on which she was allegedly assaulted" (*State v. Rippy*, 1993, 337–338).

A case involving residents in a nursing home raises interesting issues
concerning witnesses' ability to recall and narrate events. In *People v. White*
(1968), the Supreme Court of Illinois had occasion to decide whether an
elderly person who could not communicate verbally could be declared
a competent witness. In that case, Mrs. Idelle Broday shared a room
in a nursing home with Mrs. Mickey Kallick. Broday was robbed of a
ring that was taken from her with sufficient force to cause a cut on her
finger. The defendant, a nurse's aid, was accused of the crime. Broday was

incompetent to testify because she was apparently not conscious at the time of the crime. The only witness, Mrs. Kallick, was not permitted by her doctors to be moved. As a result, a portion of the trial was held in the nursing home. Also, the only way Mrs. Kallick could communicate was to raise her right knee if her answer was "yes" and remain still if her answer was no. The trial judge declared Kallick competent as a witness, and the defendant was convicted based on her testimony. The Supreme Court of Illinois disagreed with his decision: "While the record may not establish total incompetency of the eyewitness, we are of the opinion that her condition was such that defendant could not get a fair trial. The witness had no means of originally communicating an accusation."

In summary, the ability of witnesses to observe, remember, and communicate important events is an essential element for the trier of fact. As we showed earlier, with few exceptions, most witnesses can be considered competent unless they are unable to understand questions or communicate about the events in question. The cases just reviewed suggest that certain conditions such as youth, old age, and physical and mental conditions can impair a witness's ability to remember, and they therefore lack the capacity to testify.

Dead Man's Statutes

Some states have **dead man's statutes** that prohibit witnesses from testifying about transactions with a person involved in a case if the person died prior to the trial. Such laws are based on the assumption that a survivor of a deceased person should be looked at with suspicion as someone who may, on the first opportunity, make false claims against the deceased because he or she is unable to contest or affirm them.

Basically, dead man's statutes are intended to prevent fraud against those people who are unable to testify on their own behalf because they are dead. Such laws owe their origins to the common law rule of "disqualification by interest." Early common law courts concluded that witnesses with an "interest" in the outcome of the case were prevented from giving testimony (e.g., *Vastbinder v. Spinks*, 1849). According to one source:

> The existence of the dead man statutes represents the judgment of legislative bodies that the general honesty and truthfulness of people in modern society is at a pretty low ebb and that all it takes is the motive of interest plus a good chance created by death of one of the parties to cause the majority of people to concoct false

claims to plunder the estates of dead persons. (Weinstein, Mansfield, Abrams, and Berger 1997, 272)

Many states have rejected dead man's statutes. For one thing, it is unreasonable to assume that people who stand to benefit from the death of a person will necessarily testify in a fraudulent fashion. In fact, the Federal Rules of Evidence (Rule 601) contain no rules concerning testimony within the meaning of dead man's statutes. Also, to the extent that dead man's statutes still exist in certain states, they are almost exclusively limited to civil matters, particularly cases involving wills and estates.

An example of a case dealing with dead man's statutes is *Mathews v. Hines* (1978). This case concerned a dispute over more than $10,000 between the widow and daughter of a deceased man. The plaintiff, the daughter, alleged that prior to his death the man (known as a decedent in legal terms) transferred real and personal property to his wife, which presumably reduced the daughter's share that she would have received after his death had he not transferred funds before he died. The daughter alleged that the widow breached her promise to the decedent, her dead husband, to ensure that his estate was distributed according to his will. On two occasions the daughter deposed the widow to ask her about communications made to the husband prior to his death in which, presumably, arrangements were made to hide some of his assets from other family members besides the wife. The U.S. District Court for the Middle District of Florida ruled in favor of the plaintiff and ordered the widow to testify.

Why did we choose to focus on a civil case? The fact is that there are few, if any, published criminal cases focusing on dead man's statutes. Dead man's statutes, again, are designed to protect against false witness statements against a decedent, a dead person who cannot challenge such statements. In criminal cases, however, there are no decedents, that is, no dead people who stand to be "harmed" in some fashion by statements offered by a witness. The only person who stands to lose something in a criminal action is the defendant, and the defendant clearly needs to be "alive" for the trial to commence.

When Corroboration is Required

The credibility of a witness is stronger if information exists to corroborate the witness's story. Supporting evidence is called corroboration. Do not confuse **corroborative evidence** with cumulative evidence. **Cumulative evidence** is evidence that repeats what is already known. For example, several witnesses testifying that they saw an event can be considered cumulative. Corroborative evidence is supportive, not duplicative.

Corroboration can be presented by another witness or as physical evidence. For example, if two witnesses observe a crime, then if both witnesses testify at trial, one's testimony corroborates the others'. Similarly, if a witness to a domestic assault observes that a husband hit his wife, physical evidence of injury corroborates the witness's testimony. The witness's testimony in such a case is an improvement on the mere presence of a physical injury, because such an injury may or may not be tied to the husband's criminal act. The wife could have received the injury as a result of a fall rather than at the hands of her husband.

For the most part, witnesses can give their testimony without corroboration. That is, a witness usually does not need another person or other evidence to support the statements he or she makes in court. There are exceptions, however. In fact, Article III, Section 3 of the U.S. Constitution states that "No Person shall be convicted of treason unless on the testimony of two Witnesses to the same overt Act, or on Confession in open Court." Other statutes, some of which we now consider, also require corroboration.

For example, many jurisdictions require corroboration for a conviction of perjury. In *Weiler v. United States* (1945) the Supreme Court upheld the requirement that federal law requires corroboration in federal perjury cases on the ground that "the rules of law must be so fashioned as to protect honest witnesses from hasty and spiteful retaliation in the form of unfounded perjury prosecutions." The Court's ruling seems sensible; to prove that someone is lying (the essence of perjury), some "evidence" would be necessary to support the charge.

Corroboration is also considered mandatory in some cases involving accomplices. The logic is simple: When one party testifies against the other, it is generally assumed that he or she is doing so in an effort to reduce his or her culpability or gain favors with the prosecution. For example, unless two men suspected of robbery are the best of friends, it is reasonable to assume that the first man may say something during an interrogation to implicate the second man and make himself look less culpable. Because of the motive to falsify testimony, corroboration is required for a conviction based on the testimony of an accomplice regardless of the nature of the crime.

It is generally accepted in the U.S. criminal justice system that a defendant cannot be convicted on his or her confession alone. Instead, confessions almost always have to be corroborated by other evidence (e.g., *Warszower v. United States,* 1941; *Opper v. United States,* 1954). One reason offered for this rule is that police coercion may be enough to compel a person to confess to a crime he or she did not commit. In the wake of important Supreme Court decisions such as *Miranda v Arizona* (1966), however, the reasoning for requiring corroboration is now simply that "physically uncoerced false confessions occur with sufficient regularity to justify prophylactic measures" (*Government of Virgin Islands v. Harris,* 1966, 409). Corroboration is necessary, therefore, to ensure that wrongful convictions are minimized.

Somewhat controversially, certain jurisdictions require that rape victims' testimony be corroborated by additional information. This requirement has been abandoned in several areas, but the Model Penal Code continues to retain the corroboration requirement. A comment to Section 213.6(5) of the Model Penal Code states, however, that retaining the corroboration requirement is "only a particular implementation of the general policy that uncertainty should be resolved in favor of the accused." In other words, corroboration should be viewed as a means of improving the government's case against the defendant in a rape trial for which witness corroboration is required.

In those jurisdictions that retain corroboration requirements, it is not always clear to which elements of an offense the corroboration requirement attaches. In *Smith v. United States* (1954), the Supreme Court stated that all elements of the offense must be corroborated. However, in *Wong Sun v. United States* (1963) the Supreme Court stated that when a crime involves physical damage to a person or property, corroboration is necessary only for the corpus delecti damage that is criminally caused. Corroboration was not considered essential in that case to show that the defendant was the cause of the physical damage. The decision as to the defendant's guilt or innocence was to be left to the jury.

Wong Sun et al. v. United States
Supreme Court of the United States
371 U.S. 471 (1963)

The petitioners were tried without a jury in the District Court for the Northern District of California under a two-count indictment for violation of the Federal Narcotics Laws, 21 U.S.C. § 174. n1. They were acquitted under the first count which charged a conspiracy,

(continued)

but convicted under the second count which charged the substantive offense of fraudulent and knowing transportation and concealment of illegally imported heroin. The Court of Appeals for the Ninth Circuit, one judge dissenting, affirmed the convictions. We granted certiorari. We heard argument in the 1961 Term and reargument this Term.

*****

It remains only to consider Toy's unsigned statement. We need not decide whether, in light of the fact that Toy was free on his own recognizance when he made the statement, that statement was a fruit of the illegal arrest. Since we have concluded that his declarations in the bedroom and the narcotics surrendered by Yee should not have been admitted in evidence against him, the only proofs remaining to sustain his conviction are his and Wong Sun's unsigned statements. Without scrutinizing the contents of Toy's ambiguous recitals, we conclude that no reference to Toy in Wong Sun's statement constitutes admissible evidence corroborating any admission by Toy. We arrive at this conclusion upon two clear lines of decisions, which converge to require it. One line of our decisions establishes that criminal confessions and admissions of guilt require extrinsic corroboration; the other line of precedents holds that an out-of-court declaration made after arrest may not be used at trial against one of the declarant's partners in crime.

*****

It is a settled principle of the administration of criminal justice in the federal courts that a conviction must rest upon firmer ground than the uncorroborated admission or confession of the accused. We observed in *Smith v. United States* that the requirement of corroboration is rooted in "a long history of judicial experience with confessions and in the realization that sound law enforcement requires police investigations, which extend beyond the words of the accused." In *Opper v. United States,* we elaborated the reasons for the requirement:

*****

"In our country the doubt persists that the zeal of the agencies of prosecution to protect the peace, the self-interest of the accomplice, the maliciousness of an enemy or the aberration or weakness of the accused under the strain of suspicion may tinge or warp the facts of the confession. Admissions, retold at a trial, are much like hearsay,

(continued)

that is, statements not made at the pending trial. They had neither the compulsion of the oath nor the test of cross-examination."

*****

It is true that in *Smith v. United States,* supra, we held that although "corroboration is necessary for all elements of the offense established by admissions alone," extrinsic proof was sufficient which "merely fortifies the truth of the confession, without independently establishing the crime charged..." However, Wong Sun's unsigned confession does not furnish competent corroborative evidence. The second governing principle, likewise well settled in our decisions, is that an out-of-court declaration made after arrest may not be used at trial against one of the declarant's partners in crime. While such a statement is "admissible against the others where it is in furtherance of the criminal undertaking . . . all such responsibility is at an end when the conspiracy ends." We have consistently refused to broaden that very narrow exception to the traditional hearsay rule, which admits statements of a codefendant made in furtherance of a conspiracy or joint undertaking. And where postconspiracy declarations have been admitted, we have carefully ascertained that limiting instructions kept the jury from considering the contents with respect to the guilt of anyone but the declarant. We have never ruled squarely on the question presented here, whether a codefendant's statement might serve to corroborate even where it will not suffice to convict. We see no warrant for a different result so long as the rule, which regulates the use of out-of-court statements, is one of admissibility, rather than simply of weight, of the evidence. The import of our previous holdings is that a co-conspirator's hearsay statements may be admitted against the accused for no purpose whatever, unless made during and in furtherance of the conspiracy. Thus as to Toy the only possible source of corroboration is removed and his conviction must be set aside for lack of competent evidence to support it.

We introduced corroboration in this chapter simply because additional information is sometimes necessary (even required) when the veracity of a witness's testimony is questionable. However, any good attorney will do whatever possible to corroborate witnesses' testimony. Even though the rules of evidence may not require it, both sides to a criminal case, if they are reasonably competent, will always try to introduce as much evidence as possible to corroborate the testimony of their witnesses as well as to improve their chances to "win the case."

To conclude, witness testimony can regularly stand alone, that is, it does not need corroboration most of the time. Corroboration is necessary only in specific situations depending on state law. The Federal Rules of Evidence give no mention to corroboration, so the extent that corroboration is necessary is left up to the states to decide.

Summary

Today, almost anyone can be considered a competent witness. However, competency can still be challenged on a number of grounds. Mental incapacity can render a potential witness incompetent. Young children are sometimes considered incompetent. Spouses are generally incompetent to give testimony against their partners, although there are a number of exceptions to this rule. Certain prior convictions can render a witness incompetent. Finally, judges and jurors are usually considered incompetent as witnesses at their own trials. Religious beliefs, however, cannot render a witness incompetent.

To be a competent witness, one must also be able to understand the duty to tell the truth and have the ability to observe and remember the events in question. Accordingly, this chapter devoted special attention to witness oaths and affirmations and the duty to tell the truth. The chapter also discussed certain conditions under which witnesses' ability to observe and remember have been hampered, such as being too young at the time of the crime or not having had enough time to observe the perpetrator.

Dead man's statutes, which, quickly disappearing in this day and age, prevent witnesses from giving harmful testimony on behalf of a decedent, a dead person who is unable to defend himself or herself in court. Corroboration is the extent to which additional evidence can be permitted or required in order to "back up" a witness's testimony.

Discussion Questions

1. Explain the criteria for establishing witness competency.
2. Assuming that a man and woman are currently or were previously married to each other, explain the circumstances under which the spousal privilege will or will not apply.
3. What are the five grounds for challenging witness competency?

4. Explain "dead man's statutes." What was the original purpose of this legal concept, and are these rules still in use?

5. What are the four essential requirements of a competent witness?

Further Reading

Blumenthal, J. A. (1993). "A Wipe of the Hands, A Lick of the Lips: The Validity of Demeanor Evidence in Assessing Witness Credibility." *Nebraska Law Review* 72:1157.

Caine, M. L. (2001). "Using Prior Convictions to Impeach the Credibility of a Defendant-Witness in Massachusetts, Do We Go Too Far?" *Suffolk Journal of Trial and Appellate Advocacy* 6:121.

Fishman, C. S. (1992). *Jones on Evidence, Civil and Criminal* (7th ed.). Eagon, MN: West.

Graham, M. H. (1992). *Federal Practice and Procedure: Evidence* (interim ed.). Eagon, MN: West Group.

Jackson, J. W. (1996). "Commentary: Impeachment of a Witness by Prior Convictions Under Alabama Rule of Evidence 609: Everything Remains the Same, or Does it?" *Alabama Law Review* 48:253.

Lilly, G. C. (1996). *An Introduction to the Law of Evidence* (3rd ed.). Eagon, MN: West.

McCord, D. (1986). "Expert Psychological Testimony About Child Complainants in Sexual Abuse Prosecutions: A Foray Into the Admissibility of Novel Psychological Evidence." *Journal of Criminal Law and Criminology* 77:1–68.

Morris, M. L. (2001). "Comment: Li'l People, Little Justice: The Effect of the Witness Competency Standard in California on Children Sexual Abuse Cases." *Journal pd Juvenile Law* 22:113.

Mueller, C. B., and L. C. Kirkpatrick (1999). *Evidence* (2nd ed.). New York: Aspen Publishing.

Strong, J. W. (1992). *McCormick on Evidence* (4th ed.). Eagon, MN: West Group.

Weinstein, J. B., J. H. Mansfield, N. Abrams, and M. A. Berger. *Evidence: Cases and Materials* (9th ed.). Westbury, NY: Foundation Press.

Cases Cited

Chapell v. State, 710 S.W.2d 214 (Ark. 1986)

Cross v. Commonwealth, 195 Vs. 62 (1953)

District of Columbia v. Armes, 107 U.S. 519 (1882)

United States v. Roach, 590 F.2d 181 (5th Cir. 1979)

United States v. Thomann, 609 F.2d 560 (1st Cir. 1979)

United States v. Ward, 989 F.2d 1015 (1992)

Vastbinder v. Spinks, 16 Ala. 385 (1849)

Warszower v. United States, 312 U.S. 342 (1941)

Weiler v. United States, 323 U.S. 606 (1945)

Wheeler v. United States, 159 U.S. 523 (1895)

White v. Illinois, 502 U.S. 346 (1992)

Wong Sun v. United States, 371 U.S. 471 (1963)

CHAPTER 7

CREDIBILITY AND IMPEACHMENT OF WITNESSES

Key Terms & Concepts

Accrediting	Inability to observe	Rule 608
Bias	Inconsistent statements	Rule 609
Contradictory testimony	Prejudice	Rule 610
Credibility	Prior convictions	Rule 613
Discrediting	Rehabilitation	Uncharged crimes
Immoral acts	Reputation	Witness credibility
Impeachment	Rule 607	

Chapter Learning Objectives

By the end of this chapter, the student should be able to:

- Relate the important role that witness credibility plays in criminal proceedings
- Understand the rules for accrediting and discrediting of witnesses
- Identify common methods for challenging witness credibility
- Identify strategies for rehabilitating witness credibility
- Identify areas that are "off limits" and cannot be used to challenge witness credibility
- List common crimes and convictions that may be used to impugn witness credibility

Introduction

This chapter addresses the important topic of witness credibility. To be sure, both sides in a criminal case seek to present evidence that is favorably convincing to their side of the issue. In doing so, witnesses that are called to testify before the court must be credible or, in other words, believable. If a judge or jury does not find a witness to be credible, they will place very little value on what the witness has to say regarding facts of the case. Against this backdrop, Chapter 7 considers various situations in which witness credibility can become an issue.

This chapter also discusses the impeachment of witnesses. Calling the credibility of a witness into question is not uncommon, and there are several established grounds for attempting to impeach a witness's character or testimony, including bias, prior convictions, uncharged crimes, and immoral acts.

A final topic addressed in this chapter is the manner and method of rehabilitating witness credibility. That is, once the character of a witness has been compromised, what methods or strategies can be used to restore the person's credibility? These dimensions of the criminal trial process are important because they inevitably come into play during the introduction of evidence, either real or testimonial. The rules regulating witness credibility, impeachment, and rehabilitation are referenced throughout the chapter, along with various external sources for informational purposes.

Witness Credibility

We now turn our attention to the topics of credibility and impeachment. First off, we must distinguish credibility from *competency*, which refers to the ability of a witness to remember events, communicate effectively, and understand the importance of both telling the truth and the consequences for not doing so. **Credibility** asks whether the testimony offered by a witness should be believed. In other words, are the statements made by a witness such that they can be judged as truthful? If the witness is able to remember events, communicates clearly to the jury, and comes across as convincing, he or she will probably be regarded as credible.

http://www.decisionquest.com/litigation_library.php?NewsID=255

When discussing competency, courts often refer to the processes of "accrediting" and "discrediting." **Discrediting** occurs when the prosecution or defense challenges the witness's credibility. **Accrediting** is the opposite: It occurs when the prosecution or defense attempts to support, bolster, or improve a witness's credibility.

A number of specific rules govern the processes of accrediting and discrediting. First, it is universally agreed that in absence of an attack on a witness's credibility, no evidence may be introduced to support or bolster credibility. According to one court (*United States v. Price,* 1983), "[T]here is no reason why time should be spent in proving that which may be assumed to exist. Every witness must be assumed to be of normal moral character for veracity, just as he is assumed to be of normal sanity . . . Good character, therefore, in his support is excluded *until his character is brought into question* and it thus becomes worthwhile to deny that his character is bad" (p. 90). Simply put, a witness generally cannot be accredited until someone (prosecution or defense) attempts to *discredit* the witness.

Consider the situation in which a witness is asked to introduce himself or herself and describe his or her background. The prosecution or defense may ask direct questions about the witness's familiarity with the case or, in the situation of expert witnesses, questions about the witness's occupation, background, and professional accomplishments. This type of questioning would appear to be accrediting, but a certain amount of background information can be supplied by introductory witness questioning without it being considered accreditation. However, there is a point at which accrediting must stop, lacking an attack on the witness's credibility. Unfortunately, there are few answers as to what amount of accrediting "background" information is permissible. According to one court (*Government of Virgin Islands v. Grant,* 1985):

> The jurisprudence of "background" evidence is essentially undeveloped. "Background" or "preliminary" evidence is not mentioned in the evidence codes, nor has it received attention in the treatises. One justification for its admission, at least in terms of the background of a witness qua witness, is that it may establish absence of bias or motive by showing the witness's relationship (or non-relationship) to the parties or to the case . . . (p. 513)

It is safe to conclude, though, that when the introduction process turns aggrandizing, that is, into more than an introduction, the accrediting of a witness must stop.

In one interesting case (*Pointer v. State,* 1954) the prosecutor, during his closing statements, noted that if the prosecution witness had been of bad character, the defense would have raised the issue. The court reversed the ensuing conviction, holding that because the witness's credibility was not attacked during trial, the prosecutor was not permitted to bolster the witness's credibility (see also *Poole v. Commonwealth,* 1970).

A controversial issue with regard to accrediting concerns what can be done to bolster a witness's credibility when he or she cannot remember important events. If, for example, a witness testifies to a series of events but states that she is unable to remember everything, can another witness be called to offer reasons for the woman's memory lapse? A similar question was raised in *United States v. Awkward* (1979). In that case, the

Ninth Circuit Court of Appeals ruled that it was wrong for a prosecution witness to testify that he had been hypnotized and to permit a prosecution expert who had hypnotized the first witness to testify about the effects of hypnosis on that witness. There, the court stated:

> unless an adverse party attacks the witness's ability to recall by bringing out or exploring the fact of hypnosis, the use of expert testimony to support the efficacy of hypnosis is improper. The party calling a witness should not be permitted to inquire in any way into the witness's ability to recall, or methods of pretrial memory refreshment, until such questions have been raised by the adversary. (p. 679)

In sum, witness accrediting is permissible but usually "only after the character of the witness for truthfulness has been attacked by opinion or reputation evidence or otherwise" (*Blake v. Cich,* 1978, 403). In legal language, accrediting of this sort is also known as witness rehabilitation, which we address following our discussion of impeachment. Note, however, that this restriction on the accrediting rule is not recognized in most modern evidence statutes, except with regard to character evidence. That is, most modern statutes do not allow accrediting of a witness's character but are silent as to other types of accrediting (see Rule 608(a)(2) of the Federal Rules of Evidence).

Rule 608. Evidence of Character and Conduct of Witness

(b) Opinion and reputation evidence of character.

The credibility of a witness may be attacked or supported by evidence in the form of opinion or reputation, but subject to these limitations: (1) the evidence may refer only to character for truthfulness or untruthfulness, and (2) evidence of truthful character is admissible only after the character of the witness for truthfulness has been attacked by opinion or reputation evidence or otherwise.

(b) Specific instances of conduct.

Specific instances of the conduct of a witness, for the purpose of attacking or supporting the witness' character for truthfulness, other than conviction of crime as provided in Rule 609, may not be proved by extrinsic evidence. They may, however, in the discretion of the court, if probative of truthfulness or untruthfulness, be inquired into on cross-examination of the witness (1) concerning the witness' character for truthfulness or untruthfulness, or (2) concerning the character for truthfulness or untruthfulness of another witness as to which character the witness being cross-examined has testified.

The giving of testimony, whether by an accused or by any other witness, does not operate as a waiver of the accused's or the witness' privilege against self-incrimination when examined with respect to matters that relate only to character for truthfulness.

http://www.law.cornell.edu/rules/fre/ACRule608.htm

Impeachment

Impeachment is the formal term for attacking a witness's credibility. The prosecution or defense may decide, when faced with a witness who is not believed to be telling the truth, to challenge the witness's believability before the jury. The jury will then draw its own conclusions as to the witness's truthfulness and believability.

Rule 607. Who May Impeach

The credibility of a witness may be attacked by any party, including the party calling the witness.

http://www.law.cornell.edu/rules/fre/ACRule607.htm

How does impeachment occur? Generally, the process begins on cross examination. Several established and well-founded reasons exist for attacking witness credibility. However, there is little value in attempting to impeach a witness if the witness's testimony does not carry much weight or is unpersuasive to the jury. Alternatively, if no basis exists for an attack on a witness's credibility, but the opposing side attempts to attack the witness's credibility anyway, an impeachment effort could backfire. .

http://members.aol.com/richrwg/advtt/hbcross.htm
http://www.ncids.org/Defender%20Training/Drug%20Case%20Training/Cross%20Exam%20the%20Snitch.pdf

Almost without exception, impeachment occurs when the prosecution attacks the credibility of a defense witness or vice versa. However, there are certain situations in which the prosecution or the defense may wish to impeach its own witness. Indeed, **Rule 607** states, "The credibility of a witness may be attacked by any party, including the party calling the witness." Why might a party wish to impeach its own witness? The primary and perhaps only reason is surprise (*Hickory v. United States,* 1894). "Surprise" occurs when the witness's testimony is contrary to that anticipated by the party calling the witness (*United States v. Miles,* 1969).

To illustrate the notion of surprise, consider the case of *Sullivan v. United States* (1928), in which three persons pled guilty to participation in a mail robbery. All three men then served as prosecution witnesses against the defendant, a fourth man who had not pled guilty. To the surprise of the prosecution, though, one of the three men gave testimony that exculpated the defendant. Accordingly, the prosecution could have impeached the witness because of the surprise.

In another case (*People v. Spinosa,* 1953), the witness at first stated prior to trial that he had not committed the offense but then later stated that he had committed the offense. At trial, the witness testified that he had not committed the crime. The court held that the prosecution was surprised because the prosecution had the right to assume that the witness would testify in accordance with his latest story. A second reason for one party to impeach its own witness is to lessen the blow imposed by cross examination (see *United States v. Shields,* 1993).

Despite rule 607's statement to the effect that a party may impeach its own witness, there are significant restrictions on doing so. For example, the government or the prosecution cannot impeach its own witnesses by presenting what would otherwise be considered impermissible hearsay (*United States v. Ince,* 1994). Nigel D. Ince was convicted by a jury for assault with a dangerous weapon. The Fourth Circuit Court of Appeals reversed Ince's conviction because the government's only purpose for impeaching one of its own witnesses was to circumvent the hearsay rule and expose the jury to otherwise inadmissible evidence.

Impeachment is most often used by one party against another. The prosecution or the defense can attack a witness's credibility for a number of well-established reasons, including (1) bias or prejudice, (2) certain prior convictions, (3) uncharged crimes and immoral acts, (4) prior inconsistent statements, (5) inability to observe or remember events, and (6) reputation. See Table 7.1 for a summary.

Bias or Prejudice

Perhaps the most effective way of calling into question a witness's credibility is to introduce evidence of **bias** or **prejudice**. If, for example, a witness for the defense is a close personal relative of the defendant, there would seem to be strong bias in *favor* of the defendant (that is, assuming the defendant and witness are on good terms). Any motive for the witness to falsify his or her testimony, or to testify in an untruthful fashion so as to benefit or harm the defendant, can be raised by the opposing side as evidence of bias or prejudice.

One especially well-known example of a witness's credibility being attacked for prejudice was in the O.J. Simpson case. Recall that Detective Mark Fuhrman was cross examined regarding his prejudice against blacks.

Table 7.1 **Common Grounds for Challenging Witness Credibility**

Grounds	Description
Bias or prejudice	If a witness is inclined to favor or oppose one party for any reason (such as an interest, corruption, or intimidation), the witness is said to be biased. Witnesses can also be biased because of friendship, family ties, animosity, or prejudice.
Prior convictions	With some exceptions, convictions for felonies and crimes involving deception can be used to discredit a witness.
Uncharged crimes and immoral acts	A witness facing uncharged crimes can be impeached if the crimes (1) have probative value in the eyes of the judge, (2) reflect upon the ability of the witness to tell the truth, and (3) cannot be proved by extrinsic evidence.
Contradictions and prior inconsistent statements	Such statements can be called to attention at trial.
Inability to observe	Defects in the ability of a witness to perceive, recollect, or narrate events can be used to discredit her/him.
Reputation	The witness's reputation can be called into question but is limited to her/his propensity for telling the truth.

The prosecution fought to avoid the questioning of F. Lee Bailey (one of Simpson's defense attorneys) to this effect, but Judge Ito permitted it. As a result, Bailey was able to introduce evidence supporting Detective Fuhrman's racially prejudicial sentiments.

In another case (*McKnight v. State,* 1994), the court held that the examination of the defendant's wife concerning her withdrawal of previous complaints against the defendant was permissible in order to impeach her as to her bias.

One important reason to impeach a witness for evidence of bias occurs when a prosecution witness is offered promises of leniency. The bias motive is clear: If the witness knows that his or her testimony will garner favor with the prosecution, the witness may be inclined to tell the prosecution what it wants to hear. In one case, a Tennessee court ruled that the defendant had the right to attack a prosecution witness's credibility because of promises of favorable treatment made by the prosecution (*State v. Spurlock,* 1993).

In an interesting Supreme Court case, *United States v. Abel* (1984), the issue of cross- examining for bias was raised. John Abel was charged in federal court with robbery. Two of his accomplices had pled guilty to the crime, and one, Kurt Ehle, agreed to testify against Abel. At trial, Ehle implicated Abel in the robbery. However, Abel called a witness, Robert Mills, to testify that Ehle had planned to implicate Abel falsely. Mills and Ehle had both spent time together in prison. Under cross examination the prosecution asked Mills if he was, like Ehle, a member of a prison gang, the Aryan Brotherhood. Mills denied that he was. The prosecution then called Ehle back to the stand, who testified that Mills was a member of the prison gang and that the gang's tenets required its members to "lie, cheat, steal [and] kill" to protect each other. The jury convicted Abel, and the Supreme Court upheld the conviction. In the Court's words, "We hold that the evidence showing Mills' and respondent's membership in the prison gang was sufficiently probative of Mills' possible bias towards respondent [Abel] to warrant its admission into evidence."

In a more recent decision, *Banks v. Dretke* (2004), the U.S. Supreme Court reversed a 24-year-old murder conviction because of the failure of the prosecution to disclose information that could have been used by the defense to impeach the credibility of a key prosecution witness.

Banks v. Dretke
Supreme Court of the United States
540 U.S. 668 (2004)

Petitioner Delma Banks, Jr., was convicted of capital murder and sentenced to death. Prior to trial, the State advised Banks's attorney there would be no need to litigate discovery issues, representing: "[W]e will, without the necessity of motions provide you with all discovery to which you are entitled." Despite that undertaking, the State withheld evidence that would have allowed Banks to discredit two essential prosecution witnesses. The State did not disclose that one of those witnesses was a paid police informant, nor did it disclose a pretrial transcript revealing that the other witness' trial testimony had been intensively coached by prosecutors and law enforcement officers.

Furthermore, the prosecution raised no red flag when the informant testified, untruthfully, that he never gave the police any statement and,

(continued)

indeed, had not talked to any police officer about the case until a few days before the trial. Instead of correcting the informant's false statements, the prosecutor told the jury that the witness "had been open and honest with you in every way," and that his testimony was of the "utmost significance." Similarly, the prosecution allowed the other key witness to convey, untruthfully, that his testimony was entirely unrehearsed. Through direct appeal and state collateral review proceedings, the State continued to hold secret the key witnesses' links to the police and allowed their false statements to stand uncorrected.

Ultimately, through discovery and an evidentiary hearing authorized in a federal habeas corpus proceeding, the long-suppressed evidence came to light. The District Court granted Banks relief from the death penalty, but the Court of Appeals reversed. In the latter court's judgment, Banks had documented his claims of prosecutorial misconduct too late and in the wrong forum; therefore he did not qualify for federal-court relief. We reverse that judgment. When police or prosecutors conceal significant exculpatory or impeaching material in the State's possession, it is ordinarily incumbent on the State to set the record straight.

*****

Here, the State elected to call Farr as a witness. Indeed, he was a key witness at both guilt and punishment phases of Banks's capital trial. Farr's status as a paid informant was unquestionably "relevant"; similarly beyond doubt, disclosure of Farr's status would have been "helpful to [Banks's] defense." Nothing in *Roviaro*, or any other decision of this Court, suggests that the State can examine an informant at trial, withholding acknowledgment of his informant status in the hope that defendant will not catch on, so will make no disclosure motion.

*****

. . .[I]n sum, one can hardly be confident that Banks received a fair trial, given the jury's ignorance of Farr's true role in the investigation and trial of the case. On the record before us, one could not plausibly deny the existence of the requisite "reasonable probability of a different result" had the suppressed information been disclosed to the defense. Accordingly, as to the suppression of Farr's informant status and its bearing on "the reliability of the jury's verdict regarding punishment," all three elements of a Brady claim are satisfied.

Prior Convictions

Rule 609 provides specific guidance on the use of evidence regarding prior convictions to impeach the credibility of witnesses. The rule, in pertinent part, states as follows:

Rule 609. Impeachment by Evidence of Conviction of Crime

(a) General rule.

For the purpose of attacking the credibility of a witness,

(1) evidence that a witness other than an accused has been convicted of a crime shall be admitted, subject to Rule 403, if the crime was punishable by death or imprisonment in excess of one year under the law under which the witness was convicted, and evidence that an accused has been convicted of such a crime shall be admitted if the court determines that the probative value of admitting this evidence outweighs its prejudicial effect to the accused; and

(2) evidence that any witness has been convicted of a crime shall be admitted if it involved dishonesty or false statement, regardless of the punishment.

(b) Time limit.

Evidence of a conviction under this rule is not admissible if a period of more than ten years has elapsed since the date of the conviction or of the release of the witness from the confinement imposed for that conviction, whichever is the later date, unless the court determines, in the interests of justice, that the probative value of the conviction supported by specific facts and circumstances substantially outweighs its prejudicial effect. However, evidence of a conviction more than 10 years old as calculated herein, is not admissible unless the proponent gives to the adverse party sufficient advance written notice of intent to use such evidence to provide the adverse party with a fair opportunity to contest the use of such evidence.

(c) Effect of pardon, annulment, or certificate of rehabilitation.

Evidence of a conviction is not admissible under this rule if (1) the conviction has been the subject of a pardon, annulment, certificate of rehabilitation, or other equivalent procedure based on a finding of the rehabilitation of the person convicted, and that person has not been convicted of a subsequent crime which was punishable by death or imprisonment in excess of one year, or (2) the conviction has been the subject of a pardon, annulment, or other equivalent procedure based on a finding of innocence.

(d) Juvenile adjudications.

Evidence of juvenile adjudications is generally not admissible under this rule. The court may, however, in a criminal case allow evidence of a juvenile adjudication of a witness other than the accused if conviction of the offense would be admissible to attack the credibility of an adult and the court is satisfied that admission in evidence is necessary for a fair determination of the issue of guilt or innocence.

(e) Pendency of appeal.

The pendency of an appeal therefrom does not render evidence of a conviction inadmissible. Evidence of the pendency of an appeal is admissible.

http://www.law.cornell.edu/rules/fre/ACRule609.htm

Under the first limitation, prior felony convictions can be introduced to impeach the credibility of witnesses other than the defendant only if the court (through the eyes of the judge) determines that testimony to this effect is not prejudicial to the defendant. Under the second limitation, a conviction can be introduced against any witness, including the defendant, assuming it was for a crime involving dishonesty or some variation thereof. With regard to the second limitation, the Supreme Court of California has stated that "The case law is clear: The only relevant consideration is whether the prior conviction contains as a necessary element the intent to deceive, defraud, lie, cheat, steal, etc." (*People v. Spearman,* 1979).

Other limitations on the use of prior convictions also exist. First, evidence of a prior conviction is not admissible if a period of more than ten years elapsed between the trial for which the person is to be a witness and the prior conviction or from confinement for that conviction, whichever is the later date. The purpose of this time restriction is to guard against remoteness. For example, a 30-year-old conviction is typically too remote to be of any value. If, however, the court sees that value in such evidence outweighs prejudice to the defendant, evidence regarding the conviction will be admitted. However, the party seeking admission of a conviction more than 10 years old must convince the judge that the interests of justice weigh in favor of the admission. Second, evidence of a prior conviction will not be admissible if the conviction has been the subject of a pardon, annulment, or certificate of rehabilitation.

Third, evidence of prior convictions is generally not permissible with regard to juvenile witnesses. The admissibility of juvenile adjudications to attack the credibility of witnesses was specifically addressed by the Supreme Court in *Davis v. Alaska* (1974). In *Davis*, the Court reversed a burglary conviction where the trial court denied defense counsel the opportunity to thoroughly cross examine a trial witness regarding a juvenile adjudication. In reversing the conviction, the Supreme Court held that the defense attorney should have been allowed to examine the witness regarding his adjudication of delinquency for burglary and therefore reveal any possible biases, prejudices, or ulterior motives related to the case.

Finally, the fact that an appeal from the prior conviction is pending will not affect the admissibility of the conviction. Thus, as long as there is substantial probative value in doing so, the conviction may be introduced.

If a defendant takes the stand in his or her own defense, the prosecution may seek to impeach the defendant on the grounds of his or her having previously been convicted of a crime, but not if the prosecution's motive is to prove that the defendant committed the crime for which he or she is on trial. Thus, evidence regarding prior convictions may not be used to prove that the defendant "did it again." Rather, evidence of prior convictions can be used only to cast doubt on the defendant's credibility. Clearly, it must be difficult for jury members to separate one motive from the other, but the prosecution's motive should nevertheless be aimed at impeachment. Judges will generally be cautious about admitting into evidence the defendant's prior conviction(s) because of the potentially prejudicial effect doing so may have.

Non-defendant witnesses who have been convicted of crimes, on the other hand, are more likely to see their prior records introduced at trial for impeachment purposes. The ordinary witness will probably be asked a question along the lines of, "Have you ever been convicted of a felony?" or "Have you ever been convicted of a misdemeanor involving moral turpitude?" If the answer is yes, evidence of the witness's prior convictions has been introduced. However, the judge can restrict the questions asked by the prosecution, assuming the defense objects. Alternatively, the prosecution can object to defense questioning of state witnesses concerning prior convictions. Separate hearings (out of earshot of the jury) can be held in which the judge determines whether evidence of witnesses' prior convictions can be introduced at trial.

A conviction for a trivial offense, such as shoplifting, may be introduced for the purpose of impeaching a witness, because such an offense involves a significant degree of dishonesty that may cast doubt on his or her credibility. Other examples of crimes of dishonesty and false statements include forgery and embezzlement, because both are classic examples of offenses that call into question a witness's ability to be honest.

Even bank robbery (a felony) has been considered one of the offenses within the meaning of Rule 609 (see Table 7.2); however, some courts have been hesitant to admit evidence of bank robbery convictions because this crime is less deceptive than less-serious crimes involving illegitimate means of obtaining money. A bank robber simply communicates something along the lines of "Give me the money or I'll shoot you," a statement that is rather direct and confrontational. Convictions for offenses such as smuggling and tax evasion can usually be admitted, however, because they involve surreptitious activity and deception.

Table 7.2　**Crimes Subject to the Prior Conviction Rule**

Common FRE 609 (a)(2) Crimes

Shoplifting
Perjury
Grand larceny
Petit larceny
Auto theft
Tax evasion
Forgery
Embezzlement
Bank robbery

Convictions for serious offenses are not admitted for the purpose of impeaching a witness as often as less-serious offenses are. The logic is that most serious offenses, with rare exceptions, do not shed light on a witness's motive to give false or misleading testimony. One could argue, for instance, that a witness previously convicted of robbery has such contempt for the laws of a civilized society that he could not possibly be inclined to tell the truth on the stand, but this is a risky assumption. Just because a person has been convicted of a serious crime does not mean that the person will necessarily lie on the stand (even if such a person is the defendant). Instead, the only way that evidence of a serious conviction can be admitted for impeachment purposes is if it passes a balancing test comparing its probative value to certain risks of misuse, particularly prejudice that could influence the jury negatively.

Consider a hypothetical example involving a conviction for a serious offense: The defense calls a witness to testify on the defendant's behalf. On cross examination the prosecution asks the witness, "Have you ever been convicted of a felony?" The witness answers, "Yes, for grand theft auto." Assuming this questioning passes muster with the judge, it is not difficult to see how the jury could be influenced by this evidence. Not only is the witness's credibility now damaged, but the jury may assume that "birds of a feather flock together. "In other words, because the witness is affiliated with the defendant and the witness is a convicted criminal, then the defendant must be a criminal too. It is quite likely that the judge would not permit such evidence to be presented to the jury; however, if the evidence of the prior conviction has substantial probative value, as it would appear to (because grand theft auto is clearly a crime involving deception), the judge may allow it.

Uncharged Crimes and Immoral Acts

Evidence about uncharged crimes or prior immoral acts is generally *not* admissible for the purpose of impeachment. If it turns out that a witness is a habitual shoplifter but has never been convicted of one such offense, this information would seem to bear substantially on the witness's credibility, but such evidence would probably not be admissible at trial. The exception to this general rule is to be found in **Rule 608**.

http://www.law.cornell.edu/rules/fre/ACRule608.htm

These exceptions may seem convoluted, but they are actually quite straightforward. For example, if the prosecution wishes to impeach a defense witness and wants to introduce evidence of prior acts of deception that did not result in convictions, the prosecutor may do so assuming the judge believes the line of questioning to have probative value. Similarly, if a witness testifies to another witness's character, evidence of untruthfulness may be admitted.

Two significant restrictions are placed on questions of witnesses concerning prior immoral or deceptive acts for which there was no conviction. First, there must be a basis in fact in such questioning. Second, the party seeking to impeach a witness cannot: (1) call other witnesses to refute the witness's testimony, or (2) produce other evidence to prove that such acts were committed. In essence, prosecutors and defense attorneys should not go on "fishing expeditions" to find evidence of witnesses' prior immoral or deceptive acts that did not result in convictions. There needs to be a factual basis for the questions, and any evidence as to the witness's prior acts is strictly limited to what the witness says in response to questions concerning such acts.

An interesting case that illustrates these limitations is *People v. Sorge* (1950). This case involved a prosecution for abortion (note that the date is prior to the 1973 decision of *Roe v. Wade*). The Court of Appeals of New York had occasion to determine whether prejudicial error was committed by the district attorney in conducting his cross examination of the defendant. The defendant, the woman charged with the crime of performing abortion, was questioned by the prosecutor about abortions that she had allegedly performed on four other women. She testified that she did not perform the abortions, but the prosecutor pressed further in an effort to get her to testify that she had performed the abortions. The court affirmed the woman's conviction because, even though the prosecutor questioned the woman extensively about performing previous abortions, he did not seek to call other witnesses or to introduce other evidence to this effect. The court stated that negative answers to the prosecutor's questions should not bar subsequent questioning because, if it did, "the witness would have it within his power to render futile most cross examination."

Contradictions and Prior Inconsistent Statements

For any number of reasons, witnesses may forget or may misinterpret important facts surrounding a case. At the other extreme, some witnesses may intentionally offer **contradictory testimony**. In either case, the party cross examining the witness may seek to call the jury's attention to the statement it believes to be contradictory. In other words, contradictory statements made by witnesses can be introduced for the purpose of impeachment. This is another way of saying that when witnesses make statements that appear contradictory, the opposition may take steps to attack the witness's credibility. This type of impeachment is governed by **Rule 613** of the Federal Rules of Evidence.

Rule 613. Prior Statements of Witnesses

(a) Examining witness concerning prior statement.
   In examining a witness concerning a prior statement made by the witness, whether written or not, the statement need not be shown nor its contents disclosed to the witness at that time, but on request the same shall be shown or disclosed to opposing counsel.
(b) Extrinsic evidence of prior inconsistent statement of witness.
   Extrinsic evidence of a prior inconsistent statement by a witness is not admissible unless the witness is afforded an opportunity to explain or deny the same and the opposite party is afforded an opportunity to interrogate the witness thereon, or the interests of justice otherwise require. This provision does not apply to admissions of a party-opponent as defined in rule 801(d)(2).

http://www.law.cornell.edu/rules/fre/ACRule613.htm

It is not permissible for the party cross examining the witness to point to *any* mistake or false statement made by the witness. It would take too much of the court's time if the opposition spent a great deal of time pointing to trivial inconsistencies or contradictions in a witness's testimony. For example, assume a witness testifies that "I was at the corner of Main and Broadway, and I saw the defendant run out of the National Bank carrying a gun and a bag of money." What if the bank on the corner is actually First National Bank? Would the jury benefit from being informed of this contradiction? Probably not, especially if the witness is able to accurately recall the other facts.

If, on the other hand, a contradictory statement is significant, the jury would clearly benefit from learning of it. For example, assume a defense witness testifies that "I saw the robber the afternoon of the robbery and he had a full beard." If it turns out that the robber did not have a beard, this is information the jury should probably hear. Accordingly, the prosecution would probably call eyewitnesses to testify that that robber did not have a beard. The prosecution's witnesses would be contradicting the defense witness's statements. Moreover, the evidence of the robber's physical appearance would be of significant value to the jury, because the evidence bears directly on the defendant's guilt or innocence.

What happens when a witness is hesitant or evasive when it comes to admitting to a contradictory statement? In this situation, the party cross examining the witness will be permitted to press the issue by asking detailed questions. Assume that a wife testifies at her husband's criminal trial for assault and says "He did not hit me." Assume also that prior to trial when being questioned by the police that she said, "He hit me." If the prosecution points out this contradiction but the woman refuses to admit it, the prosecution will be permitted to press the issue in order to get the witness to admit that she made a contradictory statement. The prosecutor may ask, "Did you not state during questioning that your husband did hit you?" If the woman still refuses to admit to the contradiction, the prosecutor may be entitled to admit additional evidence to prove that the contradictory statement was made (assuming all other requirements for the admissibility of evidence are met). For example, the prosecutor may call one of the police officers who questioned the woman prior to trial to testify that he or she heard the prosecution's witness make the contradictory statement.

A witness's prior inconsistent statements can also be introduced for the purpose of impeachment. When is a statement **inconsistent** as compared to contradictory? In *United States v. Barrett* (1976), a witness testified that after the defendant's arrest he said, "[I]t was a shame that Bucky [the defendant] got arrested on this matter . . . Bucky didn't have anything to do with it." The witness was testifying for the prosecution, but when his prior statement came to light at trial, there was evidence of an inconsistency. How could he testify for the prosecution given his earlier statement that he believed the defendant to be innocent?

So far we have pointed out that contradictions and inconsistencies can be based on mistakes and deliberate falsehoods, but what if a witness has been entirely silent regarding an issue that he or she later testifies about at trial? This issue has been raised in a number of significant cases. For example, in *United States v. Hale* (1975), the defendant was pointed out to the police by a robbery victim. The defendant was arrested, taken to the police station, and advised of his right to remain silent. He was searched and found in possession of $158. When asked where the money came from, he did not reply. At trial, the defendant took the stand and testified that the money the police recovered was money that his wife had given him after she cashed her welfare check. On cross examination the prosecution got the defendant to admit that he had not offered this explanation to the police at the time of his arrest. The Supreme Court held that this cross examination was impermissible. The Court offered several reasons for its finding, including the observation that the defendant had been advised that he had a right not to speak and that anything he said could be used against him.

It is important to understand that while impeachment provides opportunities to introduce a variety of evidence regarding the credibility and character of a witness, it may not be used to introduce evidence that would otherwise be inadmissible. In *United States v. Morlang* (1975), the appellate court specifically held that "impeachment by prior inconsistent statement may not be permitted where employed as a mere subterfuge to get before the jury evidence which is not otherwise admissible." Thus, expectation and obligation of good faith attends the introduction of impeachment evidence.

In *Harris v. New York* (1971), the U.S. Supreme Court was called on to examine an interesting case involving the use of impeachment evidence that was otherwise inadmissible at trial pursuant to *Miranda v. Arizona* (1966). In Harris, the defendant took the stand and gave his account regarding an alleged drug transaction. While testifying, Harris admitted that he had sold bags of what appeared to be heroin to an undercover officer. However, at trial Harris claimed that the bags did not contain heroin, only baking soda. On cross examination, the prosecutor questioned Harris regarding statements he made following his arrest but prior to receiving the *Miranda* warnings. The prior statements contradicted Harris' trial testimony. The prosecution agreed that the statements were otherwise inadmissible pursuant to *Miranda v. Arizona,* but contended that they were admissible for purposes of impeachment.

Following review, the Supreme Court upheld Harris' conviction and the use of the prior inconsistent statements. Justice Burger, writing for the majority, explained:

> Every criminal defendant is privileged to testify in his own defense or refuse to do so. But that privilege cannot be construed

to include the right to commit perjury. Having voluntarily taken the stand, petitioner was under an obligation to speak truthfully and accurately, and the prosecution here did no more than utilize the traditional truth-testing devices of the adversary process. Had inconsistent statements been made by the accused to some third person, it could hardly be contended that the conflict could not be laid before the jury by way of cross-examination and impeachment. The shield provided by Miranda cannot be perverted into a license to use perjury by way of a defense, free from the risk of confrontation with prior inconsistent statements. (*Harris v. New York*, 1971, 225–226)

In another interesting case, the Supreme Court held that the pre-arrest silence of a suspect may be used to impeach a defendant. In *Jenkins v. Anderson* (1980), the defendant testified at trial and claimed his actions were in self-defense. On cross examination, the prosecution questioned Jenkins regarding his silence during a two-week period prior to his arrest. During closing arguments, the prosecution again referred to the defendant's silence, arguing that if the killing had truly been in self-defense the defendant would not have remained silent. After review, the Supreme Court concluded that no governmental action induced Jenkins to remain silent prior to his arrest. The failure to speak occurred before the petitioner was taken into custody and given *Miranda* warnings. As such, the use of the defendant's silence for purposes of impeachment was not improper.

However, it is important to note that the result of *Jenkins* would have been different if his silence occurred after he was given *Miranda* warnings (*See Doyle v. Ohio*, 426 U.S. 610, 1976).

Inability to Observe

Another method of impeaching a witness relates closely to our earlier discussion of competency. As we indicated, a witness can be declared incompetent because of an inability to observe or recall the events under question. Witnesses can also be impeached based on the argument that they were unable to observe or recall the events in question. If a witness whose eyesight is poor testified that she saw the defendant fleeing the scene of the crime, the defense may wish to call attention to the woman's vision problem. Witnesses may also be questioned regarding use of drugs or alcohol at or near the time of the event about which they are testifying. Obviously, the use of drugs or alcohol may impair the sensory ability of the witness and is thus a viable area for cross-examination.

As indicated in the previous section, witnesses do not need to have a perfect ability to recall events. Insignificant "holes" in a witness's testimony may not be relevant to the determination of the defendant's guilt or innocence. Nevertheless, on cross examination the opposition may wish to call attention to a witness's inability to observe or remember if it is believed that the witness's shortcomings will influence the jury.

A witness's inability to observe can also be hampered by physical obstructions at the scene of the crime. Assume that a witness reports that he saw the defendant flee the scene of a carjacking in the victim's vehicle, but the victim's vehicle had darkly tinted windows. If the witness had not seen the defendant prior to his entering the vehicle, the defense on cross examination may wish to question the witness's ability to observe the defendant given that the windows of the vehicle made it difficult to see inside.

The party cross examining a witness cannot challenge the witness's ability to observe if it is not relevant. For example, a witness's hearing problem is not relevant if the witness's testimony concerns something she saw. Obviously the witness's hearing problem has nothing to do with her ability to observe, because her testimony is not based on what she heard.

Reputation

Generally speaking, the defendant's **reputation** cannot be called into question at trial. However, when the defendant calls a character witness to testify as to the defendant's upstanding character, the witness can be subject to an attack by the prosecution. The prosecution can seek to impeach the witness based on the witness's reputation. Likewise, character witnesses for the prosecution can be subject to impeachment by the defense during cross examination.

How is a witness's credibility attacked? Typically, the side seeking to impeach the witness will call its own witness to testify to the other witness's propensity for telling the truth. For example, assume that a murder defendant takes the stand in his own defense. The prosecution may elect to call its own witnesses to challenge the defendant's propensity for telling the truth. Indeed, if a friend of the defendant took the stand to testify on his behalf (to support the defendant's alibi, for instance), the prosecution could call its witnesses to attack the character of the defense witness. Except in rare circumstances deemed appropriate by the court, the questioning should be limited to the general reputation of the witness for honesty, not specific acts of misconduct.

Religion

While we've discussed several areas which may provide valuable impeachment of a witness, the Federal Rules of Evidence do not allow inquiry into the area of religion. Specifically, **Rule 610** bars attacks on credibility on the basis of the witnesses' religious beliefs or their opinions regarding religion.

Rule 610. Religious Beliefs or Opinions

Evidence of the beliefs or opinions of a witness on matters of religion is not admissible for the purpose of showing that by reason of their nature the witness' credibility is impaired or enhanced.

http://www.law.cornell.edu/rules/fre/ACRule610.htm

Rehabilitation

When the credibility of a witness is attacked, the side that produced the witness can take steps to bolster the witness's credibility, either by calling other witnesses or introducing other evidence. This process is known as **rehabilitation.** Rehabilitation typically occurs during redirect examination following cross examination. For example, assume the defense calls a witness. The defense attorney will question the witness in an effort to absolve the defendant of guilt. If the prosecution sees fit to impeach the defense witness and succeeds in doing so, the defense attorney will work to rehabilitate its witness during the redirect examination stage.

In discussing the importance of rehabilitation, one court observed that "it is well recognized that once a witness's credibility has been attacked, whether it be by the introduction of evidence of bad reputation, conviction of crime, inconsistent statements, evidence of misconduct, or by incisive cross-examination, the party calling the witness has a right to present evidence designed to rehabilitate the witness's credibility" (*State v. Bowden,* 1982).

However, in cases where the side calling the witness anticipates impeachment, the best strategy in most cases is to address those issues during direct examination. This, in turn, allows the jury to hear the damaging evidence from the witness followed by a "reasonable explanation" rather than hearing the information during cross examination. Such a strategy will, in many cases, help diffuse the impact of the information and will convey to the jury that the witness was open about past troubles or other negative information. Examples of issues which may be best addressed on direct examination are expert witness fees, plea bargaining, immunity from prosecution, previous convictions, and bias or connection with other parties in the case.

In cases where the impeachment is not anticipated, three common approaches are used to rehabilitate witnesses. The first is to argue that the witness was untruthful in the past but is telling the truth now. Perhaps the witness was once a deceptive miscreant but has seen the error of his ways and has changed his life to the extent that he can now be trusted. Alternatively, if a witness lies in order to avoid prosecution, it is possible that evidence could be admitted to show that the witness has a reputation for telling the truth (*United States v. Lechoco,* 1976).

Second, the party seeking to rehabilitate its own witness may argue that a contradictory or inconsistent statement alluded to by the other side was taken out of context. For example, if part of a police report is used to impeach the officer who is giving testimony, the party seeking to rehabilitate the officer may introduce other portions of the police report that shed light on the part of the report used to impeach the officer (see *Short v. United States,* 1959).

Another way to rehabilitate a witness is to introduce other evidence to bolster the witness's credibility. For example, if a witness makes a statement prior to trial that contradicts her statement at trial, the other side may elect to introduce additional pretrial statements supportive of her statements at trial. Federal Rule of Evidence 608(a) allows the introduction of opinion or reputation evidence that supports the credibility of the witness after his or her character for truthfulness has been attacked. Thus, following an attack on the character of the witness, evidence of the good character of the witness may be admitted for purposes of rehabilitation. Referring back to the infamous O. J. Simpson case, recall that Mark Fuhrman was impeached by the defense because of his prior racially discriminatory statements. Had the prosecution called other police witnesses to testify as to Fuhrman's objectivity with regard to race (if there were any), their testimony may have rehabilitated Fuhrman as a witness.

Summary

Credibility pertains to whether a witness should be believed. When the prosecution or defense has reason to believe a witness cannot be considered credible, it may seek to impeach the witness. Common grounds for impeachment include bias or prejudice, prior convictions, uncharged crimes and immoral acts, contradictions and inconsistent statements, the inability to observe events, and reputation. Once a witness is impeached on cross examination, the party that called the witness can seek to rehabilitate the witness by introducing additional testimony that seeks to bolster the witness's credibility. It is important to note, though, that a witness's credibility cannot be supported or "rehabilitated" unless it is first challenged.

Discussion Questions

1. What factors may taint the credibility of a witness?
2. After a witness has been impeached, what methods may be used to rehabilitate him or her?
3. Explain FRE 609.
4. What are the most common grounds for impeaching a witness?
5. What subject is not an acceptable ground for impeachment?

Further Reading

Blumenthal, J. A. (1993). "A Wipe of the Hands, A Lick of the Lips: The Validity of Demeanor Evidence in Assessing Witness Credibility." *Nebraska Law Review* 72:1157.

Caine, M. L. (2001). "Using Prior Convictions to Impeach the Credibility of a Defendant-Witness in Massachusetts, Do We Go Too Far?" *Suffolk Journal of Trial and Appellate Advocacy* 6:121.

Fishman, C. S. (1992). *Jones on Evidence, Civil and Criminal* (7th ed.). Eagon, MN: West.

Graham, M. H. (1992). *Federal Practice and Procedure: Evidence* (interim ed.). Eagon, MN: West Group.

Jackson, J. W. (1996). "Commentary: Impeachment of a Witness by Prior Convictions Under Alabama Rule of Evidence 609: Everything Remains the Same, or Does it?" *Alabama Law Review* 48:253.

Lilly, G. C. (1996). *An Introduction to the Law of Evidence* (3rd ed.). Eagon, MN: West.

McCord, D. (1986). "Expert Psychological Testimony About Child Complainants in Sexual Abuse Prosecutions: A Foray Into the Admissibility of Novel Psychological Evidence." *Journal of Criminal Law and Criminology* 77:1–68.

Morris, M. L. (2001)."Comment: Li'l People, Little Justice: The Effect of the Witness Competency Standard in California on Children Sexual Abuse Cases." *Journal of Juvenile Law* 22:113.

Mueller, C. B., and L. C. Kirkpatrick (1999). *Evidence* (2nd ed.). New York: Aspen Publishing Inc.

Strong, J. W. (1992). *McCormick on Evidence* (4th ed.). Eagon, MN: West Group.

Weinstein, J. B., J. H. Mansfield, N. Abrams, and M. A. Berger. *Evidence: Cases and Materials* (9th ed.). Westbury, NY: Foundation Press.

Cases Cited

Banks v. Dretke, 540 U.S. 668 (2004)

Blake v. Cich, 79 F.R.D. 398, 403 (D. Minn. 1978)

Davis v. Alaska, 415 U.S. 308 (1974)

Doyle v. Ohio, 426 U.S. 610 (1976)

Government of Virgin Islands v. Grant, 775 F.2d 508 (3rd Cir. 1985)

Harris v. New York, 401 U.S. 222 (1971)

Hickory v. United States, 151 U.S. 303 (1894)

Jenkins v. Anderson, 447 U.S. 231 (1980)

McKnight v. State, 874 S.W.2d 745 (Tex. 1994)

Miranda v. Arizona, 384 U.S. 436 (1966)

People v. Sorge, 301 N.Y. 198 (1950)

People v. Spearman, 157 Cal. 883 (1979)

People v. Spinosa, 252 P.2d 409 (Cal. Ct. App. 1953)

Pointer v. State, 74 So.2d 615 (Ala. Ct. App. 1954)

Poole v. Commonwealth, 176 S.E.2d 917 (Va.1970)

Roe v. Wade, 410 U.S. 113 (1973)

Short v. United States, 271 F.2d 73 (9th Cir. 1959)

State v. Bowden, 439 A.2d 263 (R.I. 1982)

State v. Spurlock, 874 S.W.2d 602 (Tenn. 1993)

Sullivan v. United States, 28 F.2d 147 (9th Cir. 1928)

United States v. Abel, 469 U.S 45 (1984)

United States v. Awkward, 597 F.2d 667, cert. denied, 444 U.S. 885 (9th Cir. 1979)

United States v. Barrett, 539 F.2d 244 (1st Cir. 1976)

United States v. Hale, 422 U.S. 171 (1975)

United States v. Ince, 21 F.3d 576 (4th Cir. 1994)

United States v. Lechoco, 542 F.2d 84 (D.C. Cir. 1976)

United States v. Miles, 413 F.2d 34 (3rd Cir. 1969)

United States v. Morlang, 531 F.2d 183 (4th Cir. 1975)

United States v. Price, 722 F.2d 88 (5th Cir. 1983)

United States v. Shields, 999 F.2d 1990 (7th Cir. 1993)

CHAPTER 8

EXAMINATION OF WITNESSES

Key Terms & Concepts

Abuse of witness	Opinion evidence	Rule 701
Affidavits	Opinion rule	Rule 702
Collective facts doctrine	Opinion testimony	Rule 704
Compulsory process clause	Overruled objection	Rule of exclusion
Confrontation clause	Past recollection recorded	Rule of preference
Cross examination	Personal knowledge rule	Scope of direct rule
Declarations	Present memory revived	Specific question
Depositions	Recross examination	Subpoena
Direct examination	Redirect examination	Subpoena duces tecum
Expert witness	Rule 412	Substantive objection
Hostile witness	Rule 611	Sustained objection
Lay opinion	Rule 612	Ultimate issue rule
Lay witness	Rule 614	Witness exclusion
Leading question	Rule 615	Witness sequestration

Chapter Learning Objectives

By the end of this chapter, the student should be able to:

- Understand procedures for examining witnesses in criminal proceedings
- Explain mechanisms for securing the attendance of witnesses
- Identify various types of witnesses
- Specify the order and scope of questions
- Distinguish between specific and leading questions
- Identify acceptable methods for refreshing a witness's memory
- List objections commonly raised during the questioning of witnesses
- Explain when it is appropriate to sequester or exclude witnesses

Introduction

Criminal trials inevitably involve the testimony of witnesses. This fact requires that all parties to the proceeding be familiar with the procedures for securing the attendance of witnesses as well as the phases of witness examination. Of particular importance is an understanding of the difference between specific and leading questions. Attorneys, whether they represent the defendant or the government, must also work within the established parameters for refreshing a witness' memory in the event that immediate recall has lapsed. The most common objections raised during the questioning of witnesses are also important to know, as is the need to know when to sequester or exclude them.

In a criminal trial in the United States, the witness (or witnesses) must appear in front of the defendant. This requirement stems from the Sixth Amendment to the Constitution, which states in relevant part that "In all criminal prosecutions, the accused . . . shall be confronted with the witnesses against him." This is known as the **confrontation clause.** There are a few exceptions, but witnesses are generally required to appear in the courtroom.

The confrontation clause imposes important restrictions on the role witnesses play in criminal trials. For example, witness statements in the form of affidavits, declarations, or depositions are often frowned on because they are made out of the presence of the defendant. **Affidavits** and **declarations** are sworn written statements; **depositions** are sworn testimony given prior to trial, usually in an office outside the courtroom in the presence of attorneys. All three are common in civil trials but not in criminal trials because of the Sixth Amendment's confrontation clause.

Witnesses are not afforded much privacy in criminal proceedings because of the confrontation clause. They are almost always required, when called on to testify in court, to do so in the presence of the defendant. Of course, witnesses may be hesitant (and even resistant) to testify in sensitive criminal trials, but the Sixth Amendment usually requires them to be present and "in the open." In a recent case, the U.S. Supreme Court reaffirmed its reluctance to diminish the confrontation clause of the Sixth Amendment.

Securing the Attendance of Witnesses

The Sixth Amendment also contains what is known as the **compulsory process clause.** Stated simply, this clause provides that individuals can be compelled, or forced, to serve as a witness. To ensure that a witness

Crawford v. Washington
Supreme Court of the United States
541 U.S. 36 (2004)

Petitioner Michael Crawford stabbed a man who allegedly tried to rape his wife, Sylvia. At his trial, the State played for the jury Sylvia's tape-recorded statement to the police describing the stabbing, even though he had no opportunity for cross-examination. The Washington Supreme Court upheld petitioner's conviction after determining that Sylvia's statement was reliable. The question presented is whether this procedure complied with the Sixth Amendment's guarantee that, "[i]n all criminal prosecutions, the accused shall enjoy the right . . . to be confronted with the witnesses against him."

*****

Where testimonial statements are involved, we do not think the Framers meant to leave the Sixth Amendment's protection to the vagaries of the rules of evidence, much less to amorphous notions of "reliability." Certainly none of the authorities discussed above acknowledges any general reliability exception to the common-law rule. Admitting statements deemed reliable by a judge is fundamentally at odds with the right of confrontation. To be sure, the Clause's ultimate goal is to ensure reliability of evidence, but it is a procedural rather than a substantive guarantee. It commands, not that evidence be reliable, but that reliability be assessed in a particular manner: by testing in the crucible of cross-examination. The Clause thus reflects a judgment, not only about the desirability of reliable evidence (a point on which there could be little dissent), but about how reliability can best be determined.

*****

[The failings of the rationale announced in *Ohio v. Roberts* failings were on full display in the proceedings below. Sylvia Crawford made her statement while in police custody, herself a potential suspect in the case. Indeed, she had been told that whether she would be released "depend[ed] on how the investigation continues." In response to often leading questions from police detectives, she implicated her husband in Lee's stabbing and at least arguably undermined his self-defense claim. Despite all this, the trial court admitted her statement, listing several

(continued)

reasons why it was reliable. In its opinion reversing, the Court of Appeals listed several other reasons why the statement was not reliable. Finally, the State Supreme Court relied exclusively on the interlocking character of the statement and disregarded every other factor the lower courts had considered. The case is thus a self-contained demonstration of Roberts' unpredictable and inconsistent application.

Each of the courts also made assumptions that cross-examination might well have undermined. The trial court, for example, stated that Sylvia Crawford's statement was reliable because she was an eyewitness with direct knowledge of the events. But Sylvia at one point told the police that she had "shut [her] eyes and . . . didn't really watch" part of the fight, and that she was "in shock." The trial court also buttressed its reliability finding by claiming that Sylvia was "being questioned by law enforcement, and, thus, the [questioner] is . . . neutral to her and not someone who would be inclined to advance her interests and shade her version of the truth unfavorably toward the defendant." The Framers would be astounded to learn that ex parte testimony could be admitted against a criminal defendant because it was elicited by "neutral" government officers. But even if the court's assessment of the officer's motives was accurate, it says nothing about Sylvia's perception of her situation. Only cross-examination could reveal that.

*****

Where nontestimonial hearsay is at issue, it is wholly consistent with the Framers' design to afford the States flexibility in their development of hearsay law as does *Roberts*, and as would an approach that exempted such statements from Confrontation Clause scrutiny altogether. Where testimonial evidence is at issue, however, the Sixth Amendment demands what the common law required: unavailability and a prior opportunity for cross-examination. We leave for another day any effort to spell out a comprehensive definition of "testimonial." Whatever else the term covers, it applies at a minimum to prior testimony at a preliminary hearing, before a grand jury, or at a former trial; and to police interrogations. These are the modern practices with closest kinship to the abuses at which the Confrontation Clause was directed.

*****

In this case, the State admitted Sylvia's testimonial statement against petitioner, despite the fact that he had no opportunity to cross-

(continued)

examine her. That alone is sufficient to make out a violation of the Sixth Amendment. *Roberts* notwithstanding, we decline to mine the record in search of indicia of reliability. Where testimonial statements are at issue, the only indicium of reliability sufficient to satisfy constitutional demands is the one the Constitution actually prescribes: confrontation.

appears at trial, the prosecution or defense will often issue a subpoena. A **subpoena** is an official court document issued by a judge, the clerk of a court, or an attorney. It is delivered to, or "served upon," the witness, who must then appear at trial. A variation on a subpoena is a **subpoena duces tecum**, which requires the witness to bring certain documents or material to the trial. Failure to appear after being subpoenaed can result in a number of serious sanctions.

Many witnesses are asked to testify and do so voluntarily. In such instances, subpoenas are obviously not required. And, if a witness fails to appear after a simple request to testify (as opposed to a subpoena), no sanctions can be imposed. However, the prosecution or defense has the leverage of compulsory process in such a situation. See Figure 8.1 for a sample witness subpoena.

Any witness, other than the accused, has the privilege to refuse to disclose any information that may "tend to incriminate" him or her. The reason is that the witness is not on trial. The witness is only on the stand to provide information about what happened. Thus, witnesses cannot "plead the Fifth" simply because they are nervous about answering questions (perhaps out of fear of retaliation by the defendant or his or her cronies). Only if the answer to a question tends to incriminate the witness may he or she assert Fifth Amendment protection. For example, if the prosecution asks a witness, "Did you, Mr. Smith, sell narcotics with the defendant?" Smith would be within his rights to refuse to answer such a question. Indeed, the question need not be so explicit. For the Fifth Amendment privilege against self-incrimination to apply, the answer need only furnish a link in the chain of evidence needed to prosecute.

Types of Witnesses

It is useful to distinguish among three types of witnesses. The first type is an expert witness. The second type is a lay witness. Expert and lay

SAMPLE SUBPOENA

NAME OF ATTORNEY
1234 EAST 5678 SOUTH
SALT LAKE CITY, UT 84121
PHONE: 456-7890

BEFORE THE DIVISION OF OCCUPATIONAL AND PROFESSIONAL LICENSING
DEPARTMENT OF COMMERCE, STATE OF UTAH

JOHN DOE,	)
	)
Petitioner,	) **SUBPOENA DUCES TECUM**
	)
vs.	)
	)
RICHARD ROE, M.D.	)
	)
Respondent.	) Case No. _____
	)

TO: Richard Roe, M.D.
000 Medical Plaza
Anytown, U.S.A. 84100

RE: John Doe
Date of Birth: 8/28/48

YOU ARE COMMANDED to produce at the offices of (Name), (Address), on or before (Date), a complete copy of your medical records, pertaining to the above-referenced individual who has requested the Division of Occupational and Professional Licensing, to conduct a prelitigation panel review of a claim of medical malpractice. Attendance is not required if records are timely forwarded to the indicated address.

DATED this _____ day of _____, 2004.

DEPARTMENT OF COMMERCE

By: _____
W. Ray Walker, Regulatory & Compliance Officer
Division of Occupational & Professional Licensing

Figure 8.1

witnesses are people other than the defendant. It is also possible, however, for the accused to serve as a witness. As such, we devote a brief section later in the chapter to the role of the defendant as a witness. The accused never has to testify, but once the decision to testify is made, several important issues arise.

Expert Witnesses

Modern statutes do not actually define what it means to be an expert; nevertheless, an **expert witness** can be defined as anyone who knows more about the subject testimony than the average juror would. **Rule 702** of the FRE states that a witness is an "expert" if he or she is "qualified" to help the jury "understand the evidence" or "determine a fact in issue" by virtue of his or her "knowledge, skill, experience, training, or education." Similarly, the California Evidence Code (Section 720), like that of most states, describes an expert as one who "has special knowledge, skill, experience, training or education sufficient to qualify him as an expert on the subject to which his testimony relates."

Rule 702. Testimony by Experts

If scientific, technical, or other specialized knowledge will assist the trier of fact to understand the evidence or to determine a fact in issue, a witness qualified as an expert by knowledge, skill, experience, training, or education, may testify thereto in the form of an opinion or otherwise, if (1) the testimony is based upon sufficient facts or data, (2) the testimony is the product of reliable principles and methods, and (3) the witness has applied the principles and methods reliably to the facts of the case.

http://www.law.cornell.edu/rules/fre/ACRule702.htm

The use of expert witnesses will be more thoroughly addressed in Chapter 10: "Expert Witnesses and Scientific Evidence."

Lay Witnesses

A **lay witness** is an ordinary person who has personal knowledge about the facts of the case at hand. Rule 701 of the FRE defines a lay witness as one who "is not testifying as an expert." Lay witnesses run the gamut from mere observers of criminal activity to police officers. Lay witnesses are called to testify as to the facts only. Lay witness opinions are severely restricted. Accordingly, we devote a later section of this chapter to lay witness opinion.

Most people testify as lay witnesses. These are people who state that the crime occurred, who talked to the suspect before or after the crime, or who observed what happened or supplied information to law enforcement officials. Even a person who regularly testifies as an expert can also testify as a lay witness. If, for example, a ballistics expert observed an assault while driving home, he or she would be allowed to testify as a lay witness, assuming that a ballistic analysis is not required.

Rule 701. Opinion Testimony by Lay Witnesses

If the witness is not testifying as an expert, the witness' testimony in the form of opinions or inferences is limited to those opinions or inferences which are (a) rationally based on the perception of the witness, and (b) helpful to a clear understanding of the witness' testimony or the determination of a fact in issue, and (c) not based on scientific, technical, or other specialized knowledge within the scope of Rule 702.

http://www.law.cornell.edu/rules/fre/ACRule701.htm

Because of the confrontational nature of criminal trials, witnesses are provided with a number of protections. Most important, witnesses in criminal trials enjoy the Fifth Amendment's protection against self-incrimination. That is, even though witnesses provide testimony designed to prove the defendant's guilt (or, if they act on behalf of the defense, to exculpate the defendant), they cannot be compelled to answer questions that incriminate themselves. The Fifth Amendment's protection against self-incrimination is not limitless, however. Witnesses can be compelled to answer questions about the case at hand. Witnesses can "plead the Fifth" only when their statements are self-incriminating, that is, when they implicate themselves in a crime different from that for which the defendant is being tried.

The Accused as a Witness

The Fifth Amendment expressly provides that "no person . . . shall be compelled in any criminal case to be a witness against himself." This guarantee is designed to restrain the government from using force, coercion, or other controversial methods to obtain statements from criminal suspects. However, that the Fifth Amendment's self-incrimination clause applies only to testimonial evidence. As such, real or physical evidence (or things knowingly exposed to the public) does not enjoy constitutional protection. Also, several restrictions exist concerning the procedures law enforcement officials can rely on for the purpose of eliciting confessions.

What about Fifth Amendment protection at trial? The defendant in a criminal case has a privilege of the accused not to take the stand and not to testify. Thus, the Fifth Amendment ensures that an accused is not required to act as a witness against himself or herself. Additionally, prosecutors cannot comment on the accused's refusal to testify. That is, the jury cannot infer guilt from mere silence on the defendant's part.

The Supreme Court has recognized a fair response rule, which allows the prosecutor to comment, during closing arguments, on the defendant's refusal to take the stand. However, such a comment is allowed only if the defense argues that the government did not allow the defendant to explain his or her side of the story (*United States v. Robinson*, 1988).

United States v. Robinson
United States Supreme Court
485 U.S. 25 (1988)

During the course of respondent Robinson's mail fraud trial in the Middle District of Tennessee, his counsel urged in closing argument that the Government had not allowed respondent to explain his side of the story. The prosecutor during his summation informed the jury that respondent "could have taken the stand and explained it to you. . . ." We hold that the comment by the prosecutor did not violate respondent's privilege to be free from compulsory self-incrimination guaranteed by the Fifth Amendment to the United States Constitution.

*****

Respondent did not testify at trial. In his closing argument to the jury, the theme of respondent's counsel was that the Government had breached its "duty to be fair." Several different times, counsel charged that the Government had unfairly denied respondent the opportunity to explain his actions. Counsel concluded by informing the jury that respondent was not required to testify, and that although it would be natural to draw an adverse inference from respondent's failure to take the stand, the jury could not and should not do so.

*****

In *Griffin v. California*, supra, the defendant, who had not testified, was found guilty by a jury of first-degree murder. The prosecution had emphasized to the jury in closing argument that the defendant, who had been with the victim just prior to her demise, was the only person who could provide information as to certain details related to the murder and yet, he had "not seen fit to take the stand and deny or explain." In accordance with the California Constitution, the trial court had instructed the jury that although the defendant had a constitutional right not to testify, the jury could draw an inference unfavorable to the

(continued)

defendant as to facts within his knowledge about which he chose not to testify. This Court reversed the conviction ruling that the prosecutor's comments and the jury instruction impermissibly infringed upon the defendant's Fifth Amendment right to remain silent:

[Comment on the refusal to testify] is a penalty imposed by courts for exercising a constitutional privilege. It cuts down on the privilege by making its assertion costly. It is said, however, that the inference of guilt for failure to testify as to facts peculiarly within the accused's knowledge is in any event natural and irresistible, and that comment on the failure does not magnify that inference into a penalty for asserting a constitutional privilege. What the jury may infer, given no help from the court, is one thing. What it may infer when the court solemnizes the silence of the accused into evidence against him is quite another.

The Court said that the Fifth Amendment "forbids either comment by the prosecution on the accused's silence or instructions by the court that such silence is evidence of guilt."

We think that the Court of Appeals' holding in this case rests both upon too broad a reading of Griffin and upon too restrictive a reading of the closing comments of respondent's counsel. Taking up the second of these points first, we think the reasoning of the opinion of the Court of Appeals necessarily rests on the assumption that the references by defendant's counsel to the Government's failure to provide respondent an opportunity to "explain" were directed only to the period during which the offenses were being investigated, and not the trial itself. Respondent understandably mirrors this position in his brief here. While we agree that defense counsel's remarks could have been interpreted in this manner, we do not think that an appellate court may substitute its reading of ambiguous language for that of the trial court and counsel. The colloquy quoted earlier shows that the trial court, immediately after hearing counsel's comment, understood them to mean that the Government had not allowed respondent to explain his side of the story either before or during trial. While respondent now contends that this interpretation is incorrect, he did not while the matter was being considered by the trial judge offer the explanation which he now supports. If counsel's remarks were, as respondent now argues, so clearly limited to the pre-trial period, we think it unusual, to say the least, that counsel would have stood silently by when the trial court made clear its contrary interpretation. We accept what we

(continued)

regard as a reasonable interpretation of the remarks adopted by the trial court.

We hold that the prosecutor's statement that respondent could have explained to the jury his story did not in the light of the comments by defense counsel infringe upon respondent's Fifth Amendment rights. The Court of Appeals and respondent apparently take the view that any "direct" reference by the prosecutor to the failure of the defendant to testify violates the Fifth Amendment as construed in *Griffin*. We decline to give *Griffin* such a broad reading, because we think such a reading would be quite inconsistent with the Fifth Amendment, which protects against compulsory self-incrimination. The *Griffin* court addressed prosecutorial comment, which baldly stated to the jury that the defendant must have known what the disputed facts were, but that he had refused to take the stand to deny or explain them. We think there is considerable difference for purposes of the privilege against compulsory self-incrimination between the sort of comments involved in *Griffin* and the comments involved in this case.

It is critical to note, however, that once an accused makes the decision to testify, that is, to take the stand, he or she waives Fifth Amendment protection. This means that the accused must answer *all* inquiries (from the prosecution and the defense) about the crime for which he or she is charged. A defendant who decides to testify cannot claim "immunity from cross examination on the matters he has himself put in dispute" because this would make the Fifth Amendment "a positive invitation to mutilate the truth" (*Brown v. United States*, 1958). For this reason, many defense attorneys do not encourage their clients to take the stand. To do so opens up any number of potentially damaging questions. For example, if the accused has a *dubious* past, the prosecution may bring this up.

In summary, even though many evidence texts discuss only two types of witnesses (lay and expert), it is possible for the accused to serve as a witness for or against himself or herself. The decision is solely the defendant's, and the Fifth Amendment guarantees that an accused cannot be compelled to testify.

How Witnesses Are Examined

By custom, the plaintiff in a civil case has the burden of persuasion, so he or she goes first. That is, the plaintiff calls all witnesses and presents the evidence required to build the case. When the plaintiff rests, the defense has its turn. Criminal cases are similarly choreographed; first the prosecutor presents the state's case, then the defendant has an opportunity to present his or her case. The process of examining witnesses, however, is much more complicated than this simple description. The following sections are designed to shed light on this often-confusing aspect of evidentiary procedure. The discussion draws heavily from **Rule 611** of the Federal Rules of Evidence, which describes how testimony is to be presented in federal court.

Order and Scope of Questions

Witness testimony proceeds in a series of stages. Each examination is conducted by a particular party to the case (state/defendant, plaintiff/defendant), and each is subject to limitations in terms of scope. In other words, the stages must occur sequentially, and there are limitations as to what types of questions are permissible.

The four stages of witness examination are (1) direct, (2) cross, (3) redirect, and (4) recross. Thus, every witness called to the stand in either a criminal or civil case may be questioned four separate times. To understand how these stages of witness examination fit into the typical criminal case, see Table 8.1.

Direct and Cross Examination

The first examination of a witness is called **direct examination**. Direct examination is usually conducted by the party calling the witness. The scope of direct examination is broad. In general, questions about any consequential facts that may prove or disprove a certain point are permissible.

The next step in examining witnesses is **cross examination**. Cross examination is conducted by a party other than the party who called the witness. For example, the state may call a witness in a criminal trial.

Table 8.1   Phases of a Case

---

1. Plaintiff or prosecutor presents case, then rests

2. Defendant presents case, then rests

3. Plaintiff or prosecutor presents case in rebuttal

4. Defendant presents case-in-rejoinder, also referred to as case-in-rebuttal

5. Each side may then present further cases-in-rebuttal or rejoinder

---

Once direct examination concludes, the defense will have an opportunity to cross examine the state's witness.

http://www.criminaldefense.homestead.com/Direct.html
http://www.criminaldefense.homestead.com/Cross.html

Whereas the scope of questioning in a direct examination is broad, the scope of questioning on cross is restricted. In particular, cross examination is limited to matters covered on direct examination. Inquiries into the credibility of the witness are also permissible. Together, these two restrictions constitute the **scope of direct rule**. The scope of direct rule helps ensure that the opposing party (the party conducting the cross examination) cannot use cross examination of the witness to direct the jury's attention to issues not raised by the party calling the witness.

Perhaps an example will bring the scope of direct rule into clear focus. Assume that in a robbery trial a defense witness testifies about the defendant's whereabouts on the day of the robbery. Assume further that on cross examination the prosecutor asks whether the defendant expressed the desire to rob a bank on the day before the robbery. This question is not permissible because it is beyond the scope of the defense's direct questioning (assuming, of course, that the defense did not ask its witness about the defendant's feelings the day before the robbery).

Redirect Examination

Redirect examination is conducted by the party calling the witness *after* cross examination. Redirect examination is subsequent to the first cross examination. The scope of questioning on redirect is limited to the scope of questioning on cross examination. Suppose on cross examination a burglary victim is asked about persons who have permission to enter his residence while he is away. Assume further that on redirect the prosecutor asks the burglary victim about an incident that occurred several days prior to the burglary in which he saw the defendant "casing" the neighborhood. This question is not permissible because it is beyond the scope of the cross examination (assuming, again, that the prior incident did not come to light during the defense cross examination).

Recross Examination

The last stage in witness questioning is known as **recross examination**. Recross includes any subsequent examination of a witness by a party who has previously cross examined the witness. Recross examination is also limited in scope to the subject matter of the examination that preceded it. That is, the party engaged in recross examination cannot probe into issues not raised during redirect examination.

Assume that an eyewitness to an accident who is testifying for the plaintiff is asked on cross examination whether she was wearing her prescription glasses. If during redirect examination it is determined that the witness could see fine *without* her glasses, the defense cannot question the witness on recross examination about her relation to the plaintiff.

The four stages of witness examination follow a pattern of "progressive narrowing." That is, subsequent examination should become narrower and narrower such that there is little left to ask the witness. In short, the four stages of examination should clarify rather than confuse. See Table 8.2 for a summary of the order and scope of witness questioning.

The Form of Questioning: Specific and Leading Questions

As a general rule, on direct examination the questions must be specific but not leading. First, a **specific question** is one that does not call for a narrative. If the party calling the witness says, "Tell us what happened on the day of the incident," the opposing side will probably object. Instead, it is proper to ask something along the lines of, "Were you the victim of a burglary on August 6th of this year?"

At the other extreme, it is possible to be too specific, such that a question becomes leading. A **leading question** is, according to the California Evidence Code (Section 764), one "that suggests to the witness the answer that the examining party desires." Leading questions are generally impermissible on direct examination (subject to some exceptions described next) but are permissible on cross examination. Further, leading questions are permissible on redirect examination but not on recross examination.

Identifying a Leading Question

Determining whether a question is leading is not an easy task. Whether a question is leading is, according to some commentators, a matter of degree. For example, a request of a witness to "tell us anything about anything" is not specific and not leading. At the other extreme, a question

---

Table 8.2   Order and Scope of Witness Examination

---

1. Direct examination by party calling the witness

2. Cross examination by adverse party

3. Redirect examination by the calling party

4. Recross by adverse party

---

such as "You drank one beer per hole when you were golfing, didn't you?" is clearly leading. So, what of the gray area in between? Courts have tried to devise tests to determine when questions are leading, but these tests have proven ineffective.

http://www.wendwell.co.uk/Resources/Leading.htm

A safe rule, however, is to consider a question as "leading" when it inherently suggests an answer. For example, the question "Is it true that you locked your door when you left the house?" would be leading because it suggests a particular answer, namely that the door was locked. This question can be rephrased, however, so that it is not leading, "What, if anything, did you do as you left the house?" Another example of a leading question is "You wouldn't say you're in favor of abortion, would you?" This question can also be restated so that it is no longer leading: "What is your position on abortion, for or against?"

Leading Questions During Direct Examination

As we have seen, leading questions are generally not permissible on direct examination. However, there are a few exceptions. As the California Evidence Code attests, leading questions on direct examination are permissible "where the interests of justice" require (C.E.C. Section 767). Similarly, the Federal Rules of Evidence [Rule 611(c)] permit leading questions on direct examination when it is "necessary to develop testimony."

Rule 611. Mode and Order of Interrogation and Presentation

(c) Leading questions.
Leading questions should not be used on the direct examination of a witness except as may be necessary to develop the witness' testimony. Ordinarily leading questions should be permitted on cross-examination. When a party calls a hostile witness, an adverse party, or a witness identified with an adverse party, interrogation may be by leading questions.

http://www.law.cornell.edu/rules/fre/ACRule611.htm

Leading questions are permissible on direct examination under the following circumstances: (1) in questioning on preliminary or undisputed matters for which accuracy of the witness's response is more important than efficiency; (2) when the witness is difficult to control without the use of leading questions (e.g., children, people with mental problems, experts, and so on); (3) for the purpose of refreshing the recollection of a forgetful witness (see below for further discussion of the refreshing process); and (4) when eliciting testimony from hostile witnesses.

The fourth exception requires that we define the term hostile witness. A **hostile witness** need not be (and rarely is) a person who is physically hostile. Instead, witnesses of this type are considered either "hostile in fact" or "hostile in law." A witness is hostile in fact when he or she is resistant or uncooperative and exhibits hostility toward the examiner. For example, a witness who acts as though she does not understand a simple question may be considered hostile in fact. A witness who is hostile in law, by contrast, is one who identifies with an adverse party. For example, the widow of a deceased partner is "identified with" the plaintiff-estate and thus is considered hostile in law to the defense (e.g., surviving children, as in a dispute over the deceased's estate).

Leading Questions on Cross Examination

Cross examination is commonly characterized by leading questions. As the Federal Rules of Evidence put it, "Ordinarily leadings questions should be permitted on cross examination" (Rule 611c). Further, as the FRE attest, the use of leading questions on cross examinations "conforms to tradition in making the use of leading questions on cross examination a matter of right."

Leading questions during cross examination serve a number of important purposes. First, leading questions appeal to the conscience and awaken the witness's memory. The hope is to get the witness to tell the truth. Second, leading questions expose inaccuracies or falsehoods expressed during direct examination. Finally, leading questions help the witness focus attention on what is important.

There are a few circumstances in which leading questions are viewed as improper on cross examination. First, if the questioner goes beyond the scope of direct examination, he or she should not ask leading questions (see, e.g., *MDU Resources Group v. W.R. Grace & Co.*, 1994). Second, when a party in a civil case calls an adverse party as a witness, the usual method of questioning is reversed. Say, for example, that in a civil asset forfeiture case the government calls the defendant's wife, an adverse witness, to the stand to testify concerning her husband's marijuana grow room. In this instance, the direct examination proceeds by leading questions (because the questioner is counsel for the adversary), then cross examination proceeds by nonleading questions. Third, if the calling party is allowed for some reason to lead on direct examination (see the exceptions outlined previously), it is likely that cross examination will be limited to nonleading questions. If a witness is hostile to both parties, leading questions will probably be permitted on both direct and cross examination.

Refreshing a Witness's Memory

Witnesses frequently forget the facts to which they are supposed to testify, particularly if a great deal of time has elapsed between the event witnessed and the witness's in-court testimony. To remedy this problem, **Rule 612** of the FRE provides that a witness's prior experience may be "revived" by referral to the witness's prior statements. Of course, a witness who has no memory whatsoever of the event to which he or she is to testify is an incompetent witness. But if a "refresher" is all the witness needs, the examining party should be able to remind the witness of what he or she said in the past.

Rule 612. Writing Used to Refresh Memory

Except as otherwise provided in criminal proceedings by section 3500 of title 18, United States Code, if a witness uses a writing to refresh memory for the purpose of testifying, either--

(1) while testifying, or

(2) before testifying, if the court in its discretion determines it is necessary in the interests of justice, an adverse party is entitled to have the writing produced at the hearing, to inspect it, to cross-examine the witness thereon, and to introduce in evidence those portions which relate to the testimony of the witness. If it is claimed that the writing contains matters not related to the subject matter of the testimony the court shall examine the writing in camera, excise any portions not so related, and order delivery of the remainder to the party entitled thereto. Any portion withheld over objections shall be preserved and made available to the appellate court in the event of an appeal. If a writing is not produced or delivered pursuant to order under this rule, the court shall make any order justice requires, except that in criminal cases when the prosecution elects not to comply, the order shall be one striking the testimony or, if the court in its discretion determines that the interests of justice so require, declaring a mistrial.

http://www.law.cornell.edu/rules/fre/ACRule612.htm

The process of refreshing a witness's memory involves two important concepts: (1) present memory revived and (2) past recollection recorded. With regard to **present memory revived,** the testimony of the witness is the evidence. By contrast, with **past recollection recorded** writing is the evidence, not the witness's in-court testimony.

Let us first consider present memory revived. Stated simply, a witness's present memory is revived when, for example, the witness is asked to refer to records or other written documents. After the witness views the document and has his or her memory refreshed, the witness's statement to this effect is admitted as evidence. The document shown to the witness is not read or shown to the jury, because the document is not evidence, only the witness's testimony. Assume, for example, that a witness to a car accident is asked whether she remembers the license plate number of the car that sped away from the scene. She replies that she is uncertain but may be able to recall the number if she can consult some notes she had written on the day she witnessed the car leaving the scene. If the witness is permitted to rely on her notes and she then remembers the license plate number, she will be permitted to testify to this effect under a theory of present memory revived.

A somewhat controversial method of refreshing a witness's present memory is hypnosis. In the case of *State v. Beachum* (1967), a court in New Mexico developed a six-prong test for determining whether the results of a hypnosis session can be used to refresh a witness's memory:

1. The session must be conducted by a qualified professional.
2. The professional conducting the session should be independent and not regularly employed by the prosecution or defense.
3. Any information given to the hypnotist before the hypnotic session should be recorded.
4. Before inducing hypnosis, the hypnotist should obtain a detailed description of the facts as the witness remembers them.
5. All contacts between the hypnotist and the person hypnotized should be recorded.
6. Only the hypnotist and the person hypnotized should be present during any stage of the hypnotic session.

http://www.usdoj.gov/usao/eousa/foia_reading_room/usam/title9/ crm00287.htm

http://www.usdoj.gov/usao/eousa/foia_reading_room/usam/title9/crm00288.htm

When a document is introduced to refresh a witness's present memory, it is usually required that the opposing side have an opportunity to view it. Under the Federal Rules of Evidence, in fact, the adverse party is entitled to see and ask questions about the document used to refresh the witness's memory. Does this rule also apply to writing consulted by a witness *in advance* of trial? In such an instance, the document does not necessarily need to be disclosed to the opposing side (see, for example, *United States v. Blas,* 1991; *United States v. Williams,* 1989). There are exceptions, however. In the case of *United States v. Sheffield* (1995), a detective returned a file to the office because he "had trouble keeping up with it on breaks and did not want to carry it with him to the stand" and did not need it to refresh on any point to which he testified. The defense in that case was not allowed to view the file. Generally, it is within the discretion of the court to decide whether documents viewed prior to trial should be disclosed to the other side.

With the "past recollection recorded" approach to refreshing a witness's memory, it is the recording itself that is admitted as evidence. That is, the jury considers the document as opposed to the witness's testimony. The written document essentially becomes a substitute for the witness's memory.

Before a past recollection recorded will be admitted into evidence, it must meet certain requirements. First, the witness must testify that he or she had personal knowledge of the facts at one point in time. Second, the witness must testify that the recording was accurate. Finally, the witness must testify that he or she does not have adequate recollection of the facts such that he or she could testify to them in court. The trial judge must then be satisfied with the document for it to be admissible into evidence. Finally, once a past recollection recorded is admissible into evidence, the opposing side should have the opportunity to view the document (see *United States v. Kelly,* 1965; *People v. Banks,* 1974).

Objections to Questions

Notwithstanding what we have discussed so far, the court has the discretion to control the types of questions posed by both parties to a case. However, the court will exercise its discretion to exclude a question only if an objection is raised. For ease of exposition it is useful to distinguish between two categories of objections: substantive and formal.

Before considering them, it is important to recall that objections are either sustained or overruled. An objection is **sustained** when the judge prohibits the witness from answering the specific question posed. By contrast, an objection is **overruled** when the judge permits the witness to answer the question.

Substantive Objections

Substantive objections are those relying on particular rules of evidence. They are raised for the purpose of excluding evidence when its admission does not conform to established rules. For example, assuming no exceptions apply, a hearsay objection is a substantive one because it is based on a rule of evidence that excludes hearsay in the courtroom.

Most forms of evidence are admissible unless a substantive objection is raised by either party to the case. There are as many substantive objections as there are rules of evidence, so we will not delve further into the varieties of substantive objections, in the interest of keeping this chapter as brief and introductory as possible.

Other Objections

Most objections apart from substantive ones are objections to form. That is, the objecting party believes there is a problem with the way its adversary posed the question to a witness. There are eight fairly common objections of this nature:

1. *Asked and answered.* The question simply asks the witness to repeat testimony previously offered in response to a question. Often the examining party will pose the same question over and over to force the desired response. In such a situation, the opposition will probably have his or her "asked and answered" objection sustained, and the examining party will be ordered to move on.

2. *Assumption of facts not in evidence.* If a witness is questioned concerning some fact not in evidence, a successful objection can be raised. For example, if the examiner asks a witness, "Where was Mr. Smith when he signed the contract?" the question would be objectionable if no evidence has been introduced that Mr. Smith signed the contract.

3. *Argumentative.* Argumentative questions are those designed to win over the jury rather than elicit critical information. Questions such as, "You expect the jury to believe that cockamamie story?" are clearly argumentative. Sarcastic, patronizing questions and attorney "grandstanding" commonly lead to objections on argumentative grounds.

4. *Compound.* Compound questions consist of more than one question followed by a single question mark. "Did you leave your house and were you drunk?" is a compound question. Another example is, "Did you read the instructions and use the hairdryer properly?" If the witness responds "Yes" to such a question, the answer may obscure the truth. This is especially true if both "yes" and "no" answers would have been offered if the compound questions had been separated.

5. *Misleading.* Questions based on mistakes of evidence or misinterpretation are considered misleading. For example, if a witness testifies on direct examination that while driving he had rolled through a stop sign, a misleading question on cross examination would be, "Why did you speed through the stop sign without stopping?" The examining party would likely have an objection to this question sustained.

6. *Speculation and conjecture.* Witnesses, especially lay witnesses, are supposed to answer questions with what they know, not with a guess or expectation. For example, questions that ask witnesses what they

"would have done" if the opportunity to share an experience had presented itself would be objectionable.

7. *Uncertain, ambiguous, and unintelligible.* Questions that have either many meanings or none at all fall within the scope of this type of objection. Such a question might be, "After you stopped the suspects, you searched some suspects and not others, and arrested some and not others, and your decisions were based on the suspects' race, were they not?" Clearly, this is an awkward and nearly unintelligible question that should be rephrased.

8. *Nonresponsive to the question.* If, when asked a yes/no question, the witness responds evasively or vaguely, an objection can be raised. Assume that when asked whether he was under the influence of alcohol while driving, the witness responds, "Maybe, but I wasn't drunk, and your client is at fault for the accident." Opposing counsel will raise an objection to the effect that the witness was nonresponsive. Further, opposing counsel will ask that the witness's response be stricken from the record.

Countless other objections exist. One important category left untouched in this section concerns questions that call for opinions. Because opinion testimony is a fairly complex topic, we revisit it toward the end of this chapter. We now turn our attention to methods for protecting witnesses from abuse and humiliation.

Preventing Abuse of Witnesses During Examination

As noted in *Alford v. United States* (1931, 694), courts have a duty "to protect [witnesses] from questions which go beyond the bounds of proper cross examination merely to harass, annoy, or humiliate." It is not *essential* but still desirable to ensure that witnesses not be unduly harassed or embarrassed. This is because witnesses are not on trial; there is little need to "beat them down," only to elicit factual responses. Of course, it is useful on occasion to discredit a witness, but impeachment can occur in a tactful manner.

One way that witnesses are protected during examination is to place restrictions on evidence of prior acts (such as criminal acts) engaged in by the witness. As a general rule, when prior acts have no bearing on the witness's truthfulness, they should not be exposed through the witness's testimony. In fact, rape shield laws (and FRE Rule 412) completely prohibit opposing counsel from delving into a victim's sexual history.

Rule 412. Sex Offense Cases; Relevance of Alleged Victim's Past Sexual Behavior or Alleged Sexual Predisposition

(a) Evidence generally inadmissible.

    The following evidence is not admissible in any civil or criminal proceeding involving alleged sexual misconduct except as provided in subdivisions (b) and (c):

    (1) Evidence offered to prove that any alleged victim engaged in other sexual behavior.

    (2) Evidence offered to prove any alleged victim's sexual predisposition.

(b) Exceptions.

    (1) In a criminal case, the following evidence is admissible, if otherwise admissible under these rules:

        (A) evidence of specific instances of sexual behavior by the alleged victim offered to prove that a person other than the accused was the source of semen, injury, or other physical evidence;

        (B) evidence of specific instances of sexual behavior by the alleged victim with respect to the person accused of the sexual misconduct offered by the accused to prove consent or by the prosecution; and

        (C) evidence the exclusion of which would violate the constitutional rights of the defendant.

    (2) In a civil case, evidence offered to prove the sexual behavior or sexual predisposition of any alleged victim is admissible if it is otherwise admissible under these rules and its probative value substantially outweighs the danger of harm to any victim and of unfair prejudice to any party. Evidence of an alleged victim's reputation is admissible only if it has been placed in controversy by the alleged victim.

(c) Procedure to determine admissibility.

    (1) A party intending to offer evidence under subdivision (b) must

        (A) file a written motion at least 14 days before trial specifically describing the evidence and stating the purpose for which it is offered unless the court, for good cause requires a different time for filing or permits filing during trial; and

        (B) serve the motion on all parties and notify the alleged victim or, when appropriate, the alleged victim's guardian or representative.

    (2) Before admitting evidence under this rule the court must conduct a hearing in camera and afford the victim and parties a right to attend and be heard. The motion, related papers, and the record of the hearing must be sealed and remain under seal unless the court orders otherwise.

http://www.law.cornell.edu/rules/fre/ACRule412.htm

If the cross examining party appears to bully the witness, the court may step in and order that such questioning be halted. If, for example, the cross examiner leans close to the witness and speaks in a condescending and sarcastic manner, the judge may interrupt the questioning in the interest of preserving the witness's dignity. If the humiliation is such that the witness "caves" and answers the question falsely just to get off the stand, the court will almost certainly intervene. Of course, there is a fine line between unnecessary humiliation and "uncomfortable" testimony. In questioning a hostile witness, the examining party may have to resort to intimidation in order to elicit a truthful response from the uncooperative witness. Questions that expose falsehood, deception, uncertainty, or bias are perfectly acceptable, as long as they are not "over the top."

Finally, witnesses are protected by the courtsometimeswhen the answers to questions bear on especially sensitive topics. Questions about sexual abuse, mental disorders, and so on require special care. A good cross examiner knows that to badger and harass a witness about something sensitive may not curry favor with the jury. Consider an extreme example: Assume a witness reported on direct examination that he stopped a car with the license plate "GETAWAY" fleeing the scene of a crime. If the cross examiner asks, "You couldn't possibly have noted the correct license plate number because you are so totally and hopelessly dyslexic, right?" the jury may be less than impressed.

Calling and Questioning by the Court

Rule 614 of FRE provides that "The court may, on its own motion or at the suggestion of a party, call witnesses. . . ." Further, "The court may interrogate witnesses, whether called by itself or by a party." Judges frequently question witnesses, although they rarely call witnesses. Nevertheless, both occur.

Rule 614. Calling and Interrogation of Witnesses by Court

(a) Calling by court.
   The court may, on its own motion or at the suggestion of a party, call witnesses, and all parties are entitled to cross-examine witnesses thus called.
(b) Interrogation by court.
   The court may interrogate witnesses, whether called by itself or by a party.
(c) Objections.
   Objections to the calling of witnesses by the court or to interrogation by it may be made at the time or at the next available opportunity when the jury is not present.

http://www.law.cornell.edu/rules/fre/ACRule614.htm

Questioning of witnesses by the court is a common practice because it helps with the clarification of testimony. One illustrative case is *Logue v. Dore* (1997, 1045–1047), in which it was noted that a lower court's decision to question a witness was "little more than the judge's [effort] to clarify testimony, expedite the trial, and maintain courtroom decorum." Judge-initiated questioning is not constrained in the same fashion that the typical witness examination process is, that is, judges are not confined by the fact that their questions were not put by counsel. They have freedom to pursue matters already discussed as well as explore new ones. In questioning a witness, the court will usually notify the jury that the question is for clarification and not designed to belittle or weaken either party's case. It is critical that a judge maintain the image of neutrality and impartiality during questioning; otherwise, his or her role may become compromised in the eyes of the jury, and the judge may be seen as arguing in favor of one side's case to the detriment of the other's.

Judges may also call their own witness, wholly on their own initiative. There are several reasons for doing so. First, if one party to the case is hesitant to call a witness and fails to do so (perhaps because of fears that the witness will be loathed by the jury) but the witness has important information to contribute, the judge may call the witness anyway. Second, the judge may be more concerned with the "truth" than with facts that either party chooses to present. As such, he or she may call a witness not called by either counsel in the interest of ensuring that the truth comes out at trial.

Witness Sequestration and Exclusion

Rule 615 of the Federal Rules of Evidence states, "At the request of a party the court shall order witnesses excluded so that they cannot hear the testimony of other witnesses, and may make the order of its own motion." This situation is known as **witness exclusion.** Witnesses are excluded so they cannot hear other witnesses, not so the accused is denied the constitutional right to witness confrontation. The purpose for excluding witnesses from the courtroom is to encourage honest testimony, uninfluenced by others. Because humans can be susceptible creatures, witnesses are occasionally influenced, even on a subconscious level, by the testimony of others.

Rule 615. Exclusion of Witnesses

At the request of a party the court shall order witnesses excluded so that they cannot hear the testimony of other witnesses, and it may make the order of its own motion. This rule does not authorize exclusion of (1) a party who is a natural person, or (2) an officer or employee of a party which is not a natural person designated as its representative by its attorney, or (3) a person whose presence is shown by a party to be essential to the presentation of the party's cause, or (4) a person authorized by statute to be present.

http://www.law.cornell.edu/rules/fre/ACRule615.htm

Witness sequestration is the process of separating witnesses while they are outside the courtroom. Sequestration is sometimes done to discourage witnesses from speaking to each another and unduly influencing each another's testimony. Often, witnesses will be excluded and sequestered as opposed to sequestered or separated. The reason should be clear; just because a witness is excluded from the courtroom out of fears that he or she will influence other witnesses does not ensure that the witness will not be in contact with other witnesses outside the courtroom. When witnesses are excluded or sequestered, the court will usually order them not to talk with other witnesses.

http://www.manatt.com/newsevents.aspx?id=252&folder=24

What happens when a witness is excluded but in contact with counsel? Further, what if counsel conveys to the witness the substance of another witness's testimony? The answer to the first question is that this action is perfectly valid. The answer to the second question, however, is that Rule 615 will be violated. Counsel should not defeat an order of exclusion (or sequestration) by conveying to a witness the testimony of others. This includes reading court transcripts to a witness (see, for example, *United States v. Friedman,* 1988).

What happens when a witness violates an order of exclusion? Several remedies are available. First, the witness could be held in contempt. Another remedy is to let counsel question the witness about the violation and make arguments during the trial about the witness's out-of-court behavior. Finally, courts can exclude the testimony of witnesses who are in violation of exclusion/sequestration orders (see *Holder v. United States,* 1893). This last remedy is rarely invoked, because it punishes one of the parties to the case, not so much the witness who violates the exclusion order.

It should be pointed out that certain witnesses are exempt from orders of exclusion and sequestration. Under the first exemption, specified in Rule 615, the court should not exclude "a party who is a natural person" and a party to the case. Doing so raises questions about confrontation and effective assistance of counsel.

Second, the court cannot exclude "an officer or employee" of either party who is designated as its representative by its attorney. Government agents, law enforcement officers, officers and employees of corporations, partnerships, and other associations all fall within this exemption.

Third, exemption is open ended: The court cannot exclude a person whose presence is shown "to be essential to the presentation." Experts frequently fall within this exemption; it makes little sense to exclude two experts for fear that they are collaborating outside the courtroom. This does not mean that such witnesses are always exempt, only that in most situations orders of exclusion and sequestration are issued for them (for an exception see *Opus 3 Ltd. v. Heritage Park, Inc.,* 1996).

Finally, exemption four includes any person "authorized by statute to be present." Victims of crimes occasionally fall within this fourth exemption. In the past, there were few statutes that formally authorized victim attendance at a criminal trial; victims were permitted regardless. One recently passed federal statute, however, provides that a crime victim has the right "to be present at all public court proceedings related to the offense, unless the court determines that testimony by the victim would be materially affected if the victim heard other testimony at trial" [42 U.S.C. Section 10606(b)]. A similar statute states that in noncapital cases, federal courts "shall not order any victim of an offense excluded from the trial" because such victim may later "make a statement or present any information" during sentencing; in capital cases, federal courts shall not exclude victims because they may testify during sentencing on "the effect of the offense" on the victim and her family or on "any other factor for which notice is required" (18 U.S.C. Section 3510).

Opinion Testimony

When a witness takes the stand and testifies, his or her testimony is usually limited to the facts within his or her personal knowledge. For example, a witness may testify that she observed the defendant fleeing the scene of the crime. Here, the witness is communicating to the jury what she observed, not what she believes. However, there are occasions in which witnesses can testify as to what they believe, in essence by offering an opinion. If no better evidence can be obtained, a witness's opinion may aid the jury in reaching its decision. In other words, opinion evidence is not *desirable*, but it may have to suffice from time to time in order to avoid a miscarriage of justice.

Opinion evidence, as defined in *Black's Law Dictionary*, is "evidence of what the witness thinks, believes, or infers in regard to facts in dispute, as distinguished from his personal knowledge of the facts themselves."

The term *opinion evidence* refers to opinions offered by in-court witnesses and is to be distinguished from opinions offered by people outside of a courtroom setting.

The rules regarding opinion evidence differ depending on the type of witness giving the opinion. Generally, lay witnesses are not allowed to offer opinions, except in rare circumstances. Expert witnesses, on the other hand, frequently testify as to their opinions. We will focus on lay and expert opinions, but first we consider the so-called "opinion rule." It guides the discussion throughout the remainder of this chapter.

The Opinion Rule

At common law, opinion evidence was governed by a **rule of exclusion**. Opinions were excluded because they usurped the role of the jury to draw its own inferences from the facts. The modern approach to opinions is a **rule of preference**. A rule of preference differs from a rule of exclusion because it focuses on priorities, not absolute rules (the "best evidence" rule is another rule of preference). In a way, the **opinion rule** is not really a rule at all. Instead, what is presented to the jury should be the most concrete form of evidence possible. If "facts" are not available, opinion evidence can suffice. Rule 701 of the Federal Rules of Evidence permits opinion evidence, particularly lay opinion, if it is helpful to the trier of fact.

Facts and Opinions

There is often a fine line between opinion and fact. The distinction is usually a matter of degree. For example, if a person testifies that he smelled burning marijuana, is he offering an opinion or factual testimony? On the one hand, the smell of burning marijuana is distinct and unmistakable. On the other hand, since marijuana is an illegal substance, not everyone has had occasion to smell it. What if, furthermore, the witness testifies, "I think I smelled burning marijuana" is this an opinion? The short answer is no, but one can clearly see the fine line to be drawn. In the end, it is up to the court to decide when opinions will be admissible.

Consider another example: A witness testifies that she saw a blue car speed away from the scene of the crime. This seems like factual testimony, but opposing counsel may argue that what one person calls blue another may call blue-green, or greenish-blue, or even green. Clearly the testimony in this example is more likely than not to be considered factual, but it is impossible to say that no opinion is associated with the identification of colors. However, because the distinction between fact and opinion is a matter of degree, the testimony in this example would almost certainly be admissible.

Personal Knowledge and Opinion

The so-called **personal knowledge** rule is at the heart of the opinion rule. Witnesses should, in general, state facts based on personal knowledge rather than on inferences or conclusions drawn from such facts. For example, the witness to a robbery can testify that the robber brandished a handgun. Such testimony is based on personal knowledge. The witness probably cannot testify as to the caliber of the gun, because it is difficult (unless one is very familiar with guns) to know the caliber of a handgun without careful examination.

Lay Witness Opinions

Lay opinion is evidence given by a witness who has not been presented as and is not qualified to be an expert. In the past (and even today), witnesses were not supposed to give their opinions or draw conclusions about the facts (e.g., that the defendant is guilty). Under modern statutes, however, witnesses are allowed to offer opinions if the opinion is helpful to the trier of fact.

As indicated earlier, police officers often serve as lay witnesses. Thus, if Officer X testifies that the substance she found on the defendant felt and looked like cocaine, she will most likely be permitted to testify that the substance was cocaine. She begins by presenting facts, then draws a conclusion from those facts. Of course, the opposing side may question the officer as to her conclusions. And because of this likelihood, the prosecution will probably have the substance tested in a laboratory to determine that it is in fact cocaine.

The Collective Facts Doctrine

Some common law courts allowed witnesses to draw conclusions when they are difficult to separate from the facts. This **collective facts doctrine** allowed witnesses to offer an opinion when recitation of factual perceptions would not convey to the jury what the witness heard or observed. For example, a witness testifying that he heard a woman sing "The Itsy, Bitsy Spider" would be basing his testimony on collective facts. The witness would not be required to recite every word in the song.

In a similar vein, a witness could have testified that the defendant was drunk. If the witness were required to testify that she observed a person whose speech was slurred, who had bloodshot eyes, and who staggered around, the jury may not have understood that the person was drunk (maybe the person had a speech disorder and happened to have just gotten out of bed). The collective facts doctrine survives to this day but is not necessarily referred to as such.

The Basis for Lay Opinions

Notwithstanding the collective facts doctrine, the opinions of lay witnesses must be based on facts of which they have personal knowledge. This means that lay opinions based on hearsay are impermissible. Furthermore, some courts have required that opinion based on personal knowledge be "rationally" based, but this requirement is not embodied in evidence law.

Subjects of Lay Opinion

Lay opinion, when permissible, can consist of several subjects. For example, lay witnesses have been permitted to testify concerning a person's age. "The opinion of a lay witness concerning the age of an accused is admissible into evidence when the witness has had adequate opportunity to observe the accused" (*State v. Cobb*, 1978). Lay witnesses can also testify to people's appearance. In one illustrative case, the court accepted a lay person's opinion that the teller who handed the money over to a bank robber was "distraught and upset" (*Cole v. United States*, 1964). A third subject of lay opinion involves conduct. That is, lay witnesses can sometimes offer opinion about the nature of people's conduct. For example, testimony that the defendant was "trying to get away" has been allowed (*Lewis v. State*, 1871).

Lay opinion as to distance and space is permissible as well. However, if the jury can draw an inference as to distance, the lay opinion will not be required (again, because lay opinion is preferred only where needed; see *Alabama Power Co. v. Brown*, 1921). Lay opinion concerning time and duration is also permissible, subject to the same restrictions. Similarly, lay witnesses can offer opinion as to speed. Testimony, for example, that the car was traveling at an excessive speed will probably be allowed, whereas testimony that the car was traveling at 45 miles per hour will not.

In some situations, lay witnesses can even offer opinions about handwriting. In particular, if the handwriting in question belongs to an acquaintance of the witness, conclusions regarding the author of the handwriting may be allowed. In one Seventh Circuit Court of Appeals case, lay testimony concerning the identity of the defendant's testimony was admissible because the witness had become familiar with the defendant's handwriting on several previous occasions (*United States v. Tipton*, 1992).

Finally, lay witnesses have been permitted to offer opinions about sanity and mental condition. In most situations, lay witnesses cannot opine about such topics, but when a witness clearly demonstrates an acquaintance with the person whose mental condition is in question, such opinion may be permitted. Some courts also require that the witness's conclusion be based on specific instances of behavior or conduct. Indeed, one court required that *three* factors be considered in determining whether lay opinion about mental disorders and sanity will be admissible: (1) the witness's acquaintance with the person, if any; (2) the time during which the observation occurred; and (3) the nature of the behavior observed (*State v. Walls*, 1994).

The Ultimate Issue Rule

Our discussion of opinion evidence would not be complete without some attention to the common law **ultimate issue rule**. Though it is largely abandoned nowadays, the ultimate issue rule prohibited experts from expressing opinions on final issues of which the judge or jury was charged with deciding. Rule 704(a) is testament to the disliked ultimate issue rule, "testimony in the form of an opinion or inference otherwise admissible is not objectionable because it embraces an ultimate issue to be decided by the trier of fact."

Rule 704. Opinion on Ultimate Issue

(a) Except as provided in subdivision (b), testimony in the form of an opinion or inference otherwise admissible is not objectionable because it embraces an ultimate issue to be decided by the trier of fact.

(b) No expert witness testifying with respect to the mental state or condition of a defendant in a criminal case may state an opinion or inference as to whether the defendant did or did not have the mental state or condition constituting an element of the crime charged or of a defense thereto. Such ultimate issues are matters for the trier of fact alone.

http://www.law.cornell.edu/rules/fre/ACRule704.htm

The logic behind Rule 704(a) is simple: Witnesses should not be able to testify that "the defendant is guilty" or that the "defendant should lose," but to exclude all opinions as to ultimate issues seemed unfair to the authors of the Federal Rules of Evidence. It is helpful, for instance, to occasionally allow witnesses to testify to such issues as "the defendant was drunk" or "the car was traveling too fast." A blanket rule prohibiting all conclusions as to ultimate issues seemed a bit excessive. Rule 704(b), however, does prohibit expert witnesses from drawing conclusions on ultimate issues, but only with regard to mental conditions. This rule is discussed more thoroughly in Chapter 10.

Summary

There are two types of witnesses: expert and lay. Experts are relied on when (1) there is need, (2) there is a sufficient scientific basis for their testimony, and (3) they are sufficiently educated or qualified to offer testimony. Experts can also be appointed by the court if the need arises. Lay witnesses are nonexperts, individuals who have personal knowledge concerning the facts at issue. In a criminal trial there can be a third type of witness: If the accused chooses to do so, he or she can testify.

Witnesses in criminal trials enjoy a number of important protections. Lay and expert witnesses enjoy privilege against self-incrimination. That is, they are under no obligation to answer questions that implicate themselves in criminal activity. The accused also enjoys protection. In fact, the accused is not required to testify. However, once he or she decides to take the stand, questions posed by the prosecution must be answered.

Witness questioning is a carefully choreographed event. First, questions proceed through four stages: (1) direct, (2) cross, (3) redirect, and (4) recross. The scope of questions that can be asked at each stage varies. Next, the form of questions is restricted. In general, leading questions are impermissible on direct examination but are acceptable on cross. There are exceptions, however. Finally, a number of objections can be raised to questions posed. Substantive objections are based on the rules of evidence. Other objections often relate to the form of the questioning and include "argumentative," "misleading," and the like.

A controversial issue surrounding witness testimony concerns the role of opinions. Expert witnesses are given the greatest latitude in offering opinion. Lay witnesses, by contrast, are not permitted to offer opinions unless necessary. If, for example, no factual testimony is possible, or if additional facts are not available, lay witnesses will be permitted to offer their opinions.

Discussion Questions

1. Name the different types of witnesses.
2. When are expert witnesses used in trials? Why?
3. What protection does the Fifth Amendment give to witnesses?
4. In what circumstance during trial will the defendant be required to answer the questions put to him or her by the prosecution?
5. When are leading questions allowed?
6. Explain the concepts of "present memory revived" and "past recollection recorded."
7. Give three substantive objections and explain each one.
8. What is abuse of a witness, and how is it prevented?
9. When and by whom is opinion evidence admissible?
10. Name the four stages of questioning and explain each.

Further Reading

Fishman, C. S. (1992). *Jones on Evidence, Civil and Criminal* (7th ed.). Eagan, MN: Lawyers Coop.

Graham, M. H. (1992). *Federal Practice and Procedure: Evidence* (interim ed.). Eagan, MN: West Group.

Lilly, G. C. (1996). *An Introduction to the Law of Evidence* (3rd ed.). Eagan, MN: West Group.

Mueller, C. B. and L. C. Kirkpatrick. (1999). *Evidence* (2nd ed.). New York: Aspen.

Strong, J. W. (1992). *McCormick on Evidence* (4th ed.). Eagan, MN: West Group.

Weinstein, J. B., J. H., Mansfield, N. Abrams, and M. A, Berger. (1997). *Evidence: Cases and Materials* (9th ed.). Westbury, NY: Foundation Press.

Cases Cited

Alabama Power Co. v. Brown, 250 Ala. 167 (1921)

Alford v. United States, 282 U.S. 687 (1931)

Brown v. United States, 356 U.S. 148 (1958)

Cole v. United States, 327 F.2d 360 (9th Cir. 1964)

Crawford v. Washington, U.S. 541 36 (2004)

Holder v. United States, 150 U.S. 91 (1893)

Lewis v. State, 49 Ala. 1 (1871)

Logue v. Dore, 103 F.3d 1040 (1st. Cir. 1997)

MDU Resources Group v. W.R. Grace & Co., 14 F.3d 1274, 1282 (8th Cir. 1994)

Opus 3 Ltd. v. Heritage Park, Inc., 91 F.3d 625 (4th Cir. 1996)

People v. Banks, 50 Mich. App. 622 (1974)

State v. Beachum, N.M. Lexis 2746 (1967)

State v. Cobb, 295 N.C. 1 (1978)

State v. Walls, 445 S.E.2d 515 (W.Va. 1994)

United States v. Blas, 947 F.2d 1320 (7th Cir. 1991)

United States v. Friedman, 854 F.2d 535 (2nd Cir. 1988)

United States v. Kelly, 349 F.2d 720 (2nd Cir. 1965)

United States v. Robinson, 485 U.S. 25 (1988)

United States v. Sheffield, 55 F.3d 341 (8th Cir. 1995)

United States v. Tipton, 964 F.2d 650 (7th Cir. 1992)

United States v. Williams, 875 F.2d 846, 854 (11th Cir. 1989)

SECTION THREE

Introducing Criminal Evidence in Court

CHAPTER 9
FORMS OF EVIDENCE

Key Terms & Concepts

Admissions doctrine

Attestation

Authentication test

Best evidence rule

Collateral writings

Competent evidence

Conditional relevance

Demonstrative evidence

Documentary evidence

Documentary originals rule

Duplicate

Execution

Eyewitness testimony

Incidental matters

Inscribed chattels

Legally operative conduct

Material evidence

Official writings

Original

Real/physical evidence

Recorded transactions

Relevant evidence

Rule 401

Rule 901

Rule 902

Rule 1001

Rule 1002

Rule 1003

Rule 1004

Rule 1007

Scientific evidence

Secondary evidence

Self-authenticating
documents

Voluminous writings

Writing

Chapter Learning Objectives

By the end of this chapter, the student should be able to:

- Distinguish between testimonial, documentary and real/physical forms of evidence
- Explain the concept of relevance as defined by the Federal Rules of Evidence
- Distinguish between the "authentication" and "best evidence" admissibility tests, explaining how each rule operates in practice
- Identify the types of situations where authentication is necessary
- Identify various methods for authenticating evidence under Rule 901
- Explain the procedures used to authenticate documents, objects, voices, etc.
- Understand the concept and forms of self-authenticating evidence
- Distinguish between the best evidence rule and hearsay
- Identify alternate procedures for submitting evidence when an original cannot be obtained

- Explain the relationship between real evidence and the Fifth Amendment
- Relate the requirements for establishing admissibility
- Identify various types of real/physical evidence

Introduction

There are three broad types of evidence: (1) testimonial evidence, (2) documentary evidence, and (3) real/physical evidence. We have already focused in detail on testimonial evidence; this chapter considers the other two forms of evidence. **Documentary evidence** consists of documents and writings. **Real/physical evidence** (the terms will be used synonymously from here on out) consists of actual tangible items that can be displayed. Think of it this way: Anything that is not testimonial or documentary is probably real/physical.

Indeed, there are several types of physical evidence. We focus on three in this chapter. First, we discuss on the usual types of physical evidence, including displays of items used in crimes, photographs, sound recordings, and so on. Next, we discuss **demonstrative evidence**. The term "demonstrative" refers to a demonstration, typically using physical evidence (such as a crime scene reconstruction) to demonstrate a point. The third type of real evidence consists of that resulting from scientific experiments and procedures. These include DNA analysis, mental diagnoses, and the like.

Before we delve into the rules concerning demonstrative and real evidence we focus on two important admissibility tests: the authentication test and the best evidence test. For documentary or real evidence to be admissible, it must be authenticated and it must be the best possible evidence (the original, for instance, in the case of documentary evidence).

We do not devote a special section to documentary evidence. Instead our discussion of documentary evidence is woven into the authentication and best evidence rule sections. The reason for doing so is that authentication and the best evidence rule most frequently apply in the documentary context. However, as we will see, real/physical evidence often needs to be authenticated and can be bound by the best evidence rule.

Authentication

Authentication means "the introduction of evidence sufficient to sustain a finding that [an object or document] is the [object or document] that the proponent of the evidence claims it is" (FRE Rule 901[a]). In other words, only authentic evidence, as opposed to a fake or fabricated, is admissible.

Rule 901. Requirement of Authentication or Identification

(a) General provision.

The requirement of authentication or identification as a condition precedent to admissibility is satisfied by evidence sufficient to support a finding that the matter in question is what its proponent claims.

http://www.law.cornell.edu/rules/fre/ACRule901.htm

At common law the authentication requirement was limited strictly to writings. To this day many evidence texts discuss authentication only as it applies to documentary evidence. Modern evidence statutes, however, have expanded the authentication requirement to include not only all writings but also all evidence related to proving some point. Rule 901(a) attests that authentication is a prerequisite to admissibility to ensure that the "matter in question is what the proponent claims." Similarly, California's Evidence Code defines "writing" to include such things as photographs, computerized records, and similar items.

There are several keys to understanding the authentication process. First, it is important to understand that authentication is required only when the proponent (the person seeking to introduce evidence) wants to prove a point. For example, if a witness testifies that "I called Bob's Automotive and Bob told me that the price to repair my transmission was $1,400," the proponent will be required to prove that Bob spoke to the witness. In other words, the proponent will be required to authenticate the phone call to prove that Bob in fact answered the phone. If, however, the witness testifies that the "person on the other end of the phone line told me . . .," authentication is not required. Thus, it may behoove the proponent to minimize what needs authentication, as doing so could prove difficult.

The second key to understanding authentication is to realize that it is not required when it serves little purpose. For example, if the proponent seeks to introduce a photograph into evidence, the photographer who took the picture is not needed to authenticate the picture. Similarly, representations such as maps do not require authentication; it makes little sense to call the mapmaker to authenticate the map. However, if something in the photograph or map (or similar item) is in dispute, authentication may be required. If it is argued, for instance, that a photograph is a fabrication, authentication may be required. On that note, the process of authentication sometimes includes *non*authentication. If the proponent (or opponent) seeks to prove that "the photograph is a fake," proof of its "inauthenticity" will be required.

Yet another key to understanding authentication is to see it is analogous to conditional relevancy. Items have **conditional relevance** when they give the jury the responsibility of determining whether a fact has been proven. In other words, authentication is a preliminary fact that is determined by the jury, not the judge. This means that the proponent does not need to satisfy the court that the document (or item) is authentic. Instead, the proponent need only introduce sufficient evidence that a "reasonable juror" could find that the matter is authentic.

The fact that authentication is needed only to appease the jury is sometimes controversial and confusing, because it is possible for both parties to a case to authenticate two (perhaps conflicting) items as the true ones. In a contract case, for example, one proponent could seek to authenticate a contract specifying that Ace's Air Conditioning would do the work for free, while the other proponent could seek to authenticate a similar contract specifying that Ace's Air Conditioning would do the work for $200. In such a situation it would be up to the jury to decide which contract was authentic.

Finally, the best way to understand the authentication process is to compare it to the process for establishing relevance. In general, authentication is a higher hurdle to clear than that of relevancy. FRE **Rule 401** provides that evidence is relevant if it has a "tendency" to prove a fact in issue. For example, a letter with what seems to be university letterhead and a professor's signature has a "tendency" to prove that the letter was written by a professor. Authentication, however, will require something more, namely that the letter was written by a professor. It is entirely possible that someone else (perhaps a student) acquired some university letterhead and forged a professor's signature at the end of the letter.

The Federal Rules of Evidence address relevancy in Rules 401403. Rule 401 provides the definition of **relevant evidence**. Rule 402 (and the comment to the Rule) suggests that relevant evidence is generally admissible unless the evidence is privileged, is hearsay, or violates the Constitution. Finally, Rule 403 lists several situations where, despite relevancy, certain evidence may be excluded in the discretion of the court: situations (1) where the prejudicial value of the evidence outweighs its probative value; (2) where admission of the evidence would confuse the issues or mislead the jury; (3) where admission of the evidence would produce undue delay or would be a waste of time, or (4) where the evidence is cumulative.

Rule 401. Definition of "Relevant Evidence"

"Relevant evidence" means evidence having any tendency to make the existence of any fact that is of consequence to the determination of the action more probable or less probable than it would be without the evidence.

http://www.law.cornell.edu/rules/fre/ACRule401.htm

Rule 402. Relevant Evidence Generally Admissible; Irrelevant Evidence Inadmissible

All relevant evidence is admissible, except as otherwise provided by the Constitution of the United States, by Act of Congress, by these rules, or by other rules prescribed by the Supreme Court pursuant to statutory authority. Evidence which is not relevant is not admissible.

Rule 403. Exclusion of Relevant Evidence on Grounds of Prejudice, Confusion, or Waste of Time

Although relevant, evidence may be excluded if its probative value is substantially outweighed by the danger of unfair prejudice, confusion of the issues, or misleading the jury, or by considerations of undue delay, waste of time, or needless presentation of cumulative evidence.

How, then, is evidence authenticated? **Rule 901** lists several examples of how evidence is authenticated. As Rule 901 attests, though, this list is not exhaustive.

Rule 901. Requirement of Authentication or Identification

(b) Illustrations.

By way of illustration only, and not by way of limitation, the following are examples of authentication or identification conforming with the requirements of this rule:

(1) Testimony of witness with knowledge. Testimony that a matter is what it is claimed to be.

(2) Nonexpert opinion on handwriting. Nonexpert opinion as to the genuineness of handwriting, based upon familiarity not acquired for purposes of the litigation.

(3) Comparison by trier or expert witness. Comparison by the trier of fact or by expert witnesses with specimens which have been authenticated.

(4) Distinctive characteristics and the like. Appearance, contents, substance, internal patterns, or other distinctive characteristics, taken in conjunction with circumstances.

(5) Voice identification. Identification of a voice, whether heard firsthand or through mechanical or electronic transmission or recording, by opinion based

upon hearing the voice at any time under circumstances connecting it with the alleged speaker.

(6) Telephone conversations. Telephone conversations, by evidence that a call was made to the number assigned at the time by the telephone company to a particular person or business, if (A) in the case of a person, circumstances, including self-identification, show the person answering to be the one called, or (B) in the case of a business, the call was made to a place of business and the conversation related to business reasonably transacted over the telephone.

(7) Public records or reports. Evidence that a writing authorized by law to be recorded or filed and in fact recorded or filed in a public office, or a purported public record, report, statement, or data compilation, in any form, is from the public office where items of this nature are kept.

(8) Ancient documents or data compilation. Evidence that a document or data compilation, in any form, (A) is in such condition as to create no suspicion concerning its authenticity, (B) was in a place where it, if authentic, would likely be, and (C) has been in existence 20 years or more at the time it is offered.

(9) Process or system. Evidence describing a process or system used to produce a result and showing that the process or system produces an accurate result.

(10) Methods provided by statute or rule. Any method of authentication or identification provided by Act of Congress or by other rules prescribed by the Supreme Court pursuant to statutory authority.

http://www.law.cornell.edu/rules/fre/ACRule901.htm

Evidence is authenticated by:

1. Testimony of a witness with knowledge. A witness can testify, for example, "that is my signature on the letter."
2. Nonexpert opinion on handwriting. A witness can testify that "I believe the signature on that letter is that of my spouse."
3. Comparison by trier or expert witness to previously authenticated document. An expert witness could testify that in her opinion the handwriting exemplar before her was written by the same person who presumably wrote a previously authenticated document (e.g., one authenticated earlier in the trial).
4. Distinctive characteristics. A writing can be authenticated by its "[a]ppearance, contents, substance, internal patterns, or other distinctive characteristics."
5. Voice identification. A witness may testify that the voice on a certain recording is that of a particular person.

6. Outgoing telephone conversations. Authentication may be required if a witness claims that he called a particular business. In one case *United States v. Portsmouth Paving Corp.* (1982), testimony by R that he "called Mr. Saunders' office" was sufficient to "authenticate the occurrence of the telephone call in accordance with the standard illustrated by Rule 901 . . ."

7. Public records or reports. Certain documents can be authenticated by showing that they are from the public office where items of a similar type are normally kept. For example, in *United States v. Wilson* (1982), a receipt for a federal prisoner "signed by the director" and "identified by her at trial" was properly authenticated.

8. Ancient documents or data compilations. The authentication requirement can also be satisfied when, according to Rule 901(b)(8), evidence that a document or data compilation, in any form, is in such condition as to create no suspicion concerning its authenticity, was in a place where it, if authentic, would likely be, and has been in existence 20 years or more at the time it is offered. A witness could testify, for instance, that he found the document inside an Egyptian pyramid, and the authentication requirement would be satisfied.

9. Process or system. This example often applies to tape recordings. The case of *United States v. Lance* (1988) is illustrative. Tapes consisting of voice recordings were "adequately authenticated" by testimony . . . that they "contained accurate recordings of the conversations that occurred."

10. Methods provided by statute or rule. This is the residual category. Statutes and/or court decisions providing for other forms of authentication must be recognized.

We now turn to some of these methods of authentication in some more detail. We divide the remainder of our discussion concerning authentication into three categories: authentication of documents, authentication of objects, and authentication of voices. We will conclude with a discussion of self-authentication.

Authentication of Documents

Documents are most often authenticated by direct evidence, that is, by someone who has personal knowledge of the document's authenticity. If a person saw a document written by another, then that person can serve as a witness testifying to the document's authenticity. Documents can also be authenticated by lay or expert witness opinion. A lay witness familiar with the handwriting of the supposed author can testify that, in his or her opinion, a document was written by the author. Familiarity with the author's handwriting can come from having seen the author write other documents, from having received letters from the author, or by similar means. Experts can also authenticate documents; however, they need not necessarily see the document being written by the supposed author (or even be familiar with the supposed author's handwriting). Instead, experts can testify to a document's authenticity by comparing the document to another one. This method assumes, though, that the document used as a base of comparison has itself been authenticated. Other sophisticated techniques (such as by using computer technology or ink analysis) can also be used to authenticate documents.

Next, documents can be authenticated by circumstantial evidence. First, a document can be authenticated by evidence that it was received in response to a communication sent to its supposed author. Second, a writing can be authenticated by evidence that it states facts that are unlikely to be known to anyone but its supposed author. Third, a document can be authenticated by admission, that is, by evidence that the adversary admitted it was authentic or behaved as if it was such. For example, if in a letter between two co-conspirators X tells Y to run like hell and Y then runs like hell, the letter will be authenticated if evidence is offered that Y ran like hell. Fourth, documents can be authenticated by custody. If the document is filed or recorded in a public office authorized to file such a record and the document is obtained from said office, it will be authenticated.

There are countless other ways to authenticate documents. Understand that the methods for authentication discussed in the Federal Rules of Evidence (and in other evidence codes) are not exhaustive. Any relevant evidence that would lead a reasonable juror to conclude that a document is authentic will suffice.

Authentication of Objects

The rules for the authentication of objects are essentially the same as those for documents, taking into account the differences between objects and writings. An expert in electric guitars, for instance, can testify that the guitar in question is not a 1957 American-made Stratocaster but rather a cheaper imported version of the same guitar. As with documents, the expert may testify that in his or her opinion the guitar is not a '57. The expert would then point to unique features of a '57 Stratocaster, not to writing samples.

There are additional means for authenticating objects besides having to rely on expert opinion. For example, witnesses with knowledge can testify that objects are authentic. Mary's fiancé Craig could testify that Mary's diamond is real because Craig was with her when she bought the stone from a reputable jeweler. Or, a witness could testify that the bicycle the defendant was riding when he was arrested is hers because it has a driver's license number inscribed on the frame that is the same number as on the witness's driver's license.

Authentication of Voices

Voices can be authenticated in ways similar for those of objects or documents. First, a person with knowledge of another's voice can testify concerning that person's voice. For example, if X works for Y and is in regular communication with him, X can testify that the voice on a tape recording making death threats to the president sounds like Y's voice because she has become familiar with Y's voice.

Different rules apply in the case of telephone calls. A telephone conversation with a person can be authenticated if the caller testifies (1) that he or she called the number listed in the phone book for the person called, or (2) the person on the other end identified himself or herself as the one called. The same applies to business, with one added exception: If the call is related to business that normally takes place over the phone, testimony that the call took place will authenticate the call.

Self-Authentication

Rule 902 of the FRE creates a category of **self-authenticating documents**. Such documents require no extrinsic evidence, such as witness testimony, as to their authenticity. They are deemed authentic on their face, or at first glance. However, no such rule existed at common law.

Rule 902. Self-authentication

Extrinsic evidence of authenticity as a condition precedent to admissibility is not required with respect to the following:

(1) Domestic public documents under seal. A document bearing a seal purporting to be that of the United States, or of any State, district, Commonwealth, territory, or insular possession thereof, or the Panama Canal Zone, or the Trust Territory of the Pacific Islands, or of a political subdivision, department, officer, or agency thereof, and a signature purporting to be an attestation or execution.

(2) Domestic public documents not under seal. A document purporting to bear the signature in the official capacity of an officer or employee of any entity included in paragraph (1) hereof, having no seal, if a public officer

having a seal and having official duties in the district or political subdivision of the officer or employee certifies under seal that the signer has the official capacity and that the signature is genuine.

(3) Foreign public documents. A document purporting to be executed or attested in an official capacity by a person authorized by the laws of a foreign country to make the execution or attestation, and accompanied by a final certification as to the genuineness of the signature and official position (A) of the executing or attesting person, or (B) of any foreign official whose certificate of genuineness of signature and official position relates to the execution or attestation or is in a chain of certificates of genuineness of signature and official position relating to the execution or attestation. A final certification may be made by a secretary of an embassy or legation, consul general, consul, vice consul, or consular agent of the United States, or a diplomatic or consular official of the foreign country assigned or accredited to the United States. If reasonable opportunity has been given to all parties to investigate the authenticity and accuracy of official documents, the court may, for good cause shown, order that they be treated as presumptively authentic without final certification or permit them to be evidenced by an attested summary with or without final certification.

(4) Certified copies of public records. A copy of an official record or report or entry therein, or of a document authorized by law to be recorded or filed and actually recorded or filed in a public office, including data compilations in any form, certified as correct by the custodian or other person authorized to make the certification, by certificate complying with paragraph (1), (2), or (3) of this rule or complying with any Act of Congress or rule prescribed by the Supreme Court pursuant to statutory authority.

(5) Official publications. Books, pamphlets, or other publications purporting to be issued by public authority.

(6) Newspapers and periodicals. Printed materials purporting to be newspapers or periodicals.

(7) Trade inscriptions and the like. Inscriptions, signs, tags, or labels purporting to have been affixed in the course of business and indicating ownership, control, or origin.

(8) Acknowledged documents. Documents accompanied by a certificate of acknowledgment executed in the manner provided by law by a notary public or other officer authorized by law to take acknowledgments.

(9) Commercial paper and related documents. Commercial paper, signatures thereon, and documents relating thereto to the extent provided by general commercial law.

(10) Presumptions under Acts of Congress. Any signature, document, or other matter declared by Act of Congress to be presumptively or prima facie genuine or authentic.

(11) Certified domestic records of regularly conducted activity. The original or a duplicate of a domestic record of regularly conducted activity that would be admissible under Rule 803(6) if accompanied by a written declaration of its custodian or other qualified person, in a manner complying with any Act of Congress or rule prescribed by the Supreme Court pursuant to statutory authority, certifying that the record:

(A) was made at or near the time of the occurrence of the matters set forth by, or from information transmitted by, a person with knowledge of those matters;

(B) was kept in the course of the regularly conducted activity; and

(C) was made by the regularly conducted activity as a regular practice.

A party intending to offer a record into evidence under this paragraph must provide written notice of that intention to all adverse parties, and must make the record and declaration available for inspection sufficiently in advance of their offer into evidence to provide an adverse party with a fair opportunity to challenge them.

(12) Certified foreign records of regularly conducted activity. In a civil case, the original or a duplicate of a foreign record of regularly conducted activity that would be admissible under Rule 803(6) if accompanied by a written declaration by its custodian or other qualified person certifying that the record:

(A) was made at or near the time of the occurrence of the matters set forth by, or from information transmitted by, a person with knowledge of those matters;

(B) was kept in the course of the regularly conducted activity; and

(C) was made by the regularly conducted activity as a regular practice.

The declaration must be signed in a manner that, if falsely made, would subject the maker to criminal penalty under the laws of the country where the declaration is signed. A party intending to offer a record into evidence under this paragraph must provide written notice of that intention to all adverse parties, and must make the record and declaration available for inspection sufficiently in advance of their offer into evidence to provide an adverse party with a fair opportunity to challenge them.

http://www.law.cornell.edu/rules/fre/ACRule902.htm

Following are some examples of self-authenticating documents.

1. *Sealed writings.* If a document has the apparent seal of a state or federal governmental entity or official, it is self-authenticating. In addition to a seal, however, the document must bear "a signature purporting to be an attestation or execution." **Execution** means that the document was written or adopted by the signer; **attestation** means

that the signer examined the document after the fact and found it to be a genuine document or public record. A college diploma, for example, contains at least one signature (usually of the college president) "attesting" that the person named on the diploma satisfied certain requirements and has graduated.

2. *Public documents.* Unsealed public documents are also self-authenticating. However, the document must be signed by an officer or employee of the public agency and bear a sealed attestation that the signature is genuine. In other words, there will be one signature followed by a second signature (usually by another individual higher up in the chain of command) verifying that the first individual's signature is genuine.

3. *Diplomatic documents.* A foreign public document is self-authenticating if it satisfies three requirements: (a) it must be executed or attested to by someone authorized to do so; (b) the person's authority is certified; and (c) the validity of the document is then certified by a U.S. diplomatic officer. The last requirement can be abandoned, however, if there is good cause to do so. The court will make this determination.

4. *Certified copies of public records.* A certified copy of a public record or a recorded and filed private document is self-authenticating, but it must (a) be certified as a correct copy by the custodian of the original and (b) comply with applicable rules. Copies are acceptable under certain circumstances because of the difficulty (or impossibility) of obtaining the original document.

5. *Official publications.* Any publication issued by a public authority is self-authenticating. It is not always clear, however, what constitutes a "public authority." Further, such documents may be excludable on hearsay grounds. Nevertheless, the reason for allowing official publications to be self-authenticating is that forgery or misrepresentation of such publications is unlikely.

6. *Newspapers and periodicals.* Any newspaper or periodical is self-authenticating. The newspaper or periodical need not be popular, well known, or widely circulated. The only requirement is that it appear with some regularity. The reason for the self-authentication of newspapers and periodicals is that falsification or forgery is unlikely. Most such sources have distinctive layouts, logos, and other characteristics, making misrepresentation a difficult task indeed.

7. *Trade inscriptions.* A tag or label on a commercial product is sufficient to authenticate the product as that of its source. The tag or label must appear to have been affixed during the course of business, *and* the tag or label must appear to indicate ownership, control, or origin. A painting of a bottle of Coca-Cola would not be self-authenticating, because the label indicated in the painting would not have been

"affixed" during the normal course of business and, as such, would not be self-authenticating.

8. *Acknowledged documents.* This term applies most frequently to documents bearing the seal of a notary. A writing is self-authenticated if the author of the writing acknowledges it is genuine before an authorized notary public. The reason for allowing notarized documents to be self-authenticating is that notaries are legally obligated to take reasonable steps to ensure the true identity of the person who appears before him or her.

9. *Statutory authenticity.* Finally, a document will be self-authenticating if the provision of the Uniform Commercial Code or similar statute so provides. Several federal statutes provide for the self-authentication of documents, some of which include legislative records, records of judicial proceedings, documents filed with federal agencies, published statutes, tax returns, and so forth.

Best Evidence Rule

The **best evidence rule** is also sometimes called the "documentary originals rule." It is a rule of preference requiring that when the contents of a writing are at issue, the contents should be proved by the original writing and not by secondary evidence. In other words, the original writing is preferable unless it is not easily obtainable. The best evidence rule actually encompasses several rules listed in the Federal Rules of Evidence, specifically Rules 1001–1008.

The preference for original documents arises in two circumstances. First, as indicated, an original writing is desirable when the contents of a copy are in dispute. That is, if one party argues that a copy is not the same as an original, it is preferable to obtain the original for purposes of comparison. Second, original documents are preferable when witnesses are asked to recall the contents of such documents.

The logic for the best evidence rule is efficiency. It would be a waste of time to draw on secondary evidence to determine whether the contents of a document are identical to the original or whether a witness adequately recalls the contents of an original document. When the original is obtainable, the question as to recollection of contents can be easily resolved.

The Best Evidence Rule Is Not Authentication

The best evidence rule is separate and distinct from the authentication process. A simple way to distinguish between "best evidence" and authentication is to think in terms of the oft-cited metaphor of the forest and the trees. Authentication concerns the forest: Is the writing an original, or is the evidence in question genuine? Or, equivalently, is the evidence what its proponent says it is? The best evidence rule, by contrast, concerns the trees: Are the contents of a writing the same as those found in the original?

It is possible for the best evidence rule to apply in a case and also require authentication. If the concern is with the forest, not the trees, the best evidence rule will not apply. Alternatively, if the concern is with the trees and not the forest (say, for instance, the document is self-authenticating), authentication will not be required. The forest-trees metaphor may be somewhat crude, but it is designed to emphasize that the distinction between the best evidence rule and authentication is really one of priority and preference; whether both doctrines apply depends on what is at issue in a case.

Another way to understand the difference between authentication and best evidence is to note that the former determines whether a document or writing is an original or a copy, whereas the latter determines whether the document or writing has to be an original or a copy. Authentication asks if the evidence is an original or a copy. The best evidence rule asks if the evidence needs to be an original, or if a copy can suffice.

Distinguishing Best Evidence from Hearsay

The best evidence rule focuses on the accuracy of the contents of writings submitted to the trier of fact. The hearsay rule, by contrast, concerns the truth or falsity of those contents. Both hearsay and best evidence problems can be raised in the same case. If a writing is offered to prove the truth of its contents, hearsay objections may be raised and the best evidence rule implicated. However, if the truth of a writing's contents is not at issue, only the existence of such contents, then hearsay problems are circumvented. If, for example, a witness testifies that the marriage is invalid because there was never an official marriage certificate and a second witness produces the marriage certificate, hearsay concerns are not raised, because the truth or falsity of what is contained in the marriage certificate is not at issue. In all likelihood, the best evidence rule will not apply either, because of the "memorialized and recorded transactions" exception, to be discussed later.

Best Evidence Definitions

Rule 1001 of the FRE defines the basic terminology used with the best evidence rules.

Rule 1001. Definitions

For purposes of this article the following definitions are applicable:

(1) **Writings and recordings**. "Writings" and "recordings" consist of letters, words, or numbers, or their equivalent, set down by handwriting, typewriting, printing, photostating, photographing, magnetic impulse, mechanical or electronic recording, or other form of data compilation.

(2) **Photographs**. "Photographs" include still photographs, X-ray films, video tapes, and motion pictures.

(3) **Original**. An "original" of a writing or recording is the writing or recording itself or any counterpart intended to have the same effect by a person executing or issuing it. An "original" of a photograph includes the negative or any print therefrom. If data are stored in a computer or similar device, any printout or other output readable by sight, shown to reflect the data accurately, is an "original."

(4) **Duplicate**. A "duplicate" is a counterpart produced by the same impression as the original, or from the same matrix, or by means of photography, including enlargements and miniatures, or by mechanical or electronic re-recording, or by chemical reproduction, or by other equivalent techniques which accurately reproduces the original.

http://www.law.cornell.edu/rules/fre/ACRule1001.htm

So far we have been referring to documents as though they are the same as writings. This is not always the case. A **writing**, as far as the best evidence rules is concerned, includes "every means of recording upon any tangible thing any form of communication or representation" (CEC. Section 250).

California's Evidence Code states that the means of recording include handwriting, typewriting, photo copying, and photographing. The Federal Rules of Evidence (Rule 1001[1]) extends this list to include "magnetic impulse, mechanical or electronic recording or other forms of data compilation."

The forms of communication or representation listed in modern evidence codes include "letters, words, numbers, or their equivalent," according to the Federal Rules of Evidence. California's Evidence Code adds "pictures, sounds, or symbols, or combinations thereof" to the list of possible communications or representations.

The definition of **original** as it pertains to the best evidence rule is "the writing itself or recording itself or any counterpart intended to have the same effect by a person executing or issuing it" (FRE 1001[3]); CEC Section 255). An "original" of a photograph "includes the negative or any print therefrom." As for computers, any printout or other readable output from a computer is an "original."

Rule 1002. Requirement of Original

To prove the content of a writing, recording, or photograph, the original writing, recording, or photograph is required, except as otherwise provided in these rules or by Act of Congress.

http://www.law.cornell.edu/rules/fre/ACRule1002.htm

As we have seen, originals are preferable in place of "secondary evidence" to prove the contents of a writing. **Secondary evidence** in this case refers to any evidence of the contents of a writing other than the original. If, for instance, a witness testifies as to the terms of a contract, this is secondary evidence. The original contract would of course be the original. The Federal Rules of Evidence mention "other evidence," not "secondary evidence." This seems to indicate that circumstantial evidence could even be used to prove the contents of a writing if the original is unobtainable.

Rule 1001(4) recognizes that a **duplicate** can occasionally serve in place of an original. "A 'duplicate' is a counterpart produced by the same impression as the original, or from the same matrix, or by means of photography, including enlargements and miniatures, or by mechanical or electronic rerecording, or by chemical reproduction, or by other equivalent technique which accurately reproduces the original." An "impression" can be a carbon copy. "Matrix" refers to an impression from, for example, a printing plate, mimeograph stencil, or similar device. Photographs of originals can suffice, as can photographic enlargements (blown-up pictures) or miniatures (such as microfilm). "Rerecordings" include, but are not limited to, digital cleaning up of recordings from informants. The rules do not define "chemical" copies, and several other unmentioned techniques can be properly relied upon.

The Rule in Operation

The purpose of the best evidence rule is to prove content. This is why the rule does not apply to other physical evidence. It does not require, for instance, that a party produce the best physical evidence (e.g., the murder weapon instead of the defendant's hair sample found at the scene of the murder). Only when the contents of writings (which now seems to include photographs and recordings), are in dispute does the rule apply. If the contents of such evidence are not in dispute, the rule will not apply.

In the following subsections we briefly describe situations in which the best evidence rule does and does not apply. The rule applies, as indicated, when the content of a writing is at issue. In the remaining situations, legally operative conduct and the like, the rule usually does not apply, although there are exceptions (e.g., for testimony about written rules).

Proving Content

If the party seeks to use writings, recordings, or photographs to prove other matters besides content, doing so does not violate the best evidence rule. For example, if a party seeks to prove that John owned a car by introducing a copy of a car title with John's name on it, the rule does not apply. In such an instance the original title is not required because the content of the title is not at issue. If, however, one party argues that the title is in fact a fraud, the original would be required.

The rule also does not apply when writings serve as the basis for expert opinion. If an expert refers to a scholarly study as the basis for her opinion, the best evidence rule is not triggered. However, if the expert dwells considerably on the content of the study and the contents come into dispute, an original may be required. In such a situation a copy of the original will suffice regardless.

These examples notwithstanding, it is often difficult to determine when someone is attempting to "prove the content" of a writing. A safe rule of thumb for making this determination is whenever the jury is required to decide or infer that the writing contains a particular statement, the best evidence rule applies.

Legally Operative Conduct

The best evidence rule also applies when a writing is **legally operative conduct.** This term applies to words that affect the legal relationship of the parties. Most often, "legally operative conduct" consists of words in written contracts. If, for example, two parties enter into a written contract and one party sues the other for breach of contract, the best evidence rule applies.

Matters Incidentally Recorded

Sometimes statements asserted in writings, recordings, or photographs are "incidental"—that is, not purposeful. For example, assume two customers in a bank teller's line get in a verbal altercation, which then leads to a physical fight over their position in line. Because banks record virtually every event that takes place inside their premises, a recording capturing the fight would be incidental. In other words, the recording was not set up to capture the fight. Instead, it just so happens that the fight was recorded on videotape.

The rule governing these types of recordings is that an original is not required. Indeed, simple testimony from witnesses that the fight took place (or from the victims) could suffice. The videotape of the fight is not considered "best evidence" because it caught the fight by chance. This does not mean, of course, that the video would not be introduced as evidence in addition to witness testimony, only that the best evidence rule does not apply to matters incidentally recorded.

Memorialized and Recorded Transactions

A party can prove a nonwritten transaction that is memorialized in writing without producing the original writing. Ownership of property can be shown without having to produce a title. Proof of a person's employment or income level need not be accompanied by written proof of employment. A party can show that he or she is married without having to produce the marriage license. Courts even permit testimony that dealers are licensed without requiring that they always produce their licenses, and proof that goods cost a particular amount can be offered with testimony, not the original receipt. All such transactions (and countless others) are "memorialized" in writing and are not bound by the best evidence rule. As before, however, if the contents of the writings memorializing such transactions are in dispute, originals may have to be produced.

Witnesses can testify to facts or events of which there is a record without producing the record. For example, police officers can testify to a defendant's confession without producing the tape on which the confession was recorded. Witnesses can testify to the former testimony of a person without producing a transcript of the earlier testimony. Witnesses of car accidents, crimes, and other violent events can testify to what they saw without producing photographs taken at the scene. Witnesses can testify as to what occurs in meetings without having to produce the transcripts from such meetings. Recorded transactions are similar to memorialized transactions; however, the former are recorded whereas the latter are often documented in written form.

Testimony About Rules

Usually a witness cannot testify about the contents of written rules without producing those rules. For example, in *Conway v. Consolidated Rail Corp.* (1983) a conductor's proposed testimony that he did not "have any authority to stop a passenger from boarding a train with a footlocker" was properly excluded as not best evidence. However, in situations where a writing records preexisting rules, such as with an employee's copy of the rules, the original will not need to be provided. Further, in situations where rules are oral rather than written, originals need not be provided. This was illustrated in the case of *Hood v. Itawamba County, Miss.* (1993). There, testimony concerning a sheriff's policy of dealing with detainees with mental problems was properly admitted where the actual policies were oral instead of written.

Admissibility of Duplicates

Duplicates of originals are admissible unless one of two things occur. First, if the authenticity of the duplicate is questioned, the original should be produced if it is obtainable. Second, if it would be unfair to admit a duplicate writing in lieu of the original, the latter should be produced. If, for example, a duplicate does not bear all of the elements of the original, admission of the duplicate may result on an unfair outcome for a party to the case.

Rule 1003. Admissibility of Duplicates

A duplicate is admissible to the same extent as an original unless (1) a genuine question is raised as to the authenticity of the original or (2) in the circumstances it would be unfair to admit the duplicate in lieu of the original.

http://www.law.cornell.edu/rules/fre/ACRule1003.htm

Special Problems

Some confusion exists concerning the relationship between the best evidence rule and so-called inscribed chattels. **Inscribed chattels** include badges, logos on automobiles, and the like. What if, for instance, the plaintiff in a civil rights action argues that the person who assaulted her stepped out of an automobile bearing the inscription "to protect and serve" and was wearing a badge with the name Smiley? Should the plaintiff in this instance be required to produce the car or the badge? Most courts would probably say the best evidence rule does not apply, but a literal interpretation of the best evidence rule may lead one to conclude otherwise; the plaintiff in our example is in essence trying to prove the contents of the writing.

The inscription on the car would lead one to believe that the person who stepped out of it was a police officer, so the content of the inscription would seem of particular importance. Understood in a different way, the plaintiff is trying to prove the "contents" of the car by the inscription on the door. However, if a witness testifies that the plaintiff rode her bicycle headlong into the side of a car bearing the inscription "to protect and serve," the car would not need to be produced and the best evidence rule would not apply, because the content of the writing is not at issue.

Another best evidence rule problem arises with writings within writings. Many times documents contain excerpts from other documents. Textbooks often contain quotes from other sources; hospital records and the like often contain diagnoses or quotes from other individuals. To what extent should the originals be required in these situations? If the content of the message within a message is in dispute, the best evidence rule will apply.

Finally, is the best evidence rule implicated when it needs to be determined whether the contents of a writing do not contain a certain entry or statement? For example, would the original writing be required if a witness testifies that "I have no record of an appointment for Patient X on September 5th"? In this situation, the best evidence rule would not apply, because the purpose of the testimony in this example is not to prove contents but to prove the absence of contents.

When the Original Cannot Be Obtained

The best evidence rule is a rule of preference, so original writings are not *required* when, for some reason, they cannot be acquired. Modern evidence statutes describe several circumstances under which secondary evidence of writings (e.g., witness testimony as to contents) can serve in lieu of original writings. The most common circumstances are (1) when the original is lost, (2) when the original is unavailable, (3) when the original is in the possession of an opponent, and (4) when the writing is one characterized as collateral, official, voluminous, or produced.

Rule 1004. Admissibility of Other Evidence of Contents

The original is not required, and other evidence of the contents of a writing, recording, or photograph is admissible if:

(1) **Originals lost or destroyed**. All originals are lost or have been destroyed, unless the proponent lost or destroyed them in bad faith; or

(2) **Original not obtainable**. No original can be obtained by any available judicial process or procedure; or

(3) **Original in possession of opponent**. At a time when an original was under the control of the party against whom offered, that party was put on notice, by the pleadings or otherwise, that the contents would be a subject of proof at the hearing, and that party does not produce the original at the hearing; or

(4) **Collateral matters**. The writing, recording, or photograph is not closely related to a controlling issue.

http://www.law.cornell.edu/rules/fre/ACRule1004.htm

Lost Original

Secondary evidence of the contents of a writing is permissible when the original is lost or when the original has been destroyed without bad faith or "fraudulent intent" (CEC Section 1501) on the part of the proponent. The proponent will need to prove by a preponderance of the evidence that the original was lost. Further, the court may require a fairly intense search for the original if the original is of particular importance or if fraudulent intent is suspected.

Unavailable Original or Beyond Reach of Judicial Process

If the original cannot be obtained by any available judicial process or procedure and is not lost, secondary evidence is acceptable. Even if the original is obtainable by judicial process, it may not be required if acquiring the original would be too arduous a task. For example, it would be ridiculous for a court to require the proponent to produce a 20-ton statue bearing a plaque with the inscription "All who enter these premises shall never return." If a writing or photograph is in the possession of a third party, a subpoena duces tecum may be used to acquire the original, but not if the third party successfully asserts a privilege blocking production of the original.

Original in Possession of Opponents

The contents of a writing may be proved by secondary evidence when the original is in possession of an opponent and the opponent is given proper notice that the contents would be proven at trial. The logic underlying this exception is that if the opponent is given notice that the contents of a writing will be proved with secondary evidence, the opponent can correct any erroneous testimony by producing the original. This exception only applies when (1) the opponent is given reasonable notice that the contents will be proved with secondary evidence, (2) the opponent is in possession or control of the original at the time of the notice, and (3) the opponent does not produce the original at the hearing. Modern evidence statutes do not define "reasonable notice," and the time period for giving notice is not altogether clear.

Collateral, Official, and Voluminous Writings

Secondary evidence of the contents of a writing is permissible if it is "not closely related to a controlling issue" (Rule 1004[4]). For example, if a witness testifies that the defendant was driving down the road at a high rate of speed speaking into a hand-held tape recorder, the tape recording would be collateral, that is, not a controlling issue, and so would not be required.

Copies of official writings are acceptable if the original is a recorded document. The rationale for this exception is that it would be burdensome for courts to require the originals of official copies, but this is only if the proponent does not have a copy of the original and could not obtain one with reasonable care.

Next, secondary evidence in the form of a chart or a summary is acceptable in lieu of the original when the original is too voluminous to be "conveniently examined." If, for example, the original is a 3,000-page accounting record but only a handful of sections are at issue, a summary will probably suffice. Two key restrictions to this exception are that the original be accessible for inspection by both parties and that the summary be authenticated. Do not confuse this exception with the demonstrative evidence discussion later in this chapter. This exception to the best evidence rule is merely geared toward summarizing information. Demonstrative evidence, by contrast, concerns tools and techniques for illustrative or pedagogical purposes.

The Admissions Doctrine

Rule 1007 provides that the "contents of writings, recordings, or photographs may be proved by the testimony or deposition of the party against whom it is offered or by that party's written admission, without accounting for the non-production of the original." What this rule means is that production of the original is unnecessary where the opponent admits to the contents of the writing, recording, or photograph. An oral or written admission will suffice under this rule, which is termed the **admissions doctrine**.

Rule 1007. Testimony or Written Admission of Party

Contents of writings, recordings, or photographs may be proved by the testimony or deposition of the party against whom offered or by that party's written admission, without accounting for the nonproduction of the original.

http://www.law.cornell.edu/rules/fre/ACRule1007.htm

Best Evidence Procedure

Procedures surrounding the best evidence rule can be somewhat confusing. This is because a number of preliminary questions must be decided by either the judge or the jury. The Federal Rules of Evidence require that judges decide a number of such preliminary issues. See Table 9.1 for examples.

The lines between the role of the judge and the jury become blurry when the best evidence rule and the authentication doctrine collide. In particular, the factual issues that govern admissibility under the best

Table 9.1   Preliminary "Best Evidence" Issues Decided by Judges

Judges Must Decide Whether:

1. An Item constitutes a writing, recording, or photograph

2. A writing, recording, or photograph is "original"

3. A "duplicate" meets the requirements of Rule 1001(4)

4. A "genuine question" has been raised about authentication of the original

5. It would be "unfair" to rely on a duplication in place of the original

6. The original has been "lost" or "destroyed"

7. The original has been lost or destroyed in "bad faith"

8. The original is unobtainable by judicial process

9. The original is in possession of the opponent and proper notice was given

10. The evidence goes to a "collateral" matter

11. A copy of a public record has been properly certified

12. A copy of a public record cannot be obtained with "reasonable diligence"

13. Writings are too "voluminous" to be examined by the jury

evidence rule, which are usually decided by a judge, can be the same used to determine authentication, which the jury is supposed to decide. As such, juries occasionally decide (1) whether a writing that a party seeks to introduce ever existed, (2) which of two writings introduced at trial is the original, and (3) whether a copy or duplicate "accurately reflects" the original. Suppose, for example, one party argues that its document is the original contract while the opposing party argues that *its* document is the original contract. Here, a question of authentication arises, so the jury decides. As a general rule, if the decision goes directly to the matter being litigated, the jury should decide, not the judge. Judges make legal decisions; juries make factual ones.

Real/Physical Evidence

Real evidence and physical evidence are forms of evidence that are discernible by the senses without the use of witnesses. From here on we will refer strictly to real evidence. Understand that when we refer to real evidence we are also discussing physical evidence; the terms are used interchangeably.

Real evidence is usually the most persuasive type of evidence. Witness testimony can come across as unbelievable, requiring that the jury decide who and what to believe, but real evidence is often black and white. For example, a murder weapon with the defendant's fingerprints on it is much more believable than a witness's testimony to the effect that the defendant murdered the victim.

Real Evidence and the Fifth Amendment

People who are unfamiliar with the laws of evidence and rules of criminal procedure often get upset when a suspect's testimony is excluded because of a *Miranda* (1966) violation or other Fifth Amendment violation. These people often forget that testimonial evidence (that protected by the Fifth Amendment) is not the only type of evidence required to secure criminal convictions. Even if a defendant's confession is thrown out because of a Fifth Amendment violation, he or she can still be convicted with real evidence.

Real evidence is not protected by the Fifth Amendment because of the Supreme Court's decision in *Schmerber v. California* (1966) (discussed more thoroughly in Chapter 11). There the Court decided that the Fifth Amendment's self-incrimination protection applied to evidence of a testimonial or communicative nature but did not apply to real evidence. In the Court's words:

> Courts have usually held that it [the Fifth Amendment] offers no protection against compulsion to submit to fingerprinting, photographing, or measurements, to write or speak for identification, to appear in court, to stand, to assume a stance, to walk, or to make a particular gesture.

Furthermore:

> Compulsion which makes a suspect or accused the source of real or physical evidence does not violate it [the Fifth Amendment].

Of course, when it comes to acquiring real evidence, law enforcement officials (and the courts) are bound by the Fourth Amendment. Even though the Fifth Amendment does not offer protection to criminal defendants in the case of real evidence, the Fourth Amendment's search and seizure provisions still apply. Probable cause, or a similar level of justification, depending on the conduct in question, is still required for officials to obtain real evidence during a search or seizure. If real evidence is obtained by means other than a search or seizure, Fourth Amendment protections do not apply.

Admissibility Requirements

In legal parlance, a proper "foundation" must be in place before real evidence can be considered admissible in court. Real evidence must first meet the requirements of relevancy, competency, and materiality.

First, real evidence is **relevant** when it sheds some light on a contested matter. According to a Georgia court, "relevancy is a logical relationship between evidence and a fact in issue or to be established" (*Continental Trust Co. v. Bank of Harrison,* 1926). Understood differently, evidence is relevant when it throws or tends to throw light on the guilt or innocence of the accused even though its tendency to do so is minimal.

Second, real evidence is **competent** when, in particular, it is not obtained illegally. If evidence is obtained in violation of the Fourth Amendment, for instance, it cannot be considered competent. If real evidence is not competent, it is not admissible.

Third, real evidence is material when it significantly affects that matter at issue in a case. According to one court, **material evidence** is that which is relevant and goes to substantial matters in dispute or has legitimate influence or bearing on the decision of the case (*Hill v. State,* 1981). Materiality and relevance are not the same; the former refers to the significance of the evidence, whereas the latter suggests that evidence merely relates to the issue in question.

If necessary, real evidence may need to be authenticated. Authentication is particularly relevant in the case of written documents, but as we have seen, real evidence sometimes needs to be authenticated as well. Finally, the evidence must follow a proper chain of custody. In other words, the evidence must have been in constant possession or custody of one or more persons typically charged with handling evidence. If the evidence was tampered with at some point between where the evidence was taken in custody and the trial, authentication may not be possible.

For example, a videotape of an ATM robbery was "misplaced" for a time while it was supposed to be in custody. A strong case could be made that the videotape to be introduced at trial is not authentic because of the potential for tampering. Consider what one federal appeals court stated with regard to the chain of custody:

> As to the chain of custody for the proper admission of a physical exhibit, there must be a showing that the physical exhibit is in substantially the same condition as when the crime was committed . . .

When there is no evidence of tampering, a presumption of regularity attends the official acts of public officers in custody of the evidence; the courts presume they did their jobs correctly . . . All the government must show is that reasonable precautions were taken to preserve the original condition of evidence; an adequate chain of custody can be shown even if all possibilities of tampering are excluded . . . Merely raising the possibility of tampering is not sufficient to render the evidence inadmissible; the possibility of a break in the chain of custody of evidence goes to the weight of the evidence, not its admissibility. (*United States v. Harrington,* 1991)

Types of Real Evidence

It would be impossible to cover all the types of real evidence completely. Instead, we focus on the most common forms of real evidence encountered in criminal cases: (1) the exhibition of a person, (2) items connected to the crime, (3) photographs, (4) sound recordings, (5) videotapes/motion pictures, and (6) the results from X-rays.

Exhibition of a Person

In cases involving physical injury to a victim (in either a civil or criminal case), it is useful to present the actual victim to the jury. Of course, if a great deal of time has elapsed between the infliction of the injury and the trial date, photographs may be necessary to document the injury. But if the injury is lasting, allowing the victim to "show" himself or herself to the jury may be of substantial probative value. However, if the injury is too serious or potentially inflammatory, the trial judge may decide that the exhibition of the victim is not acceptable.

The flipside of displaying the victim to the jury is displaying the defendant to the jury. As a general rule, judges should not allow criminal defendants to appear before the jury in leg irons or handcuff unless there is clear justification for doing so. One court stated that the defendant may not be placed in any form of physical restraint while in the presence of the jury unless there is some compelling reason for doing so (see *People v. Duran,* 1976). The reason for this rule is that placing a defendant in shackles, handcuffs, leg irons, or the like makes the defendant look guilty.

Items Connected to the Crime

By far the largest category of physical evidence includes items connected with the crime. Any device or object used to facilitate any crime can fall into this category, including weapons, items used during the crime other than weapons, clothing, drugs and drug paraphernalia, and so on.

Weapons can range from guns and knives to blunt objects and even simulated explosives. Interestingly, if the specific type of weapon used to commit a homicide is not known, any weapons found in the defendant's possession that could have been used to commit the homicide will be considered admissible. However, if the prosecution argues that a specific type of weapon was used (such as a .38 caliber pistol), weapons of other types found in the defendant's possession will not be considered admissible (see *People v. Riser,* 1956).

Items other than weapons used to commit crimes are also admissible, but with special care. Items such as burglary tools fall into this category, but their identification must be certain. If the prosecution argues that the defendant used a crowbar to burglarize the victim's apartment, the mere fact that the defendant possesses a crowbar may not be enough to render it admissible. If no evidence is left behind to connect the specific crowbar with the crime, the prosecution will be hard-pressed to build a case with physical evidence.

Clothing is another form of real evidence. Everyone remembers the famous "bloody glove" in the O. J. Simpson case. In other cases, clothing identified by a witness that was worn by the accused during the commission of a crime can be admitted into evidence. In one case, a hat, jacket, and pants found in a washing machine shortly after a robber had entered a house wearing similar clothing were admissible and did not violate the Fifth Amendment (*Warden v. Hayden,* 1967). According to an appellate court decision:

> Evidence is relevant and admissible if it tends to logically prove or disprove facts in issue, or if it corroborates other material evidence. . . . The articles were found by the police at the crime scene. The robe and sheets contained seminal stains while the nightgown was torn and bloody. This evidence corroborated the victim's story that she had been raped and that her lip had been cut during the struggle. (*State v. Atkins,* 1985, 227)

Among the largest varieties of items connected with a crime are narcotics and narcotics paraphernalia. Narcotics seized from suspects, as well as containers, records, scales, packages, chemicals, and similar items, are frequently admitted against defendants in drug cases. In one case, a gun and pager found on the defendant during a search incident to arrest were considered relevant to the drug trafficking charges against the defendant (*United States v. Brown,* 1994).

Photographs

We have seen that photographs frequently need to be authenticated and can be bound by the best evidence rule. In instances where photographs are authenticated and constitute best evidence, they can be particularly useful and convey important information to the jury to aid in its decision. In criminal cases, photographs must be relevant to an issue in the case. For example, the proponent of the photograph must be able to relate the photograph to corpus delecti, identification, the nature and/or location of an injury, or the degree of atrocity to illustrate or explain testimony or to corroborate the theory of the case.

Photographs can also be controversial. This is especially the case with gruesome and graphic photographs. In deciding whether, for example, a graphic photograph of a murder victim should be admitted into evidence, courts will make a cost-benefit analysis determining whether the probative value of the photograph outweighs the potential for prejudice to the defendant. In other words, the court must determine whether the probative value of the photograph outweighs it prejudicial or inflammatory nature. Thus, if the trial court finds that a photograph, although prejudicial, is probative, it may be admitted into evidence. As one court explained it, gruesome photographs are admissible if they assist the jury in any of the following ways:

> [b]y shedding light on some issue; by proving a necessary element of the case; by enabling a witness to testify more effectively, by corroborating testimony, or by enabling the jurors to better understand the testimony. (*Sanders v. State,* 1994)

In criminal cases where the state will attempt to introduce gruesome photographs, a common defense strategy is to request that black and white photographs be used instead of color; to request that the photographs be censored in some manner to exclude gruesome elements; or to stipulate to the point or issue that the photograph is offered to prove. A common example of an issue to which defendants will stipulate is the cause of death. Thus, rather than have the prosecution enter a photograph depicting the victim lying in a pool of blood with a knife in her body, the defense will stipulate (agree) that the victim was stabbed to death. As a result, the jury will not view the photograph, which could potentially prejudice them against the defendant.

Sound Recordings

The use of sound recordings as evidence raises a number of issues. For example, electronic eavesdropping and similar techniques used to obtain incriminating information are protected by the Fifth Amendment. Indiscriminate sound recording activities can result in the evidence thereby obtained being declared inadmissible. Even if sound recordings are obtained legally, several evidence questions still remain. According to one court, seven steps must be taken before a sound recording will be considered admissible (*State v. Toomer,* 1984):

1. The recording was legally obtained.
2. The device used was capable of recording statements and was operating properly.
3. The operator of the device was competent and operated it properly.
4. The recorded voices were identified.
5. The accuracy and authenticity of the recording is verified.
6. No changes, additions, or deletions have been made to the recording,
7. Evidence is introduced showing an acceptable chain of custody.

Videotapes and Motion Pictures

Videotapes and similar "motion pictures" are often admitted into evidence. Bank robbery videotapes, for example, can be of particular value to the prosecution's case. Videotapes of crime scenes have also been properly admitted (e.g., *Seibert v. State,* 1989). However, at least one court has cautioned against the potential damage that can be done with videotape/motion picture evidence:

> Motion pictures should be received as evidence with caution, because the modern art of photography and the devices of an ingenious director frequently produce results which may be quite deceiving. Telescopic lenses, ingenious settings of the stage, the elimination of unfavorable portions of a film, and angle from which a picture is taken, the ability to speed up the reproduction of the picture and the genius of a director may tend to create misleading impressions. (*Harmon v. San Joaquin L. & P. Corp.,* 1940)

X-rays

Photographs can be authenticated with relative ease. Usually witness testimony to the effect that a photograph genuinely depicts a particular event or thing will suffice. X-rays, however, present a special problem. Because X-ray photographs show only shadows of internal parts of the body, they are not as easy to authenticate. In recent years, courts have held that X-ray photographs can be admitted into evidence if a qualified expert testifies that they are genuine.

Viewing the Crime Scene

As yet another form of real evidence, some jurisdictions actually permit the jury to exit the courtroom and physically view the crime scene. The purpose of doing so is, in part, to surmount some of the problems inherent in other types of real evidence, such as photographs. The argument for these so-called jury views is to enable jurors to more adequately understand the evidence in question as well as the location in which the crime took place. Photographs may not do the scene justice, so an actual visit to the scene may help fill in the gaps. In some criminal cases the accused is allowed to be present; in others he or she is not. Regardless, special care must be taken in facilitating jury views because of their potentially prejudicial and inflammatory effects.

Scientific Evidence

The careful reader is by now asking, what about **scientific evidence?** Such evidence includes blood, hair, DNA, and other samples as well as polygraphs, criminal profiles, spectography, hypnosis, narcoanalysis, statistical analysis, and countless other techniques. Several strict rules govern the admissibility of scientific evidence. As such, we devote a full section in Chapter 10 to scientific evidence. For now, though, we turn to demonstrative evidence, that is, the use of demonstrations and other exercises to help the jury make its decision.

Demonstrative Evidence

The term "demonstrative evidence" appears nowhere in the rules of evidence. Nevertheless, it is well known that charts, drawings, pictures, and other tools can help jurors sort through a complex matter. Some have called demonstrative evidence anything that appeals to the senses. Others have opted for a narrower definition, claiming that demonstrative evidence is that which is conveyed with a "firsthand sense impression" (Strong, 1992). This definition excludes witness testimony, because witness testimony is secondhand. Yet another source calls demonstrative evidence "illustrative evidence" (Brain and Broderick, 1992).

Even though the Federal Rules make no mention of demonstrative evidence, it is still bound by Rules 401 and 403. In particular, the demonstrative evidence in question must be relevant, that is, it must have a tendency to make the existence of a consequential fact more or less probable than it would be without the evidence. Furthermore, demonstrative evidence can be excluded under Rule 403 if its benefits are substantially outweighed by the potential for unfair prejudice, delay, or confusion. These rules notwithstanding, courts are cautious when it comes to considering the admissibility of demonstrative evidence, because of the potential to mislead jurors or mistakenly convey important information.

Drawings and Diagrams

Drawings, diagrams, and similar devices are perhaps the most common forms of demonstrative evidence. For example, the prosecution may rely on a diagram showing where and how the defendant entered the house for the purpose of committing a murder. Similarly, a doctor providing expert testimony may rely on a drawing or illustration of a human body to point out an important feature. The potential uses for drawings and diagrams is limited only by the imagination.

The only barrier to the admissibility of drawings and diagrams (beyond the Rule 401 and 403 concerns discussed above) is authentication. Drawings and diagrams are required to be authenticated. Doing so ensures that a drawing accurately depicts what it is supposed to depict. Authentication of drawings and diagrams is frequently accomplished by testimony from the person who prepared it. Authentication is not always required. For instance, a doctor's reliance on a commonly used drawing of the interior of the human body rarely needs to be accompanied by witness testimony to the effect that the drawing is accurate.

Displays and Demonstrations

Displays and demonstrations are also commonly used to aid the jury with its decision. It would be easier for a jury to understand the severity of a plaintiff's wounds by being able to *see* the wounds as opposed to relying on the plaintiff's testimony. To use a real-world example, one appellate court held that the plaintiff in a civil action should have been allowed to display injuries to her breasts (*Hillman v. Funderburk,* 1986).

Displays and demonstrations are restricted, of course, by standards of decency. It is possible, in other words, to go too far in trying to make a point to the jury. In *Bates v. Newman* (1954), for example, an appellate court held that the trial court properly refused the plaintiff's offer to demonstrate to the jury his ability to hold an erection.

Displays and demonstrations are not limited to physical characteristics of human beings. Demonstrations that depict mechanical processes are also permitted. A witness could use a model of a working engine, for instance, to show the jury precisely what goes on inside the engine when it is running.

Courts are rightly cautious when it comes to admitting displays and demonstrations. Demonstrations might appeal to the jury's sympathies unfairly. They might distort the facts somewhat and "reenact" important events in a manner different from what originally occurred. Demonstrations can also be fabrications. Either way, one court has stated that demonstrations "should be carefully staged" with "the widest opportunity allowed for cross examination" (*United States v. Skinner,* 1970).

One controversial form of demonstrative evidence is known as a "day-in-the-life film." Plaintiffs in workers compensation cases, for example, may wish to demonstrate the effects of a work-related injury (such as a back injury) on their daily lives. Such films need to be authenticated as accurately depicting the true extent of the injuries in question. Further, day-in-the-life films raise hearsay concerns, because the plaintiff may, in the video, make nonverbal "assertions" about his or her injuries.

Computer Animations

According to one author, "Computer animation is likely to become the single most powerful evidentiary tool used by trial lawyers in the [twenty-first century]" (D'Angelo 1998). Even so, computer animation requires authentication under FRE Rule 907(b)(9). Computer animations often amount to "assertions" of their creators, so hearsay concerns are raised with their use. Such concerns are often overcome, however, if the creator of the animation is present in the trial and subject to cross examination.

Computer animations have been used to re-create shooting incidents, car accidents, and countless other events. As one example, the Ninth Circuit Court of Appeals held that a lower court did not abuse its discretion by admitting a computer animation of a shooting with all the facial expressions of the participants removed, even though there was an objection that one simulated party looked like a "nutty android" or "somebody who is crazed" (*Byrd v. Guess,* 1998). In another case, the Tenth Circuit Court of Appeals held that there was no abuse of discretion where a video animation of a train-automobile accident was admitted and where an instruction was given to the jury that the animation was not an actual re-creation of the accident (*Robinson v. Missouri Pac. R. Co.,* 1994). Because computer imagery can have a powerful impact on the jury, courts are and should be cautious about its admission.

Experiments

Experiments of various forms are also used to demonstrate important points to the jury. The term "experiment" is used broadly here; it does not necessarily refer to laboratory experiments conducted under strict conditions of control. For example, one court permitted a film showing a car approaching an inclined ramp, becoming airborne, and landing, all in an effort to show the trajectory of the car (*Bannister v. Town of Noble,*

Okla., 1987). Nearly everyone has seen videos on the news of automobile safety experiments. Videos resulting from such experiments could be used for demonstrative purposes.

In another case (*Brandt v. French,* 1981), the court held that it was appropriate to admit a film of a motorcycle passing cars in order to show how the motorcycle leans when it turns. Another videotaped experiment of a driver of a truck traveling 35 miles per hour and taking his foot off the accelerator one-quarter mile from a curve was properly admitted in order to show that the truck would come to a stop before hitting the curve (see *Champeau v. Fruehauf Corp.,* 1987).

In all the experiment examples thus far, the experiments were conducted out of view of the jury and replayed for them via videotape or film. Of course, it is also possible for an experiment to be conducted before the jury's eyes. An example of this technique can be found in the case of *United State v. Rackley* (1984). The court in that case ruled that the lower court acted appropriately by conducting an experiment in front of the jury of how Biff, a narcotics dog, could sniff out cocaine hidden in closed containers.

Courts are also cautious when it comes to the use of experiments. The most important requirement is that the experiment be conducted under circumstances similar to the event in question. The conditions do not have to be identical, but they should be close. Also, the results from experiments may be excluded if they are unfairly prejudicial or misleading. And, of course, the relevancy requirement still attaches.

Summary

Authentication refers to the originality of evidence. Forms of evidence that frequently require authentication are documents, objects, and voice recordings. Some evidence, however, is self-authenticating. The best evidence rule is related to authentication but is not the same. Whereas authentication focuses on whether evidence is an original, the best evidence rule is concerned with whether the original is required. The best evidence rule is a rule of preference; if an original is available, it should be used.

Real evidence must satisfy the requirements of relevancy, competency, and materiality. It must also follow a proper chain of custody. In addition to evidence such as items connected with a crime, demonstrative and scientific evidence are also considered "real." Because of the complexity and potential problems associated with demonstrative evidence, we devoted special attention to its forms and admissibility requirements.

Discussion Questions

1. What are the ways in which documents can be authenticated?
2. Explain self-authentication. Give examples.
3. Explain the best evidence rule. What is it? What is it not? How does this rule relate to hearsay?
4. Is real evidence protected by the Fifth Amendment? Why or why not?
5. What foundation must be in place before real evidence may be admitted in court? Explain each requirement.
6. Give examples and brief explanations of the six types of real evidence named in the text.
7. Name and explain the types of demonstrative evidence named in the text.

Further Reading

Aitken, C. G. G. (1995). Statistics and the Evaluation of Evidence for Forensic Scientists. New York: John Wiley and Sons.

Brain, R. D., and D. J. Broderick. (1992). "The Derivative Relevance of Demonstrative Evidence: Charting Its Proper Evidentiary Status." University of California, Davis, Law Review. 25:957, 968–969.

D'Angelo, C. (1998). "The Snoop Doggy Dogg Trial: A Look at How Computer Animation Will Impact Litigation in the Next Century." University of San Francisco Law Review 32:561, 585.

Downs, D. A. (1998). More Than Victims: Battered Women, the Syndrome Society, and the Law. Chicago: University of Chicago Press.

Foster, K. W. and P. W. Huber. (1999). Judging Science: Scientific Knowledge and the Federal Courts. Cambridge, MA: MIT Press.

Goldstein, E. (1995). Visual Evidence: A Practitioner's Manual. Toronto, ON: Carswell.

Imwinkelried, E. J. (1992). Methods of Attacking Scientific Evidence (2nd ed.). Charlottesville, NC: Michie.

Moenssens, A. A. (1995). Scientific Evidence in Criminal Cases (4th ed.). Westbury, NY: Foundation Press.

Robertson, B. J. and G. A. Vignaux. (1995). Interpreting Evidence: Evaluating Forensic Science in the Courtroom. New York: John Wiley and Sons.

Rychlak, R. J. (1995). Real and Demonstrative Evidence: Application and Theory. Charlottesville, NC: Michie Butterworth.

Strong, J. W. (1992). McCormick on Evidence (4th ed.). Eagan, MN: West.

Cases Cited

Bannister v. Town of Noble, Okla., 812 F.2d 1265 (10th Cir. 1987)

Bates v. Newman, 121 Cal. App. 2d 800 (1954)

Brandt v. French, 638 F.2d 209 (10th Cir. 1981)

Byrd v. Guess, 137 F.3d 1126 (9th Cir. 1998)

Champeau v. Fruehauf Corp., 814 F.2d 1271 (8th Cir. 1987)

Continental Trust Co. v. Bank of Harrison, 36 Ga. App. 149 (1926)

Conway v. Consolidated Rail Corp., 720 F.2d 221 (1st Cir. 1983)

Harmon v. San Joaquin L. & P. Corp., 37 Cal. App. 2d 1064 (1940)

Hill v. State, 159 Ga. App. 489 (1981)

Hillman v. Funderburk, 504 A.2d 596 (D.C. App. 1986)

Hood v. Itawamba County, Miss., 819 F. Supp. 556 (N.D. Miss. 1993)

Miranda v. Arizona, 384 U.S. 436 (1966)

People v. Duran, 16 Cal. 3d 282 (1976)

People v. Riser, 47 Cal. 2d 566 (1956)

Robinson v. Missouri Pac. R. Co., 16 F.3d 1083 (10th Cir. 1994)

Sanders v. State, 317 Ark. 328 (1994)

Schmerber v. California, 384 U.S. 757 (1966)

Seibert v. State, 555 So. 2d 772 (Ala. 1989)

State v. Atkins, 697 S.W.2d 226 (Mo. App. 1985)

State v. Toomer, 311 N.S. 183 (1984)

United States v. Brown, 16 F.3d 423 (D.C. Cir. 1994)

United States v. Harrington, 923 F.2d 1371 (9th Cir. 1991)

United States v. Lance, 853 F.2d 1177 (5th Cir. 1988)

United States v. Portsmouth Paving Corp., 694 F.2d 312 (4th Cir. 1982)

United States v. Rackley, 742 F.2d 1266 (1984)

United States v. Skinner, 425 F.2d 552 (D.C. Cir. 1970)

United States v. Wilson, 690 F.2d 1267 (9th Cir. 1982)

Warden v. Hayden, 387 U.S. 294 (1967)

CHAPTER 10

EXPERT WITNESSES AND SCIENTIFIC EVIDENCE

Key Terms & Concepts

Bases for expert opinions	Polygraph evidence	Rule 706
Court-appointed expert	Profile	Scientific evidence
Daubert test	Reliability	Statistics
DNA evidence	Rule 702	Syndrome
Expert witness	Rule 703	Ultimate issue rule
Frye test	Rule 704	Validity
Opinion evidence	Rule 705	Voir dire

Chapter Learning Objectives

By the end of this chapter, the student should be able to:

- Relate the prerequisites for establishing expertise
- List the types of subject matter about which experts commonly testify
- Explain the difference between the *Frye* and *Daubert* tests
- Understand the controversy surrounding polygraph evidence
- Identify factors that affect the reliability of eyewitness testimony
- Explain how expert testimony regarding various syndromes (battered woman, rape trauma, child abuse) is handled by the courts
- Identify the typical characteristics of drug couriers through the use of criminal profiles

Introduction

The use of expert testimony in criminal cases has increased in recent years. This reliance is commensurate with the significant technological and scientific developments that our world has experienced. As such, understanding the manner in which expert testimony is presented is essential to students. This chapter will examine the use of experts and the manner in which expert testimony must be presented. However, it is important to keep in mind material from Chapter 8 regarding the order of questioning, objections, and other matters presented. While these topics are not reexamined here, they play an important role in the use of expert witnesses.

More specifically, this chapter identifies the criteria necessary for establishing expertise. Whether experts are called by a party to the case or are appointed by the court, they must meet certain criteria. The chapter explains the types of subject matter to which expert witnesses can testify and devotes attention to the various forms of scientific evidence, statistical, DNA, and polygraph. It also considers debate surrounding the use of eyewitness testimony. In sum, the chapter seeks to provide students with a solid working knowledge of how expertise is established and the role of expert witnesses in the evidentiary world.

Expert Witnesses

Modern statutes do not actually define what it means to be an expert; nevertheless, an expert witness can be defined as anyone who knows more about the subject testimony than the average juror would. The Federal Rules of Evidence (Rule 702) state that a witness is an "expert" if he or she is "qualified" to help the jury "understand the evidence" or "determine a fact in issue" by virtue of his or her "knowledge, skill, experience, training, or education." Similarly, the California Evidence Code (Section 720), like most states, describes an expert as one who "has special knowledge, skill, experience, training or education sufficient to qualify him as an expert on the subject to which his testimony relates."

Rule 702. Testimony by Experts

If scientific, technical, or other specialized knowledge will assist the trier of fact to understand the evidence or to determine a fact in issue, a witness qualified as an expert by knowledge, skill, experience, training, or education, may testify thereto in the form of an opinion or otherwise, if (1) the testimony is based upon sufficient facts or data, (2) the testimony is the product of reliable principles and methods, and (3) the witness has applied the principles and methods reliably to the facts of the case.

http://www.law.cornell.edu/rules/fre/ACRule702.htm

Types of Experts

There are two types of expert witnesses: (1) degree-bearing experts, and (2) non-degree-bearing experts. Degree-bearing experts are those individuals conjured up in most people's minds when they think of the term "expert." There are persons who have been certified by some educational institution as knowledgeable in some subject. The educational institution does not necessarily have to be a university or college. Non-degree-bearing experts include individuals who through education or *experience* know something that jurors do not.

The Prerequisites for Expert Testimony

http://www.daubertontheweb.com/

For an expert witness to be used, three prerequisites must be in place. First, there must be a *need* for expert testimony. If the facts can be understood by lay jurors, there is no need for an expert. For example, common knowledge (e.g., that objects fall toward earth when dropped) does not need expert testimony. However, specific knowledge—say, of what type of track a certain tire will leave behind—often requires expert interpretation.

The second prerequisite for expert testimony is that a sufficiently established body of knowledge exists on the subject about which the expert will testify. In other words, the expert's field must be one requiring specific scientific or technical knowledge. Several tests are in place to determine whether a relevant knowledge base exists. In *Daubert v. Merrell Dow Pharmaceuticals, Inc.* (1993) the Supreme Court created a test for determining whether the expert's field has reached the level of "scientific knowledge." The so-called *Daubert* **test** requires that the trial judge make the determination based on two primary factors: (1) The science must be valid, and (2) the evidence must "fit" the case. Prior to the *Daubert* test, the Supreme Court relied on the *Frye* **test,** which required that expert testimony be based on scientific knowledge "generally accepted as reliable in the relevant scientific community."

Often the courts will deem a certain body of knowledge, for lack of a better word, "unscientific." A good example is polygraphs. Many people believe that a well-trained polygraph operator can tell when a person is lying, but the courts have been reluctant to rely on polygraph evidence. In a similar vein, courts do not rely on psychic testimony or astrology, because both fields lack a scientific base.

The third prerequisite is that the witness must be shown to have a background necessary to qualify as an expert in the field. Because the process can be somewhat complicated and arduous, we reserve the next subsection for a discussion of what it takes to qualify as an expert witness.

Daubert v. Merrell Dow Pharmaceuticals, Inc.
Supreme Court of of the United States
509 U.S. 579 (1993)

Petitioners Jason Daubert and Eric Schuller are minor children born with serious birth defects. They and their parents sued respondent in California state court, alleging that the birth defects had been caused by the mothers' ingestion of Bendectin, a prescription antinausea drug marketed by respondent. Respondent removed the suits to federal court on diversity grounds.

After extensive discovery, respondent moved for summary judgment, contending that Bendectin does not cause birth defects in humans and that petitioners would be unable to come forward with any admissible evidence that it does. In support of its motion, respondent submitted an affidavit of Steven H. Lamm, physician and epidemiologist, who is a well-credentialed expert on the risks from exposure to various chemical substances. Doctor Lamm stated that he had reviewed all the literature on Bendectin and human birth defects, more than 30 published studies involving over 130,000 patients. No study had found Bendectin to be a human teratogen (i.e., a substance capable of causing malformations in fetuses). On the basis of this review, Doctor Lamm concluded that maternal use of Bendectin during the first trimester of pregnancy has not been shown to be a risk factor for human birth defects.

*****

The United States Court of Appeals for the Ninth Circuit affirmed. Citing *Frye v. United States* (1923), the court stated that expert opinion based on a scientific technique is inadmissible unless the technique is "generally accepted" as reliable in the relevant scientific community. The court declared that expert opinion based on a methodology that diverges "significantly from the procedures accepted by recognized authorities in the field . . . cannot be shown to be 'generally accepted as a reliable technique.'"

The court emphasized that other Courts of Appeals considering the risks of Bendectin had refused to admit re-analyses of epidemiological studies that had been neither published nor subjected to peer review. Those courts had found unpublished re-analyses "particularly problematic in light of the massive weight of the original published studies

(continued)

supporting [respondent's] position, all of which had undergone full scrutiny from the scientific community." Contending that reanalysis is generally accepted by the scientific community only when it is subjected to verification and scrutiny by others in the field, the Court of Appeals rejected petitioners' re-analyses as "unpublished, not subjected to the normal peer review process and generated solely for use in litigation." The court concluded that petitioners' evidence provided an insufficient foundation to allow admission of expert testimony that Bendectin caused their injuries and, accordingly, that petitioners could not satisfy their burden of proving causation at trial.

We granted certiorari in light of sharp divisions among the courts regarding the proper standard for the admission of expert testimony.

*****

The primary locus of this obligation is Rule 702, which clearly contemplates some degree of regulation of the subjects and theories about which an expert may testify. "If scientific, technical, or other specialized knowledge will assist the trier of fact to understand the evidence or to determine a fact in issue" an expert "may testify thereto." The subject of an expert's testimony must be "scientific . . . knowledge." The adjective "scientific" implies a grounding in the methods and procedures of science. Similarly, the word "knowledge" connotes more than subjective belief or unsupported speculation. The term "applies to any body of known facts or to any body of ideas inferred from such facts or accepted as truths on good grounds." Of course, it would be unreasonable to conclude that the subject of scientific testimony must be "known" to a certainty; arguably, there are no certainties in science. But, in order to qualify as "scientific knowledge," an inference or assertion must be derived by the scientific method. Proposed testimony must be supported by appropriate validation (i.e., "good grounds") based on what is known. In short, the requirement that an expert's testimony pertain to "scientific knowledge" establishes a standard of evidentiary reliability.

*****

To summarize: "General acceptance" is not a necessary precondition to the admissibility of scientific evidence under the Federal Rules of Evidence, but the Rules of Evidence, especially Rule 702, do assign to the trial judge the task of ensuring that an expert's testimony both rests on a reliable foundation and is relevant to the task at hand.

(continued)

Pertinent evidence based on scientifically valid principles will satisfy those demands.

*****

The inquiries of the District Court and the Court of Appeals focused almost exclusively on "general acceptance," as gauged by publication and the decisions of other courts. Accordingly, the judgment of the Court of Appeals is vacated, and the case is remanded for further proceedings consistent with this opinion.

It is so ordered.

The Third Prerequisite in Depth: Deciding Who Is an Expert

Once it is clear that an expert is needed and that a sufficient body of scientific knowledge exists, the decision as to who will be considered an expert is left to the judge. However, before the judge can make his or her decision as to whether a person will be allowed to testify as an expert, a voir dire process must take place. **Voir dire** in this context is a questioning process in which the expert's "expertise" is established or refuted.

The party calling the supposed expert must begin by qualifying the witness as an expert. Usually the calling party does so without reservation, because qualifying the expert lends credibility to the witness's testimony. This qualification process takes place when the witness answers questions posed by the calling party. The calling party will ask questions about the witness's education, experience, training, and work in order to establish that he or she is an expert. Indeed, the calling party may go to great lengths in questioning the witness (above and beyond education and experience) to convince the trial judge that the witness is in fact an expert in his or her field.

After this preliminary questioning, many jurisdictions require that the calling party formally tender the witness. This means that (1) the qualification process has been concluded, and (2) the calling party is asking the court to recognize this witness as an expert. The opposing attorney can then conduct his or her on voir dire examination of the witness. The opposing side's questions are usually asked before the witness offers opinions, as we will see later. This procedure allows the opposing attorney to convince the judge that the supposed expert is not actually an "expert" in the field. For example, opposing counsel may attempt to show that the witness lacks the necessary education and qualification to serve as an expert witness. It is advisable, therefore, that the party seeking to qualify an expert go to lengths to ensure that the witness's expertise cannot be refuted by the opposing side.

An expert witness need not be renowned in his or her field (e.g., *United States v. Rose*, 1984, 1346). On the other hand, minimal preparation or experience should not be viewed as sufficient to qualify one as an expert. Unfortunately, there are no hard and fast rules as to what level of experience and training is sufficient. In the end, the trial judge will make the determination as to whether a witness can be considered an expert. Once the decision is made to recognize a witness as an expert, the jury then decides what amount of weight will be given to the witness's testimony.

Court-Appointed Experts

It is easy for jury members to become confused when experts for opposing sides testify as to the same issue. For example, the prosecution's expert may argue that an automobile accident was caused by the defendant. The defense attorney's expert may argue, on the contrary, that the defendant could not possibly have been responsible. Who is the jury to believe? This quandary can be especially significant if the prosecution and defense both call several expert witnesses. One solution to this problem is a court-appointed expert.

The Federal Rules of Evidence (**Rule 706**) state, in part that, "the court may on its own motion or on the motion of any party enter an order to show cause why expert witnesses should not be appointed, and may request the parties to submit nominations." Further, "The court may appoint any expert witnesses agreed upon by the parties, and may appoint expert witnesses of its own selection." A court-appointed expert is supposedly one who is neutral and objective and so inclined not to side, a priori, with either the prosecution or the defense.

Rule 706. Court Appointed Experts

(a) Appointment.

The court may on its own motion or on the motion of any party enter an order to show cause why expert witnesses should not be appointed, and may request the parties to submit nominations. The court may appoint any expert witnesses agreed upon by the parties, and may appoint expert witnesses of its own selection. An expert witness shall not be appointed by the court unless the witness consents to act. A witness so appointed shall be informed of the witness' duties by the court in writing, a copy of which shall be filed with the clerk, or at a conference in which the parties shall have opportunity to participate. A witness so appointed shall advise the parties of the witness' findings, if any; the witness' deposition may be taken by any party; and the witness may be called to testify by the court or any party. The witness shall be subject to cross-examination by each party, including a party calling the witness.

(b) Compensation.

Expert witnesses so appointed are entitled to reasonable compensation in whatever sum the court may allow. The compensation thus fixed is payable from funds which may be provided by law in criminal cases and civil actions and proceedings involving just compensation under the Fifth Amendment. In other civil actions and proceedings the compensation shall be paid by the parties in such proportion and at such time as the court directs, and thereafter charged in like manner as other costs.

(c) Disclosure of appointment.

In the exercise of its discretion, the court may authorize disclosure to the jury of the fact that the court appointed the expert witness.

(d) Parties' experts of own selection.

Nothing in this rule limits the parties in calling expert witnesses of their own selection.

http://www.law.cornell.edu/rules/fre/ACRule706.htm

The decision of whether to select a court-appointed expert (as opposed to one or several called by the parties to the case) is entirely discretionary; courts are not under any obligation to do so. However, in situations in which the prosecution and defense experts fail to produce evidence of clear probity, a court-appointed expert may be desirable (e.g., *Students of California School for Blind v. Honig*, 1984).

As a general rule, court-appointed experts should be relied upon only when absolutely necessary, because the prosecution and the defense bear the main responsibility for presenting their sides of the case. Courts decide matters of law and usually know less about the evidence and issues than the lawyers representing the government and the accused. However, when court-appointed experts *are* used, it is best if the wheels are set in motion long before trial. Stopping a trial for the purpose of selecting a court-appointed expert can be quite disruptive.

The procedure for selecting court-appointed experts established by Rule 706 contains five elements:

1. The trial judge has broad discretion in deciding whether and whom to appoint, but both parties to the case should be able to be heard on the matter if they so desire. Actions by the court in accordance with this rule do not affect the rights of the opposing parties to call their own experts.

2. Court-appointed experts must consent to testify. In other words, courts should avoid compelling witnesses to serve as court-appointed

experts. However, the court's (like the opposing side's) subpoena power can ensure that a witness serve as a court-appointed expert (see *Kaufman v. Edelstein*, 1976, 820–821).

3. The court-appointed expert must be notified of his or her duties in advance of testimony. This notice is to be provided in writing.

4. The court-appointed expert is to advise the parties of his or her findings. Either party may take the expert's deposition. The witness may also be called to testify by the court or by either party to the case.

5. Finally, the court-appointed expert shall be subject to cross examination by both parties to the case.

Subjects of Expert Witness Testimony

Experts can testify to countless subjects, but we briefly consider several common subjects here.

1. *Automobile accidents.* For example, a police officer with several years of experience investigating accidents and who is extensively trained in accident investigation may serve as an expert (see *Bonner v. Polacari*, 1965).

2. *Physical and mental condition.* Experts often testify to the defendant's mental condition (such as after ingesting drugs), but courts usually do not allow experts to render opinions in such situations. For example, an expert in the effects of a drug on a person's mental condition could testify as to the likely effect that a certain amount of drugs will have on a person generally. However, such a witness will probably not be allowed to offer an opinion as to whether the defendant was affected in the same way (see, for example, *People v. Cronin*, 1983).

3. *Handwriting comparisons.* Experts will occasionally testify that a piece of handwriting was written by a certain person. For example, in a prosecution for conspiracy to import marijuana, the trial court allowed a handwriting expert to testify that he had a "high degree of belief" that the handwriting on a motel bill was that of one of the defendants. Of course, it is up to the jury in such situations to decide whether the expert's testimony should carry weight.

4. *Typewriter comparisons.* Prior to the advent of computers, experts would testify that a typewritten documents came from a specific typewriter. Experts could even determine that a document came from a specific model of typewriter without actually having to see or handle the particular typewriter responsible for the document. In some cases, courts have even allowed typewriter comparison experts to draw opinions about the identity of the operator of the typewriter (see, for example, *Thomas v. State*, 1946).

5. *Voice print identification.* Some states authorize the use of spectrographic voice print evidence. Devices are used to compare the defendant's voice with a voice print recorded from an earlier conversation (such as during a telephone call). In *United States v. Williams* (1978), the Second Circuit noted that, "spectrographic voice analysis evidence is not so inherently unreliable or misleading as to require its exclusion from the jury's consideration in every case." Understand, however, that voice print identification is not permissible in every (or even most) jurisdiction throughout the country.

6. *Neutron activation analysis.* On some occasions suspects in shootings have their hands swabbed with a nitric acid solution. Then a neutron activation analysis is used to determine whether the suspect fired a gun recently. In one case, *State v. Spencer* (1974), the Minnesota Supreme Court upheld an expert's testimony as to the results of neutron activation analysis. In that case, a suspect was accused of shooting a police officer. After the suspect was taken into custody, his hands were swabbed with the solution. The swabs were then sent to the Treasury Department laboratory in Washington, D.C. The court concluded:

We believe that neutron activation analysis is a useful law enforcement technique and that the increasing use of technology in criminal investigation should not be inhibited but encouraged where consistent with the rights of the accused. (pp. 461–462)

The court also expressed concern, however, about unrestricted use of neutron activation analysis:

An expert witness could be permitted to testify that in his opinion the chemicals present on the defendant's hand may have resulted from the firing of a gun. He should not have been permitted to state, as he did, that this defendant had definitely fired a gun. To allow this testimony to stand without a cautionary instruction to the jury was technical error. (p. 461)

7. *Fingerprint identification.* To show that fingerprints lifted from a crime scene are that of the defendant usually requires expert testimony. In an illustrative case, one court found that a police officer, who was a veteran of the sheriff's department and who had extensive training in footprints and latent prints, was qualified to testify as an expert (*State v. Oliver,* 1987). Not just any law enforcement officer will be permitted to testify as an expert for the purpose of fingerprint identification; special training and expertise are usually required.

8. *Insanity.* Experts are required when mental disorders are raised as defenses to criminal liability. Perhaps the best example of a mental disorder raised at trial (albeit rarely) is insanity. The expert, usually a trained psychiatrist, will explain to the jury the effect of the condition on the personality and likely behavior of the accused. The defense expert will argue that the defendant could not form the requisite mens rea required for criminal liability; the prosecution's expert, on the other hand, will argue that the defendant should be found guilty of the crime with which he or she is charged.

9. *Ballistics.* When a bullet slug is recovered from the scene of a crime, an expert is necessary to convince the jury that the slug came from a particular gun. The pattern of marks and grooves in the barrel of a gun leaves a particular pattern on the bullet fired. If the gun is recovered, a ballistics expert can test-fire the gun, then conduct a microscopic comparison of the two bullets to find a positive match.

10. *Testimony concerning drug operations.* Expert witnesses are often called on to testify about the price of narcotics, the language used by drug dealers, and the nuances of complex drug manufacturing operations. In several cases, the courts have permitted expert opinions as to the meaning of "drug lingo" (e.g., *United States v. Nunez,* 1987). In another case, a trial court properly admitted a police officer's expert testimony regarding the countersurveillance techniques used by a drug dealer to avoid apprehension (*United States v. DeSoto,* 1989).

11. *Others.* Experts are relied for a wide variety of other determinations. Some of these include the modus operandi of offenders, such as in serial killing cases (e.g., *Johninson v. State,* 1994); cause of death (e.g., *State v. Vining,* 1994); blood and tissue matching; and polygraph examinations, where permissible (e.g., *United States v. Miller,* 1989).

United States v. DeSoto
Seventh Circuit
885 F.2d 354 (1989)

The defendants, Gustavo Chaverra Cardona, Ruth Urrego Chaverra, and Maria Urrego DeSoto, appeal their convictions for various drug trafficking offenses; a jury found each defendant guilty of conspiring to distribute cocaine in violation of 21 U.S.C. §846 and of several

(continued)

counts of possession of cocaine with intent to distribute in violation of 21 U.S.C. §841(a)(1). The defendants appeal on a multitude of grounds. We affirm.

*****

Lieutenant Dailey testified as an expert with respect to "countersurveillance" techniques employed by drug dealers to avoid detection by competitors or the police. As an example of such a technique, the Lieutenant noted that when "on the street when they are on foot they constantly stop and look back and forth at the street traffic to see if anyone is watching them." Later on in his testimony, while describing the events of October 16, Lt. Dailey recounted how he twice witnessed Sanchez emerge from Ms. DeSoto's building (once accompanied by Ms. DeSoto) and look up and down the street while standing on the stoop. When asked by the prosecutor to describe Sanchez' activity more precisely, Lt. Dailey stated that Sanchez "was looking for either us, the police, or any type agents or, again, competitors that may be concerned what his activities were." Sanchez' actions "definitely" constituted countersurveillance, in Lt. Dailey's opinion. Mr. Chaverra now submits that Lt. Dailey's interpretation of these outwardly commonplace and innocuous actions, looking up and down a street, was based on mere speculation and improperly imposed the imprimatur of expert testimony on an otherwise straightforward narrative. Therefore, the defendant further argues, Lt. Dailey's testimony should have been excluded as intruding on the exclusive province of the jury. Under the circumstances set forth in this record, we cannot agree.

As we have noted earlier, testimony by law enforcement officers regarding drug countersurveillance may be admitted as expert testimony. For example, in *United States v. Stewart*, the Ninth Circuit "upheld admission of DEA agents' opinion testimony that the defendant's activities were similar to the modus operandi of persons conducting counter-surveillance while transporting drugs." The particular conduct as to which the agents testified in Stewart and Maher was the manner in which the defendants drove their carscircuitously touring the drop-off point several times before stopping. Such activity, especially in city streets with congested parking spaces, may appear, to the outside observer, to be perfectly normal and innocent, just like looking up and down a street. As the Ninth Circuit concluded, however, the everyday appearance of the activity is not an automatic bar to the admission of expert testimony, which may attribute a more sinister motive to the actions.

(continued)

However, because such activities are usually innocent, the district court must be especially vigilant in ensuring that a law enforcement expert's testimony does not unfairly prejudice the defendant or usurp the jury's function. Consequently, there are limits to admission of this type of testimony: the expert must not base his opinion on mere speculation; nor can he speak, as an expert, to matters that the jury can evaluate for itself.

Our review of the record convinces us that, in this case, the district court was well aware of its special responsibilities and proceeded with the utmost caution. Immediately before Lt. Dailey testified, the district court carefully considered the defendants' arguments to exclude this expert testimony. It stated that:

> What we're dealing with here, as I understand it, is the projected testimony of someone who has observed a lot of narcotics trans-actions, and has observed conduct that might, to someone who has not had that as part of his or her common experience, appear either perfectly innocuous or perhaps with argument might view that with some degree of suspicion.

After that characterization of Lt. Dailey's proposed testimony, the court allowed admission of the evidence. However, later on, during the testimony of Lt. Dailey, the district court admonished the jury "that the fact that an expert has given an opinion does not mean that it[']s binding on you. . . . You should assess the weight that's to be accorded to this expert opinion in the light of all of the evidence in the case." This instruction was repeated to the jury at the conclusion of the trial. Finally, and most importantly, the jury had an opportunity to hear the defendants' arguments, which cast all these activities in an innocent light. ("An American jury needs something more than a policeman saying looking up and down a street is countersurveillance and he was engaged in countersurveillance and that's it.") On this record, we cannot say that the district court abused its discretion in admitting Lt. Dailey's testimony regarding countersurveillance.

Protection Under the Fifth Amendment

Any witness, other than the accused, has the privilege to refuse to disclose any information that may "tend to incriminate" him or her. The witness is not on trial; the witness is only on the stand to provide information about what happened. Thus, witnesses cannot "plead the Fifth" simply because they are nervous about answering questions (perhaps out of fear of retaliation by the defendant or his or her cronies). Only if the answer to a question tends to incriminate the witness may he or she assert Fifth Amendment protection. For example, if the prosecution asks a witness, "Did you, Mr. Smith, sell narcotics with the defendant?" Smith would be within his rights to refuse to answer such a question. Indeed, the question need not be so explicit. For the Fifth Amendment privilege against self-incrimination to apply, the answer need only furnish a link in the chain of evidence needed to prosecute.

Expert Witness Opinions

As indicated earlier, an expert is anyone who knows more about the subject of his or her testimony than the typical juror would. Of great importance in criminal cases are the opinions of expert witnesses. Because expert testimony can be instrumental in the jury's decision, special rules apply to their opinions. For example, Rules 702 through 706 of the Federal Rules of Evidence all govern the testimony of expert witnesses.

The rules governing expert witness opinions arise, in part, from fears that expert witnesses may unfairly influence the jury. For one thing, experts (unlike lay witnesses) are not required to have personal knowledge of what they testify about (e.g., experts do not need to be insane to testify about a party's supposed insanity). This means that the potential exists for nearly unlimited numbers of expert witnesses in a given trial, taking up valuable time. Second, because experts are generally paid for their testimony, their "opinion" may be motivated by the payment. Lay witnesses do not enjoy the same compensation, so judges occasionally fear the potential influence of expert opinions on jurors. Experts can also serve as channels for a great deal of hearsay evidence, again, because their testimony does not have to be based on personal knowledge.

As a result of these and other fears, courts have placed great restrictions on expert opinions. This does not mean that courts restrict the "substance" of expert testimony. Rather, courts are especially cautious about the "techniques" experts have at their disposal to win over the jury. For example, a prosecution expert in a criminal case may have the knowledge to testify that the likelihood of the defendant being insane is one in 300 million (numbers may exist to back this or a similar claim), but it has been held that an expert witness, especially one who specializes in probability theory, cannot explain to jurors how he or she may go about calculating the probability of the defendant's guilt (see

People v. Collins, 1968). The courts prefer that there be a "valid scientific connection" between X and Y, not a mere probability.

Bases for Expert Opinions

Lay witness testimony generally requires personal knowledge. With experts, this is not the case. The basis of expert opinion can be of several forms. Under **Rule 703**, an expert's opinion can be based on one or more of the following source.

Rule 703. Bases of Opinion Testimony by Experts

The facts or data in the particular case upon which an expert bases an opinion or inference may be those perceived by or made known to the expert at or before the hearing. If of a type reasonably relied upon by experts in the particular field in forming opinions or inferences upon the subject, the facts or data need not be admissible in evidence in order for the opinion or inference to be admitted. Facts or data that are otherwise inadmissible shall not be disclosed to the jury by the proponent of the opinion or inference unless the court determines that their probative value in assisting the jury to evaluate the expert's opinion substantially outweighs their prejudicial effect.

http://www.law.cornell.edu/rules/fre/ACRule703.htm

1. *Personal knowledge acquired prior to trial.* Rule 703 provides that an expert may rely on "facts or data perceived or made known to the expert before the hearing." This information includes, for example, that gained from physical inspection of a person or thing. For instance, a physician who conducted the autopsy prior to a criminal trial may testify as to the supposed cause of death.
2. *Personal knowledge acquired at trial.* Rule 703 provides furthermore that experts may rely on "facts or data perceived by the expert at the hearing." For example, the expert may watch the conduct of the accused at trial and opine that the defendant was insane. Or, the examining party may ask the expert a hypothetical question based on knowledge acquired at trial. This approach involves asking the expert to assume the truth of a prior witness's (or witnesses') opinion, then offer an opinion.
3. *Hearsay statements of others/secondhand information.* An expert might read scientific literature, read police reports, examine records, review depositions, or engage in any number of similar activities to gain knowledge. If the secondhand information is unpersuasive, however,

the court may restrict expert opinion testimony based on such information. Allowing hearsay as a basis for expert opinion raises questions about confrontation rights. In particular, expert testimony relying on out-of-court statements can invite challenge, particularly in criminal trials, under the confrontation clause discussed earlier. To date, however, the Supreme Court has not decided on this matter. Finally, an expert who relies on a scholarly publication, when expressing his or her opinion can be cross examined concerning statements in the publication that are inconsistent with the expert's opinion. For example, if an expert opines that based on his reading of X's treatise on automotive repair that transmissions should be serviced every 30,000 miles, he or she can be confronted on cross concerning X's recommendation that engine oil be changed every 100,000 miles, which is obviously wrong. The intent of this form of cross examination is to cast doubt on the credibility of the information supplied in the source, thereby weakening the persuasiveness of the expert's opinion.

4. *Testimony at trial.* A person may testify at trial to a particular fact, and the expert could formulate an opinion based on such testimony. For example, a witness may testify that she saw the defendant exchange small baggies for cash with another person. The expert may testify that her opinion is that the other witness observed an illicit drug transaction.

5. *Exception.* None of the four bases for expert opinion just introduced can serve as the basis for an expert opinion if it cannot be reasonably relied on (i.e., if there is no scientific basis for such opinion). For example, a defense expert cannot testify that she read a study indicating that the "stars determine one's destiny," because there is no scientific basis for astrology.

Disclosing Facts and Data

Assume that an expert for the plaintiff in a civil rights action argues that, "the majority of law enforcement agencies in the United States are dependent on the monies generated from civil asset forfeiture in the war on drugs." Assume further that this expert's opinion is based on a survey he conducted of several hundred law enforcement agencies across the country. Should he be required to make available to the court the data used to support his opinion? The short answer to this question is no, but it is within the discretion of the court to decide whether such information should be required.

Rule 705. Disclosure of Facts or Data Underlying Expert Opinion

The expert may testify in terms of opinion or inference and give reasons therefore without first testifying to the underlying facts or data, unless the court requires otherwise. The expert may in any event be required to disclose the underlying facts or data on cross-examination.

http://www.law.cornell.edu/rules/fre/ACRule705.htm

Rule 705 provides that "The expert may testify in terms of opinion or inference and give reasons therefore without first testifying to the underlying facts or data, unless the court requires otherwise." The reason that experts are rarely required to disclose the facts and/or data responsible for their opinions is that it would take too long (and be too confusing to the jury, perhaps) to require the details. Also, this "shorthand" approach to expert testimony provides the party calling the witness with some flexibility. That is, the expert is given a measure of creative license with regard to an opinion when he or she is not required to spell out all the details forming the basis of the opinion.

This does not mean that the expert can offer an opinion that is unsupported. As in other areas of evidence law, a fine line exists here. This line weighs the benefits of efficiency, expediency, and clarity against the costs of sacrificing the details of potential interest to the trier of fact.

In which situations would the court require disclosure? First, disclosure is needed if the expert's opinion is based on "cutting edge" research, that is, research that is on the frontier of scientific understanding. If the knowledge base is relatively new and undeveloped, some attention to the details underlying an expert's opinion may be desirable. Second, it may be essential that underlying facts and/or data be supplied in order to understand the expert's opinion. For example, if the expert testifies as to a person's mental condition, the jury would probably want to hear some of the reasons for such a diagnosis. Either way, underlying facts and data can be required at trial or at a pretrial hearing of some sort.

The Ultimate Issue Rule

Our discussion of opinion evidence would not be complete without some attention to the common law **ultimate issue rule**. Although it is largely abandoned nowadays, the ultimate issue rule prohibited experts from expressing opinions on final issues of which the judge or jury was charged with deciding. **Rule 704** is testament to the disliked ultimate issue rule: ". . . testimony in the form of an opinion or inference otherwise admissible is not objectionable because it embraces an ultimate issue to be decided by the trier of fact."

Rule 704. Opinion on Ultimate Issue

(a) Except as provided in subdivision (b), testimony in the form of an opinion or inference otherwise admissible is not objectionable because it embraces an ultimate issue to be decided by the trier of fact.

(b) No expert witness testifying with respect to the mental state or condition of a defendant in a criminal case may state an opinion or inference as to whether the defendant did or did not have the mental state or condition constituting an element of the crime charged or of a defense thereto. Such ultimate issues are matters for the trier of fact alone.

http://www.law.cornell.edu/rules/fre/ACRule704.htm

The logic behind Rule 704(a) is simple: Witnesses should not be able to testify that "the defendant is guilty" or that the "defendant should lose," but to exclude all opinions as to ultimate issues seemed unfair to the authors of the Federal Rules of Evidence. It is helpful, for instance, to occasionally allow witnesses to testify to such issues as "the defendant was drunk" or "the car was traveling too fast." A blanket rule prohibiting all conclusions as to ultimate issues seemed a bit excessive.

Rule 704(b), however, does prohibit witnesses from drawing conclusions on ultimate issues, but only with regard to mental condition:

No expert witness testifying with respect to the mental state or condition of a defendant in a criminal case may state an opinion or inference as to whether the defendant did or did not have the mental state or condition constituting an element of the crime charged or of a defense thereto.

What this means is that an expert witness in a criminal case cannot testify that the defendant was insane. This exception to Rule 704(a) was revived in light of the highly public trial of John Hinckley, Jr., who was charged with attempting to assassinate President Ronald Reagan. In 1984, Congress reinstated the M'Naghten rule, which states that a criminal defendant will succeed with an insanity plea if he or she is "unable to appreciate the nature and quality or the wrongfulness of his acts." The jury, not the expert witness, should make such a determination.

There are also reasons for Rule 704(b). First, it is designed to eliminate conflicting expert testimony, at least as far as sanity is concerned. At common law, jurors could become confused by expert testimony for the defense and the prosecution in a trial in which the insanity defense was raised; one side could conclude that the defendant was sane, the other that the defendant was insane. Allowing the jury to decide this issue supposedly makes the guilty/not guilty decision an easier one. Second, Rule 704(b) also helps ensure that the jury hears full information concerning an expert's diagnosis, not just an uninformative statement that, for instance, "the defendant is insane." Finally, Rule 704(b) ensures that the expert witnesses do not overstep their bounds and take the decision-making function away from the trier of fact.

Recently, Rule 704(b) has been interpreted to include not just insanity but all mental conditions that constitute elements of the charged offense. For example, in *United States v. DiDomenico* (1993), the Second Circuit barred testimony that the defendant suffered from a condition that would prevent her from knowing that equipment was stolen. Indeed, the rule prohibits any expert testimony that the defendant could (or could not) form the requisite mens rea of the offense charged. The rule also prohibits expert testimony as to the mental state required to succeed with criminal defenses such as duress, intoxication, and entrapment. Even so, Rule 704(b) does not apply to lay testimony, and it only restricts expert testimony on the mental state of criminal defendants, not third parties or the parties to any civil action.

Scientific Evidence

Earlier we examined the important case of *Daubert v. Merrell Dow Pharmaceuticals* (1993). In it the Supreme Court declared that scientific testimony must be "supported by appropriate validation" and must have a "valid scientific connection" or "fit" with the issues in the case. The *Daubert* decision did away with the earlier *Frye* (1923) decision, namely that scientific validity was shown if the science had gained "general acceptance."

There are two critical requirements for meeting the *Daubert* standard. First, the science in question must be "valid." According to the Supreme Court, this means that the evidence is "reliable" or "trustworthy." It is useful to distinguish validity from reliability. **Validity** is concerned with actually measuring some underlying construct. In this context, a technique is valid if it actually measures what it purports to measure. **Reliability** is concerned with producing consistent results. Validity is not easy to determine. As such, courts rely on several factors. See Table 10.1 for a list of these factors.

"Fit" is the next requirement under the *Daubert* test. This requirement is closely related to relevancy in that the results of the scientific technique should be closely connected to the facts in dispute. As the Supreme Court

Table 10.1   Factors Considered in Determining Scientific Validity

1. Whether the theory or technique has been tested

2. Whether the theory or technique has been subjected to peer review

3. The error rate (and types of errors) involved in application of the theory or technique

4. Whether the standards are in place that govern use of the technique

5. The degree of acceptance within the scientific community regarding the theory or technique

6. The "newness" or novelty of the technique

7. The qualifications and stature of the technique or witness

8. Whether a body of professional literature exists concerning the theory or technique

stated in *Daubert*, the evidence must be "sufficiently tied to the facts of the case that it will aid the jury."

Other considerations should go into determining whether "scientific" evidence is appropriate in a courtroom. If the technique is exceedingly technical or complicated, for example, the jury may become confused. Alternatively, if the technique or theory in question is nascent, undeveloped, and prone to error, special care should be taken in basing important decisions on the resultant evidence.

Several types of scientific evidence have led to much confusion and controversy in the courts (some more than others). Certain techniques probably do not require much validation, but we focus here on the techniques that do. These include statistics, DNA evidence, polygraph results, evidence concerning the reliability of eyewitness testimony, and evidence of syndromes and profiles. The admissibility of these types of evidence is essentially controlled by rules 702 and 703 of the Federal Rules of Evidence presented earlier in the chapter, even though the FRE contain no direction mention of scientific evidence.

Statistics

http://www.cas.lancs.ac.uk/short_courses/notes/stat_inf/session1.pdf

The problem of statistical evidence was clearly illustrated in the case of *People v. Collins* (1968). An eyewitness in that case testified that a black man and a blonde woman mugged a woman in an alley in Los Angeles.

The prosecutor argued that the statistical probability of two such people being together was so minute that the defendants had to be responsible for the mugging (the witness also pointed out other characteristics of the suspects, but these are beside the point). The California Supreme Court, however, overturned one of the convictions.

There are several reasons that statistical evidence is usually not admissible. The first is that it is impossible to state with confidence the odds of an event occurring without knowing how likely the event is. Consider a simple example: We know how likely it is that two heads will result from two flips of a coin because we know that there are only two possible outcomes associated with any given flip of a coin. At the other extreme, though, and to stick with the *Collins* case illustration, no one knows how likely a black man and blonde woman are to associate with each other. We have enough trouble trying to count the number of people in this country, not to mention the odds of different individuals associating with one another!

Another problem with statistical evidence stems from the so-called product rule. Going back to the coin example, we know that in flipping a coin the likelihood of two heads is one-fourth. This result is calculated by the product of the likelihood of both events occurring in isolation (one-half times one-half). The product rule becomes problematic when it is used to calculate the probability of nonindependent events. We know that two coin tosses are independent; there is no way that the result of one toss will somehow influence the result of the second toss.

To illustrate nonindependence, assume we have a group of 20 people, of which 5 are black (so the probability of being black is 5/20, which reduces to one-fourth); and 15 are white. Further, 2 are women and 18 are men (the probability of being a woman is 2/20, which reduces to 1/10). Finally, 3 are wearing red, 7 are wearing yellow, and 10 are wearing blue (probability of wearing red is 3/20). It would be wrong to predict the likelihood of selecting a black woman wearing red by multiplying one-fourth by 1/10 by 3/20. The result is 1/800, but we know that since there are only 20 people, the odds of any one person being selected cannot possibly be less than 1/20. In our example, the qualities of being black or white, male or female, and wearing any of the three colors are not independent, so the product rule is inappropriate. The rule exaggerates the probability of events and would mislead a jury.

There are several other reasons for viewing statistical evidence cautiously, but they can become technical and quite mathematical. Following the example of the misuse of the product rule requires careful attention, so it is no wonder that jurors can become confused and overwhelmed when presented with too many numbers.

One of the most important reasons for excluding statistical evidence is that it seems to conflict with the notion of proof beyond a reasonable doubt. As the system currently stands (and students of legal topics are taught), proof beyond a reasonable doubt is not quantifiable. This standard does not mean 99 or 95 percent certainty, or even any level of likelihood below or above these points. To attach specific probabilities raises some ethical dilemmas. Would we be satisfied with 95 percent certainty, or even 99 percent certainty? What is the appropriate cutoff point? It is naive to assume that judges, prosecutors, defense attorneys, and jurors could all agree on the same level of certainty, so it is safe to leave the definition of "proof beyond a reasonable doubt" open ended.

In sum, think of statistics as just another method of drawing inferences. As we have seen earlier in this book, circumstantial evidence is similar. It requires arriving at the "truth" through inferences of probabilities arising from the association of certain facts. An example of circumstantial evidence is the testimony of a witness in an adultery case that she saw the accused and a woman who was not his wife together in a hotel room. Such testimony should not lead anyone to conclude with 100 percent certainty that adultery was taking place, but most jurors will probably infer that it was taking place.

Statistics constitutes a family of sophisticated techniques for making inferences. Statistics, in our view, take "common sense" out of play and try to substitute relatively formal and "objective" tools for making decisions. Unfortunately, statistics can often be confusing as well as manipulated (everyone's heard the homily, "You can prove anything with statistics"), so courts should be especially careful in deciding whether evidence resulting from statistical analysis should be admitted to prove consequential facts.

DNA Evidence

> http://www.scientific.org/tutorials/articles/riley/riley.html
> http://www.usdoj.gov/ag/dnapolicybook_cov.htm

In recent years, **DNA evidence** has gained popularity in both criminal trials and paternity cases. The reason is its unsurpassed ability to point to particular individuals. What is interesting, though, is that DNA evidence frequently goes hand in hand with statistics. One often hears about the "probability" of the DNA not belonging to the defendant, or the probability of the DNA match between a parent and child being of a certain level. Despite the language of probability, the use of DNA evidence has been approved by all courts across the country.

DNA evidence is fully acceptable under the *Daubert* standards discussed earlier, but it still raises potential problems. Special care needs to be given to the handling of DNA evidence. Laboratory protocol also needs to be followed with special care. Statistics need to be applied cautiously, and the information needs to be communicated to the jury in clear and understandable terms.

A recent DNA-evidence development of some controversy is that of DNA dragnets. In the wake of a serious crime, all people in the town where the crime was committed and who fit the profile of the offender are asked to voluntarily submit DNA samples. This sampling can be accomplished by swabbing the inside of a person's cheek with a cotton swab. Then, by process of elimination, the suspect is found. Usually, the suspect is one of the few who fail to submit to DNA testing.

DNA dragnets have been used successfully in a handful of European countries. Some attempts have been made to "import" them to the United States, but they are highly controversial here because of constitutional concerns. Taking a DNA sample from a person constitutes a search and is therefore protected by the Fourth Amendment. Thus, if DNA dragnets are to gain acceptance within our borders, they need to be voluntary. Just because a person refuses to consent should not mean that that he or she is a suspect. Another reason DNA dragnets face potential problems in the United States is that their success abroad has mostly been in small, isolated towns. It would be nearly impossible to obtain voluntary samples from people fitting the profile of a criminal suspect in a town as big as New York City.

Polygraph Evidence

http://www.usdoj.gov/usao/eousa/foia_reading_room/usam/title9/crm00259.htm

http://www.usdoj.gov/usao/eousa/foia_reading_room/usam/title9/crm00262.htm

Another variety of scientific evidence that has been particularly controversial is expert testimony based on the results of polygraph examinations. *Frye v. United States* (1923), one of the leading cases that established the standard for scientific evidence that prevailed for several years, did not consider polygraph testing a science. Most courts have followed suit; today most jurisdictions have rules against permitting polygraph-based testimony. Even in light of the more recent *Daubert* decision, which was more liberal than *Frye* in terms of its test for the admissibility of scientific evidence, most courts avoid polygraph evidence. There are exceptions, however (e.g., *United States v. Cordoba*, 1997; *United States v. Posado,* 1995).

Some courts permit polygraph testimony if both parties agree to it (e.g., *United States v. Gordon,* 1982), but others will still exclude it even if both parties agree because of a perception that such evidence is unreliable (e.g., *People v. Baynes,* 1981). As one court noted, agreement by both parties "neither enhances the uncertain reliability of the polygraph examination nor blunts the prejudicial effect" (*State v. Lyons,* 1987).

In a more recent case (*United States v. Scheffer,* 1998), the Supreme Court held that criminal defendants have no constitutional right to introduce expert testimonial evidence that they passed a polygraph examination. A key feature of this decision was that the Court only considered whether polygraph evidence must be admitted. The decision suggests, then, that polygraph evidence can be admitted at trial, but it does not need to be. The Court did note, however, that because the scientific community is still in disagreement over the reliability of polygraph evidence, a rule providing for its exclusion is perfectly acceptable, but it is up to the lower courts to decide.

Some commentators believe that even if polygraph testing were an infallible truth-seeking technique, admitting such evidence would bypass the role of the judge or jury in determining guilt. As one court noted, criminal defendants should be "treated as persons to be believed or disbelieved by their peers rather than as electrochemical systems to be certified as truthful or mendacious" (*State v. Lyons,* 1987).

United States v. Scheffer
United States Supreme Court
523 U.S. 303 (1998)

On April 30, Edward Scheffer, a member of the United States Air Force, unaccountably failed to appear for work and could not be found on the base. He was absent without leave until May 13, when an Iowa state patrolman arrested him following a routine traffic stop and held him for return to the base. OSI agents later learned that respondent's urinalysis revealed the presence of methamphetamine.

Respondent was tried by general court-martial on charges of using methamphetamine, failing to go to his appointed place of duty, wrongfully absenting himself from the base for 13 days, and, with respect

(continued)

to an unrelated matter, uttering 17 insufficient funds checks. He testified at trial on his own behalf, relying upon an "innocent ingestion"
theory and denying that he had knowingly used drugs while working
for OSI. On cross-examination, the prosecution attempted to impeach
respondent with inconsistencies between his trial testimony and earlier
statements he had made to OSI.

Respondent sought to introduce the polygraph evidence in support
of his testimony that he did not knowingly use drugs. The military
judge denied the motion, relying on Military Rule of Evidence 707,
which provides, in relevant part:

(a) Notwithstanding any other provision of law, the results of a
polygraph examination, the opinion of a polygraph examiner, or
any reference to an offer to take, failure to take, or taking of a
polygraph examination, shall not be admitted into evidence.

*****

A defendant's right to present relevant evidence is not unlimited,
but rather is subject to reasonable restrictions. A defendant's interest
in presenting such evidence may thus "'bow to accommodate other
legitimate interests in the criminal trial process." As a result, state
and federal rulemakers have broad latitude under the Constitution to
establish rules excluding evidence from criminal trials. Such rules do
not abridge an accused's right to present a defense so long as they are
not "arbitrary" or "disproportionate to the purposes they are designed
to serve." Moreover, we have found the exclusion of evidence to be
unconstitutionally arbitrary or disproportionate only where it has
infringed upon a weighty interest of the accused.

*****

State and federal governments unquestionably have a legitimate interest in ensuring that reliable evidence is presented to the trier of fact
in a criminal trial. Indeed, the exclusion of unreliable evidence is a
principal objective of many evidentiary rules.

The contentions of respondent and the dissent notwithstanding,
there is simply no consensus that polygraph evidence is reliable.
To this day, the scientific community remains extremely polarized
about the reliability of polygraph techniques. Some studies have concluded that polygraph tests overall are accurate and reliable. Others
have found that polygraph tests assess truthfulness significantly less

(continued)

accurately, that scientific field studies suggest the accuracy rate of the "control question technique" polygraph is "little better than could be obtained by the toss of a coin," that is, 50 percent.

*****

The approach taken by the President in adopting Rule 707 excluding polygraph evidence in all military trials is a rational and proportional means of advancing the legitimate interest in barring unreliable evidence. Although the degree of reliability of polygraph evidence may depend upon a variety of identifiable factors, there is simply no way to know in a particular case whether a polygraph examiner's conclusion is accurate, because certain doubts and uncertainties plague even the best polygraph exams.

*****

It is equally clear that Rule 707 serves a second legitimate governmental interest: Preserving the jury's core function of making credibility determinations in criminal trials. A fundamental premise of our criminal trial system is that "the jury is the lie detector." Determining the weight and credibility of witness testimony, therefore, has long been held to be the "part of every case [that] belongs to the jury, who are presumed to be fitted for it by their natural intelligence and their practical knowledge of men and the ways of men."

By its very nature, polygraph evidence may diminish the jury's role in making credibility determinations. The common form of polygraph test measures a variety of physiological responses to a set of questions asked by the examiner, who then interprets these physiological correlates of anxiety and offers an opinion to the jury about whether the witness, often, as in this case, the accused, was deceptive in answering questions about the very matters at issue in the trial. Unlike other expert witnesses who testify about factual matters outside the jurors' knowledge, such as the analysis of fingerprints, ballistics, or DNA found at a crime scene, a polygraph expert can supply the jury only with another opinion, in addition to its own, about whether the witness was telling the truth. Jurisdictions, in promulgating rules of evidence, may legitimately be concerned about the risk that juries will give excessive weight to the opinions of a polygrapher, clothed as they are in scientific expertise and at times offering, as in respondent's case, a conclusion about the ultimate issue in the trial. Such jurisdictions may legitimately determine that the aura of infallibility attending

(continued)

polygraph evidence can lead jurors to abandon their duty to assess credibility and guilt. Those jurisdictions may also take into account the fact that a judge cannot determine, when ruling on a motion to admit polygraph evidence, whether a particular polygraph expert is likely to influence the jury unduly. For these reasons, the President is within his constitutional prerogative to promulgate a per se rule that simply excludes all such evidence.

*****

A third legitimate interest served by Rule 707 is avoiding litigation over issues other than the guilt or innocence of the accused. Such collateral litigation prolongs criminal trials and threatens to distract the jury from its central function of determining guilt or innocence. Allowing proffers of polygraph evidence would inevitably entail assessments of such issues as whether the test and control questions were appropriate, whether a particular polygraph examiner was qualified and had properly interpreted the physiological responses, and whether other factors such as countermeasures employed by the examinee had distorted the exam results. Such assessments would be required in each and every case.

In light of the debate over the reliability of polygraph evidence, Congress has even become involved. For example, the Employee Polygraph Protection Act places restrictions on the use of polygraphs in the employee context. It should prove interesting to follow future court decisions and congressional actions concerning the admissibility of polygraph evidence in criminal and civil trials.

The Reliability of Eyewitness Testimony

Psychologists routinely testify (as experts) to the effect that eyewitnesses are notoriously inaccurate in terms of their recollections. This testimony is another variety of "scientific" evidence and, like polygraph evidence, is viewed with some caution because the research suggesting that eyewitnesses misinterpret and fail to remember events is not conclusive. Experts in this area often testify to such commonly agreed-upon facts (*United States v. Curry*, 1992, 1050–1052):

1. Memory diminishes quickly
2. Stress causes inaccurate recollections
3. Witnesses often include inaccurate information in their testimony

4. Conversations witnesses have following events reinforce flawed perceptions
5. Even accurate descriptions are not necessarily indicative of guilt
6. Cross-racial identifications are frequently inaccurate

Some courts approve testimony concerning the inaccuracy of eyewitness testimony (e.g., *People v. Enis,* 1990). A handful of decisions have even resulted in reversals because of such evidence (*United States v. Stevens,* 1991). Other courts, however, are skeptical and may hold separate hearings on whether such testimony is admissible. Still others exclude altogether expert testimony that eyewitnesses are notoriously inaccurate in what they observe (e.g., *United States v. Larkin,* 1992).

In general, it is up to the judge to decide on the admissibility of expert testimony in this area. If, for example, a witness identifies the defendant after he or she had seen the defendant at great length (or if the witness knew the defendant), the testimony will probably prove reliable. Furthermore, if eyewitness testimony is tangential and not the "whole" of the prosecution's case, there is not really any advantage to allowing an expert to testify that the witness may have been wrong; a guilty verdict could be arrived at regardless. At the other extreme, however, where identity is crucial and a substantial portion of the prosecution's case, expert testimony may be desirable. This is particularly true if the witness caught no more than a fleeting glimpse of the perpetrator.

Syndromes and Profiles

Experts are often called on to testify as to a syndrome shared by a witness or party to the case. The term **syndrome** simply refers to a pattern of behavior or mental attitude exhibited by a particular person. Prosecutors often offer evidence of a syndrome as it relates to a victim. Other times, the defense will argue that the defendant's actions can best be understood in terms of some debilitating condition. Either way, the courts are not surprisingly cautious about such testimony. The question of scientific validity is often raised because many "syndromes" that experts would testify to are not universally recognized. Examples of such syndromes are battered woman syndrome, rape trauma syndrome, and abused child syndrome.

Battered Woman Syndrome

The idea behind this syndrome is that a woman party to an abusive relationship develops a sense of helplessness that keeps her in the relationship. Experts will also testify that women in abusive relationships develop considerable rage that they ultimately "release," resulting in significant injury or death to the abusing partner. This syndrome is often raised in trials involving abused women who have killed their partners. Many courts admit evidence of battered woman syndrome to establish a "social framework" that places the events in context (*Bechtel v. State,* 1992), but other courts suggest that it is difficult to believe testimony concerning what a woman might be expected to do in an abusive relationship (e.g., *Hill v. State,* 1986).

http://www.divorcenet.com/states/oregon/or_art02

Rape Trauma Syndrome

Rape trauma syndrome exists when women go through specific, identifiable stages after being raped. Experts will testify that rape victims first experience an acute, negative reaction to being raped, then progress through a series of stages akin to posttraumatic stress disorder. Testimony concerning rape trauma syndrome is often presented to refute a defense claim that the victim consented to the sexual encounter. This approach has been accepted by a number of courts (e.g., *Henson v. State,* 1989). A more controversial use of rape trauma syndrome testimony, however, occurs when there is no physical evidence linking the defendant to the presumed victim. In such cases, the prosecution may argue that because the "victim" exhibits symptoms consistent with rape trauma, the defendant should be found guilty. Courts are generally quick to reject this approach (e.g., *People v. Taylor,* 1990).

http://www.rapevictimadvocates.org/trauma.html

Battered or Abused Child Syndrome

When children are abused or sexually assaulted, they often develop common symptoms, such as nightmares and behavioral problems. Testimony concerning abused child syndrome has been admitted for such purposes as explaining questionable behavior. When the focus shifts from the child to, for example, a parent or guardian, the courts become a bit nervous about allowing expert testimony. This approach essentially asks the jury to infer the guilt or innocence of an adult's alleged abusive actions from the behavior or conditions exhibited by a child. Courts do admit this testimony, but sometimes grudgingly (e.g., *State v. Hester,* 1988).

http://www.healthatoz.com/healthatoz/Atoz/common/standard/transform.
jsp?requestURI=/healthatoz/Atoz/ency/battered_child_syndrome.jsp

Criminal Profiles

By comparison to the aforementioned syndromes are criminal profiles. In general, the term **profile** refers to common characteristics shared by certain types of offenders. Whereas syndromes are usually offered to *excuse* questionable conduct on the part of someone (battered spouse, rape victim, etc.), criminal profiles are intended to lead to a conclusion that because someone fits a certain description, he or she is guilty.

For example, because Mr. Smith bought a one-way plane ticket with cash, was traveling to a city known as a "hub" of drug activity, did not carry any luggage, looked nervous, and walked briskly through the terminal, he may fit the profile of a "drug courier." Courts do not permit expert testimony that because a person fits a criminal profile, he or she should be found guilty. The courts often consider profiling, but not explicitly. The subject is commonly raised during appellate review of stop-and-frisk encounters in which the question of whether authorities had reasonable suspicion to stop is raised.

Because every person walking through an airport, for example, can realistically be stopped, law enforcement officials are forced to look to specific characteristics of drug couriers. This is because, as the Supreme Court observed in *United States. v. Mendenhall* (1980), "Much . . . drug traffic is highly organized and conducted by sophisticated criminal syndicates . . . And many drugs . . . may be easily concealed. As a result, the obstacles to detection . . . may be unmatched in any other area of law enforcement" (pp. 545–546). Further, one of the most significant impediments in the war on drugs is the "extraordinary and well-documented difficulty of identifying drug couriers" (*Florida v. Royer,* 1983).

The drug courier profile is generally attributed to Paul Markonni, a DEA agent who identified a number of suspicious characteristics of likely drug couriers when he was assigned to a drug interdiction unit at the Detroit Airport. The drug courier profile has since been described as an "informally compiled abstract of characteristics thought typical of persons carrying illicit drugs" (*United States v. Mendenhall,* 1980). There is no single, nationally recognized drug courier profile or set of characteristics indicative of drug courier profiling. Instead, one must look at specific cases to ascertain which types of characteristics fit the drug courier profile.

The first drug courier profile case of note, *United States v. Van Lewis* (1976), listed several characteristics to be used in identifying drug couriers. They include (1) the use of small denominations of currency for ticket purchase, (2) travel to and from major drug import centers, (3) the absence of luggage or use of empty suitcases on trips that normally require extra clothing, and (4) travel under an alias.

In a similar case, the Fifth Circuit in *Elmore v. United States* (1979) described common characteristics of drug couriers:

(1) arrival from or departure to an identified source city; (2) carrying little or no luggage; (3) unusual itinerary, such as rapid turnaround

time for a very lengthy airplane trip; (4) use of an alias; (5) carrying unusually large amounts of currency in the many thousands of dollars, usually on their person, or in briefcases or bags; (6) purchasing airline tickets with a large amount of small denomination currency; and (7) unusual nervousness beyond that ordinarily exhibited by passengers. (p.1039, n3)

Some secondary characteristics of drug couriers have also been identified. They include "(1) the almost exclusive use of public transportation, particularly taxicabs, in departing from the airport; (2) immediately making a phone call after deplaning, (3) leaving a false or fictitious call-back

---

Table 10.2   Typical Characteristics of Drug Couriers

1. Use of small cash denominations of currency for ticket purchase

2. Travel to and from major drug importation centers/countries/cities

3. Absence of luggage or use of empty suitcases on trips that normally require extra clothing

4. Travel under an alias/assumed name

5. Unusual itinerary, such as rapid turnaround time for a very lengthy airplane trip

6. Carrying unusually large amounts of currency (e.g., in the thousands of dollars)

7. Unusual nervousness beyond that ordinarily exhibited by passengers

8. The almost exclusive use of public transportation upon departing the airport

9. Immediately making a phone call after exiting the airplane

10. Leaving a false or fictitious call-back telephone number with the airline

11. Unusual dress

12. Age between 25 and 35

13. Extreme paleness consistent with being extremely nervous

14. Failure to use identification tags on luggage

15. Purchase of tickets on the day of flight

16. Exiting first or last from the plane

17. Walking quickly through the terminal while continuously checking over one's shoulder

18. Quickly leaving the airport upon arrival

telephone number with the airline being utilized, and (4) excessively frequent travel to source or distribution cities" (*Elmore v. United States,* 1979; See also, *Illinois v. Wardlow,* 528 U.S. 119, 2000). See Table 10.2 for a list of common characteristics associated with drug couriers.

It is important not to confuse profile evidence with the investigative technique of criminal profiling. Criminal profilers, such as those who "profiled" the individual responsible for mailing anthrax-tainted letters in 2001, seek to narrow the list of potential suspects. In fact, this technique is the exact opposite of expert testimony concerning profiles. Whereas profile testimony starts with a list of characteristics criminals display and concludes that anyone fitting that description is a criminal, investigative profiling seeks to a develop a list of characteristics that can lead authorities to a single individual. If an investigative profile is accurate enough and leads to apprehension of the perpetrator, the criminal trial will proceed as usual, without any testimonial evidence to the effect that the defendant was apprehended because of the work of a criminal profiler.

Summary

An enduring issue in criminal trials is the role of the expert witness, namely, the question of determining who qualifies as such. Over time, the standard for establishing scientific expertise as a legal concept has shifted, from that which was initially elaborated in the *Frye* case, to that which prevails according to the *Daubert* case and its progeny. Expert witnesses, once ordained by the court, are allowed to testify on a number and variety of subjects ranging from accident reconstruction to neuron activation and just about every topic in between. The matter of scientific admissibility and expertise becomes important, especially when one considers the controversy surrounding DNA, polygraph, and other forms of evidence.

Discussion Questions

1. What is an expert witness?
2. What are the two types of expert witnesses?
3. What is meant by "qualification" of an expert witness?
4. What does the *Daubert* rule require?
5. What is the ultimate issue rule? Why does this rule exist?
6. Why is eyewitness testimony considered unreliable?

7. What is a court-appointed expert?
8. Explain "syndromes" and give examples.
9. Explain the difference between criminal profiles and the investigative technique of criminal profiling.
10. According to the text, what are the common characteristics of drug couriers? What type of evidence is this? Is it admissible?

Further Reading

Aitken, C. G. G. (1995). Statistics and the Evaluation of Evidence for Forensic Scientists. New York: John Wiley and Sons.

Brain, R. D., and D. J. Broderick. (1992). "The Derivative Relevance of Demonstrative Evidence: Charting Its Proper Evidentiary Status." University of California, Davis, Law Review. 25:957, 968–969.

D'Angelo, C. (1998). "The Snoop Doggy Dogg Trial: A Look at How Computer Animation Will Impact Litigation in the Next Century." University of San Francisco Law Review 32:561, 585.

Downs, D. A. (1998). More than Victims: Battered Women, the Syndrome Society, and the Law. Chicago: University of Chicago Press.

Foster, K. W. and P. W. Huber. (1999). Judging Science: Scientific Knowledge and the Federal Courts. Cambridge, MA: MIT Press.

Goldstein, E. (1995). Visual Evidence: A Practitioner's Manual. Toronto, ON: Carswell.

Imwinkelried, E. J. (1992). Methods of Attacking Scientific Evidence (2nd ed.). Charlottesville, NC: Michie.

Moenssens, A. A. (1995). Scientific Evidence in Criminal Cases (4th ed.). Westbury, NY: Foundation Press.

Robertson, B. J. and G. A. Vignaux. (1995). Interpreting Evidence: Evaluating Forensic Science in the Courtroom. New York: John Wiley and Sons.

Rychlak, R. J. (1995). Real and Demonstrative Evidence: Application and Theory. Charlottesville, NC: Michie Butterworth.

Strong, J. W. (1992). McCormick on Evidence (4th ed.). Eagan, MN: West.

Cases Cited

Bechtel v. State, 840 P.2d 1 (Okla. Crim. App. 1992)
Bonner v. Polacari, 350 F.2d 493 (10th Cir. 1965)
Daubert v. Merrell Dow Pharmaceuticals, 509 U.S. 579 (1993)
Elmore v. Untied States, 595 F. 2d 1036 (5th Cir. 1979)
Florida v. Royer, 460 U.S 491, 519 (1983)

Frye v. United States, 54 App D.C 46 (CADC 1923)

Henson v. State, 535 N.E.2d 1189 (Ind. 1989)

Hill v. State, 507 S.2d 554 (Ala. Crim. App. 1986)

Illinois v. Wardlow, 528 U.S. 119 (2000)

Johninson v. State, 878 S.W. 2d 727 (Ark. 1994)

Kaufman v. Edelstein, 539 F.2d 811 (2nd Cir. 1976)

People v. Baynes, 430 N.E.2d 1070 (Ill. 1981)

People v. Collins, 438 Cal.P.2d 33 (Cal. 1968)

People v. Cronin, 60 N.Y.2d 430 (1983)

People v. Enis, 564 N.E.2d 1155 (Ill. 1990)

People v. Taylor, 552 N.E.2d 131 (N.Y. 1990)

State v. Hester, 760 P.2d 27 (Idaho 1988)

State v. Lyons, 744 P.2d 231 (Or. 1987)

State v. Oliver, 742 P.2d 999 (Mont. 1987)

State v. Spencer, 216 N.W.2d 131 (Minn. 1974)

State v. Vining, 645 A.2d 20 (Me. 1994)

Students of California School for Blind v. Honig, 736 F.2d 538 (9th Cir. 1984)

Thomas v. State, 197 Okla. 450 (1946)

United States v. Cordoba, 104 F.3d 225 (9th Cir. 1997)

United States v. Curry, 977 F.2d 1042 (7th Cir. 1992)

United States v. DeSoto, 885 F.2d 354 (7th Cir. 1989)

United States v. DiDomenico, 985 F.2d 1159 (1993)

United States v. Gordon, 688 F.2d 42 (8th Cir. 1982)

United States v. Larkin, 978 F.2d 964 (7th Cir. 1992)

United States v. Mendenhall, 446 U.S. 544, 547 (1980)

United States v. Miller, 874 F.2d 1255 (9th Cir. 1989)

United States v. Nunez, 658 F.Supp. 828 (D. Colo. 1987)

United States v. Posado, 57 F.3d 428 (5th Cir. 1995)

United States v. Rose, 731 F.2d 1337 (8th Cir. 1984)

United States v. Scheffer, 118 S.Ct. 1261 (1998)

United States v. Stevens, 935 F.2d 1380 (3rd Cir. 1991)

United States v. Van Lewis, 409 F.Supp. 535 (E.D Mich. 1976)

United States v. Williams, 583 F.2d 1194 (2nd Cir. 1978)

CHAPTER 11

TESTIMONIAL PRIVILEGES

Key Terms & Concepts

Adverse testimony

Agency privilege

Attorney-client privilege

Beneficial testimony

Clergy-penitent privilege

Client perjury

Crime fraud exception

Dead man's act

Defendant's privilege

Derivative use immunity

Doctor-patient privilege

Executive privilege

Freedom of Information Act

Holder of the privilege

Husband-wife privilege

In camera

Informant's privilege

Involuntary disclosure

Journalist's privilege

Law enforcement privilege

Marital communications privilege

Marital testimony privilege

Military and diplomatic secrets privilege

News reporter source privilege

Privilege

Privilege for required reports

Privileged communication

Psychotherapist-patient privilege

Religious/spiritual adviser

Religious privilege

Rule 501

Shield laws

State secrets privilege

Testimonial privilege

Transactional immunity

Use immunity

Waiver

Chapter Learning Objectives

By the end of this chapter, the student should be able to:

- Identify the various testimonial privileges extended to witnesses
- Explain the history and purpose of testimonial privileges
- Describe the various forms of immunity
- List the criteria used to determine whether a testimonial privilege exists
- Relate the most common testimonial privileges and the type of circumstances under which they may be exercised
- Explain the attorney-client privilege and its limitations
- Identify limitations and exceptions to the doctor-patient & psychotherapist-patient privileges

- Describe the need for a "state secrets" privilege in contemporary society
- Explain the significance of the reporter-source privilege and how it has been previously used

Introduction

The general rule, both at common law and in today's courts, is that it is the duty of every witness called to testify to provide a complete and accurate accounting of the events of which he or she has personal knowledge. As an esteemed evidence scholar put it long ago, the courts have "a right to every man's evidence" (Younger, Goldsmith, and Sonenshein 2000). However, there are occasions when persons with extremely relevant knowledge about a case may not be required or permitted to testify. A criminal defendant has the right, guaranteed under the Fifth Amendment, not to incriminate himself or herself, and that includes the right to choose not to testify. Other witnesses may also have a right to refrain from testifying or they may be prohibited from testifying.

Shielding or barring a witness from testifying is referred to as a **testimonial privilege.** A testimonial privilege excludes evidence (usually testimony about a communication between two parties) without regard for the trustworthiness, reliability, or importance to the trial outcome. The legal protection of certain communications from being revealed in court is referred to as **privileged communication.** Several types of testimonial privileges have been created by either court decision or statutory enactment. Some testimonial privileges have existed for many years, while others are of relatively recent origin.

A privilege is a rule that gives a witness the option not to testify or that gives another person the option to prevent the witness from testifying. The person who has the right to keep certain information from being revealed is the **holder of the privilege.** It may be the witness or another person, usually the person with whom the witness has spoken. The holder of the privilege may exercise the privilege by requesting the court to prevent the testimony. This request may occur at trial or in pretrial proceedings. The privilege is not limited to trial; it applies to any judicial proceeding in which the witness is under oath. A failure to exercise the privilege at the appropriate time constitutes a waiver of the privilege.

Rules of evidence generally apply only in court proceedings, such as the trial. Privileges, however, are an exception to this general rule. They are recognized in all judicial proceedings, including grand jury hearings and preliminary hearings.

Privileges and Witness Competency

There is some overlap between privileges and competency. Competency, recall from Chapter 6, relates to classes of persons and is absolute. Incompetent persons are those considered unable, by virtue of who they are, to give reliable evidence and are not allowed to testify. A **privilege,** on the other hand, is a right held by a person who was a party to a confidential relationship, the sanctity of which the law values above even the search for truth. A person deemed incompetent by the court is not allowed to testify at all, while a holder of testimonial privilege may simply be restricted on what he or she can testify about. A privilege may be *qualified*, meaning it is not absolute.

Waiver

A privilege may be waived by its holder, expressly or by implication, intentionally or inadvertently. Failing to assert a privilege when the holder is able to do so constitutes a **waiver** of the privilege. Waiver of the privilege for *any* purpose waives the privilege for *all* purposes. Consenting to the disclosure of the contents of the communication to a third party is a waiver of the privilege. In many instances the privilege rests with only one member of the relationship, and that person has the sole authority to waive the privilege. The other party may have an obligation to assert the privilege on behalf of the other party, however.

Disclosure of a significant portion of the conversation to a third party is generally treated as a waiver, although there is some debate as to what constitutes a "significant" portion of the conversation. An **involuntary disclosure** (when overheard by an unknown third party or compelled by the court) is generally not treated as a waiver. At common law, an eavesdropper overhearing an otherwise privileged communication would destroy the privilege, even if the parties were unaware of the eavesdropper and took reasonable precautions to prevent disclosure. The modern trend is to continue the privilege.

History of Testimonial Privileges

Testimonial privileges have existed in some form since Roman times. A number of the privileges used today were developed at common law, as courts struggled to balance the competing interests of protecting valued relationships (such as husband and wife or priest and penitent) and encouraging the efficient administration of justice in the courts. As states began in the mid-eighteenth century to codify the common law, many of the common law testimonial privileges were written into evidence codes or court rules.

The original draft of the Federal Rules of Evidence, presented to Congress by the Supreme Court in 1972, contained a comprehensive set of nine types of privileged communications, including attorney-client, husband-wife, doctor-patient, psychotherapist-patient, clergy-penitent, and state secrets. These privileges were largely derived from privileges that existed at common law.

Congress chose not to adopt specific testimonial privileges, however, and instead and adopted FRE **Rule 501**, which states that testimonial privileges "shall be governed by the principles of the common law as they may be interpreted by the courts of the United States in the light of reason and experience." This means that the only testimonial privileges recognized under the Federal Rules of Evidence are those that existed in the federal common law at the time of the passage of FRE 501, along with any privileges later recognized by federal courts. Since the passage of the Federal Rules of Evidence, the Supreme Court has adopted one new privilege, that of psychotherapist-patient (*Jaffe v. Redmond*, 1996). The Court has also altered the husband-wife privilege (*Trammel v. United States*, 1980).

Rule 501. General Rule

Except as otherwise required by the Constitution of the United States or provided by Act of Congress or in rules prescribed by the Supreme Court pursuant to statutory authority, the privilege of a witness, person, government, State, or political subdivision thereof shall be governed by the principles of the common law as they may be interpreted by the courts of the United States in the light of reason and experience. However, in civil actions and proceedings, with respect to an element of a claim or defense as to which State law supplies the rule of decision, the privilege of a witness, person, government, State, or political subdivision thereof shall be determined in accordance with State law.

http://www.law.cornell.edu/rules/fre/ACRule501.htm

Purpose of Testimonial Privileges

There are several rationales for creating a testimonial privilege. The first is that doing so protects the confidentiality of communications that take place in certain relationships, relationships that society so values that we are willing to hinder the fact-finding process at trial to protect that relationship. The absence of a privilege would hinder open and honest communication within the relationship. Common examples include communication between attorney and client, husband and wife, and doctor and patient.

A second reason for creating a testimonial privilege is that the courts realize that the law cannot force certain individuals to disclose confidences they became privy to as part of their vocation. Thus, where a member of the clergy has taken a vow to maintain the confidentiality of the confessional, the law early on recognized that it could not, and should not, force the clergy to violate that pledge. To force persons to reveal such information would force them to make a difficult choice between the dictates of the law and the moral and ethical obligations of their professions; it would also place the courts in the position of appearing to force people to renounce their promises to others.

Testimonial privileges are sources of much controversy because they operate to exclude often important, relevant evidence. In the words of then-Chief Justice Burger, "These exceptions to the demand for every-man's evidence are not lightly created nor expansively construed, for they are in derogation of the search for truth" (*United States v. Nixon,* 1974). This situation is particularly problematic in criminal cases, where the exclusion of statements by the defendant may result in a factually guilty person being found not guilty. Testimonial privileges generally do not receive as much public attention as the defendant's privilege against self-incrimination, but they have a significant impact on both civil and criminal trials.

http://www.csustan.edu/cj/evidence/chap10.htm

The positive aspect of testimonial privileges is that they encourage open and honest communication in relationships where such communication is essential. If the substance of such conversations could be revealed by either person in the relationship, it is reasoned, people would be less likely to speak openly and forthrightly, which would in turn damage the relationship. Spouses would hide their thoughts from each other, creating suspicion and mistrust in what should be the closest of relationships. Clients would not tell their attorney everything, thus hindering the attorney's ability to adequately represent them. According to the Supreme Court, a privilege is warranted only for "public good transcending the normally predominant principle of utilizing all rational means for ascertaining the truth" (*Elkins v. United States,* 1980). Supporters of testimonial privileges argue that the "public good" is well served by promoting open communication in certain relationships.

Testimonial privileges keep some otherwise admissible evidence from the jury because the courts and legislatures have determined that protection of particular relationships is more important than making all relevant evidence admissible. This is clearly a policy decision, the competing interests have been weighed and a value judgment has been made. As you read about the various privileges, think about whether a particular privilege is a good idea or whether that privilege should be eliminated. Also ask yourself whether there are other relationships that deserve protection but do not receive it.

The Privilege Against Self-Incrimination

The Fifth Amendment to the Constitution includes the privilege against self-incrimination, commonly referred to as the right to remain silent. Every state constitution recognizes a privilege against self-incrimination, and the Supreme Court has held that the Fifth Amendment applies to both the state and federal governments (see *Malloy v. Hogan,* 378 U.S. 1, 1964). This privilege protects both criminal defendants and any witness who is testifying under oath in a court proceeding. Court proceedings include the trial, grand jury proceedings, and pretrial depositions. The privilege applies only to criminal trials; civil defendants have no right not to testify and can be called to the witness stand by the plaintiff.

The U.S. Supreme Court has interpreted the privilege against self-incrimination to mean that a criminal suspect has the right not to speak to the police during the investigation or to testify at trial. Additionally, the prosecution is barred from calling the defendant as a witness or commenting adversely on the defendant's decision not to testify (*Griffin v. California,* 1965). This is sometimes referred to as the **defendant's privilege.**

The Court has endorsed a fair response rule, which allows prosecutors to address, during closing arguments, the defendant's invocation of his or her Fifth Amendment rights. However, prosecutors may comment on the refusal to testify if the defendant claims he or she was denied the opportunity to explain his or her actions.

However, the privilege against self-incrimination is not absolute. Rather, it applies only to testimonial self-incrimination, which means being compelled to speak one's guilt. The Supreme Court has made it clear that the privilege does not apply to nontestimonial acts, such as the

Griffin v. California
United States Supreme Court
380 U.S. 609 (1965)

Following a jury trial, Griffin was convicted of murder in the first degree. He did not testify at the trial on the issue of guilt, though he did testify at the penalty phase of the proceedings. The trial court instructed the jury on the issue of guilt, stating that a defendant has a constitutional right not to testify. However, the trial court further instructed the jury as follows:

As to any evidence or facts against him which the defendant can reasonably be expected to deny or explain because of facts within his knowledge, if he does not testify or if, though he does testify, he fails to deny or explain such evidence, the jury may take that failure into consideration as tending to indicate the truth of such evidence and as indicating that among the inferences that may be reasonably drawn therefrom those unfavorable to the defendant are the more probable.

*****

The trial court added, however, that no such inference could be drawn as to evidence respecting which he had no knowledge. It stated that failure of a defendant to deny or explain the evidence of which he had knowledge does not create a presumption of guilt nor by itself warrant an inference of guilt nor relieve the prosecution of any of its burden of proof.

Griffin had been seen with the deceased the evening of her death, the evidence placing him with her in the alley where her body was found. The prosecutor made much of the failure of petitioner to testify:

The defendant certainly knows whether Essie Mae had this beat up appearance at the time he left her apartment and went down the alley with her. What kind of a man is it that would want to have sex with a woman that beat up if she was beat up at the time he left? He would know that. He would know how she got down the alley. He would know how the blood got on the bottom of the concrete steps. He would know how long he was with her

(continued)

in that box. He would know how her wig got off. He would know whether he beat her or mistreated her. He would know whether he walked away from that place cool as a cucumber when he saw Mr. Villasenor because he was conscious of his own guilt and wanted to get away from that damaged or injured woman. These things he has not seen fit to take the stand and deny or explain. And in the whole world, if anybody would know, this defendant would know. Essie Mae is dead, she can't tell you her side of the story. The defendant won't.

The death penalty was imposed and the California Supreme Court affirmed. The Supreme Court granted the petition for writ of certiorari to consider whether comment on the failure to testify violated the Self-Incrimination Clause of the Fifth Amendment.

*****

We said in *Malloy v. Hogan,* . . . that, "the same standards must determine whether an accused's silence in either a federal or state proceeding is justified." We take that in its literal sense and hold that the Fifth Amendment, in its direct application to the Federal Government, and in its bearing on the States by reason of the Fourteenth Amendment, forbids either comment by the prosecution on the accused's silence or instructions by the court that such silence is evidence of guilt.

police taking fingerprints, conducting lineups, drawing blood, or using breathalyzer machines, as the evidence obtained via these methods, while potentially incriminating, is nontestimonial. Additionally, the compelled production of tangible items, such as documents or personal property, is not included within the privilege.

Immunity from Prosecution

The privilege against self-incrimination is waived if the court grants the witness immunity from prosecution. Typically, a witness called to the stand, when asked a question, will assert his or her right not to incriminate him or herself. This is often referred to as "taking the Fifth." The prosecutor may then request the court to grant the witness immunity from prosecution and order the witness to either answer the question or be held in contempt of court. If the court grants immunity, the witness cannot refuse to accept the immunity. He or she must testify or risk being held in contempt.

Schmerber v. California
Supreme Court of the United States
384 U.S. 757 (1966)

Schmerber was convicted in Los Angeles Municipal Court of the criminal offense of driving an automobile while under the influence of intoxicating liquor. He was arrested at a hospital while receiving treatment for injuries suffered in an accident involving the automobile that he had apparently been driving. At the direction of a police officer, a blood sample was then withdrawn from petitioner's body by a physician at the hospital. The chemical analysis of this sample revealed a percent by weight of alcohol in his blood at the time of the offense, which indicated intoxication, and the report of this analysis was admitted in evidence at the trial. Petitioner objected to receipt of this evidence of the analysis on the ground that the blood had been withdrawn despite his refusal, on the advice of his counsel, to consent to the test. He contended that in that circumstance the withdrawal of the blood and the admission of the analysis in evidence denied him due process of law under the Fourteenth Amendment, as well as specific guarantees of the Bill of Rights secured against the States by that Amendment; his privilege against self-incrimination under the Fifth Amendment; his right to counsel under the Sixth Amendment; and his right not to be subjected to unreasonable searches and seizures in violation of the Fourth Amendment. The Appellate Department of the California Superior Court rejected these contentions and affirmed the conviction. In view of constitutional decisions since we last considered these issues in *Breithaupt v. Abram,* we granted certiorari. We affirm.

*****

As the passage in *Miranda* implicitly recognizes, however, the privilege has never been given the full scope, which the values it helps to protect suggest. History and a long line of authorities in lower courts have consistently limited its protection to situations in which the State seeks to submerge those values by obtaining the evidence against an accused through "the cruel, simple expedient of compelling it from his own mouth. . . . In sum, the privilege is fulfilled only when the person is guaranteed the right 'to remain silent unless he chooses to speak in the unfettered exercise of his own will.'" The leading case in this Court is *Holt v. United States,* 218 U.S. 245. There the question

(continued)

was whether evidence was admissible that the accused, prior to trial and over his protest, put on a blouse that fitted him. It was contended that compelling the accused to submit to the demand that he model the blouse violated the privilege. Mr. Justice Holmes, speaking for the Court, rejected the argument as "based upon an extravagant extension of the Fifth Amendment," and went on to say: "The prohibition of compelling a man in a criminal court to be witness against himself is a prohibition of the use of physical or moral compulsion to extort communications from him, not an exclusion of his body as evidence when it may be material. The objection in principle would forbid a jury to look at a prisoner and compare his features with a photograph in proof." 218 U.S., at 252–253.

*****

It is clear that the protection of the privilege reaches an accused's communications, whatever form they might take, and the compulsion of responses which are also communications, for example, compliance with a subpoena to produce one's papers. On the other hand, both federal and state courts have usually held that it offers no protection against compulsion to submit to fingerprinting, photographing, or measurements, to write or speak for identification, to appear in court, to stand, to assume a stance, to walk, or to make a particular gesture. The distinction which has emerged, often expressed in different ways, is that the privilege is a bar against compelling "communications" or "testimony," but that compulsion which makes a suspect or accused the source of "real or physical evidence" does not violate it.

*****

Although we agree that this distinction is a helpful framework for analysis, we are not to be understood to agree with past applications in all instances. There will be many cases in which such a distinction is not readily drawn. Some tests seemingly directed to obtain "physical evidence," for example, lie detector tests measuring changes in body function during interrogation, may actually be directed to eliciting responses which are essentially testimonial. To compel a person to submit to testing in which an effort will be made to determine his guilt or innocence on the basis of physiological responses, whether willed or not, is to evoke the spirit and history of the Fifth Amendment. Such situations call to mind the principle that the protection of the privilege "is as broad as the mischief against which it seeks to guard."

(continued)

*****

In the present case, however, no such problem of application is presented. Not even a shadow of testimonial compulsion upon or enforced communication by the accused was involved either in the extraction or in the chemical analysis. Petitioner's testimonial capacities were in no way implicated; indeed, his participation, except as a donor, was irrelevant to the results of the test, which depend on chemical analysis and on that alone. Since the blood test evidence, although an incriminating product of compulsion, was neither petitioner's testimony nor evidence relating to some communicative act or writing by the petitioner, it was not inadmissible on privilege grounds.

There are three types of immunity: use immunity, derivative use immunity, and transactional immunity.

Use immunity means that anything the witness says on the stand cannot be used against him or her in a criminal proceeding. This is the most limited form of immunity, as it applies only to specific criminal acts mentioned by the witness on the witness stand.

Derivative use immunity means that the state cannot use any evidence derived from the immunized testimony against the witness. This form of immunity is slightly broader than use immunity because it applies to both specific criminal acts mentioned by the witness and other criminal acts that the police are able to uncover as a result of the testimony.

Transactional immunity means that the witness cannot be prosecuted for any activities about which the witness testifies. This is the broadest form of immunity. It applies to any criminal acts the witness mentions and any criminal acts that are in any way related to the testimony.

Privileged Communications

At early common law, there were no testimonial privileges, but courts soon began to create them as they saw a need to protect certain special relationships. Because excluding privileged communications from trial obviously impedes the fact-finding process, courts have historically been reluctant to extend the privileged communication rule to many relationships. According to Younger, Goldsmith, and Sonenshein (2000), the rule was that courts "start with the primary assumption that there is a general duty to give what testimony one is capable of giving, and that any exemptions which may exist are distinctly exceptional."

Four conditions must be established before a court will determine that a testimonial privilege exists:

1. The parties to a conversation must intend that the conversation be confidential.
2. Confidentiality must be essential to the maintenance of the relationship between the parties.
3. The relationship must be one that society believes should be promoted and protected.
4. The injury that would be caused by disclosure of the confidential communication must be greater than the value of the conversation to the resolution of the trial.

Major Forms of Testimonial Privileges

The development of testimonial privileges, like other evidence rules, has been inconsistent among the states. Different states have different testimonial privileges. And since the Federal Rules of Evidence are largely silent on the matter, there has not been the wholesale adoption of privileges and move toward consolidation that occurred with other evidence rules spelled out by the FRE. Nonetheless, while the privileges contained in the proposed Rule 501 were not adopted by Congress, a number of states did adopt these privileges in whole or in part. Thus, there now exists greater uniformity among the states than existed prior to 1972.

There are several generally accepted testimonial privileges. Some occur primarily in criminal cases, while others occur more frequently in civil cases. We focus our attention on the privileges that are most frequently asserted in criminal cases and that are most frequently recognized by state courts. They include (1) husband and wife, (2) attorney and client, (3) doctor and patient (including psychotherapist and patient), (4) clergy and penitent, (5) government secrets (including informants), and (6) news reporter and source.

Husband and Wife Privilege

It is axiomatic that family relationships are highly valued in American society. Cultural institutions such as the church and schools reaffirm this principle daily. Courts have long acknowledged the primacy of the family, in particular the marital relationship. In *Griswold v. Connecticut* (1965), the Supreme Court held that within the marital relationship is a right to privacy that the government cannot violate.

The husband-wife privilege has a long history. It is actually two distinct privileges. The first privilege involves testimony by one spouse against the other and is often referred to as the **marital testimony privilege.** The second privilege, which protects confidential marital communications from disclosure, is commonly referred to as the **marital communications privilege.** These two are often inaccurately lumped together, but they are in fact different privileges, applicable to different circumstances.

Marital Testimony Privilege

At common law, a party to a lawsuit was deemed incompetent and barred from testifying. This was based on the assumption that an interested party could not give unbiased, accurate testimony. Similarly, courts initially held that neither spouse was a competent witness either for or against the other. This rule was based on the premise that a husband and wife were essentially one person. Consequently, if one spouse was a defendant in a criminal case, the other spouse was treated as an interested and therefore incompetent party.

The rule that a spouse was generally incompetent to testify was gradually replaced in some jurisdictions by one stating that a spouse could choose to testify for the other in a criminal trial but could not testify against the other spouse if either spouse objected. This created a testimonial privilege that either spouse could assert. Thus, a woman called to testify against her husband could refuse to testify or her husband could refuse to allow her to testify. This became known as the **marital testimony privilege,** or the **husband-wife privilege.**

The justification for this privilege was the need to protect marital harmony. It was assumed that allowing one spouse to give testimony against the other would damage the marital relationship. The marital testimony privilege thus excludes from trial testimony by one spouse against the other spouse. The privilege covers only testimony that would be against the interests of the party spouse, or **adverse testimony.** It does not cover **beneficial testimony.**

This restriction originally allowed either spouse to claim the privilege, even in cases in which one spouse was charged with a crime against the other spouse, as when a husband was charged with assaulting his wife. The courts struggled with the perception of unfairness created by allowing a defendant spouse to assert a privilege to prevent the victim spouse from testifying against the defendant spouse.

The marital testimony privilege was adopted by many early American courts. In many states, the privilege was modified to permit only the spouse called as a witness to assert the privilege. This change allowed spouses who were the victims of criminal acts by their spouses to testify against that spouse, if they were willing to do so. This seemed a logical modification of the rule; otherwise a husband who assaulted his wife could prevent his wife from testifying against him by asserting a privilege intended to protect the marital relationship. Courts reasoned that there was likely no marital relationship to salvage at this point, so the privilege was not necessary in such instances.

The Supreme Court, in *Trammel v. United States* (1980), adopted the majority rule and held that the spousal privilege is held only by the spouse acting as a witness and not by the other spouse. This ruling permits one spouse to choose to testify against the other in a criminal trial but does not mandate it. The Court reasoned that allowing the non-testifying spouse to exercise the privilege did not serve a valid purpose, because if a spouse is willing to testify against the other, there is no need to protect the marital relationship as it "is almost certainly in disrepair." Prior to the *Trammel* (1980) decision, the Court relied on *Hawkins v. United States*, (1958), which required the consent of both spouses prior to one testifying against the other in a criminal case.

Some states still hold that a spouse is incompetent to testify for or against the other spouse. Most states have done away with spousal incompetency and have implemented spousal privilege in some form.

Originally, the marital testimony privilege applied to communications that occurred both before and during the marriage. This situation allowed a person to marry someone into silence. The modern trend is to not extend privilege to premarital communications. Additionally, persons must be married when privilege is exercised. If the persons are no longer married, there is no marriage to protect and so there is no need for the privilege. Most jurisdictions limit this privilege to criminal cases or cases in which the nonwitness spouse is a party (such as a civil damage claim).

Marital Communications Privilege

The **marital communications privilege** protects against the disclosure of confidential communications between the spouses. The rationale for this privilege, like that for the marital testimony privilege, is the protection of the marital relationship, as well as the promotion of open and honest marital conversations. Some courts have also noted that forcing a spouse to give testimony about a confidential marital communication places the court in an unfavorable light. There may also exist a constitutional right to privacy regarding marital communications following the decision in *Griswold v. Connecticut* (1965), although the Supreme Court has never explicitly addressed this issue.

The privilege covers both verbal and nonverbal communications. Most courts require that the verbal conduct be intended as a substitute for verbal communication. Some jurisdictions do not protect nonverbal communication and hold strictly to the verbal requirement.

The marital communications privilege covers only confidential communications made during the marriage. The privilege does not apply to nonmarital relationships that fail to meet common law marriage requirements. As such, the privilege does not cover same-sex relationships.

The privilege does not apply to communications made prior to a marriage. Thus, if a man says something in confidence to a woman to whom he is not married and later marries the woman, neither person may claim the privilege. Additionally, the privilege does not apply to communications made after the spouses are divorced.

In most states, the privilege applies to communications made during the marriage, even if the spouses later divorce. Thus, a confidential communication made by a wife to her husband during their marriage is privileged both during the course of the marriage and afterward. The minority rule is that divorce destroys the privilege, and a handful of courts have held that the privilege does not apply if the spouses are separated.

The modern rule is that the communicating spouse is the holder of the privilege. If the communicating spouse wishes to reveal what he or she said, the rationale does not apply. Most states allow a witness spouse to assert the privilege on behalf of the communicating spouse, unless the communicating spouse waives the privilege. The minority rule gives the privilege to both spouses.

Generally, any communication between a husband and wife is privileged, as long as there is evidence that the spouses intended for the communication to be private. Thus, the privilege is limited to confidential communications. Courts are split on whether the presence of an eavesdropper who overhears a marital communication destroys the privilege. At common law, an eavesdropper could testify as to what he or she heard, even if the spouses attempted to keep their conversation confidential. A number of states still follow the common law, but a significant number of states hold that the presence of an eavesdropper does not destroy the privilege. If the spouses were unaware that a third party could hear their conversation, the communication remains privileged.

The presence of third parties, even children, destroys the privilege. If spouses speak to each other in front of other family members, there is no privilege. There is no "family privilege," although many people have mistakenly thought otherwise. Communications between a parent and child are not covered under the privilege either.

Another important limitation on the privilege involves marital communications regarding criminal acts. A number of states do not allow the exercise of the privilege when the husband and wife are charged with engaging in a criminal conspiracy and the communication involves the conspiracy. This is because the privilege is an attempt to balance the competing interests of protection of the marital relationship with the smooth administration of justice, and in this instance, courts have determined that the privilege should not apply if it will serve to allow a person to hide criminal conduct.

As with the marital testimony privilege, the modern rule is that the marital communications privilege does not extend to proceedings between the spouses or to cases in which one spouse is charged with crime against the other.

Attorney and Client Privilege

http://www.enotes.com/everyday-law-encyclopedia/attorney-client-privilege

The **attorney-client privilege** is the oldest testimonial privilege (*Upjohn Company v. United States,* 1981). It was recognized in early Roman law. The privilege is designed to protect the confidentiality of communications between an attorney and a client. The general rule is that confidential communications made in the course of professional employment between an attorney and a client cannot be revealed by the attorney without the consent or waiver of the privilege by the client. Additionally, the client cannot be compelled to testify as to what was said in the course of the attorney-client relationship.

There are several justifications for the privilege. The primary justification is that clients will be encouraged to be honest with and to trust their attorney if they know that whatever they tell the attorney will remain confidential. This protection, it is assumed, will lead to more orderly and efficient litigation, as clients will be willing to tell the truth, thus allowing their attorney to prepare the best possible representation, based on the facts of the case. If it were otherwise, persons might be reluctant to tell the entire story, impairing the attorney's ability to represent his or her client. Also, persons might be reluctant to hire an attorney and might attempt to represent themselves. This was the case at early common law. Courts believed trials would be more efficient if trained specialists conducted them and so created the privilege to encourage individuals to hire attorneys.

Today, the Supreme Court has held that a defendant has the right to self-representation at trial, but only if the court is convinced that the defendant can do an adequate job. Incidentally, while the Supreme Court has held that the Sixth Amendment includes the right to represent oneself at trial, the Court has recently held that this right does not extend to an appeal of a criminal conviction. Only licensed attorneys can represent someone; the one exception to this rule allows inmates to assist other inmates in the preparation of legal documents.

The attorney-client privilege applies not only to any communications made during the business relationship but also to any preliminary discussions about hiring the attorney. The privilege applies even to communications in which a client seeks to employ the attorney but the attorney decides not to take the case or the client decides not to hire the attorney. The privilege is created as soon as a person consults with an attorney about legal matters. The privilege applies to both criminal and civil matters.

The privilege includes not only oral communications but also any written communications or physical actions. Thus, it applies to documents such as letters passed between the attorney and the client discussing the case. The privilege does not apply, however, to tangible evidence of a crime transferred to the attorney by the client. An attorney cannot be used to conceal evidence.

The privilege does not apply to the fact that a communication occurred. Thus, an attorney may properly be asked to reveal who his client is or to reveal his fee for services rendered, if the issue is relevant.

The privilege also applies to communications made to agents of the attorney whose presence is necessary, such as a secretary, paralegal, or investigator. If third parties who do not work for the attorney are present, however, the privilege is destroyed. Thus, if a friend accompanies the client to a meeting with an attorney, the communications between the attorney and client at that meeting would not be privileged if the friend overheard the conversation.

The attorney-client privilege rests with the client. As with other privileges, only the holder of the privilege (i.e., the client) can waive it. The client may do so by discussing the confidential communication, either outside of court with a third party, or in court during testimony. The attorney may assert the privilege on behalf of the client, unless instructed by the client not to do so. However, if the client waives the privilege, the attorney cannot reassert it.

Crime Fraud Exception

As mentioned above, an important limitation on the attorney-client privilege is that it does not cover criminal evidence turned over to the attorney by the client. Thus, if a client gives the attorney evidence, such as a murder weapon, the privilege does not apply. The attorney has an obligation as an officer of the court to turn that evidence over to the court. The attorney does not have to reveal how he or she obtained the evidence, however, that is protected by the privilege.

A related exception exists when a defendant consults with an attorney about a possible future crime or about concealing a crime. Recall that the purpose of the attorney-client privilege is to promote the efficient administration of justice. Providing a client with information on how to commit or conceal a crime does not promote justice, and hence this sort of communication is not protected. If an attorney provides advice about how to commit a crime, he or she may also be charged with conspiracy.

Client Perjury

Relatedly, a criminal defendant may confess his guilt to his attorney. Such a confession is protected by the attorney-client privilege, and the attorney is barred from disclosing the contents of that conversation. The client cannot be compelled to testify, because he is protected by the privilege against self-incrimination. But what if a client attempts to take the witness stand and deny his involvement in the crime charged? The attorney is barred from revealing to the court what he knows, but at the same time, he is aware that his client is about to commit perjury. The attorney is obligated, as an officer of the court, to not knowingly permit his client to commit perjury. Thus, he must either convince the defendant not to lie or inform the court that he is ethically unable to continue to represent the defendant. The court will likely allow him to withdraw at this point.

There is nothing wrong, on the other hand, with an attorney allowing a defendant to plead not guilty and then trying to get the client a lesser sentence through a plea bargain or have the client found not guilty at trial. While the attorney knows the client is guilty, he or she has an ethical obligation to zealously represent the client, within the rules of court and the rules of evidence. It is not considered a breach of legal ethics to represent someone who has committed a crime. If an attorney is unwilling to represent a client he or she knows committed a crime, the attorney is free to refuse to do so.

There are several exceptions to the attorney-client privilege. The privilege does not cover the attorney's statements regarding the client's mental or physical condition, and if the attorney is accused of wrongdoing by the client, the privilege does not prevent the attorney from disclosing information necessary to defend himself or herself.

Doctor and Patient Privilege

Doctor-patient privilege did not exist at common law. The privilege was not recognized until 1828, when the New York legislature adopted a statutory privilege. While the privilege was slow to be created, it eventually gained widespread acceptance, either by statute or court decision. Only a handful of states, mostly in the South, have refused to adopt the privilege. Some federal courts recognize the privilege, while others do not. Interestingly, the proposed Rules of Evidence did not include a doctor-patient privilege, although they did include a psychotherapist-patient privilege.

http://law.enotes.com/everyday-law-encyclopedia/doctor-patient-confidentiality

The privilege prevents a doctor from testifying about confidential communications made by a patient in the course of the professional relationship. The purpose of the privilege is to protect the doctor-patient relationship and encourage the patient to be truthful in seeking treatment so as to aid the doctor in making an informed diagnosis. The assumption is that a patient is more likely to be open and forthcoming when discussing his or her condition if he or she knows that the doctor cannot reveal any information that would embarrass the patient.

The doctor-patient privilege has been harshly criticized by some commentators and courts (including the Supreme Court in *Jaffee v. Redmond*, 1996). Critics of the privilege assert that there is no compelling reason for the privilege, as adequate treatment may often be provided by the doctor without discussion of the problem with the patient.

A number of modern courts have acknowledged that there is another justification for the doctor-patient privilege: the protection of the patient's privacy. This justification may prove more compelling than the original justification for the privilege.

While most states recognize the doctor-patient privilege, there are significant limitations and exceptions. Many states do not recognize the privilege in criminal cases, for instance. The privilege is asserted more frequently in civil cases, particularly ones involving personal injury claims. Also, the privilege applies only to communications made for the purpose of, and relevant to, obtaining treatment of a disease or injury. The privilege does not extend to communication unrelated to treatment or diagnosis. Many states limit the privilege to communications, while some extend it to observations by the doctor and other material, such as test results.

The identity of the patient and the fact that a doctor was consulted are generally not considered privileged, unless revelation would reveal the nature of the communication regarding treatment (for instance, if the doctor was a specialist in treating a particular disease). Privilege survives the death of the patient.

For the privilege to apply, the communication must have been intended to be confidential. The presence of third parties destroys the privilege, unless these third parties are office staff assisting the doctor or are close family members of the patient.

The privilege is for the protection of the patient, not the doctor. Thus, the patient is the holder of the privilege. The patient may waive the privilege by testifying concerning the consultation, by calling the doctor to testify, or by consent. The doctor may assert the privilege on behalf of the patient until the patient waives it. If the patient waives the privilege, the doctor cannot assert it on behalf of the patient.

The most common exception to the privilege occurs when the patient sues his or her doctor and any part of the claim or defense to the claim places the medical condition at issue. This makes sense, as it would be unfair to allow a patient to sue a doctor and allege the doctor mistreated him but not allow the doctor to prove that his or her treatment was based on what the patient told him or her.

Other common exceptions include statutes that require the doctor to report suspected child abuse or to report to the police the treatment of any wounds inflicted by a deadly weapon. In both instances, courts have determined that the justification for the doctor-patient privilege does not extend to allow patients to prevent doctors from revealing information that is necessary for the protection of society generally.

A majority of states hold that the patient does not waive the privilege by bringing a lawsuit in which his or her physical condition is at issue or by testifying to his or her physical condition. Some states, however, hold that putting one's medical condition at issue constitutes a waiver of the privilege. This is often the case in criminal cases, when the defense to the crime charged is insanity. Some states hold that a plea of not guilty by reason of insanity is an automatic waiver of the doctor-patient privilege, while some other states hold that the privilege is not waived until the defense actually puts on evidence of insanity.

Psychotherapist-Patient Privilege

A 1996 Supreme Court case (*Jaffee v. Redmond*) extended the doctor-patient privilege to psychotherapists. This decision conforms with the original draft of the Federal Rules of Evidence, which included such a privilege, and with the rules of evidence in the states. This is the only instance in which the Supreme Court has created a privilege since the adoption of the Federal Rules of Evidence. While this privilege is of more recent origin than the doctor-patient privilege, it was recognized in all 50 states prior to the Supreme Court decision.

http://jaffee-redmond.org/

The privilege applies to communications between a psychotherapist and patient, similar to the doctor-patient privilege. The more difficult aspect of the privilege is determining who is a psychotherapist and who is a patient. A patient is anyone who consults with a psychotherapist for the treatment and/or diagnosis of a mental or emotional condition. A psychotherapist is generally defined as (1) a person who is authorized and licensed to practice medicine and who devotes a significant portion of his or her time to the practice of psychiatry; or (2) a person licensed as a psychologist. Additionally, many jurisdictions extend the privilege to other licensed professionals who engage in psychotherapy or counseling, such as social workers and counselors.

There is a greater justification for this privilege than the doctor-patient privilege, as a communication between a psychotherapist and a patient is more likely to involve the transmittal of embarrassing or damaging information than a communication between a doctor and a patient. Those with psychological problems are often shunned by the public, so revealing communications at trial would likely deter visits to a doctor. Thus, an absence of the privilege is seen as more likely to deter patients from seeking assistance from psychotherapists than from doctors.

Additionally, total candor between a patient and psychotherapist is thought to be more necessary than between a doctor and patient, as a doctor can often make an adequate diagnosis without discussion with the patient, while such is not the case with mental problems.

An important aspect of the privilege is that it covers confessions of criminal misconduct, as long as the confession occurs in the course of treatment. This means that if a person admits to a psychotherapist that he or she committed a crime, the psychotherapist is barred from revealing that information unless the patient waives the privilege.

However, if a psychotherapist reasonably believes a patient may be a danger to himself or herself or to others, the privilege does not apply and the psychotherapist has a duty to disclose this information to the proper authorities. Obviously, this situation requires the psychotherapist to make a difficult judgment.

Clergy and Penitent Privilege

The early common law did not recognize a privilege for communications between a member of the clergy and a parishioner. Nonetheless, clergy

Jaffee v. Redmond
Supreme Court of the United States
518 U.S. 1 (1996)

After a traumatic incident in which she shot and killed a man, a police officer received extensive counseling from a licensed clinical social worker. The question we address is whether statements the officer made to her therapist during the counseling sessions are protected from compelled disclosure in a federal civil action brought by the family of the deceased. Stated otherwise, the question is whether it is appropriate for federal courts to recognize a "psychotherapist privilege" under Rule 501 of the Federal Rules of Evidence.

Petitioner is the administrator of the estate of Ricky Allen. Respondents are Mary Lu Redmond, a former police officer, and the Village of Hoffman Estates, Illinois, her employer during the time that she served on the police force. Petitioner commenced this action against respondents after Redmond shot and killed Allen while on patrol duty.

*****

On June 27, 1991, Redmond was the first officer to respond to a "fight in progress" call at an apartment complex. As she arrived at the scene, two of Allen's sisters ran toward her squad car, waving their arms and shouting that there had been a stabbing in one of the apartments. Redmond testified at trial that she relayed this information to her dispatcher and requested an ambulance. She then exited her car and walked toward the apartment building. Before Redmond reached the building, several men ran out, one waving a pipe. When the men ignored her order to get on the ground, Redmond drew her service revolver. Two other men then burst out of the building, one, Ricky Allen, chasing the other. According to Redmond, Allen was brandishing a butcher knife and disregarded her repeated commands to drop the weapon. Redmond shot Allen when she believed he was about to stab the man he was chasing. Allen died at the scene. Redmond testified that before other officers arrived to provide support, "people came pouring out of the buildings," and a threatening confrontation between her and the crowd ensued.

Petitioner filed suit in Federal District Court alleging that Redmond had violated Allen's constitutional rights by using excessive

(continued)

force during the encounter at the apartment complex. The complaint sought damages under Rev. Stat. § 1979, 42 U.S.C. § 1983 and the Illinois wrongful death statute, Ill. Comp. Stat., ch. 740, § 180/1 et seq. (1994). At trial, petitioner presented testimony from members of Allen's family that conflicted with Redmond's version of the incident in several important respects. They testified, for example, that Redmond drew her gun before exiting her squad car and that Allen was unarmed when he emerged from the apartment building.

During pretrial discovery petitioner learned that after the shooting Redmond had participated in about 50 counseling sessions with Karen Beyer, a clinical social worker licensed by the State of Illinois and employed at that time by the Village of Hoffman Estates. Petitioner sought access to Beyer's notes concerning the sessions for use in cross-examining Redmond. Respondents vigorously resisted the discovery. They asserted that the contents of the conversations between Beyer and Redmond were protected against involuntary disclosure by a psychotherapist-patient privilege. The district judge rejected this argument. Neither Beyer nor Redmond, however, complied with his order to disclose the contents of Beyer's notes. At depositions and on the witness stand both either refused to answer certain questions or professed an inability to recall details of their conversations.

In his instructions at the end of the trial, the judge advised the jury that the refusal to turn over Beyer's notes had no "legal justification" and that the jury could therefore presume that the contents of the notes would have been unfavorable to respondents. The jury awarded petitioner $45,000 on the federal claim and $500,000 on her state-law claim.

*****

Guided by these principles, the question we address today is whether a privilege protecting confidential communications between a psychotherapist and her patient "promotes sufficiently important interests to outweigh the need for probative evidence . . ." Both "reason and experience" persuade us that it does.

Like the spousal and attorney-client privileges, the psychotherapist-patient privilege is "rooted in the imperative need for confidence and trust." Treatment by a physician for physical ailments can often proceed successfully on the basis of a physical examination, objective information supplied by the patient, and the results of diagnostic tests. Effective psychotherapy, by contrast, depends upon an atmosphere of

(continued)

confidence and trust in which the patient is willing to make a frank and complete disclosure of facts, emotions, memories, and fears. Because of the sensitive nature of the problems for which individuals consult psychotherapists, disclosure of confidential communications made during counseling sessions may cause embarrassment or disgrace. For this reason, the mere possibility of disclosure may impede development of the confidential relationship necessary for successful treatment. As the Judicial Conference Advisory Committee observed in 1972 when it recommended that Congress recognize a psychotherapist privilege as part of the Proposed Federal Rules of Evidence, a psychiatrist's ability to help her patients "is completely dependent upon the [patients'] willingness and ability to talk freely. This makes it difficult if not impossible for [a psychiatrist] to function without being able to assure . . . patients of confidentiality and, indeed, privileged communication. Where there may be exceptions to this general rule . . . , there is wide agreement that confidentiality is a sine qua non for successful psychiatric treatment."

By protecting confidential communications between a psychotherapist and her patient from involuntary disclosure, the proposed privilege thus serves important private interests.

*****

Our cases make clear that an asserted privilege must also "serve public ends." Thus, the purpose of the attorney-client privilege is to "encourage full and frank communication between attorneys and their clients and thereby promote broader public interests in the observance of law and administration of justice." And the spousal privilege, as modified in *Trammel*, is justified because it "furthers the important public interest in marital harmony." The psychotherapist privilege serves the public interest by facilitating the provision of appropriate treatment for individuals suffering the effects of a mental or emotional problem. The mental health of our citizenry, no less than its physical health, is a public good of transcendent importance.

routinely refused to break the sanctity of the confessional. Clergy of many faiths are required to keep confidential the matters discussed in confession or in any private communication with a member of the faith. Thus, the development of the privilege was merely a recognition that the law cannot always force people to act according to its wishes and that other forces, such as religion/morality, have a greater impact on people.

This privilege developed in Ireland during the later part of the common law period and was originally intended to protect the confessional of the Catholic Church. England never adopted the privilege. It was recognized very early on in American courts. Today, the privilege is recognized either by statute or judicial decision in all 50 states, as well as by the federal courts. The privilege today applies much more broadly than at common law and is applicable to spiritual advisors of any recognized religious organization.

The clergy-penitent privilege protects against the disclosure of confidential communications made to a member of the clergy or a similar religious person in that person's capacity as a **religious/spiritual adviser**. Also known as **clergy-penitent privilege**, and **religious privilege**, the purpose of the privilege is to allow a person to openly confess his or her sins and misdeeds and seek spiritual guidance and redemption without fear of the confessions being revealed. Were it otherwise, clergy would be hauled into court and forced to act as government agents, and the confessional atmosphere would be chilled.

Originally, the privilege applied only to statements made in confession. Today, however, most jurisdictions extend the privilege to cover any statements made for the purpose of spiritual guidance. The privilege thus covers any communications made in pursuance of a recognized church procedure that creates a confessional-like relationship.

A difficulty sometimes arises in defining what constitutes an effort to receive spiritual guidance. Asking a priest to hide evidence of a crime would not be included in the privilege, but a confession that the penitent had committed a crime would be privileged. The clergy-penitent privilege is similar in this respect to the attorney-client privilege. The privilege does not apply if the clergy person is speaking as a friend or if the communication involves matters unrelated to seeking spiritual guidance. The privilege applies to any bona fide religion. Courts are generally liberal in defining the term *clergy*. It includes priests, ministers, or anyone who has been ordained by a recognized religious denomination. Statutes codifying the privilege often use the term "religious adviser" or "spiritual adviser" to cover all possible persons.

The majority rule is that the privilege belongs to the penitent, not the clergy. The penitent has the privilege to refuse to disclose and to keep a clergyman from disclosing confidential communications made by that person to the clergyman. The priest may assert the privilege on behalf of the penitent, until the penitent waives the privilege. A minority of states extend the privilege to the clergy as well and allow a clergyman to refuse to waive it even if the penitent waives it. This policy is a recognition that some religions bar the priest from revealing confession even if the penitent reveals it. The privilege generally survives the death of the penitent.

State Secrets Privilege

Courts have long recognized a privilege for state secrets. This privilege originally allowed the government to prevent the disclosure of military and diplomatic secrets and thus was often referred to as the **military and diplomatic secrets privilege**. The purpose of the privilege is to prevent the disclosure of information that might damage the security of the state and to encourage full and honest communication within government agencies

> http://www.sourcewatch.org/index.php?title=State_secrets_privilege
> http://www.fas.org/sgp/jud/arar-memo-011805.pdf

The privilege exists today and applies to both the federal government and state governments. Additionally, the privilege has been extended to cover not only state secrets but claims of **executive privilege**, **agency privilege**, and **law enforcement privilege**.

The privilege must be asserted by the government, not a private party. When the government asserts the privilege, the court holds an *in camera* hearing to determine whether application of the privilege is necessary. This means the court will examine the documents in question and uphold the privilege if there is a "reasonable danger" that disclosure would compromise national security. The state secrets privilege was discussed by the Supreme Court in *United States v. Reynolds* (1953).

While this privilege may seem rare, it has been used in recent years. Examples include the Pentagon Papers case, the Watergate cover-up, and the Oliver North case. More important for our purposes, it is the basis for a related privilege, the confidential informant privilege (discussed below).

A number of state and federal agencies require employees to file reports of events. An example is a police report of a crime. Such reports may be privileged by statute under the **privilege for required reports**. If such reports are designated as public information, however, then they are not privileged. This exception typically applies to police reports.

The policy deliberations of state and federal agencies are often privileged to promote full and open disclosure. The **Freedom of Information Act** (FOIA) grants the public access to most, but not all government documents. Information available to the public is not subject to claims of privilege in court. Material not available under the FOIA may still be available, if the litigant can convince the court of the need for the information.

The states secret privilege differs in several important respects from other privileges. First, it is not limited to communications, it also applies to documents and acts. Second, the privilege may be qualified, requiring the court to make a determination of whether privilege should be allowed in a particular case. Additionally, the executive privilege is not just an evidentiary privilege, the Supreme Court has held that it is constitutionally based (*United States v. Nixon*, 1974).

Confidential Informant Privilege

The confidential informant privilege is related to the state secrets privilege. It is sometimes referred to as the **informant's privilege**, as it permits law enforcement agencies to refuse to disclose the identity of an informant in a criminal investigation. The privilege applies only to the identity of the informant. Contents of the communication between informant and police must be revealed if doing so can be accomplished without revealing the identity of the informant. This aspect makes it different from other privileges, which are intended primarily to prevent the disclosure of communications. The purpose of the privilege is to promote efficient law enforcement and encourage people to come forward, by removing the fear of reprisal by the defendant.

While it was a crime to fail to report a crime at common law (this was known as "misprision of a felony"), today there is no legal obligation to report knowledge of a crime, except in some limited circumstances where a duty is imposed (as when a special relationship exists between the parties). Nonetheless, courts recognize a need to encourage reporting, especially when a person is otherwise willing to do so except for fear of reprisal.

The confidential informant privilege is qualified, meaning the court will weigh the effect of permitting the privilege against the need to reveal the information in the particular case. Also, there is an exception to the privilege if disclosure of the informant's identity is necessary for the defendant to receive a fair trial. If the court determines that revealing the identity of the informant is necessary to ensure a fair trial, the identity will be revealed. This rarely happens however.

The most common situation occurs when an informant has provided information used to develop probable cause to justify a search or an arrest. The identity of informants used to develop probable cause generally need not be revealed, as police officers corroborate the information obtained from the informant and thus can testify in place of the informant. The Supreme Court held, in *McCray v. Illinois* (1967), that when a police officer testifies as to the underlying information provided by an informant supporting a probable cause determination, the officer need not identify the informant because he or she is under oath and has provided the same set of facts that the informant would have provided (see also *Roviaro v. United States,* 1957.

If it is determined that the informant is an integral part of a transaction for which the defendant is being prosecuted, his or her identity may be revealed, but only if the court determines it is necessary for an adequate defense.

McCray v. Illinois
Supreme Court of the United States
386 U.S. 300 (1967)

McCray was arrested in Chicago, Illinois, on the morning of January 16, 1964, for possession of narcotics. The Chicago police officers who made the arrest found a package containing heroin on his person and he was indicted for its unlawful possession. Prior to trial he filed a motion to suppress the heroin as evidence against him, claiming that the police had acquired it in an unlawful search and seizure in violation of the Fourth and Fourteenth Amendments. See *Mapp v. Ohio,* 367 U.S. 643. After a hearing, the court denied the motion, and the petitioner was subsequently convicted upon the evidence of the heroin the arresting officers had found in his possession. The judgment of conviction was affirmed by the Supreme Court of Illinois, and we granted certiorari to consider the petitioner's claim that the hearing on his motion to suppress was constitutionally defective.

*****

The . . . arrest occurred near the intersection of 49th Street and Calumet Avenue at about seven in the morning. At the hearing on the motion to suppress, he testified that up until a half hour before he was arrested he had been at "a friend's house" about a block away, that after leaving the friend's house he had "walked with a lady from 48th to 48th and South Park," and that, as he approached 49th Street and Calumet Avenue, "the Officers stopped me going through the alley." "The officers," he said, "did not show me a search warrant for my person or an arrest warrant for my arrest." He said the officers then

(continued)

searched him and found the narcotics in question. The petitioner did not identify the "friend" or the "lady," and neither of them appeared as a witness.

*****

The arresting officers then testified. Officer Jackson stated that he and two fellow officers had had a conversation with an informant on the morning of January 16 in their unmarked police car. The officer said that the informant had told them that the petitioner, with whom Jackson was acquainted, "was selling narcotics and had narcotics on his person and that he could be found in the vicinity of 47th and Calumet at this particular time." Jackson said that he and his fellow officers drove to that vicinity in the police car and that when they spotted the petitioner, the informant pointed him out and then departed on foot. Jackson stated that the officers observed the petitioner walking with a woman, then separating from her and meeting briefly with a man, then proceeding alone, and finally, after seeing the police car, "hurriedly walk[ing] between two buildings." "At this point," Jackson testified, "my partner and myself got out of the car and informed him we had information he had narcotics on his person, placed him in the police vehicle at this point." Jackson stated that the officers then searched the petitioner and found the heroin in a cigarette package.

Jackson testified that he had been acquainted with the informant for approximately a year, that during this period the informant had supplied him with information about narcotics activities "fifteen, sixteen times at least," that the information had proved to be accurate and had resulted in numerous arrests and convictions. On cross-examination, Jackson was even more specific as to the informant's previous reliability, giving the names of people who had been convicted of narcotics violations as the result of information the informant had supplied. When Jackson was asked for the informant's name and address, counsel for the State objected, and the objection was sustained by the court.

*****

It is the petitioner's claim, however, that even though the officers' sworn testimony fully supported a finding of probable cause for the arrest and search, the state court nonetheless violated the Constitution when it sustained objections to the petitioner's questions as to the identity of the informant. We cannot agree.

*****

(continued)

What Illinois and her sister States have done is no more than recognize a well-established testimonial privilege, long familiar to the law of evidence. Professor Wigmore, not known as an enthusiastic advocate of testimonial privileges generally, has described that privilege in these words:

A genuine privilege, on . . . fundamental principle . . ., must be recognized for the identity of persons supplying the government with information concerning the commission of crimes. Communications of this kind ought to receive encouragement. They are discouraged if the informer's identity is disclosed. Whether an informer is motivated by good citizenship, promise of leniency or prospect of pecuniary reward, he will usually condition his cooperation on an assurance of anonymity, to protect himself and his family from harm, to preclude adverse social reactions and to avoid the risk of defamation or malicious prosecution actions against him. The government also has an interest in nondisclosure of the identity of its informers. Law enforcement officers often depend upon professional informers to furnish them with a flow of information about criminal activities. Revelation of the dual role played by such persons ends their usefulness to the government and discourages others from entering into a like relationship.

That the government has this privilege is well established, and its soundness cannot be questioned.

News Reporter and Source Privilege

Some states today recognize a **news reporter source privilege,** also referred to as a **journalist's privilege,** or **shield law.** This privilege is similar to the informant's privilege; it allows news media to refuse to reveal their sources of information. News reporters were not protected from being required to reveal their sources of information at common law. The First Amendment, however, provides for freedom of the press, and it has long been argued that forcing news gatherers to reveal their sources would have a chilling effect on the press.

The Supreme Court in *Branzburg v. Hayes* (1972) rejected the First Amendment contentions of the news media, holding that journalists could be compelled to appear before a grand jury or to testify and to reveal the identity of their sources. The Court determined that news reporters were no different from other citizens and that the concerns that justified protection of a police informant's identity did not apply to news media sources. In response to this decision, a number of states have either enacted or adopted by judicial decision so-called shield laws.

http://iml.jou.ufl.edu/projects/Spring05/Vaught/state.html

Under shield laws, a news reporter may refuse to reveal the identity of his or her source if the source spoke to the reporter with the expectation of remaining anonymous. The privilege includes the identity of the source, not the information itself. The privilege means that a news media person cannot be held in contempt of court for refusing to reveal his or her source. The privilege does not apply to cases in which the news reporter is a party, as when he or she is being sued for libel. The privilege applies to criminal cases in which the news reporter has a confidential informant.

The privilege generally covers reporters from a wide range of news media, including newspaper reporters, magazine writers, television and radio journalists, as well as editors, publishers, and other persons connected with a news media outlet.

The privilege is not absolute, but qualified. This means the court will weigh the news media claim of privilege against the need for the information for a criminal prosecution. If the court determines the need for the information outweighs the claim of privilege, the reporter must provide the information or is subject to being held in contempt.

Privileges in Civil Cases

Some privileges occur more frequently in civil cases, such as the **dead man's act**. In about half the states, dead man's acts allow the estate of a deceased person to keep a party who is contesting the distribution of the estate's assets from testifying about a transaction with the deceased. Some states allow the estate to bar other interested witnesses as well.

A number of other evidentiary privileges apply only in civil cases. These include offers of settlement and statements made during settlement negotiations. These items are privileged in an effort to promote the efficient settlement of disputes and promote settlement before trial.

If offers to settle or statements made during settlement negotiations were not privileged, parties to a civil lawsuit would be reluctant to discuss the particulars of a case, as anything they said could be used against them to show they were liable for whatever injuries had occurred. Thus FRE Rule 408 provides that evidence of conduct or statements made in compromise negotiations is not admissible to prove liability or nonliability. Furthermore, the involvement of third persons in the offer to compromise or negotiation does not destroy the privilege. However, offers of settlement and statements made during negotiations are admissible for purposes other than proving liability or nonliability.

In criminal cases, offers to plead guilty and withdrawn guilty pleas are not admissible against the defendant, for a similar reason, a failure to provide these statements with a privilege would reduce the willingness of defendants to enter into plea negotiations and would hamper the efficient administration of justice.

Summary

In this chapter, we have reviewed the history and purposes of testimonial privileges as well as the major testimonial privileges. Privileges are like so much of evidence law in that they represent a compromise between the search for absolute truth and society's needs. In the case of privileges, "truth" may at times be made more difficult to discover at trial because testimonial privileges reduce the ability of some witnesses to testify as to what they know about a crime or other event. On the other hand, valued relationships are protected, such as the relationship between husband and wife and the relationship between an attorney and client. Without the ability to trust that what is said in the course of these relationships will remain between the parties, these relationships will be weakened, or so the thinking goes.

Testimonial privileges are controversial precisely because at times they serve to make the search for truth more difficult. This controversy has led to the restricting of some privileges, while others have been created as the need has arisen to protect the sanctity of a particular relationship (such as the relationship between psychotherapist and patient).

Comment at trial on the invocation of a testimonial privilege is allowed for some privileges but not others. Jurisdictions are split on this, but the trend is to bar comment on assertion of all testimonial privileges. The Supreme Court has limited the ability of prosecutors to comment on a defendant's invocation of his right to remain silent, as such commentary would affect the privilege against self-incrimination. This is in line with the general rule that when there is a clash between a nonconstitutional privilege and a constitutional right, a court will treat the privilege as qualified or will overrule the privilege completely.

Discussion Questions

1. What is the purpose of testimonial privilege?
2. Describe the major forms of testimonial privilege.
3. Why is the attorney-client privilege important? What communications or actions are not protected?

4. Describe a hypothetical situation in which the doctor-patient/psycho-therapist-patient/clergy-penitent privilege might become an issue in a criminal case.
5. Why is the news reporter source privilege important?
6. What conditions must be established before a court will determine that a testimonial privilege exists?
7. What is the purpose of the state secrets privilege, and who may assert it? In what ways does it differ from other privileges?
8. Can overheard communications between an attorney and client be used as evidence? Support your answer.
9. How has the Supreme Court altered the husband-wife privilege through passage of the Federal Rules of Evidence?
10. What are some evidentiary privileges that apply in civil cases?

Further Reading

Imwinkelried, E. J. (1980). *Evidentiary Foundations*. Charlottesville, VA: The Michie Company.

Mauet, T. A. and W. D. Wolfson. (1997). *Trial Evidence*. New York: Aspen Publishers.

Rice, P. (2001). *Best-Kept Secrets of Evidence Law*. Cincinnati, OH: Anderson Publishing.

Younger, I., M. Goldsmith, and D. S. Sonenshein. (2000). *Principles of Evidence* (4th ed.). Cincinnati: Anderson Publishing.

Cases Cited

Branzburg v. Hayes, 408 U.S. 665 (1972)
Elkins v. United States, 445 U.S. 40, 45 (1980)
Griffin v. California, 380 U.S. 609 (1965)
Griswold v. Connecticut, 381 U.S. 479 (1965)
Hawkins v. United States, 358 U.S. 74 (1958)
Jaffee v. Redmond, 518 U.S. 1 (1996)
Malloy v. Hogan, 378 U.S. 1 (1964)
McCray v. Illinois, 386 U.S. 300 (1967)
Roviaro v. United States, 353 U.S. 53 (1957)
Schmerber v. California, 384 U.S. 757 (1966)
Trammel v. United States, 445 U.S. 40, 47 (1980)
United States v. Nixon, 418 U.S. 683 (1974)
United States v. Reynolds, 345 U.S. 1 (1953)
Upjohn Company v. United States, 449 U.S. 383 (1981)

CHAPTER 12
THE HEARSAY RULE

Key Terms & Concepts

Centrality theory

Circumstantial evidence of
   a declarant's state of
   mind

Declarants

Effect on hearer

Faulty memory

Hearsay

Implicit assertions

Intentional/nonliteral
   statement

Legally operative conduct

Minimalist theory

Misperception/
   misunderstanding

Narrative ambiguity

Out-of-court statement

Prior statements

Procedural rights theory

Production theory

Reliability theory

Risk of uncertainty

Rule 801

Rule 805

Statement

Subassertions

Testimonial evidence

Truth of the matter
   asserted

Chapter Learning Objectives

By the end of this chapter, the student should be able to:

- Relate the historical origins of the hearsay rule
- Explain the concept of hearsay and why such statements are not admissible in court
- Identify the criteria for determining whether or not a statement constitutes hearsay
- Describe five theories concerning the relationship between hearsay and the Sixth Amendment's confrontation clause
- Identify criteria for determining the truth of the matter asserted
- Explain what is meant by "hearsay within hearsay"

Introduction

The hearsay rule is one of the most commonly discussed rules in evidence law. Unfortunately, there is a great deal of confusion surrounding the meaning of hearsay. Many people assume that anything that is "heard" then "said" at trial (usually by a witness who is testifying) is not admissible because it constitutes hearsay. Actually, the hearsay rule is far more complicated than that. In fact, many people argue that more hearsay evidence is actually admitted at trial than is excluded because of the many exceptions to the rule.

Against this backdrop, this chapter seeks to define hearsay as an evidentiary term. **Rule 801** of the FRE guides the use of hearsay. However, we provide a historical context surrounding its evolution. We also consider the relationship between hearsay and the Sixth Amendment confrontation clause. The chapter identifies the most common "problems" with hearsay as a form of evidence, including misperception, faulty memory, and narrative ambiguity. As if these matters do not already complicate the issue of hearsay enough, the chapter concludes with a discussion of multiple hearsay or, as it is sometimes referred to, hearsay-within-hearsay.

The Hearsay Rule

Hearsay is defined as an out-of-court statement, made by a speaker other than the in-court witness, offered in evidence to prove the truth of the matter asserted. Let us break this definition down.

Rule 801. Definitions

The following definitions apply under this article:

(a) Statement.

A "statement" is (1) an oral or written assertion or (2) nonverbal conduct of a person, if it is intended by the person as an assertion.

(b) Declarant.

A "declarant" is a person who makes a statement.

(c) Hearsay.

"Hearsay" is a statement, other than one made by the declarant while testifying at the trial or hearing, offered in evidence to prove the truth of the matter asserted.

http://www.law.cornell.edu/rules/fre/ACRule801.htm

1. To be hearsay, the statement must have been offered "**out of court**." Modern statutes do not define "out of court." Instead, they define "in-court" statements and treat anything outside that definition as hearsay. "In-court statements" are defined as statements made by a witness while testifying at the current trial. If a statement is made

by someone other than the witness, not under oath, and prior to the current trial (either at an earlier hearing or out of court), it will almost certainly be considered hearsay.

2. A **statement** is either a verbal assertion or a nonverbal act intended to be an assertion. *Verbal* means consisting of words, whether written or oral. The Federal Rules of Evidence Advisory committee stated, "It can scarcely be doubted that an assertion made in words is intended by the declarant to be an assertion. Hence verbal assertions readily fall into the category of 'statement.'" The only confusion centers around nonverbal "statements" and their role in the hearsay determination.

3. "Speakers" are commonly referred to as **declarants.** Technically, a "declarant" is anyone who makes a statement (whether in or out of court), but for the sake of simplicity we will refer to witnesses (those who testify at trial) and "declarants" or "speakers" (those whose statements witnesses seek to introduce at trial to prove a particular fact).

4. Finally, when a statement is "offered in evidence to prove the **truth of the matter asserted**," the in-court witness is "repeating" what another person said for the purpose of supporting his or her position. Two questions need to answered in determining whether a statement is offered in evidence to prove the truth of the matter asserted. First, what is the content of the statement? Second, what was the statement intended to assert? Because there are no easy answers to these two questions, we devote two full sections to answering them.

Simply put, hearsay is an attempt to get the jury to believe that something was said outside its presence, prior to the present trial. There is no easier way to understand the meaning of hearsay than with an example. Assume that John is on trial for assault with a deadly weapon. Witness Craig testifies that while he did not actually see the assault, his friend Andy did. Specifically, Craig asserts at trial that Andy said, "I saw John assault the victim." This quoted statement, having been made by a person other than Craig, the witness, is hearsay. Craig will attempt to get the jury to believe that a statement was made even though the statement was not made in the presence of the jury.

Consider another hypothetical example, this time involving a statement that is not considered hearsay. Assume Bill sues Hillary for hitting him with her car. Witness Monica testifies that her friend Linda said, "Bill hit Hillary." Assume further that Hillary never did hit Bill with her car and that the lawsuit is fraudulent. Witness Monica is now on trial for perjury, but she maintains that she told the truth when she testified that, "Linda told me that Bill hit Hillary." Monica calls Chelsea to the stand to testify that Chelsea also heard Linda say that Bill hit Hillary.

Chelsea's statement at Monica's perjury trial is not hearsay because, even though she testified the same as Monica, her statement is not offered to prove that Linda told the truth but rather to prove that Linda stated that Bill hit Hillary. In other words, Chelsea's testimony is being offered to exculpate Monica, not to prove that Bill hit Hillary. Therefore, Chelsea's statement is not hearsay.

Origins of the Hearsay Rule

The hearsay rule traces its origins to Anglo-American evidence law. Prior to the development of the hearsay rule, cases were often decided based on statements made out of court.

The modern-day hearsay rule also finds support in the confrontation clause of the Sixth Amendment, which states that in criminal cases the defendant is entitled to be "confronted with the witnesses against him." This means that the accused is entitled to be present at his or her trial and to see and hear the witness(es) against him or her. Indeed, in 1988 the Supreme Court held that the Sixth Amendment entitles the accused not only to see and hear adverse witnesses but to personally view such witnesses (*Coy v. Iowa,* 1988). There are some exceptions to the confrontation clause that the Supreme Court has carved out, such as allowing child abuse victims to testify via closed circuit television (*Maryland v. Craig,* 1990); however, such exceptions are comparatively rare and only available in extremely limited circumstances.

The trial of Sir Walter Raleigh in 1603 is illustrative of the role hearsay played in early English courts. Raleigh was on trial for conspiracy to overthrow the King of England. The prosecution relied almost exclusively on a witness who testified that another man, Lord Cobham, spoke of Raleigh's guilt. Raleigh objected to this evidence and argued that Lord Cobham should appear in court. Unfortunately, he did not succeed with his hearsay objection and was convicted of high treason. He was ultimately executed.

In 1813, Chief Justice Marshall explained the adoption of the hearsay rule when he stated that, "Our lives, our liberty, and our property, are all concerned in the support of these rules, which have been matured by the wisdom of ages, and are now revered from their antiquity and the good sense in which they are founded. One of these rules is that hearsay evidence is by its own nature inadmissible." Furthermore, hearsay's "intrinsic weakness, its incompetency to satisfy the mind of the existence of the fact, and the frauds which might be practiced under its cover, combine to support the rule that hearsay is totally inadmissible" (*Mima Queen and Child v. Heburn,* 1813).

Hearsay and the Sixth Amendment

As to the issue of hearsay, a strict interpretation of the Sixth Amendment's confrontation clause would lead one to believe that any statement intended to prove guilt that is not made in the presence of the defendant would not be admissible. The question is whether a person's out-of-court statement "against" the accused, but introduced at trial by a third party, should be considered hearsay. In other words, does the confrontation clause entitle the accused to exclude hearsay? The short answer is "no." There are some 30 exceptions to the hearsay rule that permit the use of hearsay at trial against the accused. Nevertheless, the relationship between hearsay and the confrontation clause is still debated at great length by legal scholars. We briefly outline the contours of this debate.

One perspective on the hearsay-confrontation relationship is that the confrontation clause entitles the accused to be present at trial and to face adverse witnesses but that it also permits the prosecution to take protective measures on the behalf of witnesses. An example of this perspective would be a court permitting a witness against the mob to conceal his or her identity because of the risk of retaliation.

Another view on the hearsay-confrontation relationship is that as long as the defendant has had a chance to cross examine adverse witnesses prior to the current trial, the Sixth Amendment is not violated. This was the point raised by the Supreme Court in *Pointer v. Texas* (1965), regarding an armed robbery trial in which the Court condemned the use of testimony at a preliminary hearing where the defendant was not provided with counsel. Justice Black said that the case would be "quite a different one" if the defendant had been represented by counsel and "given a complete and adequate opportunity to cross examine." Reading between the lines, it seems that the Court was suggesting that prior cross examination (if it had occurred in *Pointer*) would have satisfied the Sixth Amendment's confrontation requirement. As noted in Chapter 8, the Supreme Court has held that cross examination is an indispensable element in such situations (*Crawford v. Washington,* 2004). There, the Court held:

> Where testimonial evidence is at issue, however, the Sixth Amendment demands what the common law required: unavailability and a prior opportunity for cross-examination. We leave for another day any effort to spell out a comprehensive definition of "testimonial." Whatever else the term covers, it applies at a minimum to prior testimony at a preliminary hearing, before a grand jury, or at a former trial; and to police interrogations. These are the modern practices with closest kinship to the abuses at which the Confrontation Clause was directed.

Thus, despite the fact that hearsay evidence may be admissible pursuant to a firmly rooted hearsay exception, if that evidence is testimonial in nature, *Crawford* requires unavailability and cross examination.

At the other extreme, some commentators believe that even limited use of out-of-court statements at a trial violates the confrontation clause. The logic is that since such statements cannot be proven or disproven by cross examination, they should not be admissible as evidence against the accused. This point was raised in *Douglas v. Alabama* (1965). In that case, the prosecution desired to "refresh the recollection" of a convicted co-offender by the name of Loyd by reading his previous confession that implicated the defendant, Douglas. Loyd, however, refused to be cross examined. As such, the Court ruled that the use of the out-of-court confession violated that confrontation clause. In a similar case, *Bruton v. United States* (1968), the Supreme Court held that the introduction of a confession by defendant Evans implicating defendant Bruton violated Bruton's confrontation rights where Evans could not be cross examined.

Bruton v. United States
Supreme Court of the United States
391 U.S. 123 (1968)

A joint trial of petitioner and a co-defendant Evans in the District Court for the Eastern District of Missouri resulted in the conviction of both by a jury on a federal charge of armed postal robbery, A postal inspector testified that Evans orally confessed to him that Evans and petitioner committed the armed robbery. The postal inspector obtained the oral confession, and another in which Evans admitted he had an accomplice whom he would not name, in the course of two interrogations of Evans at the city jail in St. Louis, Missouri, where Evans was held in custody on state criminal charges. Both petitioner and Evans appealed their convictions to the Court of Appeals for the Eighth Circuit. That court set aside Evans' conviction on the ground that his oral confessions to the postal inspector should not have been received in evidence against him. That court set aside Evans' conviction on the ground that his oral confessions to the postal inspector should not have been received in evidence against him. However, the

(continued)

court, relying upon Delli Paoli, affirmed [Bruton's] conviction because the trial judge instructed the jury that although Evans' confession was competent evidence against Evans it was inadmissible hearsay against petitioner and therefore had to be disregarded in determining petitioner's guilt or innocence. Specifically, the trial judge, at the close of the Government's direct case, cautioned the jury that Evans' admission implicating petitioner "if used, can only be used against the defendant Evans. It is hearsay insofar as the defendant George William Bruton is concerned, and you are not to consider it in any respect to the defendant Bruton, because insofar as he is concerned it is hearsay."

*****

Nevertheless, as was recognized in *Jackson v. Denno,* supra, there are some contexts in which the risk that the jury will not, or cannot, follow instructions is so great, and the consequences of failure so vital to the defendant, that the practical and human limitations of the jury system cannot be ignored. Such a context is presented here, where the powerfully incriminating extrajudicial statements of a co-defendant, who stands accused side-by-side with the defendant, are deliberately spread before the jury in a joint trial. Not only are the incriminations devastating to the defendant but their credibility is inevitably suspect, a fact recognized when accomplices do take the stand and the jury is instructed to weigh their testimony carefully given the recognized motivation to shift blame onto others. The unreliability of such evidence is intolerably compounded when the alleged accomplice, as here, does not testify and cannot be tested by cross-examination. It was against such threats to a fair trial that the Confrontation Clause was directed.

*****

We, of course, acknowledge the impossibility of determining whether in fact the jury did or did not ignore Evans' statement inculpating petitioner in determining petitioner's guilt. But that was also true in the analogous situation in *Jackson v. Denno,* and was not regarded as militating against striking down the New York procedure there involved. It was enough that [the] procedure posed "substantial threats to a defendant's constitutional rights to have an involuntary confession entirely disregarded and to have the coercion issue fairly and reliably determined. These hazards we cannot ignore." Here the introduction of Evans' confession posed a substantial threat to petitioner's right to confront the witnesses against

(continued)

> him, and this is a hazard we cannot ignore. Despite the concededly clear instructions to the jury to disregard Evans' inadmissible hearsay evidence inculpating petitioner, in the context of a joint trial we cannot accept limiting instructions as an adequate substitute for petitioner's constitutional right of cross-examination. The effect is the same as if there had been no instruction at all.

A fourth perspective on the hearsay-confrontation relationship is that the confrontation clause requires, whenever possible, that the state produce at trial the person whose out-of-court statement is introduced against the accused. This issue was raised in *Barber v. Page* (1968), in which the Court held that the prosecutor who offered testimony from a preliminary hearing should have tried to produce the witness who made the statement, even though the man was in a federal prison in a neighboring state and could not be easily subpoenaed to appear before the court.

Finally, some people believe that certain types of hearsay should be admissible while other types should be excluded. For example, in *California v. Green* (1970), the Supreme Court rejected challenges to the use of statements by a witness who appeared forgetful and evasive at trial and who had previously implicated the defendant while speaking with the police and in testimony at the defendant's preliminary hearing.

Mueller and Kirkpatrick (1999) describe five theories concerning the relationship between hearsay and the Sixth Amendment's confrontation clause. **Minimalist theory** "entitles the defendant to be present and cross examine witnesses who testify but does not stop the prosecutor from offering testimonial accounts of what others said or from freely using prior statements by those who do testify." **Production theory** holds that the confrontation clause requires the prosecutor to produce the "speaker" at trial wherever possible. **Reliability theory** holds that hearsay is permissible as long as it is reliable. By contrast, unreliable or questionable statements should not be admissible. The view underlying **centrality theory** is that hearsay should be permissible insofar as it corroborates or serves as circumstantial proof of guilt, but not as direct and critical evidence. Finally, **procedural rights theory** holds that the state should gather and present as much live testimony as possible. In other words, the state should be prevented from building its case against the accused primarily with out-of-court statements by people who cannot be cross examined.

Clearly, there is little agreement among courts and legal scholars as to the relationship between the Sixth Amendment's confrontation clause and the hearsay rule. This lack of agreement is responsible in large part for the complexity of modern-day hearsay law. The many exceptions we will discuss, for example, are in response to some of the aforementioned views that some out-of-court statements are more reliable than others and, as such, should be allowed into evidence against the accused.

Problems with Hearsay

Testimonial evidence is relevant if four conditions are satisfied: (1) the witness accurately perceived the event he or she is testifying about, (2) the witness now correctly recalls that perception, (3) the witness now wishes to communicate that recollection accurately and honestly, and (4) the witness has the verbal skills to effectively narrate the events he or she is testifying about. Several trial safeguards are commonly taken to ensure that these four requirements are met: (1) taking an oath so the witness feels compelled to tell the truth; (2) subjecting witnesses to cross examination so their perceptions, ability to recollect, and sincerity can be called into question by the opposition; and (3) displaying the witness before the whole court so the judge and jury can observe the witness's demeanor and behavior.

The problem with hearsay is that it defeats all three safeguards. When a witness testifies about a statement that was made out of court, the court does not have the benefit of swearing in the person who made the statement, overseeing cross examination, or displaying that person before the judge and jury. In essence, the trier of fact is asked to assume that the out-of-court statement was true and, in fact, uttered by an honest and credible person.

Courts typically frown on hearsay evidence for several reasons. Mueller and Kirkpatrick (1999) offer four such reasons. The first and most obvious is that the speaker may misperceive or misunderstand what was said out of court. The second reason is faulty memory. The third is the risk of uncertainty. Finally, hearsay introduces the potential for narrative ambiguity. Collectively, these problems are referred to as errors of perception, errors of memory, and errors of narration. It is immaterial whether the errors are intentional or unintentional.

Misperception and Misunderstanding

The first risk concerning hearsay is that of **misperception or misunderstanding** what took place. For example, if Speaker tells Witness that she saw Defendant flee the scene of the crime, Speaker may have mistaken

Defendant for someone else. Speaker may have had poor vision, may not have been able to hear well, or may have only briefly observed who he thought was the perpetrator. Indeed, there are countless reasons that speakers or declarants can misperceive the events in question. Anything from deficient sensory capacities to deficient mental capacity to physical circumstances (such as poor lighting or distractions) can cause someone to mistakenly perceive a series of events.

Faulty Memory

The second risk, **faulty memory**, is another reason that hearsay is viewed with caution. As Mueller and Kirkpatrick observe (1999), "The acuity of memory is affected by factors operating both at the time of observation, such as attentiveness, interest, emotional involvement, and nature of the experience . . . [however,] . . . [i]t is also affected by factors that come into play when the event is later called to mind, including the type of information, the attitude of the observer, and the suggestivity of the situation" (p. 784). Clearly, in-court witnesses can have faulty memory as well, but the problem with hearsay is that the speaker is not present in court to be questioned as to his or her ability to remember the events in question. In other words, without confrontation, there can be no clarification (see, e.g., *Krist v. Eli Lilly & Co.,* 1990).

The Risk of Uncertainty

A third reason for viewing hearsay statements with caution is the **risk of uncertainty**. It is possible that, for whatever reason, a declarant has a motivation to shade or distort the truth to ensure that the defendant is the one convicted for the crime. Unfortunately, if such a motivation exists, there is no way for it to be revealed in court. For example, assume Witness Brian testifies in court that his friend Jay stated, "I saw Dan commit the crime." Assume further that Jay was insincere in his statement and, in fact, wanted to see Dan convicted of a crime. This deceptive tactic could not be revealed in court because, unless Jay is actually called to testify, the defense will not be able to question the veracity of Jay's claim.

Narrative Ambiguity

The final reason that hearsay is problematic concerns the potential for **narrative ambiguity**. In other words, the declarant may have misspoke or been misunderstood. Because he or she will not be present at the hearing, the opposing side will not be able to seek clarification. Narrative ambiguity can occur for several reasons. First, the declarant may have meant one thing but said another. We discuss this problem later in the section titled "Determining the Matter Asserted." The second reason is that the declarant may have communicated clearly and unequivocally, but the witness still misunderstood him or her. Finally, narrative ambiguity can be introduced by virtue of hearsay evidence because the declarant's statement may not be sufficiently specific, or clarified, to the point that the witness understands its true and intended meaning.

For the Truth of the Matter Asserted

As indicated in the definition of hearsay set forth at the beginning of this chapter, two questions must be answered when determining whether a statement is offered in evidence to prove the **truth of the matter asserted**. These questions focus on (1) the content of the statement, and (2) the purpose of the statement.

In many situations, the content and the purpose of a statement are the same. For example, if the witness wants to prove that the light was red and offers an out-of-court statement that "the light was red," the content of the statement is that the light was red and the statement is offered to prove that the light was red. More problematic is the situation in which the intent of a statement differs from the content. What if the same statement is offered by a witness, but only to prove there was a light at the intersection? The answer to this question requires further analysis. We begin by focusing on the "purpose" of the statement, then we move to the "content."

No other topic in hearsay law is more difficult to understand than the relevance of the "purpose" of an out-of-court statement. Formally, a statement is offered, "for the truth of the matter asserted" when its relevance requires the jury (or judge) to infer that the statement is true. If the jury is not being asked to determine whether an out-of-court statement is true, the statement is not hearsay. Put a different way, an out-of-court statement is not hearsay if it is relevant to prove the fact that it is offered to prove, regardless of whether it is true or false. For example, to prove that Dale was still alive after his car crashed into a wall, a witness testifies that as the paramedics approached the scene of the crash, one called out, "Are you alive?" and Dale called back, "No, I'm dead." Dale's statement is not hearsay because it does not require the jury to determine whether his statement was true or false (he was obviously alive because he responded to the paramedic's question).

Consider another example. Assume that Husband has motive to kill Wife because she has a large life insurance policy. At Husband's trial for murder, Witness testifies that Husband told Witness (out of court and prior to the murder), "I am sick and tired of my wife's infidelity." This statement is not hearsay because, if true, demonstrates motive. If false, it still suggests that Husband may eventually have murdered Wife. Because the jury does not need to focus on the truthfulness (or untruthfulness) of Husband's statement, Husband's statement is not hearsay. A twist on this example is this: If Husband told Witness, "I am going to kill my wife," his statement, if offered in court by Witness, would be considered hearsay because the jury will have to determine whether or not Husband's statement was true.

Four commonly recognized types of statements are not offered for the truth of the matter asserted. They are: (1) legally operative conduct, (2) effect on hearer, (3) circumstantial evidence of declarant's state of mind, and (4) prior statements.

Legally Operative Conduct

An out-of-court statement is not offered for the truth of the matter asserted when the (substantive) law makes uttering the statement a consequential fact. In the criminal context, whenever the making of some statement is an element of the crime, the statement, even if made out of court, will not be considered hearsay. For example, assume that the crime of kidnapping requires a ransom demand. Kidnapper X demands $10,000 dollars from Victim Y for the return of his daughter, Z. X's out-of-court ransom demand, if introduced by a witness at trial (most likely Y), is not hearsay. Returning to our definition concerning the truth of the matter asserted, the jury will not need to determine whether the ransom demand was legitimate or merely an empty threat. The only thing that matters is that the statement was made. Therefore, it is not hearsay.

Effect on Hearer

An out-of-court statement is not for the truth of the matter asserted (and therefore not hearsay) when it is offered to prove that it had an effect on the person who heard it. The most common type of "effect on hearer" statement is an out-of-court notice. For example, assume that Mechanic tells Driver, "Your brake pads need to be replaced." Driver ignores Mechanic's advice, leaves the shop, and crashes into a pedestrian because of brake failure. Pedestrian's surviving spouse sues Driver, and Witness is called to testify that she (who happened to be in the shop at the same time as Driver) heard Mechanic tell Driver that Driver's brake pads needed to be replaced. Witness's testimony is not hearsay because the jury does not have to determine whether it was true, only that it was said. In other words, Mechanic gave Driver "notice" that her car had a problem, which demonstrates knowledge as to the problems with Driver's vehicle. A key limitation of the "effect on hearer" doctrine, however, is that it only covers statements of others (Mechanic) to the person whose state of mind is supposed to have been affected (Driver).

Circumstantial Evidence of a Declarant's State of Mind

Circumstantial evidence of a declarant's state of mind is another situation in which a statement is offered for a reason other than to prove the truth of the matter asserted. To understand this idea, it is important to remember the definition of circumstantial evidence (see Chapter 4). Assume the prosecutor wants to prove that the defendant had the knowledge and ability to rob an armored car. Witness testifies that the defendant said, "I am going to rob Acme Armored's number 1 car when it stops in the Thriftway parking lot on December 10." Ordinarily, this statement would be hearsay; however, if the prosecutor introduces evidence that the defendant had a written record of Acme's delivery and possessed armor-piercing explosives, the defendant's statement will not be considered hearsay. The key is that the statement is offered to prove the defendant's state of mind, not to prove whether his statement was true or false.

Indeed, this example suggests there is a fine line between hearsay and nonhearsay. The thing to remember is that in certain situations, the declarant's statement alone (without additional corroborating evidence) can be admissible and not considered hearsay, but not to prove whether it was true.

Prior Statements

A fourth type of out-of-court statement not offered for the truth of the matter asserted is a prior statement. Evidence that an in-court witness made an out-of-court statement not consistent with his in-court testimony is not hearsay. If the witness testified out of court (possibly during a grand jury investigation or while being interrogated at the police station) "I was drunk" but testifies in court "I was sober," this is an example of an inconsistent statement.

Prior consistent statements can also be offered, but not for the truth of the matter asserted. In other words, the jury does not need to determine whether the statement was true or false. For example, assume that Doctor Expert testifies that Victim was raped. On cross examination, Prosecutor asks, "Dr. Expert, are you being paid for your services today?" Dr. Expert replies, "Yes, I am." On re-direct, the defense attorney introduces an out-of-court statement, made by Dr. Expert prior to his being retained as an expert witness, that "It is my opinion that this girl was raped." Such a statement can be offered to prove the truthfulness of Dr. Expert's in-court testimony, even though the jury will not have to determine the veracity of Dr. Expert's prior out-of-court statement. For a summary of this section, see Table 12.1.

Determining the Matter Asserted

The hearsay doctrine generally assumes that a statement is hearsay or not. For example, saying "It is cold outside" (an assertion) and putting on a coat (a nonverbal act) are clearly two different acts. The statement "It is cold outside" is hearsay if offered in court to prove temperature. The act of putting on a coat is not hearsay if it is not intended to show, nonverbally, that it is cold outside. In reality, though, there are situations in which nonverbal acts and explicit assertions can be both hearsay and nonhearsay when offered for one purpose. To the extent that this situation occurs, it becomes difficult to discern what the "matter asserted" is. In other words, what is the person trying to communicate?

Determining the "matter asserted" is sometimes more difficult than the hearsay rule assumes. Three types of statements pose problems. First, statements offered intentionally but not literally cause confusion. An example of an **intentional, nonliteral statement** is the response "Nice move!" to a person who trips. The statement is made intentionally, but its literal meaning is opposite from what is said. Usually, if the declarant

Table 12.1 When Prior Statements Are Admissible

Statements	Admissibility
Prior consistent statements made under oath	Admissible to rebut claims of improper influence or fabrication
Prior consist statements not made under oath	Admissible to rebut claims of improper influence or fabrication
Prior inconsistent statements made under oath	Always admissible
Prior inconsistent statements not made under oath	Not admissible

consciously intends to assert something other than the literal truth of the statement, the courts will consider it hearsay. Sarcasm, code words, and slang, therefore, will usually be considered hearsay.

Implicit assertions are the second type of confusing statement. For example, Husband is annoyed that Wife likes to keep the heat down in their house and complains, "It's freezing in here!" Clearly, Husband believes it is cold, but his statement is an implicit assertion insofar as it is really a statement of belief or opinion. In other words, the truthfulness of Husband's statement is wholly subjective.

The hearsay analysis becomes particularly complicated with regard to statements that look simple but are actually complex. In evidence parlance, several **subassertions** can be uttered in a single statement. Assume Stacy makes the following out-of-court statement: "Rod hit a water skier with his boat yesterday." This main assertion contains several subassertions. These could include (1) I know a person named Rod; (2) I saw Rod yesterday; (3) Rod was operating a boat yesterday; (4) Rod was going too fast; (5) Rod intended to hit the water skier; (6) my eyes are capable of determining who was operating the boat; (7) there was a water skier in the boat's path; and so on. On the one hand, these subassertions can be considered hearsay because they may be what was intended by the main assertion, "Rod hit a water skier with his boat yesterday." On the other hand, these subassertions may not be considered hearsay if they were not what Stacy intended to communicate.

Yet another way of understanding hearsay is to think of an assertion that the declarant wants the witness to believe is true but that in fact may not be true. Assume, for example, that a person gives false testimony to a police officer during an investigation. In one view, this statement cannot be considered hearsay because it would appear that the intent of the statement is simply to mislead the officer. However, the statement can be considered hearsay because the speaker wants the listener to believe what is being said.

One of the most confusing situations concerning determining the matter asserted is when hearsay is disguised as acts. Some courts allow parties to get around the hearsay requirement by disguising oral or written statements as an act. For example, if a doctor is allowed to testify that "the patient complained of pain," this statement would appear to be hearsay. However, if the intent with this statement is to report on an act (pain) and not to determine whether the patient actually felt pain, it may be admissible as nonhearsay.

A court case should help clarify. In *United States v. Singer* (1982), the Eighth Circuit concluded that an eviction notice sent to "Carlos Almaden" at 600 Wilshire Drive in Minnetonka, Minnesota, was *not* hearsay when offered to prove that Almaden lived at the residence. Two actions supported the contention that Almaden lived at 600 Wilshire Drive: (1) the landlord's act of *sending* the eviction notice, and (2) the actual written contents of the notice. The court said that one can rely on "the landlord's behavior" in mailing the letter rather than "the implied truth of its written contents." Had the witness referred to the written contents of the eviction notice as opposed to the landlord's act of sending the notice, the court would have decided differently.

Another example concerns drug orders and bets. Frequently, during raids and searches of drug houses or gambling operations, the police intercept calls from people seeking to place orders or make bets. Such calls can be viewed in two ways. On the one hand, the calls can be viewed in terms of their content. If an officer testifies in court by saying, "I heard Defendant X state that he would like to order one pound of marijuana," this would be considered hearsay. However, if the officer-now-witness merely wishes to demonstrate a pattern of conduct (that drug orders where taking place at the house) instead of demonstrating that what the person on the other end of the phone said was true, it would not be considered hearsay.

The point of this section is, simply, to illustrate that the question of whether a statement is hearsay is not "black and white." In many situations, determining what the "matter asserted" is depends on why and how the out-of-court statement is introduced in court. A sense of proportionality is essential. Consider the *Singer* case again. The eviction notice is clearly more of a "formal" indicator that Almaden lived at the residence. Yet the court relied on the landlord's act of mailing the notice in order to circumvent the hearsay rule. Had the court focused on the formal indicator (the eviction notice) and given it more weight, the outcome probably would have been different.

Multiple Hearsay and Nonverbal Statements

In most situations the answer to the question, "Is a statement hearsay?" is relatively simple. However, there are occasions where the answer is far from self-evident. It is more difficult to distinguish between hearsay and nonhearsay in two common situations: (1) when multiple people are involved in making a statement (i.e., one person says something, another hears it, who in turn repeats it yet another person), or (2) when a person makes a nonverbal statement.

The hearsay analysis can be more complicated than our earlier examples attest. Multiple hearsay, or hearsay within hearsay, is occasionally encountered. For instance, assume that Jack is on trial for raping Jill. Witness Bill testifies in court that he was told by his friend Will that he in turn was told by his friend Gill that Jack raped Jill. Bill's testimony would contain (Will's) hearsay within (Gill's) hearsay. In such a situation, every level of hearsay must be considered carefully. Naturally, hearsay within hearsay will be viewed with more caution than outright hearsay.

Rule 805. Hearsay Within Hearsay.

Hearsay included within hearsay is not excluded under the hearsay rule if each part of the combined statements conforms with an exception to the hearsay rule provided in these rules.

http://www.law.cornell.edu/rules/fre/ACRule805.htm

Another troubling situation arises when a "statement" offered by a witness is nonverbal. FRE Rule 801 suggests that a statement can be *nonverbal* conduct of a person if it is intended by the person as an assertion. An example will help clarify this rule. Assume that a defendant wishes to prove that it was unseasonably hot one day in August. Witness Pamela testifies that although she did not know how hot it was that day (she was inside her comfortable, air-conditioned office), she did see Dale emerge from *his* office and promptly remove his sweater. As such, Dale must have thought it was hot outside. In other words, Dale was nonverbally asserting to Pamela that it was hot outside. Dale's conduct, then, seems to be an out-of-court statement that is being offered to prove the truth of the matter asserted (that it was hot outside), but such a nonverbal act is not hearsay, at least in this example.

Had Dale stopped by Pamela's office on his way out, looked at her, and wiped his brow as though to suggest it was sweltering outside, this nonverbal statement would be intentional. Assuming Pamela testifies to the effect that Dale wiped his brow, such a nonverbal act can be considered hearsay because (1) it is intended to prove the matter asserted, namely that it was hot outside, and (2) it has an *intentional* effort on the part of Dale to suggest, albeit nonverbally, that it was in fact hot outside (see *United States v. Abou-Saada,* 1986, and *United States v. Ross,* 1963, for further examples).

Summary

The general rule is that hearsay is not admissible in court. In some situations, however, hearsay is admissible. If a statement is made out of court and is offered for the truth of the matter asserted, it may be admissible, provided that the statement is trustworthy and comes from a reliable declarant.

To recap, there are three specific steps that should be taken when analyzing a potential hearsay problem. First, identify the "statement." While this may seem easy, it often is not. The statement may not be an actual quotation, or even a declarative sentence. Instead, the statement may actually consist of some nonverbal act. When a non-verbal act is the statement, convert the nonverbal act into a statement. For example, if Harry swung a baseball bat at his lawnmower, one can safely conclude that his "statement" was, "I've had it with this lawnmower!"

The next step in the hearsay analysis is to identify the declarant as well as the time or place he or she made the statement. In our example from the previous paragraph, the declarant is obviously Harry. The determination may be considerably more complicated, however, if several people were present and engaged in similar non-verbal acts (or were making similar statements). The time frame of the statement is important, too. If the statement was made at a prior trial or a similar hearing, it is not hearsay, because it was not made "out of court."

The third step is to analyze the content of the statement, that is, to identify the consequential fact it is offered to prove. If the statement is not offered for the truth of the matter asserted, it is not hearsay. A hearsay statement to the effect that "I will take great pleasure in see-ing you die from the gunshot wound I will inflict" would obviously be offered for the truth of the matter it asserts (that one person killed or planned to kill another), but a statement to the effect that "little green men are going to kill me" would not be offered for the truth it asserts but perhaps to demonstrate that the declarant was not of sound mind when the statement was made.

Discussion Questions

1. In what way does the Sixth Amendment govern the hearsay rule?
2. What are the four requirements that must be satisfied for testimonial evidence to be relevant?
3. What are the risks concerning hearsay? Briefly explain each one.
4. Explain and give an example of a nonverbal statement. Why are these statements troublesome?

Further Reading

Choo, A. L. T. (1996). *Hearsay and Confrontation in Criminal Trials.* New York, Oxford University Press.

Coady, C. A. J. (1992). *Testimony: A Philosophical Study.* New York, Oxford University Press.

Friedman, R. D. (2002). "The Conundrum of Children, Confrontation, and Hearsay." *Law and Contemporary Problems* 65:243.

Holland, B. (2002). "Using Excited Utterances to Prosecute Domestic Violence in New York: The Door Opens Wide, or Just a Crack?" *Cardozo Women's Law Journal* 8:171.

Kirgis, P. F. (2001). "Meaning, Intention, and the Hearsay Rule." *William And Mary Law Review* 43:275.

Mueller, C. B. and L. C. Kirkpatrick (1999). *Evidence* (2nd ed.). New York: Aspen.

Cases Cited

Barber v. Page, 390 U.S 719 (1968)

Bruton v. United States, 391 U.S 123 (1968)

California v. Green, 399 U.S 149 (1970)

Coy v. Iowa, 487 U.S 1012 (1988)

Crawford v. Washington, 541 U.S. 36 (2004)

Douglas v. Alabama, 380 U.S. 415 (1965)

Krist v. Eli Lilly & Co., 897 F.2d 293 (7th Cir. 1990)

Maryland v. Craig, 497 U.S 836 (1990)

Mima Queen and Child v. Hepburn, 7 U.S. 290 (1813)

Pointer v. Texas, 380 U.S 400 (1965)

United States v. Abou-Saada, 785 F.2d 1 (1st Cir. 1986)

United States v. Ross, 321 F.2d 61 (2nd Cir. 1963)

United States v. Singer, 687 F.2d 1135 (8th Cir. 1982)

CHAPTER 13
HEARSAY: EXEMPTIONS AND EXCEPTIONS

Key Terms & Concepts

Admission by conduct

Business records exception

Contemptuous declarants

Declarations against interest

Defunct or infirm declarants

Distant declarants

Documents affecting property interest

Dying declaration

Evidence of past judgments

Excited utterance

Family records/memorabilia exception

Forfeiture by wrongdoing

Forgetful declarants

Former testimony exception

Hearsay exceptions

Hearsay exemptions

Incompetent declarants

Learned treatises

Market reports/commercial publications

Medical diagnosis exception

Necessity

Official/pubic records exception

Party opponent(s)

Party's agent/servant/employee

Past recollection recorded

Past state of mind

Present sense impression(s)

Prior consistent statements

Prior statement(s)

Prior statement of identification

Prior statements hearsay exemptions

Privileged declarants

Proponent procurement proviso

Records of religious organizations

Reliability

Representative/vicarious/authorized admissions

Reputation

Reputation evidence concerning boundaries

Reputation evidence concerning character

Reputation evidence concerning personal or family history

Residual hearsay exception

Rule 408

Rule 410

Rule 801

Rule 803

Rule 804

Rule 807

Silent hound exception

Statements in ancient documents

Statements made by a party opponent's

co-conspirator

Then-existing mental, emotional, or physical condition exception

Vital statistics exception

Vulnerable declarants

Chapter Learning Objectives

By the end of this chapter, the student should be able to:

- Distinguish between hearsay exemptions and exceptions

- List the exemptions to the hearsay rule
- List the exceptions to the hearsay rule
- Explain what is mean by unrestricted hearsay exceptions
- Identify various hearsay exceptions requiring unavailability of the declarant
- Explain the need for a residual/catch-all exception to the hearsay rule

Introduction

There are two ways that an out-of-court statement can be admitted over a hearsay objection. First, one must ask whether the statement falls within the definition of hearsay. If the answer is no, the statement is not hearsay. Because it is not hearsay, it is exempt from the hearsay rule. If the statement is hearsay, then one must ask, does the statement fall within one of the established hearsay exceptions?

Certain evidence which, on its face, appears to constitute hearsay under the definition provided in Chapter 12 may be deemed admissible under one or more exemptions or exceptions to the hearsay rule. This chapter identifies these various exemptions. Despite the collective mistrust surrounding hearsay, there are times and circumstances under which such evidence may be admissible. This chapter examines those exceptions as well the reasons for their existence. The student should understand that hearsay exemptions and exceptions are driven by public policy and the need for certain evidence to be available in court.

First, we distinguish between hearsay exemptions and exceptions. Rule 801d of the FRE regulates evidence not considered hearsay. Exemptions include prior statements and admissions by party opponents, among others. Unrestricted hearsay exceptions introduced in this chapter include present sense impressions, excited utterances, past recollection recorded, public records, vital statistics, and many more. Miscellaneous hearsay exceptions also discussed in this chapter include family records and memorabilia, documents affecting property interest, market reports and commercial publications, and learned treatises. Finally, we discuss situations in which the declarant is unavailable for one reason or another. These include privileged declarants, forgetful declarants, incompetent declarants, and vulnerable declarants, to name just a few. Dying declarations are also explored as a source of information excepted from the general hearsay rule.

Statements Not Considered Hearsay: Hearsay Exemptions

Rule 801. Definitions

(d) Statements which are not hearsay

> (1) Prior statement by witness. The declarant testifies at the trial or hearing and is subject to cross-examination concerning the statement, and the statement is (A) inconsistent with the declarant's testimony, and was given under oath subject to the penalty of perjury at a trial, hearing, or other proceeding, or in a deposition, or (B) consistent with the declarant's testimony and is offered to rebut an express or implied charge against the declarant of recent fabrication or improper influence or motive, or (C) one of identification of a person made after perceiving the person; or
>
> (2) Admission by party-opponent. The statement is offered against a party and is
>
>> (A) the party's own statement, in either an individual or a representative capacity or
>>
>> (B) a statement of which the party has manifested an adoption or belief in its truth, or
>>
>> (C) a statement by a person authorized by the party to make a statement concerning the subject, or
>>
>> (D) a statement by the party's agent or servant concerning a matter within the scope of the agency or employment, made during the existence of the relationship, or
>>
>> (E) a statement by a coconspirator of a party during the course and in furtherance of the conspiracy.
>
> The contents of the statement shall be considered but are not alone sufficient to establish the declarant's authority under subdivision (C), the agency or employment relationship and scope thereof under subdivision (D), or the existence of the conspiracy and the participation therein of the declarant and the party against whom the statement is offered under subdivision (E).

http://www.law.cornell.edu/rules/fre/ACRule801.htm

Two categories of statements are not considered hearsay. These are also known as **hearsay exemptions,** as opposed to hearsay exceptions. Some scholars also refer to these as nonhearsay (Mueller and Kirkpatrick, 1999). They correspond to FRE Rule 801(d)(1) and (d)(2) namely, prior statements by the witness and admissions by party opponents. Each category in turn has several subcategories (three for prior statements and five for admissions by party opponents). Hearsay exemptions used to be considered hearsay exceptions (and, to an extent, still are). For simplicity's sake, we distinguish between exemptions and exceptions. Statements not considered hearsay are exempt from the hearsay requirement. Statements that are considered hearsay can be admissible by way of an exception to the hearsay rule.

Prior Statements

Three types of prior statements made by a testifying witness cannot be considered hearsay. First, if a witness makes an out-of-court statement that contradicts his or her in-court testimony, the out-of-court statement is not considered hearsay. For example, assume that prior to trial, Witness tells Officer that, "Defendant committed the crime." In court, however, Witness testifies that Defendant did not commit the crime. The out-of-court statement can probably be introduced as evidence (*United States v. Matlock*, 1997). We say "probably" because the Federal Rules of Evidence state that in order for the prior statement to be considered exempt from the hearsay rule, it must have been made under oath or subjected to the penalty of perjury. In our example, had Witness signed a sworn statement prior to trial to the effect that Defendant committed the crime, the court would be correct in admitting it into evidence.

Certain types of **prior consistent statements** are also exempt from the hearsay rule. However, such statements are only admissible in order to rebut a charge of fabrication, improper influence, or motive. For example, assume that Bill is on trial for murder. Witness Pat testifies that he saw Bill commit the murder. In rebuttal, Bill's attorney calls Police Officer Jones to the stand to testify that Pat told him after the murder that Hank, not Bill, had committed the murder. This is an example of an inconsistent statement. Assume further, that following Police Officer Jones' testimony the prosecution calls witness Wilma, who states that Pat told her directly after the murder that Bill was responsible. This is an example of a prior consistent statement being introduced for the purpose of rebutting Police Officer Jones' charge that Pat's testimony was fraudulent.

A third type of statement exempt from the hearsay requirement is a **prior statement of identification**. Statements of prior identification are simply out-of-court statements identifying a person after the declarant has seen the person. For example, assume Henry testifies that he saw someone steal Lewis' car but that he cannot remember who committed the crime because his memory has faded. The prosecutor then introduces evidence that, directly following the crime, Henry accompanied Police Officer Harris on a ride-along during which Henry pointed to a person and said, "That's the person who stole Lewis' car." Henry later picked the Defendant's photo out of a photographic lineup. This is an example of a third-party identification. In general, any out-of-court identification of a suspect in a photographic lineup, actual lineup, or showup is admissible under this hearsay exemption (e.g., *United States v. Evans*, 1971; *United States v. Hallman*, 1971; *United States v. Simmons*, 1991). Note, however, that Sixth Amendment counsel requirements (if any) need to be satisfied (e.g., *Kirby v. Illinois*, 1972; *Gilbert v. California*, 1967).

In summary, each of the "prior statements" hearsay exemptions has two common and critical requirements. First, for a prior statement to be exempt from the hearsay rule, the declarant must take the stand and testify at the hearing where the statement is offered. Second, the declarant must be subject to cross examination. This means that the declarant must be subjected to cross examination as to the prior statement at the current hearing, not some previous hearing.

Admissions by Party Opponents

Admissions by **party opponents** are generally statements attributed to criminal defendants or the party named in a civil lawsuit. Statements by party opponents are not considered hearsay because such statements are not made by an unavailable out-of-court witness, but rather are admissions made by the opposing party. The are five such admissions: (1) the party's own statement, (2) the party's admission by adoption or conduct, (3) an admission by a person authorized by a party to speak, (4) a statement by the party's agent, servant, or employee, and (5) an admission by a co-conspirator of the party. Admissions can be written, spoken, or in the form of nonverbal assertions (*Tamez v. City of San Marcos, Texas*, 1997; *United States v. Seelig*, 1980).

The **party opponent's own statements** can be introduced at trial and are not considered hearsay. For example, assume that Sally sues Officer Rush for negligence following a high-speed collision between their cars. Sally offers evidence that before the accident her friend Officer Slow (who happens to work with Rush and is disgusted with Rush's reckless driving habits) told Sally that Officer Rush said to him, "I can drive as fast as I want, I'm a cop." Although this statement fits the general definition of hearsay, it is not hearsay because the statement is made by a party opponent, namely Officer Slow. Even if Slow's statement does not have any real guarantee of trustworthiness (the problem with hearsay generally), it is admissible because it is offered against the party who presumably made it (Officer Rush). Moreover, Officer Rush is present at the trial because he is a party to the litigation and may rebut the prior statement if he so chooses.

A party opponent's **admission by conduct** is also exempt from the hearsay rule. Assume Shady is on trial for narcotics offenses. Officer

Vigilant testifies that Shady fled from her when she attempted to effect an arrest. Vigilant can testify that Shady fled. This is an example of admission by conduct. It resembles hearsay; however, it is not because Vigilant is testifying *against* Shady. In our example, then, flight from a police officer (conduct) is considered an admission of guilt.

Other types of admissions by conduct are not admissible for policy reasons. If the conduct is one that society generally encourages, it would be detrimental to admit such evidence into trial. For example, if a defendant offers to pay the victim's medical bills (an implied admission of guilt), such evidence will not be admissible under a hearsay exemption because it is generally desirable, from a policy standpoint, for guilty parties to take responsibility for their actions. If evidence such as this *were* admissible, it would discourage future defendants from paying medical bills. The Federal Rules of Evidence (**Rule 408**) also exclude evidence regarding settlement negotiations.

Rule 408. Compromise and Offers to Compromise

Evidence of (1) furnishing or offering or promising to furnish, or (2) accepting or offering or promising to accept, a valuable consideration in compromising or attempting to compromise a claim which was disputed as to either validity or amount, is not admissible to prove liability for or invalidity of the claim or its amount. Evidence of conduct or statements made in compromise negotiations is likewise not admissible. This rule does not require the exclusion of any evidence otherwise discoverable merely because it is presented in the course of compromise negotiations. This rule also does not require exclusion when the evidence is offered for another purpose, such as proving bias or prejudice of a witness, negativing a contention of undue delay, or proving an effort to obstruct a criminal investigation or prosecution.

http://www.law.cornell.edu/rules/fre/ACRule408.htm

Such a rule encourages parties to resolve their disputes without litigation. If settlement negotiations were admissible, parties would be reluctant to discuss settlement prior to trial. Parties would reasonably fear that their willingness to settle a case may be considered by the jury to be an admission of liability.

A similar rule, **Rule 410**, exists for statements made during plea bargaining in criminal cases.

Rule 410. Inadmissibility of Pleas, Plea Discussions, and Related Statements

Except as otherwise provided in this rule, evidence of the following is not, in any civil or criminal proceeding, admissible against the defendant who made the plea or was a participant in the plea discussions. (1) a plea of guilty which was later withdrawn; (2) a plea of nolo contendere; (3) any statement made in the course of any proceedings under Rule 11 of the Federal Rules of Criminal Procedure or comparable state procedure regarding either of the foregoing pleas; or (4) any statement made in the course of plea discussions with an attorney for the prosecuting authority which do not result in a plea of guilty or which result in a plea of guilty later withdrawn.

However, such a statement is admissible (i) in any proceeding wherein another statement made in the course of the same plea or plea discussions has been introduced and the statement ought in fairness be considered contemporaneously with it, or (ii) in a criminal proceeding for perjury or false statement if the statement was made by the defendant under oath, on the record and in the presence of counsel.

http://www.law.cornell.edu/rules/fre/ACRule410.htm

Admissions by conduct are similar to adoptive admissions. Adoptive admissions occur when silence serves as an admission of guilt. For example, assume that X and Y approach each other on a crowded street. X points to Y and says, "That's the man who murdered my wife!" Y says nothing in response and remains silent. Witness Z testifies at trial as to Y's silence. This evidence is admissible because it is offered by a party opponent. Had Y said, "No I didn't," his statement would not be admissible. The rationale for this exemption is that it is reasonable to expect someone who is not guilty of a crime (or responsible for some other act) to make a statement to that effect.

One significant exception to the adoptive admission exemption concerns the *Miranda* warning. If police officers advise a suspect of her *Miranda* right to remain silent and she stands mute, this type of silence cannot be admitted into evidence as an implied admission of guilt. As the Supreme Court stated in *Miranda,* a defendant cannot be penalized for exercising Fifth Amendment privilege during custodial interrogation; prosecutors may not "use at trial the fact that [defendant] stood mute or claimed his privilege in the face of accusation" (*Doyle v. Ohio,* 1976, p. 627).

Further, admissions not by party opponents but by individuals authorized to speak for party opponents are also exempt from the hearsay rule. Such admissions are referred to as **representative/vicarious/authorized admissions.** Virtually anyone can act as an authorized speaker. That includes spouses, attorneys, children, business partners, and so forth. Assume, for example, that Chris sues Larry for injuries Chris suffered while shopping in Larry's store. Keith, an employee of Larry's, approached Chris and said, "My boss, Larry, sent me to apologize for your injury." If Keith's statement is authorized by Larry and is attributed to Larry, it

Doyle v. Ohio
United States Supreme Court
426 U.S. 610 (1976)

Doyle and Wood were arrested together and charged with selling 10 pounds of marijuana to a local narcotics bureau informant. They were convicted in separate trials held about one week apart. The evidence at their trials was identical in all material respects.

The State's witnesses sketched a picture of a routine marijuana transaction. William Bonnell, a well-known "street person" with a long criminal record, offered to assist the local narcotics investigation unit in setting up drug "pushers" in return for support in his efforts to receive lenient treatment in his latest legal problems. The narcotics agents agreed. A short time later, Bonnell advised the unit that he had arranged a "buy" of 10 pounds of marijuana and needed $1,750 to pay for it. Since the banks were closed and time was short, the agents were able to collect only $1,320. Bonnell took this money and left for the rendezvous, under surveillance by four narcotics agents in two cars. As planned, he met petitioners in a bar. From there, he and Wood drove in Bonnell's pickup truck to a nearby town while Doyle drove off to obtain the marijuana and then meet them at a prearranged location in New Philadelphia. The narcotics agents followed the Bonnell truck. When Doyle arrived at Bonnell's waiting truck, the two vehicles proceeded to a parking lot where the transaction took place. Bonnell left in his truck, and Doyle and Wood departed in Doyle's car. They quickly discovered that they had been paid $430 less than the agreed upon price, and began circling the neighborhood looking for Bonnell. They were stopped within minutes by New Philadelphia police acting on radioed instructions from the narcotics agents. One of those agents, Kenneth Beamer, arrived on the scene promptly, arrested petitioners, and gave them *Miranda* warnings. A search of the car, authorized by warrant, uncovered the $1,320.

At both trials, defense counsel's cross-examination of the participating narcotics agents was aimed primarily at establishing that, due to a limited view of the parking lot, none of them had seen the actual transaction but had seen only Bonnell standing next to Doyle's car with a package under his arm, presumably after the transaction. Each petitioner took the stand at his trial and admitted practically

(continued)

everything about the State's case except the most crucial point: who was selling marijuana to whom. According to petitioners, Bonnell had framed them. The arrangement had been for Bonnell to sell Doyle 10 pounds of marijuana. Doyle had left the Dover bar for the purpose of borrowing the necessary money, but while driving by himself had decided that he only wanted one or two pounds instead of the agreed-upon 10 pounds. When Bonnell reached Doyle's car in the parking lot, with the marijuana under his arm, Doyle tried to explain his change of mind. Bonnell grew angry, threw the $1,320 into Doyle's car, and took all 10 pounds of the marijuana back to his truck. The ensuing chase was the effort of Wood and Doyle to catch Bonnell to find out what the $1,320 was all about.

*****

Petitioners' explanation of the events presented some difficulty for the prosecution, as it was not entirely implausible and there was little if any direct evidence to contradict it. As part of a wide-ranging cross-examination for impeachment purposes, and in an effort to undercut the explanation, the prosecutor asked each petitioner at his respective trial why he had not told the frameup story to Agent Beamer when they were arrested.

*****

Following review, the Supreme Court reversed the convictions. Despite the importance of cross-examination, we have concluded that the *Miranda* decision compels rejection of the State's position. The warnings mandated by that case, as a prophylactic means of safeguarding Fifth Amendment rights, require that a person taken into custody be advised immediately that he has the right to remain silent, that anything he says may be used against him, and that he has a right to retained or appointed counsel before submitting to interrogation. Silence in the wake of these warnings may be nothing more than the arrestee's exercise of these *Miranda* rights. Thus, every post-arrest silence is insolubly ambiguous because of what the State is required to advise the person arrested. Moreover, while it is true that the *Miranda* warnings contain no express assurance that silence will carry no penalty, such assurance is implicit to any person who receives the warnings. In such circumstances, it would be fundamentally unfair and a deprivation of due process to allow the arrested person's silence to be used to impeach an explanation subsequently offered at trial.

(continued)

MR. JUSTICE WHITE, concurring in the judgment in *United States v. Hale*, put it very well:

> When a person under arrest is informed, as *Miranda* requires, that he may remain silent, that anything he says may be used against him, and that he may have an attorney if he wishes, it seems to me that it does not comport with due process to permit the prosecution during the trial to call attention to his silence at the time of arrest and to insist that because he did not speak about the facts of the case at that time, as he was told he need not do, an unfavorable inference might be drawn as to the truth of his trial testimony. . . . Surely Hale was not informed here that his silence, as well as his words, could be used against him at trial. Indeed, anyone would reasonably conclude from *Miranda* warnings that this would not be the case.

is an authorized admission. As such, it will not be considered hearsay. Again, the reason is that the statement in our example was made by a party opponent, namely an authorized speaker for the defendant, Larry.

Statements made by a *party's agent, servant, or employee* are also exempt from the hearsay rule. Note, however, that the difference between this exemption and the "authorized admission" exemption discussed in the previous paragraph is that speaking authority is not necessary. In other words, the speaker does not have to be given "authority" to speak for his or her employer for the statement to be admissible against the party opponent. One important qualifier, though, is that the speaker be to blame, if only in part, for the injury or crime. Assume, for example, that Jerri works for a babysitter service and is hired by the Smiths. While babysitting, she falls asleep and the Smiths' toddler wanders outside into the street and is struck by a car. When Jerri wakes up, she calls the Smiths' cell phone and says, "There's been an accident. I'm sorry, it's all my fault." The Smiths then sue Madeline, the owner of the babysitter service. Jerri's statement would be admissible against Madeline as though Madeline had made the statement herself. It is immaterial whether Jerri was authorized to speak. Moreover, her statement will not be considered hearsay because it is provided by a party opponent, the person (or persons) named in the Smiths' lawsuit.

Finally, **statements made by a party opponent's co-conspirator** are not considered hearsay. This hearsay exemption is frequently raised in criminal trials. However, two additional requirements must be satisfied for a co-conspirator's statement to be exempt from the hearsay rule. Not only must the statement be made by a co-conspirator, it must also be made (1) during the conspiracy, and (2) in furtherance of the conspiracy (e.g., *United States v. Nixon,* 1974; *Anderson v. United States,* 1974). Assume Susan is on trial for the murder of Sara. Witness Clyde testifies for the prosecution that he overheard a conversation between Fred and Barney in which Barney stated, "Susan has agreed to help us kill Sara." According to the general definition of hearsay, Barney's statement is hearsay if offered by Witness Clyde. However, Barney's statement will be admissible under the co-conspirator exemption because the statement was made by a co-conspirator (Barney) both prior to the murder and in furtherance of the conspiracy to commit murder. Were it not for this exemption, it is unlikely that secretive conversations made in furtherance of a conspiracy would ever be disclosed in a courtroom setting.

In summary, for a statement by a party opponent to be exempt from the hearsay rule, it must be offered against the party who made the statement or is otherwise responsible for the statement. A party statement is not admissible on behalf of the party who made it or did not make it. A full understanding and grasp of this hearsay exemption requires a correct answer to this important question: Who is offering the statement? If the opposing party offers the statement, it is not hearsay.

Hearsay Exceptions

Before considering whether a hearsay exception applies, it is important to answer three questions. First, is the statement relevant? If the answer is no, it does not matter whether the statement is subject to a hearsay exception or, for that matter, is hearsay at all; it will not be admissible. Second, who is the declarant? If the declarant is someone other than the witness, it is more likely that the statement will be considered hearsay. Third, is the statement offered for the truth of the matter asserted? If the answer is no, the statement is not hearsay. If the answer is yes, the statement is hearsay. At this point, when it is clear that the statement is relevant, was made out of court, and is hearsay, it is time to determine whether the statement falls within an exception to the hearsay rule.

There are so many hearsay exceptions that students of evidence law can get easily mired in the possibilities. A common approach to determining whether a hearsay exception applies is to scrutinize the facts of a case, then decide which hearsay exception is most likely to apply. This approach makes for more work than is necessary. Instead, it is useful to think in terms of categories of exceptions to the hearsay rule. The best way to do so is to first ask whether the declarant is available to testify. If the answer is yes, there are several hearsay exceptions that apply. These are known as "unrestricted" hearsay exceptions, insofar as they do not require that the declarant be inaccessible or unavailable. If the answer is no, there is another specific category of hearsay exceptions that apply only when the declarant is unavailable. We organize the remainder of this chapter around both categories of hearsay exceptions: (1) unrestricted hearsay exceptions, and (2) exceptions requiring the unavailability of the declarant.

Notwithstanding the many varieties of hearsay exceptions, a **hearsay exception** can be defined as a rule that for policy reasons permits an out-of-court statement to be used as substantive evidence of the matter it asserts. There are two reasons that justify the use of hearsay as evidence under certain circumstances. The first is **reliability**. Statements falling within established hearsay rule exceptions are thought to have the highest degrees of trustworthiness and believability. For example, a statement by a patient made to his or her doctor about symptoms of an illness are likely to have a high degree of reliability because of the patient's vested interest in being truthful (few people elect to lie to their doctors about symptoms of illness). The second reason for certain hearsay exceptions is **necessity**. In some situations hearsay is the only evidence available. In other words, hearsay is better than no evidence at all. However, with regard to necessity, it is also desirable that necessary hearsay statements be reliable. It would be unfair to convict a defendant solely on hearsay evidence with few indications of reliability.

Keep in mind the fact that hearsay statements can fall within many hearsay exceptions at the same time. For example, a **present sense impression** [FRE Rule 803(1)] that is made for the purpose of securing medical treatment [Rule 803(4)] is admissible under two specific provisions of the Federal Rules of Evidence. Also, be reminded that we are discussing *exceptions* throughout the remainder of this chapter, not exemptions. Exemptions fell into the categories of prior statements and admissions by party opponents discussed earlier in this chapter.

Unrestricted Hearsay Exceptions

There are at least nine categories of hearsay exceptions not requiring that the declarant be unavailable. We approach each of these in the order they are covered in the Federal Rules of Evidence. Our introduction to each exception will consist of approximately three paragraphs. The first will describe the exception followed by the federal rule itself, the second will offer the rationale for the exception, and the third will describe restrictions and modifications (if any) to the exception. Some of the more complex hearsay exceptions will be discussed in more detail.

Present Sense Impressions

A declarant's statement, whether or not he or she is available, is admissible if (1) the contents of the declarant's statement describe or explain an event or condition, and (2) the timing of the statement places it within the period when the declarant was observing the matter in question (Rule 803[1]). For example, Lisa sues Nicole for negligence following an automobile accident, alleging that Nicole ran a stop sign. Witness Brian testifies for Lisa that he was standing next to Jay just before the collision and heard Jay say, "Wow! That car blew through the stop sign!" Jay's statement is hearsay, but it is admissible because it was a **present sense impression,** a description of the event that sparked the lawsuit.

Rule 803. Hearsay Exceptions; Availability of Declarant Immaterial

(1) Present sense impression. A statement describing or explaining an event or condition made while the declarant was perceiving the event or condition, or immediately thereafter.

http://www.law.cornell.edu/rules/fre/ACRule803.htm

The rationale for this exception is reliability. First, courts tend to believe that there is no problem of recollection when the statement was made at the time of the perception (see *Dutton v. Evans,* 1970; *Nuttall v. Reading Co.,* 1956). In our example, Jay's statement is likely to be reliable because he both observed and commented on Nicole's driving at nearly the same point in time. Second, it is likely that statements of present sense impressions are sincere, again because they are uttered at the same point in time as the event in question (in our example, Nicole's act of running the stop sign).

Importantly, the present sense impression hearsay exception does not require that the declarant be a participant in the event described by the statement (in our example, Jay was merely an observer). Also, the declarant does not have to have direct, personal knowledge of the matter in question. Assume a witness testifies that while speaking on the phone with a murder victim he heard the victim say, "Let me call you back, my neighbor just walked in . . . no, Jim, don't shoot . . ." (BANG! BANG! BANG!). This statement is hearsay, but it is admissible as a present sense impression, even though the declarant had no direct, personal knowledge of the event (i.e., he did not technically *observe* what happened). Next, the present sense impression exception does not require that the statement be precisely contemporaneous with the event. A "slight lapse" between the event and the statement is permissible, but too much time weakens reliability. Finally, the present sense impression exception applies to statements made by identified (though not necessarily "available") and unidentified declarants; however, statements by unidentified declarants are somewhat less reliable because the declarant's statement cannot be challenged as unreliable.

Excited Utterances

A statement is admissible whether or not the declarant is available as a witness if (1) the content of the statement relates to a startling event or condition, and (2) the statement was made while the declarant was under the stress or excitement caused by the event or condition (Rule 803[2]). For example, assume Steve was severely injured by a hit-and-run driver. While he was being treated in the hospital emergency room he saw Mary walk in. He started to shake, then he shouted, "That's the woman who ran me down and nearly killed me!" Assume further that the nurse who was treating Steve testifies at trial as to Steve's emergency room statement. Steve's statement is admissible (through the nurse) as an **excited utterance** because the statement relates to a startling event and was made while the declarant, Steve, was under stress and excitement.

Rule 803. Hearsay Exceptions; Availability of Declarant Immaterial

(2) Excited utterance. A statement relating to a startling event or condition made while the declarant was under the stress of excitement caused by the event or condition.

http://www.mcacp.org/issue50.htm

The rationale for the excited utterance exception is reliability. In other words, when a person is under stress and excited about a recent event, it is less likely that he or she will fabricate the statement (*Ferrier v. Duckworth,* 1990). The excitement presumably increases the accuracy of the declarant's recollection of what happened. Also, because excited utterances are usually made in close temporal proximity to the event in question (the hit-and-run in our example), they are also less likely to be fabricated.

In the past, courts required that excited utterances "narrate, describe, or explain" the traumatic event; however, Rule 803(2) specifies that the statement merely "relate to" the event. What is an "exciting" event that can give rise to an excited utterance? The courts have not defined "exciting" qualities, but accidents and crimes usually qualify as exciting events. The excited utterance exception is two dimensional, meaning that it requires (1) that the exciting event caused the statement, and (2) that the statement must have been made while the excitement from the event persisted. Finally, like the present sense impression exception, the excited utterance exception to the hearsay rule requires that the excited utterance be made in close temporal proximity to the event in question. In some cases, however, courts allow several hours to pass between the event and the excited utterance. The logic is that excitement can persist for a relatively long period of time after a traumatic event. Such statements, if not admissible under the excited utterance exception, will be admissible under the present sense impressions exception (see, for example, *United States v. Sowas,* 1994; *United States v. Golden,* 1982).

Then-Existing Mental, Emotional, or Physical Condition

A statement of the declarant's then-existing state of mind is admissible to prove that state of mind regardless of whether the declarant is now available (Rule 803[3]). In other words, statements that describe the declarant's mental, emotional, or physical condition at the time of the statement are admissible. For example, assume Sally testifies that she heard Lewis say, "John looks really tired," just before John fell asleep at the wheel of his eighteen-wheeler and jumped the median, killing a motorist traveling in the opposite direction. Sally's testimony is admissible because it is in reference to John's state of mind at the time of the crash (he was tired). The same applies to statements concerning physical condition. If Lewis had said, "Look, John is wearing a cast. I don't know how he thinks he can drive," this statement would also be admissible. In short, the **then-existing mental, emotional, or physical condition exception** covers statements *about what a person was feeling at the time he or she spoke.*

Rule 803. Hearsay Exceptions; Availability of Declarant Immaterial

(3) Then existing mental, emotional, or physical condition. A statement of the declarant's then existing state of mind, emotion, sensation, or physical condition (such as intent, plan, motive, design, mental feeling, pain, and bodily health), but not including a statement of memory or belief to prove the fact remembered or believed unless it relates to the execution, revocation, identification, or terms of declarant's will.

The rationale for this exception to the hearsay rule is not only reliability, but necessity. Because such statements are made at or near the time of the event, there is little chance for inaccurate recollection. Also, because such statements are often made in situations where witnesses don't know that a crime has occurred, there is little incentive to fabricate a statement or to lie to ensure that the perpetrator will be convicted. Finally, because mental state is a requirement for most criminal offenses, unless the testifying witness knows of the defendant's mental state, it is often necessary to rely on the statements of third-party declarants to prove mens rea (mental state).

There are three exceptions to the hearsay rule that often get confused with the "then-existing mental, emotional, or physical condition" exception. First, do not confuse "then-existing" with "past state of mind." The past state of mind exception requires unavailability of the declarant, which we cover later in this chapter. Second, do not confuse the "then-existing mental, emotional, or physical condition" exception with the use of the statement of one person to prove the state of mind of another who heard the statement. Such exceptions are admissible because they are not offered for the truth of the matter asserted. Finally, this exception should not be confused with the nonhearsay use of the statement of the declarant together with extrinsic evidence as circumstantial evidence of the defendant's state of mind (see "Circumstantial Evidence of a Declarant's State of Mind" in Chapter 12).

A key restriction on the then-existing mental, emotional, or physical condition hearsay exception is that it does not permit statements of memory or belief. A statement of the declarant's memory or belief concerning whether something is admissible is used only to prove that the declarant remembered or believed something; it cannot be used to prove the declarant's specific memory or belief. For example, to prove that the declarant went to the movies on a Friday, an out-of-court statement on Saturday by the declarant that "I went to the movies yesterday" would be excluded as hearsay to prove that the declarant went to the movies on Friday. This is because the statement amounts to the declarant's "past memory." Declarant's statement is admissible to prove that he or she believes that he or she went to the movie but not to prove that he or she actually went to the movie. However, had the declarant stated on Friday that "I will go to the movies on Saturday," the statement would be admissible because it does not speak to belief or memory of something that happened in the past. It is strange indeed that statements about what the declarant did or actually saw have less probative value that statements about what might occur (i.e., what a person's plans are), but the drafters of the Federal Rules of Evidence apparently believed that statements about past belief/memory are less reliable than statements about planned events.

What value is there in a statement of past belief to prove that the declarant believed something, not that which he or she believed was true? Consider one of the oft-cited hearsay dilemmas, a statement that "I am the King of Mars." Such a statement is admissible under the "then-existing mental, emotional, or physical condition" exception to the hearsay rule to prove that the declarant believed he was the King of

Mars. Obviously, it is impossible (and unnecessary) to prove that the declarant is in fact the King of Mars.

Statements for Medical Diagnosis/Treatment

A statement made for the purpose of medical diagnosis of the declarant or some other person is admissible, regardless of whether the declarant is available as a witness (Rule 803[4]). The medical diagnosis exception to the hearsay rule recognizes two types of statements. The first concerns medical history, symptoms, pains, and other sensations. The second concerns "pertinent causes," the sources of the patient's condition that are reasonably pertinent to the diagnosis or treatment. In other words, the exception's coverage extends to descriptions of what caused the patient's problemsnot just the problems themselvesas long as the descriptions are relevant.

> **Rule 803. Hearsay Exceptions; Availability of Declarant Immaterial**
>
> (4) Statements for purposes of medical diagnosis or treatment. Statements made for purposes of medical diagnosis or treatment and describing medical history, or past or present symptoms, pain, or sensations, or the inception or general character of the cause or external source thereof insofar as reasonably pertinent to diagnosis or treatment.

The primary rationale for this exception is reliability. The theory is that people have a high degree of self-interest in ensuring that they speak truthfully with their health care practitioners concerning illness and injury; people desire to be cured. However, another rationale for the medical diagnosis exception is need. In some cases, such statements are necessary to provide a basis for a medical expert's testimony or to impeach that testimony.

Statements of medical diagnosis need not be made by the patient to fall within the exception. For example, if a parent or a guardian describes a child's condition to the doctor, the parent or guardian's statement will probably be admissible. This is true despite the fact that a parent's statement may be multiple hearsay (e.g., the parent tells a doctor that the child complained of a "stomachache"). Another point of clarification concerning the medical diagnosis exception is that such statements can be made to intermediaries, including hospital attendants, ambulance drivers, nurses, and others, not just doctors. The exception can also apply to non-treating physicians. For example, if a plaintiff in a medical malpractice lawsuit describes a condition to a doctor hired to testify on her behalf, anything she says to the doctor concerning her medical condition will be admissible under the medical diagnosis exception.

Past Recollection Recorded

A recorded (written or recorded on audio) statement of a declarant may be read into evidence or played for the trier of fact, provided that a number of conditions are met (Rule 803{5}). First, the declarant has to be a witness in the case. Second, the statement has to concern a matter of which the declarant would have had personal knowledge. Third, this exception applies only if the declarant cannot remember the matter such that he or she can testify accurately (see *Vicksburg & Meridian Railroad Co. V. O'Brien,* 1886; *United States v. Felix-Jerez,* 1982). Fourth, the statement had to be made or "adopted" by the declarant when the event he or she was making a statement about was still fresh in his or her memory. Finally, the statement must be an accurate reflection of the knowledge of the witness/declarant at the time that it was made. Assume, for example, that Professor Paula witnessed a mugging at a bus stop. At the time of the crime, she jotted some notes down to herself concerning the description of the perpetrator (she knew, after all, that her profession renders her "absent-minded"). Paula testifies at trial that she cannot remember what the perpetrator looks like but that she has written notes describing the defendant. Her written statements are admissible, subject to the above restrictions.

Rule 803. Hearsay Exceptions; Availability of Declarant Immaterial

(5) Recorded recollection. A memorandum or record concerning a matter about which a witness once had knowledge but now has insufficient recollection to enable the witness to testify fully and accurately, shown to have been made or adopted by the witness when the matter was fresh in the witness' memory and to reflect that knowledge correctly. If admitted, the memorandum or record may be read into evidence but may not itself be received as an exhibit unless offered by an adverse party.

The rationale for the "past recollection recorded" exception is necessity. If the witness can no longer remember the events in sufficient detail, it makes sense to admit a "recording" of the incident when no other evidence is available. To an extent, this exception is also justified by reliability. Even though the declarant does not remember the event in order to testify sufficiently at trial, his or her recollection of the event through a "recording" is probably better than any such "recording" provided by a third party.

A thorough understanding of this exception requires that one distinguish between past recollection recorded and past recollection refreshed. The distinction is a subtle but important one. A past recollection refreshed occurs when a testifying witness examines something in court that refreshes his or her memory. For example, assume that Witness Forgetful looks at a police report and says, "Now I remember. The license plate on the hit-and-run truck was BADGUY." This is past recollection refreshed and is (1) not considered hearsay, and (2) not subjected to the hearsay rule or any of its exceptions. Only past recollections recorded constitute exceptions to the hearsay rule.

Another important restriction concerning the past recollections recorded exception is that such past statements are not introduced into evidence as exhibits. Past recordings cannot be introduced into evidence by the proponent. For example, if the plaintiff in a lawsuit wishes to introduce evidence of a past recording to support his testimony, he may not do so. The rationale for this restriction is that allowing proponents to introduce evidence of past recordings may result in them simply using this exception as a method of getting a record of important testimony before the jury. In other words, the jury may give more weight to the written words than to the oral testimony of the witness. Thus, the opponent is the only party that can introduce evidence of a past recollection recorded.

The Business Records Exception

Statements recorded (again, in writing or by audio) as a matter of routine in the records of a regularly conducted business (or businesslike) activity are admissible, without regard to the availability of the declarant (Rule 803[6]). Four important restrictions govern the **business records exception**. The statement must have been recorded (1) during the regular course of business, (2) as a record of some event or condition, (3) at or near the time of the event or condition, and (4) by someone with personal knowledge of the event or condition. In addition to these four restrictions, the custodian of the record or other authorized witness must testify to or provide an affidavit showing that these four restrictions were met. Also, it needs to be shown that the sources of information and/or the method of preparation of the recording are trustworthy.

Rule 803. Hearsay Exceptions; Availability of Declarant Immaterial

(6) Records of regularly conducted activity. A memorandum, report, record, or data compilation, in any form, of acts, events, conditions, opinions, or diagnoses, made at or near the time by, or from information transmitted by, a person with knowledge, if kept in the course of a regularly conducted business activity, and if it was the regular practice of that business activity to make the memorandum, report, record or data compilation, all as shown by the testimony of the custodian or other qualified witness, or by certification that complies with Rule 902(11), Rule 902(12), or a statute permitting certification,

unless the source of information or the method or circumstances of preparation indicate lack of trustworthiness. The term "business" as used in this paragraph includes business, institution, association, profession, occupation, and calling of every kind, whether or not conducted for profit.

The justification for this exception includes both reliability and necessity. Businesses rely on their records for their operation, so it is highly likely that such records are reliable. Aside from being essential to the operation of a business, business records are also kept so that people do not need to remember every transaction or important occurrence. Without records being available, businesses would not be able to prove that transactions or events took place. In this sense, then, it is occasionally necessary for courts to rely on business records, even though they are considered hearsay.

There are several restrictions concerning the business records exception. First, such records must be in writing, although the Federal Rules of Evidence remain silent on the definition of "writing." Most modern statutes construe "writing" to include not just written documents but audio and video recordings, as well as photographs, movies, and computerized business records. Second, records associated with the "regular course" of business include those books and records that are regularly relied on in the operation of a business. These include records of receipts, orders, and so on. For example, assume that Harry Homicidal reserved a wood chipper at Acme Rentals. The record of his reservation would be admissible under the business records exception, assuming Acme regularly documents reservations in writing. Third, the definition of "business" in the business records exception is expansive. "Business" is not limited to commercial enterprises but includes government agencies, nonprofit organizations, and even criminal organizations. Virtually any record that is not purely personal falls within the business records exception. Fourth, the business record must be of an "act, condition, or event"; otherwise, it will not be admissible under the business records exception. However, Rule 803(6) now provides that even "opinions" and "diagnoses" are admissible under the business records exception.

Fifth, the record must be made "at or near" the time of the event or act. For example, a receipt documenting a purchase at the time of the purchase would be admissible. A doctor's documented opinion about a patient's condition she diagnosed 10 years ago would probably not be admissible, because the record was not made at the time of the diagnosis. Sixth, we stated that the exception applies only to people with personal knowledge of the event or condition. To clarify, the information recorded must first come from someone with personal knowledge, but his or her perception can be transmitted to and recorded by any employee authorized as part of a "business duty" to transmit such information. Unfortunately, in complex business operations, records are often transmitted through multiple parties, raising problems of multiple hearsay. To keep things as simple as possible, remember that "business duty" means that the statement must be part of the person's job to make, or record such statements. Statements that fall outside of a "business duty" (such as reports of witnesses at crime scenes) are not admissible under the business records exception.

Keep in mind the fact that business records can be admitted into evidence through other channels besides the business records exception. If, for example, a statement in a business record is offered not for the truth of the matter asserted but for another person (such as to show that the statement had an effect on the "hearer"), the record would be admissible. Such a statement would be *exempt* from the hearsay rule.

The Official (Public) Records Exception

A writing, statement, report, data compilation, or other record by a government agency (known as either "official" or "public") is admissible if it records (1) acts of the agency, (2) matters the agency is required to observe and report, and/or (3) factual findings of investigations (Rule 803{8}). Such writings are not admissible, however, if they include matters observed by police officers or are offered against the defendant. Also, such writings are not admissible if it turns out that the source of the information is not reliable and trustworthy. The **official records exception** bears striking resemblance to the business records exception, but it operates differently and is easier to use. Official records need not be routinely maintained, and no custodian of the records or other witness is usually required to testify as to their authenticity.

Official records are not admissible in criminal proceedings against the defendant. Few people think prosecutors should use police reports prepared after the crime was committed as evidence against a defendant, because such reports are often based on outsider statements and are provided by people who themselves are implicated or involved in any number of ways in the crime. This is not to say that police reports are inaccurate, they probably are in most situations, but the material they contain, if offered alone to prove guilt, threatens the Sixth Amendment's confrontation clause. In other words, if people were convicted based on evidence supplied in a police officer's report, they would be denied their Sixth Amendment right to confront adverse witnesses and cross examine them as to the truthfulness of their statements.

Rule 803. Hearsay Exceptions; Availability of Declarant Immaterial

(8) Public records and reports. Records, reports, statements, or data compilations, in any form, of public offices or agencies, setting forth (A) the activities

of the office or agency, or (B) matters observed pursuant to duty imposed by law as to which matters there was a duty to report, excluding, however, in criminal cases matters observed by police officers and other law enforcement personnel, or (C) in civil actions and proceedings and against the Government in criminal cases, factual findings resulting from an investigation made pursuant to authority granted by law, unless the sources of information or other circumstances indicate lack of trustworthiness.

Notwithstanding the problems associated with official records used to prove guilt, the rationale for the official records exception is generally reliability and necessity. By virtue of being in an official position or working in a public capacity, official/public records are assumed to be kept accurately. Also, because of the desire to allow public employees to continue working, it is often necessary to rely on the reports they prepare. For example, assume an airline passenger's surviving spouse sues the carrier for negligence following a crash that occurred because of faulty maintenance. During the course of the crash investigation, an NTSB investigator prepared a report, which was offered at trial. The official records exception ensures that the investigator can continue to go about her investigative duties while her report can be admitted at trial.

A source of controversy surrounding the official records exceptions concerns the extent to which prosecutors and others can evade the restrictions and limitations on the use of official records and instead rely on the business records exception. Many courts have said no, this cannot be done. However, given that there are several other exceptions (e.g., past recollection recorded), prosecutors have other possible channels through which they may be able to admit otherwise restricted official records. See Table 13.1 for a summary of this discussion.

Table 13.1   Admissibility of Public Records

Type of Report/Document	Admissible by Which Party
Activities of public office	Civil plaintiff and defendant; criminal prosecutor and defendant
Non-law enforcement reports/observations	Civil plaintiff and defendant; criminal prosecutor and defendant
Findings from official investigations	Civil plaintiff and defendant; criminal defendant only
Law enforcement observations/reports	Civil plaintiff & defendant only

The Vital Statistics Exception

Public records of **vital statistics**, including births, deaths, and marriages, are the subject of two separate hearsay exceptions in the Federal Rules of Evidence [Rule 803(9) and Rule 803(12)]. Such documents are usually made by people with an obligation to report and with no motive to lie. Thus, the rationale for exempting such records from the hearsay rule is reliability. Also, it would be difficult to obtain such records from other sources, so they are often necessary. As with the official records exception, the custodian of the records does not have to testify as to their authenticity; however, certified copies of vital statistics and similar records are usually required.

Rule 803. Hearsay Exceptions; Availability of Declarant Immaterial

9) Records of vital statistics. Records or data compilations, in any form, of births, fetal deaths, deaths, or marriages, if the report thereof was made to a public office pursuant to requirements of law.

The "Silent Hound" Exceptions

Rule 803(7) and 803(10) are known collectively as the **silent hound exception**. They are the mirror images of the business records and official records exceptions, respectively. Rule 803(7) says that the *absence* of records kept in accordance with the business records exception is admissible to prove the nonoccurrence or nonexistence of the matter. Similarly, Rule 803(10) says that *absence* of records kept in accordance with the official records exception is admissible to prove the nonoccurrence or nonexistence of the matter. In one view, the absence of records can be considered nonhearsay, which does not fall within any particular hearsay exception. Even so, the framers of the Federal Rules of Evidence saw fit to state that the absence of records is exempt from the hearsay rule. Assume, for example, that Carol sues the local police department for negligently failing to respond to citizen complaints that were phoned in via the department's 800 number for complaint filing. She introduces evidence at trial that no records of complaints were kept by the agency. This failure to document complaints would fall under Rule 803(10).

Miscellaneous Hearsay Exceptions

Several other, less "popular" hearsay exceptions that do not require that the declarant be unavailable as a witness deserve a brief description.

Records of religious organizations, including statements of births, marriages, divorces, deaths, legitimacy, ancestry, relationship by blood or marriage, or other similar facts of personal or family history, are not bound by the hearsay rule (rule 803[11]). In certain proceedings, such as probate hearings or litigation, it is occasionally necessary to rely on church records. Church records are viewed with a high degree of reliability because the aura of "God" (or a similar deity) is thought to discourage fabrication. This exception also holds that the use of sacramental certificates issued by a person with ecclesiastical or governmental authority to administer the sacrament are admissible to prove facts contained in the certificate regarding the ritual and its participants.

Rule 803. Hearsay Exceptions; Availability of Declarant Immaterial

11) Records of religious organizations. Statements of births, marriages, divorces, deaths, legitimacy, ancestry, relationship by blood or marriage, or other similar facts of personal or family history, contained in a regularly kept record of a religious organization.

Certain **family records and memorabilia** are also exempt from the hearsay rule (Rule 803 [12–13]). These include statements of fact concerning personal or family history contained in family Bibles, genealogies, charts, engravings on rings, inscriptions on family portraits, and engravings on urns, crypts, or tombstones and other items. The rationale for this exception is reliability. It is thought that statements concerning family history are likely to be accurate when they are made in places that are subject to inspection and are viewed as important. California law limits this exception to facts about family history of members of the family, but the Federal Rules of Evidence are silent on this issue.

Rule 803. Hearsay Exceptions; Availability of Declarant Immaterial

(12) Marriage, baptismal, and similar certificates. Statements of fact contained in a certificate that the maker performed a marriage or other ceremony or administered a sacrament, made by a clergyman, public official, or other person authorized by the rules or practices of a religious organization or by law to perform the act certified, and purporting to have been issued at the time of the act or within a reasonable time thereafter.

(13) Family records. Statements of fact concerning personal or family history contained in family Bibles, genealogies, charts, engravings on rings, inscriptions on family portraits, engravings on urns, crypts, or tombstones, or the like.

Records of and statements in **documents affecting a property interest** are admissible under yet another exception to the hearsay rule (Rule 803 [14–15]). The most common type of record of an interest in property is a title (such as a car title). Additional documents such as deeds, mortgages, and wills also affect the ownership of property. The rationale for relying on such documents is reliability; given their "official" nature, they are given a high degree of deference. Also, it is frequently necessary to rely on such documents because the original may not be available. Instead, it is useful to prove transfer of title or ownership by the record of title documents filed with the appropriate public official. There are three requirements to this exception. First, the instrument must purport to establish or affect an interest in property. Second, the statement must be relevant to the purpose of the document. Finally, later dealings with the property cannot be inconsistent with the truth of the statement or purport of the document.

Rule 803. Hearsay Exceptions; Availability of Declarant Immateria

(14) Records of documents affecting an interest in property. The record of a document purporting to establish or affect an interest in property, as proof of the content of the original recorded document and its execution and delivery by each person by whom it purports to have been executed, if the record is a record of a public office and an applicable statute authorizes the recording of documents of that kind in that office.

(15) Statements in documents affecting an interest in property. A statement contained in a document purporting to establish or affect an interest in property if the matter stated was relevant to the purpose of the document, unless dealings with the property since the document was made have been inconsistent with the truth of the statement or the purport of the document.

Another hearsay exception pertains to **statements in ancient documents** (Rule 803[16]). According to the Federal Rules of Evidence, statements in a document in existence for 20 years, the authenticity of which is established, are not bound by the hearsay rule. The rationale for this exception is twofold. First, it is occasionally necessary to rely on ancient documents because of the unlikelihood of finding a witness who recalls appropriate facts because of the passage of time. In some cases it may even be difficult to find any witness at all. The Federal Rules permit authentication of an ancient document by proof that it was found in a place and in such condition as would suggest its authenticity.

Rule 803. Hearsay Exceptions; Availability of Declarant Immaterial

(16) Statements in ancient documents. Statements in a document in existence twenty years or more, the authenticity of which is established.

Market reports and commercial publications, including business publications, are exempt from the hearsay rule as well (Rule 803[17]).

For example, a statement in a published document, such as stock market quotations, phone directories, real estate listings, or compilations of commodity sales, are admissible. A key restriction on this exception is that such documents must be relied upon by the public or by members of the same occupation. Thus, the rationale for permitting such documents is reliability; they are thought to be compiled by people with no motive to lie. Also, such documents are used by the public (or other members of the same occupation), so errors are likely to be discouraged and infrequent. Certain states place additional restrictions on this exception, including limiting reliance on business publication to other business, not the public, and excluding statements of opinion in such compilations.

Rule 803. Hearsay Exceptions; Availability of Declarant Immaterial

(17) Market reports, commercial publications. Market quotations, tabulations, lists, directories, or other published compilations, generally used and relied upon by the public or by persons in particular occupations.

Learned treatises are the subject of another hearsay exception (Rule 803[18]). This exception covers statements published in books, magazines, pamphlets and other such documents. However, the Federal Rules of Evidence require that (1) the reliability of the text be shown by the testimony of experts or judicial notice, and (2) the statement(s) be called to the attention of an expert witness either on cross examination or relied on by the expert in direct examination. Statements falling within this exception can be introduced into evidence, but the publications in which they are found cannot. Furthermore, the rationale for this exception is the need to rely on an accumulated body of knowledge rather than "reinvent" knowledge whenever a particular fact is in dispute. Assume, for example, that Coffee Addict cannot afford to hire an expert witness to prove that when coffee is too hot, it burns. When Coffee Executive testifies that it is careless people who burn themselves, not the coffee, Addict reads an excerpt from a book called *The Perils of Hot Coffee* (a highly respected and reliable treatise) to the effect that coffee, when served too hot, burns people. The statement from the book is admissible under an exception to the hearsay rule.

Rule 803. Hearsay Exceptions; Availability of Declarant Immaterial

(18) Learned treatises. To the extent called to the attention of an expert witness upon cross-examination or relied upon by the expert witness in direct examination, statements contained in published treatises, periodicals, or pamphlets on a subject of history, medicine, or other science or art, established as a reliable authority by the testimony or admission of the witness or by other

expert testimony or by judicial notice. If admitted, the statements may be read into evidence but may not be received as exhibits.

There are also three hearsay exceptions concerning reputation. **Reputation** refers to what people think about someone. Three types of reputation evidence are admissible under the Federal Rules of Evidence. First, **reputation evidence concerning personal or family history** is admissible (Rule 803[19]). This includes reputation among members of a person's family or among a person's associates or in the community as to a person's birth, adoption, marriage, divorce, death, legitimacy, or other similar fact of personal or family history. The reason for this is exception is that, in some cases, it is necessary to rely on the hearsay statements of others (besides in-court witnesses) to establish reputation.

Rule 803. Hearsay Exceptions; Availability of Declarant Immaterial

(19) Reputation concerning personal or family history. Reputation among members of a person's family by blood, adoption, or marriage, or among a person's associates, or in the community, concerning a person's birth, adoption, marriage, divorce, death, legitimacy, relationship by blood, adoption, or marriage, ancestry, or other similar fact of personal or family history.

Second, **reputation evidence concerning character** can be admitted into evidence without regard to the availability of the declarant. (Rule 803 [21]). However, character hearsay is limited to character in one's community or in a group of which he or she is a member. Moreover, hearsay statements concerning character are also bound by the rules governing the use of character evidence.

Rule 803. Hearsay Exceptions; Availability of Declarant Immaterial

(21) Reputation as to character. Reputation of a person's character among associates or in the community.

Third, **reputation evidence concerning boundaries** (community history) is also admissible without regard to the declarant's availability (Rule 803[20]). This exception is limited to statements about community history, geographic boundaries, and customs.

Rule 803. Hearsay Exceptions; Availability of Declarant Immaterial

(20) Reputation concerning boundaries or general history. Reputation in a community, arising before the controversy, as to boundaries of or customs affecting lands in the community, and reputation as to events of general history important to the community or State or nation in which located.

These three exceptions to the hearsay rule have in common the fact that they allow evidence of common repute (what people say about someone) to be offered as proof that things are just as people think, and it is not a necessary precondition that the declarant be unavailable to testify as a witness.

Finally, **evidence of past judgments** is not bound by the hearsay rule (Rule 803[22–23]). These include criminal and civil judgments. With regard to past criminal convictions, evidence of past *felony* convictions is admissible to prove any consequential fact if (1) the judgment results from a trial or guilty plea (but not a plea of nolo contendere), and (2) if offered by the prosecution in a criminal case, the judgment involves the accused. Do not confuse this rule with what we discussed in Chapter 7 about witness credibility. Next, evidence from civil judgments is admissible to prove personal, family, or general history or boundaries if (1) the fact was a consequential fact essential to the judgment, and (2) the fact is one of those described in the exceptions for reputation evidence of such history or boundaries.

Rule 803. Hearsay Exceptions; Availability of Declarant Immaterial

(22) Judgment of previous conviction. Evidence of a final judgment, entered after a trial or upon a plea of guilty (but not upon a plea of nolo contendere), adjudging a person guilty of a crime punishable by death or imprisonment in excess of one year, to prove any fact essential to sustain the judgment, but not including, when offered by the Government in a criminal prosecution for purposes other than impeachment, judgments against persons other than the accused. The pendency of an appeal may be shown but does not affect admissibility.

(23) Judgment as to personal, family or general history, or boundaries. Judgments as proof of matters of personal, family or general history, or boundaries, essential to the judgment, if the same would be provable by evidence of reputation.

Hearsay Exceptions Requiring 'Unavailability' of the Declarant

http://www.mcacp.org/issue44.htm

We now move into the second category of hearsay exceptions. The exceptions that follow can be used only if the declarant is dead or is otherwise "unavailable" to act as a witness. The reason for having a category of exception requiring the "unavailability" of the declarant is that necessity dictates the few exceptions that require it. These exceptions stem from FRE Rule 804(a).

The Federal Rules of Evidence go to great lengths to define "unavailable." Eight types of people are considered unavailable. The first includes **privileged declarants**. According to Rule 804(a)(1), "a declarant is unavailable as a witness if a privilege could be asserted to prevent her from testifying about the facts asserted in her statement."

Second, a declarant is unavailable as a witness if he or she is ordered to testify about his or her out-of-court statements but refuses to do so (a so-called **contemptuous declarant**). Obviously, a declarant who refuses to testify cannot be considered available.

Third, **forgetful declarants** are considered unavailable. The forgetful person must actually testify that he or she cannot remember the facts of his or her out-of-court statement. People may state that they have no memory, sometimes truthfully and sometimes to avoid testifying.

Fourth, **defunct or infirm declarants** are considered unavailable. This means that the person is dead or is unable to appear because of a physical illness or infirmity. Death is, of course, the ultimate form of unavailability and is responsible in large part for the "dying declaration" exception discussed below.

Fifth, the Federal Rules consider unavailable **distant declarants**. Distant declarants are those who are absent, beyond subpoena, and undeposable. An important requirement concerning distant declarants is that the proponent take reasonable steps to procure the witness's appearance and act diligently in so doing.

Sixth, **incompetent declarants** are considered unavailable. If a witness is not competent (see Chapter 6) with regard to an out-of-court statement, he or she will be considered unavailable. Recall that if a person cannot understand the duty to tell the truth and cannot narrate the events in question (or, in the case of hearsay, narrate his or her out-of-court statement), the person will be considered incompetent to act as a witness.

Seventh, **vulnerable declarants,** such as those who would likely suffer severe harm or trauma from testifying, can be considered unavailable. A problem with considering vulnerable declarants unavailable is that the Sixth Amendment's confrontation clause is compromised if the defendant does not have the opportunity to cross examine the declarant.

Finally, the Federal Rules provide for a **proponent procurement proviso**. This proviso states that a declarant is unavailable if (1) the grounds for the declarant's unavailability were caused by the proponent of the declarant's statement, and (2) the causative act was intended to prevent the declarant from testifying. In other words, the hearsay exceptions that follow may not be used by a party who intentionally prevents the declarant from being present.

Rule 804. Hearsay Exceptions; Declarant Unavailable

(a) Definition of unavailability.

"Unavailability as a witness" includes situations in which the declarant—

(1) is exempted by ruling of the court on the ground of privilege from testifying concerning the subject matter of the declarant's statement; or

(2) persists in refusing to testify concerning the subject matter of the declarant's statement despite an order of the court to do so; or

(3) testifies to a lack of memory of the subject matter of the declarant's statement; or

(4) is unable to be present or to testify at the hearing because of death or then existing physical or mental illness or infirmity; or

(5) is absent from the hearing and the proponent of a statement has been unable to procure the declarant's attendance (or in the case of a hearsay exception under subdivision (b)(2), (3), or (4), the declarant's attendance or testimony) by process or other reasonable means.

A declarant is not unavailable as a witness if exemption, refusal, claim of lack of memory, inability, or absence is due to the procurement or wrongdoing of the proponent of a statement for the purpose of preventing the witness from attending or testifying.

http://www.law.cornell.edu/rules/fre/ACRule804.htm

The Former Testimony Exception

When a person is unavailable as a witness, his or her previous testimony can be admitted into evidence in the present trial subject to the following restrictions: (1) it was made under oath and subject to direct or cross examination, and (2) the former testimony was given in a prior trial, deposition, or similar judicial hearing (Rule 804[b][1]). And unless expressly required by law, the former testimony need not be proven by a transcript of the former proceeding.

Rule 804. Hearsay Exceptions; Declarant Unavailable

(1) Former testimony. Testimony given as a witness at another hearing of the same or a different proceeding, or in a deposition taken in compliance with law in the course of the same or another proceeding, if the party against whom the testimony is now offered, or, in a civil action or proceeding, a ·predecessor in interest, had an opportunity and similar motive to develop the testimony by direct, cross, or redirect examination.

An important restriction is the direct or cross examination requirement. Assume that Jack has sued his insurance company to collect the insurance owed on his car that was stolen. Assume also that Jill testified at

Jack's earlier trial for auto theft that Jack said, "I'm going to make it look like my car was stolen so I can collect the insurance money." If Jill is "unavailable" to testify in the civil trial, her testimony will be admissible, but only because Jack (through Jack's attorney) had an opportunity to cross examine Jill at the previous criminal trial. Had Jack not been able to cross examine Jill at the previous trial, her past testimony would not be admissible in the civil trial. Note that only the *opportunity* to cross examine (or directly examine) is required. Had Jack's attorney not cross examined Jill at Jack's criminal trial, her testimony would still be admissible in the civil trial because Jack had the opportunity to cross examine her.

Dying Declarations

At common law, a dying declaration of a homicide victim was admissible against the murderer in a criminal prosecution. The rationale for the present-day version of this exception is reliability (there is no motive to lie right before one is about to die; see *Mattox v. United States,* 1892; *United Services Auto. Assn. v. Wharton,* 1965). Federal Rule of Evidence 804(b)(2) makes a **dying declaration** admissible as evidence if (1) the declarant is unavailable, (2) the declarant believed his or her death was imminent when the statement was made, (3) the statement concerns the cause and circumstances of the declarant's anticipated death, and (4) the statement is offered in a civil action or prosecution for homicide.

Rule 804. Hearsay Exceptions; Declarant Unavailable

(2) Statement under belief of impending death. In a prosecution for homicide or in a civil action or proceeding, a statement made by a declarant while believing that the declarant's death was imminent, concerning the cause or circumstances of what the declarant believed to be impending death.

These four requirements may seem restrictive, but not when compared to California's evidence code. Section 1242 of the California Evidence Code makes a dying declaration admissible if (1) the declarant is dead, (2) the declarant was actually dying when the statement was made, (3) the declarant was under a sense of immediately impending death when the statement was made, (4) the statement concerned the cause and circumstances of the declarant's death, and (5) the declarant had personal knowledge of the matters stated. Unlike the Federal Rules of Evidence, California's dying declaration exception to the hearsay rule requires that the declarant actually be dead and was actually dying when the statement was made. The Federal Rules contain no such restrictions. Technically, under the federal rules a declarant can still be alive, but unavailable, for the dying declaration exception to apply. Note, however, that neither the Federal Rules nor the California Evidence Code permit dying declarations to be admitted into evidence in any type of criminal proceeding other than a homicide trial.

Mattox v. United States
Supreme Court of the United States
146 U.S. 140 (1892)

Dying declarations are admissible on a trial for murder as to the fact of the homicide and the person by whom it was committed, in favor of the defendant as well as against him. But it must be shown by the party offering them in evidence that they were made under a sense of impending death. This may be made to appear from what the injured person said; or from the nature and extent of the wounds inflicted, being obviously such that he must have felt or known that he could not survive; as well as from his conduct at the time and the communications, if any, made to him by his medical advisers, if assented to or understandingly acquiesced in by him. The length of time elapsing between the making of the declaration and the death is one of the elements to be considered, although as stated by Mr. Greenleaf, "it is the impression of almost immediate dissolution, and not the rapid succession of death, in point of fact, that renders the testimony admissible." In *Regina v. Perkins*, the deceased received a severe wound from a gun loaded with shot, of which wound he died at five o'clock the next morning. On the evening of the day on which he was wounded, he was told by a surgeon that he could not recover, made no reply, but appeared dejected. It was held by all the judges of England that a declaration made by him at that time was receivable in evidence on the trial of a person for killing him, as being a declaration in *articulo mortis*. There the declaration was against the accused, and obviously no more rigorous rule should be applied when it is in his favor. The point is to ascertain the state of the mind at the time the declarations were made. The admission of the testimony is justified upon the ground of necessity, and in view of the consideration that the certain expectation of almost immediate death will remove all temptation to falsehood, and enforce as strict adherence to the truth as the obligation of an

(continued)

oath could impose. But the evidence must be received with the utmost caution, and if the circumstances do not satisfactorily disclose that the awful and solemn situation in which he is placed is realized by the dying man because of the hope of recovery, it ought to be rejected. In this case the lapse of time was but a few hours; the wounds were three in number and one of them of great severity; the patient was perfectly conscious, and asked the attending physician his opinion, and was told that the chances were all against him, and that the physician thought there was no "show for you [him] at all." He was then interrogated as to who did the shooting, and he replied that he did not know. All this was admitted without objection. Defendant's counsel then endeavored to elicit from the witness whether, in addition to saying that he did not know the parties who shot him, Mullen stated that he knew Clyde Mattox, and that it was not Clyde who did so. The question propounded was objected to on the sole ground of incompetency, and the objection sustained. In this, as the case stood, there was error. So long as the evidence was in the case as to what Mullen said, defendant was entitled to refresh the memory of the witness in a proper manner and bring out, if he could, what more, if anything, he said in that connection. It was inconsistent with Mullen's statement that he did not know the parties, for him also to have said that he knew Mattox was not one of them. His ignorance of who shot him was not incompatible with knowledge of who did not shoot him. We regard the error thus committed as justifying the awarding of a new trial.

Declarations Against Interest

A statement by an unavailable person (whether or not a party to the current proceedings) that, at the time it was made, would have been harmful to some interest of the declarant is admissible under another exception to the hearsay rule (Rule 804[b][3]). For example, assume Dealer is on trial for selling drugs to high school students. When a witness testified at trial that she had seen Dealer sell drugs in the cafeteria, Dealer cried out in the courtroom, "You liar! It was in the gym!" Assume further that the gym teacher is fired for having failed to intervene. If the gym teacher sues to challenge the firing, Dealer's statement would be admissible in the civil trial. The rationale for permitting this statement is, not surprisingly, reliability. A reasonable person would not make such a statement unless he or she believed it was true. Of course, for this exception to apply, the person making the statement knows that the statement is against his or her interest (see *Roberts v. Troy,* 1985).

Rule 804. Hearsay Exceptions; Declarant Unavailable

(3) Statement against interest. A statement which was at the time of its making so far contrary to the declarant's pecuniary or proprietary interest, or so far tended to subject the declarant to civil or criminal liability, or to render invalid a claim by the declarant against another, that a reasonable person in the declarant's position would not have made the statement unless believing it to be true. A statement tending to expose the declarant to criminal liability and offered to exculpate the accused is not admissible unless corroborating circumstances clearly indicate the trustworthiness of the statement.

A major source of confusion concerning this exception lies in its relationship to the exemption for party admissions. An admission must be a statement by a party, whereas a *declaration* can be made by any unavailable witness. Also, an admission does not require that the declarant be unavailable; a declaration against interest does. Moreover, an admission need not be against one's interest (it can be *in* one's interest), but a declaration against interest is always against the declarant's interest. Finally, an admission does not need to be based on personal knowledge; however, a declaration against interest must.

Determining whether a statement is against one's interest is not always easy (see Table 13.2 for some assistance in this regard). Some statements may "on their face" seem to be against interest when in fact they are not. Assume that the statement of a declarant places him at the scene of a misdemeanor. This may seem to be against the declarant's interest, but not if the declarant is also a suspect in a more serious crime. Some statements may be against one's interest but also in one's interest at the same time. For example, if a declarant says, "I have paid half the mortgage on my house," this statement is self-serving as far as payment goes but is against the declarant's interest as to the unpaid portion of the loan.

Table 13.2   Admissions and Statements Against Interest Compared

Admission	Statement Against Interest
Can only be made by party in present case	Can be made by anyone
Declarant can be available or unavailable	Declarant must be unavailable
Is adverse to party's interest at trial	Is adverse to party's interest at or beyond trial
Is admissible against declarant or co-conspirator	Is admissible against any party

An important restriction on the declaration against interest exception arises when the confession of an unavailable third person is used to exculpate a criminal defendant. The Federal Rules require that, in this situation, additional corroboration be offered to establish innocence. Assume that at his trial for first-degree murder, Mike introduces an out-of-court statement from Henrietta, who is now unavailable, that she murdered the victim. This statement alone would not be enough for Mike to be found not guilty; additional evidence would be required. According to Rule 804(b)(3), "A statement tending to expose the declarant to criminal liability and offered to exculpate the accused is not admissible unless corroborating circumstances clearly indicate the trustworthiness of the statement."

Statements of Family History

Statements of family history are admissible if (1) the declarant is unavailable, and (2) the statement concerns the declarant's own family history (Rule 804[b][4]). "Family history" refers to the declarant's birth, adoption, marriage, ancestry, or other similar fact. For example, Susan claims that her late father Don was the son of Claude. Margie testifies that she was once told by Don that he was Claude's son. Don's statement, though hearsay, is admissible for the truth of its assertion. The rationale for this exception is reliability; one is unlikely to be mistaken about one's own history or about that of persons or families with whom one is associated.

Rule 804. Hearsay Exceptions; Declarant Unavailable

(4) Statement of personal or family history. (A) A statement concerning the declarant's own birth, adoption, marriage, divorce, legitimacy, relationship by blood, adoption, or marriage, ancestry, or other similar fact of personal or family history, even though declarant had no means of acquiring personal knowledge of the matter stated; or (B) a statement concerning the foregoing matters, and death also, of another person, if the declarant was related to the other by blood, adoption, or marriage or was so intimately associated with the other's family as to be likely to have accurate information concerning the matter declared.

Forfeiture by Wrongdoing

A party forfeits the right to exclude hearsay if the party was involved in an act that wrongfully kept the declarant from being a witness at trial (Rule 804[b][6]). In other words, if a party wrongly prevents a person from testifying by bribing, intimidation, or killing, any statement that person ever made can be introduced against the party. Assume, for example, that Jean has the "dirt" on Larry, who has been charged with multiple counts of burglary. She has told her friend Cody all the details of Larry's criminal activities. She plans to testify against Larry at his criminal trial, but Larry promptly has her killed when he learns of her intent to testify. Unfortunately for Larry, Cody can testify about everything that Jean told him. Her statements are admissible not only because she is unavailable, but because her death was a result of Larry's wrongdoing.

Rule 804. Hearsay Exceptions; Declarant Unavailable

(6) Forfeiture by wrongdoing. A statement offered against a party that has engaged or acquiesced in wrongdoing that was intended to, and did, procure the unavailability of the declarant as a witness.

Past State of Mind

Some states recognize a hearsay exception for statements of a prior mental or physical state if (1) the declarant is unavailable, and (2) the physical or mental state involved in the statement is the consequential fact it is offered to prove. This exception should not be confused with the *then-existing* mental state exception discussed in the section on unrestricted hearsay exceptions. That exception prohibited statements of *past* mental state, but when the declarant is unavailable, statements concerning his or her past state of mind are admissible. The statement must, however, be trustworthy. Note also that the Federal Rules of Evidence do not recognize this exception.

The Residual (Catch-All) Hearsay Exception

Another hearsay exception exists in the Federal Rules for statements that does not fit any of the aforementioned exceptions (see Rule 807). There are six requirements for applying the catch-all exception. The statement must (1) not be covered by one of the existing, enumerated exceptions, (2) have equivalent circumstantial guarantees of trustworthiness to the enumerated exceptions, (3) be offered as evidence of a material fact, (4) be more probative than other evidence its proponent can with reasonable diligence procure, and (5) serve the general purposes of the rules and the interests of justice. Additionally, proper advance notice and opportunity to meet must also be provided.

Assume that an investigative reporter wrote a series of articles exposing abuse of force in the local police department. The articles gave hypothetical names for the officers involved, but the stories were based on observations the writer made after having been hired to work as a janitor at the stationhouse. An alleged victim of excessive force sues the department for damages. To bolster his case, the victim seeks to introduce one of the newspaper articles, along with the notes the writer made that gave the real names of the officers involved. Assume also that (1) the writer has died of natural causes since writing the articles, (2) the articles were written only two years prior to the lawsuit (so the ancient documents exception doesn't apply), and (3) a period of several months had elapsed between the abuse of force and the reporter's note taking (so the business records exception doesn't apply). What exception, if any, applies?

Rule 807. Residual Exception

A statement not specifically covered by Rule 803 or 804 but having equivalent circumstantial guarantees of trustworthiness, is not excluded by the hearsay rule, if the court determines that (A) the statement is offered as evidence of a material fact; (B) the statement is more probative on the point for which it is offered than any other evidence which the proponent can procure through reasonable efforts; and (C) the general purposes of these rules and the interests of justice will best be served by admission of the statement into evidence. However, a statement may not be admitted under this exception unless the proponent of it makes known to the adverse party sufficiently in advance of the trial or hearing to provide the adverse party with a fair opportunity to prepare to meet it, the proponent's intention to offer the statement and the particulars of it, including the name and address of the declarant.

http://www.law.cornell.edu/rules/fre/ACRule807.htm

Rule 807, the residual exception, may apply in our example. The proponent (the plaintiff in our example) would have to give notice to the defendant of the intention to introduce the notes and article and would have to establish that they are trustworthy. With regard to trustworthiness, it is reasonable to assume that reporters have an obligation to report the truth, so their notes are probably reliable. Next, the evidence in the notes and the articles would have to be more probative in terms of revealing excessive force than other evidence that could be procured through reasonable effort. Assuming that notes and articles are all that is available, they may be admissible under the residual exception.

Hearsay Procedure

It is easy to get caught up in the complexity of hearsay definitions, exemptions, and exceptions. Hearsay, however, is subject to all the usual meta rules of evidence. First, if no objection is made, the hearsay statement may be admitted and given the same weight by the jury as testimony by an in-court witness. Hearsay, though perhaps relevant, may be excluded if its probative value is substantially outweighed by the danger of prejudice. Also, if the statement is confusing, or a waste of time, the judge has the discretion to exclude it.

When hearsay is admitted, the declarant is basically treated as a witness for the purpose of impeachment. This means that evidence of felony convictions and evidence of character can be used to impeach the declarant. Also, it means that the opposing party can call the declarant to the stand and cross examine, provided that he or she is available. Of course, the declarant can also be "rehabilitated" by the proponent.

Discussion Questions

1. What is the difference between hearsay exceptions and hearsay exemptions?
2. What is an admission by conduct?
3. Explain how a statement made by an agent, servant, or employee of a person may be exempt from the hearsay rule. What is the one qualifier that must be in place in order for the statement to be accepted by the court?
4. What is a "dying declaration"? What do the Federal Rules of Evidence say about dying declarations? What does California say?
5. Explain "present sense impressions."
6. What is the rationale for the "excited utterances" exception?

Further Reading

Choo, A. L. T. (1996). *Hearsay and Confrontation in Criminal Trials.* New York, Oxford University Press.

Coady, C. A. J. (1992). *Testimony: A Philosophical Study.* New York, Oxford University Press.

Friedman, R. D. (2002). "The Conundrum of Children, Confrontation, and Hearsay." *Law and Contemporary Problems* 65:243.

Holland, B. (2002). "Using Excited Utterances to Prosecute Domestic Violence in New York: The Door Opens Wide, or Just a Crack?" *Cardozo Women's Law Journal* 8:171.

Kirgis, P. F. (2001). "Meaning, Intention, and the Hearsay Rule." *William and Mary Law Review* 43:275.

Mueller, C. B. and L. C. Kirkpatrick. (1999). *Evidence* (2nd ed.). New York: Aspen.

Rakos, R. F. and S. Landsman. (1992). "The Hearsay Rule as the Focus of Empirical Investigation." *Minnesota Law Review.* 76:655.

Cases Cited

Anderson v. United States, 417 U.S. 211 (1974)

Doyle v. Ohio, 426 U.S. 610 (1976)

Dutton v. Evans, 400 U.S. 74 (1970)

Ferrier v. Duckworth, 902 F.2d 545 (7th Cir. 1990)

Gilbert v. California, 388 U.S. 263 (1967)

Kirby v. Illinois, 406 U.S. 682 (1972)

Mattox v. United States, 146 U.S. 140 (1892)

Nuttal v. Reading Co., 235 F.2d 546 (3rd Cir. 1956)

Roberts v. Troy, 773 F.2d 720 (6th Cir. 1985)

Tamez v. City of San Marcos, Texas, 118 F.3d 1085 (5th Cir. 1997)

United Services Auto. Assn. v. Wharton, 237 F.Supp. (W.D.N.C. 1965)

United States v. Evans, 438 F.2d 162 (D.C. Cir. 1971)

United States v. Felix-Jerez, 667 F.2d 1297 (9th Cir. 1982)

United States v. Golden, 671 F.2d 369 (10th Cir. 1982)

United States v. Hallman, 439 F.2d 603 (D.C. Cir. 1971)

United States v. Matlock, 109 F.3d 1319 (8th Cir. 1997)

United States v. Nixon, 418 U.S. 683 (1974)

United States v. Seelig, 622 F.2d 207 (6th Cir. 1980)

United States v. Simmons, 923 F.2d 934 (2nd Cir. 1991)

United States v. Sowas, 34 F.3d 447 (6th Cir. 1994)

Vicksburg & Meridian Railroad Co. v. O'Brien, 119 U.S. 99 (1886)

GLOSSARY

Accrediting—The process of attempting to support, bolster, or improve the credibility of a witness by an attorney.

Actus reus—The criminal act itself.

Administrative regulations—A form of legislation that may, under certain circumstances, have the force of law.

Admission by conduct—Not conduct, but silence serves as an admission of guilt.

Adverse testimony—Testimony that is against the defendant.

Affidavit—A sworn statement.

Affirmative defense(s)—A protection from prosecution for an offense claimed by a defendant even thought the government has met its burden of proof for each element of the crime charged.

American Law Institute (ALI)—That body that drafted the Model Code of Evidence in 1942.

Appellate jurisdiction—The power of a higher court to review the decision of a lower court.

Appointed counsel—Private attorneys who are paid by the state on a case-by-case basis to represent indigent defendants.

Arraignment—An initial hearing at which time the defendant enters a plea.

Arrest—The taking of an individual into custody.

Article Three Courts—Courts established under the authority of Article Three of the Constitution.

Ascertainable fact—A fact that can be determined by researching a source, the accuracy of which cannot be easily disputed.

Assistance of counsel—A provision of the Sixth Amendment guaranteeing defendants the right to legal representation.

Attestation—Indication that the signer examined the document after the fact and found it to be a genuine document or public record.

Attorney general—An administrator who sets prosecution priorities for deputy attorney generals.

Attorney-client privilege—A testimonial privilege intended to encourage trust and confidentiality in the relationship between the individual and legal counsel.

Authentication—The introduction of evidence sufficient to sustain a finding that an object or document is what it is claimed to be.

Beneficial testimony—Testimony that is for the defendant.

Best evidence rule—A rule of preference holding that if an original writing is available, it should be used instead of a copy.

Bias—Any motive for the witness to falsify his or her testimony or to testify in an untruthful fashion so as to benefit or harm the defendant.

Bill of Rights—The primary source of individual rights under the Constitution.

Bills of attainder—Legislation imposing punishment without trial.

Blank pad rule—An assumption that the court and the jury in a criminal case know nothing about the dispute between the two parties involved.

Booking—An administrative procedure that involves entering of the suspect's name, arrest time, and offense charged into the police blotter and taking fingerprints and photographs.

Burden of production—The obligation placed on one side in a trial to produce evidence, to make a prima facie showing on a particular issue; also called *burden of going forward*.

Burden of proof—The obligation placed on the prosecution to convince a judge or jury regarding a particular issue.

Business records exception—Statements recorded as a matter of routine in the records of a regularly conducted business (or businesslike) activity are admissible, without regard to the availability of the declarant.

Castle doctrine—Individuals threatened in their own homes are not required to retreat before resorting to force in order to protect themselves.

Centrality theory—Idea that hearsay should be permissible insofar as it corroborates or serves as circumstantial proof of guilt, but not as direct and critical evidence.

Challenged for cause—The removal of a juror from the jury pool based upon some articulable reason.

Change of venue—A request by the defendant to have his or her trial take place in a different location.

Circuit courts—also referred to as courts of appeal in the federal system; There are 13 circuits in the federal judiciary.

Circumstantial evidence—testimony not based on actual personal knowledge or observation of the facts in controversy, but of other facts from which deductions are drawn.

Clear and convincing evidence—This standard is used in some civil and criminal trials and means that the facts asserted are quite likely true.

This burden lies somewhere between preponderance of the evidence and reasonable doubt.

Clergy-penitent privilege—A testimonial privilege based in common law, recognizing the notion that communications between the individual and his or her spiritual advisor should be treated as confidential.

Closing arguments—An opportunity for each side to summarize its case before the judge or jury.

Code of Hammurabi—The first known written legal code, which expressed a retribution-oriented "eye for an eye" philosophy.

Collective facts doctrine—A doctrine that allows witnesses to offer an opinion when recitation of factual perceptions would not convey to the jury what the witness heard or observed.

Common knowledge—A fact is considered as such if it is information that is generally known by informed individuals within the jurisdiction of the trial court.

Common law—The body of uncodified, judge-made law that developed in England under King Henry II.

Competency—The presence of particular characteristics and the absence of particular disabilities that render the witness legally qualified to testify in court.

Competent evidence—Evidence that is in a form the jury is permitted to hear or see; evidence not gathered illegally.

Complaint—A sworn statement alleging the commission of a criminal offense.

Compulsory process clause—Sixth Amendment provision providing that individuals can be compelled to serve as witnesses.

Conclusive presumption—A presumption that cannot be challenged by either the prosecution or the defense.

Conditional relevance—An item, object, or issue that requires the jury to determine if a given fact is important or has been proven.

Confrontation clause—A provision of the Sixth Amendment guaranteeing defendants the right to be confronted by their accusers and witnesses.

Consent—Equates to informed permission in the legal context.

Constitution—A document that creates a government.

Contradictory testimony—information presented to the court that does not agree with that previously submitted for consideration.

Corroborative evidence—Evidence in support of another witness's testimony.

Court actors—Judges, prosecutors, and defense attorneys.

Court of last resort—Another term for the Supreme Court or final arbiter of a case.

Credibility—The believability of the witness.

Crime fraud exception—An important limitation on the attorney-client privilege that does not cover criminal evidence turned over to the attorney by a client. Thus, if a client gives an attorney incriminating evidence, the privilege does not apply.

Cross examination—Examination conducted by a party other than the party who called the witness.

Cruel and unusual punishment—A provision of the Eighth Amendment that limits the type and form of punishment imposed by a state after conviction of a crime; it prohibits torture, as well as punishment that is disproportionate to the offense.

Cumulative evidence—Evidence that repeats what is already known.

***Daubert* test**—A two-pronged test used to determine whether the field of the expert witness has reached the level of "scientific knowledge."

Dead man's statutes—Statutes that prohibit witnesses from testifying about transactions with a person involved in a case if the person died prior to the trial.

Declarant—Anyone who makes a statement.

Declaration—A sworn written statement.

Declarations against interest—Statements made by an unavailable person (whether or not a party to the current proceedings) that, at the time made, would have been harmful to some interest of the declarant.

Defendant's privilege—Refers to the standing principle that the prosecution is barred from calling the defendant as a witness or commenting adversely on the defendant's decision not to testify.

Defense attorneys—Lawyers who represent their client as effectively as possible while acting within the rules of the court.

Defunct or infirm declarants—Witnesses who are unable to appear due to death, illness, or infirmity.

Demonstrative evidence—Evidence intended to demonstrate a certain point.

Demonstrative evidence—Using physical evidence (such as a crime scene reconstruction) to demonstrate a point.

Depositions—Sworn testimony given prior to trial.

Derivative use immunity—A type of immunity in which the state cannot use any evidence derived from the immunized testimony against the witness.

Direct appeal—The opportunity, generally created by state law or constitution, for convicted defendants to have their case heard, either in whole or part, by a court of higher authority.

Direct evidence—Evidence in the form of testimony from a witness who actually saw, heard or touched the subject of interrogation.

Direct examination—The line of questioning put to a witness by the side calling the witness.

Discrediting—The prosecution's or the defense's challenging of a witness's credibility.

Distant declarants—Declarants who are absent, beyond subpoena, and undeposable.

District courts—Courts that have original jurisdiction over both civil and criminal cases involving federal statutes.

Diversity of citizenship—A situation in which the opposing parties in a case are from different states.

Doctor-patient privilege—A testimonial privilege intended to encourage trust and confidentiality in the relationship between and individual and doctor.

Documentary evidence—Documents and writings used as evidence.

Documents affecting property interest—Legal records, such as car titles, mortgage papers, wills, and so forth, that are used to establish evidence of a property interest based upon their official nature and presumed relevance.

Double jeopardy—A constitutional provision prohibiting the state from prosecuting the defendant again for the same act.

Dual sovereignty doctrine—The notion that a person can be prosecuted in both federal and state courts for the same offense or in multiple state courts for the same offense.

Due process—The notion that a state or government must follow certain procedures, designed to protect individual rights, before depriving an individual of his or her liberty or property.

Duplicate—A counterpart produced by the same impression as the original, or from the same matrix, or by means of photography, including enlargements and miniatures, or by mechanical or electronic rerecording, or by chemical reproduction, or by other equivalent technique that accurately reproduces the original.

Duress—When the defendant was forced to commit the crime in question.

Durham test—The defendant is not criminally responsible if his act was "the product of mental disease or defect."

Dying declaration—At common law, a dying declaration of a homicide victim was admissible against the murderer in a criminal prosecution. The rationale for the present-day version of this exception is reliability, presumably because there is no motive to lie right before one is about to die.

Eighth Amendment—Constitutional amendment that prohibits excessive bail, and cruel and unusual punishment.

En banc—A situation in which appeals court justices sit as a collective group in order to clear up any conflicting decisions involving the same legal issue.

Equal protection clause—Rule that precludes states or governments from making unequal, arbitrary distinctions between people. It does not ban reasonable classifications, but it does prohibit classifications that are either without reason or based on race or gender.

Establishment clause—The portion of the First Amendment that created what the U.S. Supreme Court has referred to as a "wall of separation between church and state."

Evidence—The information that is presented trial that allows a jury to render verdict.

Evidence code—A compilation of the common law evidence rules, written down (or codified) by the legislature.

Evidence law—The set of rules that govern what the jury can hear (and see) during a trial. These rules place limits on the type of testimony that may be presented as well as the forms of physical evidence that may be admitted.

Ex post facto law—Legislation making prior conduct criminal.

Excessive bail—A bail amount that is higher than necessary to ensure the presence of the defendant at trial.

Excited utterance—A verbal statement made due to the stress of a situation.

Excuse defense—Protection to prosecution raised by a defendant who admits to wrongdoing, but argues that she or he is not responsible under the circumstances.

Execution of public duties—A defense to prosecution extended to officials (such as police officers) who, by necessity of their job, may have to break the law in order to accomplish some other lawful objective (i.e., exceeding the speed limit to pursue a fleeing felon).

Expert witness—A witness who is qualified to help the jury understand the evidence or determine a fact in issue by virtue of special knowledge, skill, experience, training, or education.

Faulty memory—Individuals may not clearly or immediately recall events of the past.

Federal Rules of Evidence (FRE)—The most widely known evidence code used by federal courts.

Fifth Amendment—Constitutional amendment that provides a number of protections for individual citizens, including the right to an indictment by a grand jury, freedom from double jeopardy, the right to due process and just compensation, and the privilege against self-incrimination.

First Amendment—Constitutional amendment that establishes the freedom of religion, freedom of speech, freedom of the press, and freedom of assembly.

Fleeing felon doctrine—A common law doctrine allowing the police to use deadly force to prevent escape; struck down by the U.S. Supreme Court in *Tennessee v. Garner.*

Forfeiture by wrongdoing—A party forfeits the right to exclude hearsay if he or she was involved in an act that wrongfully kept the declarant from being a witness at trial.

Forgetful declarants—This person must actually testify that he or she cannot remember the facts of his or her out-of-court statement.

Former testimony exception—When a person is unavailable as a witness, his or her previous testimony can be admitted into evidence in the present trial subject to the following restrictions: (1) it was made under oath and subject to direct or cross examination, and (2) the former testimony was given in a prior trial, deposition, or similar judicial hearing.

Fourteenth Amendment—Constitutional amendment that prohibits states from denying citizens due process of law or equal protection of the laws.

Fourth Amendment—Constitutional amendment that prohibits unreasonable searches and seizures.

Freedom of Information Act—Act granting the public access to most, but not all, government documents.

Frye **test**—A test to determine if expert testimony is based on scientific knowledge that is generally accepted and reliable in the relevant field.

Fundamental rights—Those freedoms essential to the concept of ordered liberty rights without which neither liberty nor justice would exist.

General jurisdiction—The authority of a court to hear a variety of cases; the court is not limited to only one type of case.

Geographic jurisdiction—The authority of courts to hear cases that arise within specific geographic boundaries (such as a city, county, state, or country).

Grand jury—An investigative body that determines whether adequate evidence exists to support a criminal complaint.

Habeas corpus—"You have the body"; either produce the person named in the writ or release that person from custody.

Habits of guilt—guilt can be demonstrated in several ways, including flight, concealing or destroying evidence, possession of the fruits of crime, sudden wealth, and threats against witnesses.

Hearsay—An out-of-court statement, made by a speaker other than the in-court witness, offered in evidence to prove the truth of the matter asserted.

Hierarchical jurisdiction—The division of responsibilities and functions among the various courts.

Holder of the privilege—The person who has the right to keep certain information from being revealed.

Hostile witness—A witness who is either "hostile in fact" (he or she is resistant or uncooperative) or "hostile in law" (he or she identifies with an adverse party).

Impartial jury—A jury, selected from the community where the crime occurred, that is not predisposed to believe the defendant is guilty.

Impeachment—The formal term for attacking a witness's credibility.

In camera—A private hearing; often held in the judge's chambers.

Incompetent declarants—If a declarant is not competent with regard to an out-of-court statement, he or she will be considered unavailable.

Incorporation—The process by which the Supreme Court has applied provisions of the Bill of Rights to the states via the Fourteenth Amendment's due process and equal protection clauses.

Indictment—A finding issued by a grand jury indicating that adequate evidence exists to support a criminal complaint.

Indisputable fact—A fact that speaks for itself and requires virtually no interpretation or debate as to its truthfulness.

Individual rights—Various provisions limiting the ability of the government to intrude into a person's private life.

Inference—A logical deduction or conclusion from an established fact.

Informant's privilege—Permits law enforcement agencies to refuse to disclose the identity of a confidential source in criminal investigations.

Information—A substitute for an indictment, filed directly with the court by the prosecutor.

Initial appeal—The first level of review by a court of higher authority arising from the previous decision of a lower court.

Insanity—A legal term that describes mental illness. To be found insane, defendants must prove that they have a mental illness and that they were unaware of either the consequences of their actions or that they did not know right from wrong.

Insanity Defense Reform Act of 1984—Legislation that shifted the burden of proof from requiring the government having to prove sanity beyond a reasonable doubt to requiring the defense to prove insanity by clear and convincing evidence (a tougher standard than the preponderance of the evidence standard usually applied to affirmative defenses).

Inscribed chattels—Marks of affiliation that include logos, badges, crests, and so on.

Intentional/nonliteral statement—A statement made intentionally but with a literal meaning that is opposite of the content of the statement.

Intermediate scrutiny—A legal standard that requires the state to prove (1) that the law or regulation furthers an important state interest, and (2) that the law is substantially related to the achievement of that interest.

Intoxication defense—Voluntary intoxication is not a valid defense to prosecution. Involuntary intoxication, however, may be used as a defense if the individual can prove that he or she was unaware of being drugged.

Irresistible impulse test—Test used when a defendant is unable to control his or her conduct because he or she suffers from a mental disease; this test holds that the defendant is not responsible if a mental disease kept him or her from controlling his or her conduct, even if the person knows the conduct is wrong.

Judge—A referee responsible for enforcing court rules, instructing the jury on the law, ruling on the admissibility of evidence, and determining the law.

Judicial notice—A procedure that courts use to determine the facts of a case without having to follow the normal rules of evidence.

Judicial notice of adjudicative facts—Matters of general knowledge not otherwise connected to statutes, constitutions, administrative rules, or other sources of law.

Judicial notice of law—A court's acceptance of what is written in statutes, constitutional provisions, and court cases.

Judicial notice of legislative facts—Facts that courts rely on when interpreting statutes, constitutional provisions, and the like.

Judicial review—The power of the court, specifically judges, to examine a law and determine whether it is constitutional.

Judiciary Act of 1789—The act that established Supreme Court membership at six justices and that created three federal circuit courts and thirteen district courts, one in each of the original states.

Jurisdiction—The legal authority of a court to hear a case.

Jury selection—The process of drawing eligible members of the community who are called at random, usually from voting records or automobile registration records, for purposes of hearing evidence testimony and determining guilt or innocence through a process of questioning by the judge and attorneys to determine whether there is any bias, prejudice, or interest that would prevent the potential juror from being impartiality.

Justification defense—A protection from prosecution raised by a defendant who admits to wrongdoing, but explains that guilt is mitigated by other factors (such as self-defense).

Lay opinion—Evidence given by a witness who has not been presented as and is not qualified to be an expert.

Lay witness—An ordinary person who has personal knowledge about the facts of the case at hand.

Leading question—A question that suggests to the witness the answer that the examining party desires.

Legally operative conduct—Words that affect the legal relationship of the parties, especially words in a contract.

Legislation—Rules enacted by the legislature under the authority granted it by a constitution.

Limited jurisdiction—The authority of a court to hear only a particular type of case, such as traffic court, juvenile court, or probate court.

M'Naghten test—Test that focuses on the defendant's intellectual capacity to know what he or she is doing and to distinguish right from wrong. It is a two-prong test: (1) the defendant must suffer from a disease or defect of the mind; and (2) this disease must cause the defendant either to not know the nature and quality of the criminal act or to not know right from wrong.

Magistrate judges—Judges who preside over lower-level courts and conduct preliminary proceedings in cases before the district court and issue warrants.

Marital communications privilege—Provision that protects confidential marital communications from disclosure.

Marital testimony privilege—The right of one spouse to refuse to testify against the other.

Material evidence—Evidence that significantly affects the matter at issue in a case.

Mens rea—Criminal intent.

Mental incapacity—A valid basis for challenging witness competency that focuses on the unique abilities of each individual to determine ability for offering truthful and meaningful testimony.

Mistake of fact—A defense to prosecution where the individual commits a violation based on reasonable and honest misinterpretation of facts then available.

Mistake of law—A defense to prosecution in which the individual undertakes reasonable efforts to learn the law, but remains unaware that he or she has violated some obscure, unusual law.

Mistrial—The failure of a jury to reach a unanimous verdict.

Model Code of Evidence—A set of evidence rules promulgated by the American Law Institute in 1942.

Modus operandi—Method of operation; the specific way that the crime was committed.

Motive—The reason that a crime was committed.

Narrative ambiguity—A risk of hearsay evidence based on the fact that people may misunderstand or misinterpret conversations.

News reporter source privilege—The right of news reporters to refuse to reveal their sources of information.

Ninth Amendment—Constitutional amendment stating that the listing of some rights in the Constitution should not be construed as a listing of *all* the rights retained by individual citizens.

No bill—A finding issued by a grand jury indicating that inadequate evidence exists to support a criminal complaint.

Notice of charges—A provision of the Sixth Amendment requiring that defendants be informed of the charges against them.

Official/pubic records exception—A writing, statement, report, data compilation, or other record by a government agency (known as either "official" or "public") is admissible if it records acts of the agency, matters the agency is required to observe and report, and/or factual findings of investigations.

Opening statements—Initial oral arguments offered by each side in a criminal proceeding.

Opinion evidence—Evidence of what the witness thinks, believes, or infers in regard to facts in dispute, as distinguished from his or her personal knowledge of the facts themselves.

Opinion rule—The concept that what is presented to the jury should be the most concrete form of evidence possible. If "facts" are not available, opinion evidence can suffice.

Opinion testimony—As defined in *Black's Law Dictionary*, "evidence of what the witness thinks, believes, or infers in regard to facts in dispute, as distinguished from his personal knowledge of the facts themselves." Refers to opinions offered by in-court witnesses and is to be distinguished from opinions offered by people outside of a courtroom setting.

Original—The writing itself or recording itself or any counterpart intended to have the same effect by a person executing or issuing it.

Original jurisdiction—The power of the court to hear a case initially; also refers to the place where a trial takes place.

Parens partiae doctrine—Refers to the role of the state as guardian of persons under legal disability, particularly children.

Particularity requirement—The Fourth Amendment requirement that a warrant particularly describe the place to be searched and the persons or things to be seized in response to the British practice in colonial times of issuing general warrants. General warrants allowed British customs inspectors to search for virtually anything, anywhere, at any time.

Past recollection recorded—A written document that becomes a substitute for the witnesses testimony.

Penal code—The criminal law.

Peremptory challenge—A objection to the selection of a juror for which no reason must be given.

Perjury—Lying while under oath.

Personal jurisdiction—The authority of a court over a person.

Personal knowledge rule—The concept that witnesses should, in general, state facts based on personal knowledge rather than their inferences or conclusions drawn from such facts.

Plea—A response by the defendant of his or her counsel to criminal charges: not guilty, guilty, or no contest.

Precedent—Previous decisions of another court or judge that are relied on as a justification for present or future decisions.

Prejudice—Any motive for the witness to falsify his or her testimony or to testify in an untruthful fashion so as to benefit or harm the defendant.

Preliminary hearing—A hearing that is conducted for purposes of determining whether or not a person who has been charged with a crime should be held over for trial.

Preponderance of the evidence—The standard of proof used in civil trials requiring that the facts asserted are more probably true than false.

Present memory revived—Allowing a witness to refresh his or her memory by reviewing certain documents.

Present sense impressions—Statement made regarding action observed; it must be contemporaneous to the action.

Presentence investigation/report—A report compiled by a court-appointed official containing information regarding a defendant's background, generally for sentencing purposes.

Presumption—A procedural device that not only permits an inference of the presumed fact but also shifts to the opposing party the burden of producing evidence to disprove the presumed fact.

Presumption against suicide—The presumption that a dead person did not die by his or her own hand.

Presumption of death upon unexplained absence—A presumption that someone is dead after he or she has been missing for several years.

Presumption of fact—A presumption that does not require the jury to draw an inference or deduction regarding evidence or testimony.

Presumption of innocence—The legal requirement that all defendants are presumed innocent until proven guilty.

Presumption of law—A presumption of law requiring that an inference or deduction be drawn by the jury regarding evidence or testimony.

Presumption of regularity of official acts—The assumption that public officials going about their official duties do so in good faith.

Presumption of sanity—The presumption that every person tried in a criminal case is of sound mind until evidence to the contrary is presented.

Presumption that young people are not capable of crime—The legal notion that some states that children under a certain age are incapable of committing crime.

Pretrial motions—A legal request filed before a case begins regarding the disclosure, or suppression, of evidence.

Prima facie showing—Latin for "on its face," referring to a lawsuit or criminal prosecution in which the prosecution's evidence is sufficient to prove the case unless there is substantial contradictory evidence presented at trial.

Prior statement of identification—Out-of-court statements identifying a person after the declarant has seen the person.

Privilege—A right held by a person who was a party to a confidential relationship, the sanctity of which the law values above even the search for truth.

Privileged communication—Certain communications that are protected from being revealed in court.

Probable cause—Facts or circumstances that would lead a reasonable and prudent person to believe that a crime has been or is being committed.

Procedural rights theory—Idea that the state should gather and present as much live testimony as possible.

Production theory—Idea that the confrontation clause requires the prosecutor to produce the "speaker" at trial whenever possible.

Profile—Compilations of common characteristics shared by certain types of offenders.

Proof beyond a reasonable doubt—The standard used in criminal trials holding that the facts asserted are highly probable; a difficult burden to meet.

Proponent procurement proviso—States that a declarant is unavailable if the grounds for the declarant's unavailability were caused by the proponent of the declarant's statement, and the causative act was intended to prevent the declarant from testifying.

Prosecutors—Attorneys responsible for prosecuting cases on behalf of the state.

Public defenders—Attorneys hired by the state to work for defendants who cannot afford to have their own lawyer.

Public trial—A provision of the Sixth Amendment, prohibiting secret trials.

Rational basis review—A method of determining whether a state may abridge someone's fundamental rights; a lesser standard of proof is required than with strict scrutiny, and the courts generally find in favor of the state.

Real/physical evidence—Actual tangible items that can be displayed.

Rebuttable presumption—Presumption for which the party against whom it operates may introduce evidence to disprove the presumption.

Recross examination—The last stage in witness questioning; it includes any subsequent examination of a witness by a party who has previously cross examined the witness.

Redirect examination—Examination conducted by the party calling the witness *after* cross examination; redirect examination is subsequent to the first cross examination.

Rehabilitation—The act of introducing evidence or calling additional witnesses to reinstate the credibility of a witness who has been impeached.

Relevance—Logical relationship between evidence and a fact in issue or to be established.

Relevant evidence—Evidence that pertains to the matter at hand and has some bearing on the trial.

Reliability—Producing consistent results.

Reliability theory—The idea that hearsay is permissible as long as it is reliable.

Reputation—What people think about a person and his or her character.

Retained counsel—Attorney selected and paid by the defendant.

Retreat doctrine—A person must retreat rather than use deadly force if it is possible to do so without endangering the retreating party.

Risk of uncertainty—A risk of hearsay evidence based on the fact that unchecked testimonial evidence can be subject to distortion where only one side is presented.

Roman Twelve Tables—The first entirely secular written legal code promulgated around 450 B.C.

Rule of exclusion—A common law principle stipulating that opinions be excluded from evidence because they usurp the role of the jury to draw its own inferences from the facts.

Rule of four—The idea that in order for the Supreme Court to accept a case, four or more justices must vote to accept it.

Scope of direct rule—Cross examination is limited to matters covered on direct examination. Inquiries into the credibility of the witness are also permissible. Together, these two restrictions constitute the "scope of direct" rule.

Second Amendment—Constitutional amendment that provides citizens with the right to "keep and bear arms," stating that this right shall not be "infringed."

Secondary evidence—Any evidence of the contents of a writing other than the original.

Selective incorporation—The process of how some, but not all, of the Bill of Rights were made applicable to the states through the due process clause of the Fourteenth Amendment.

Self-defense—A defense to prosecution raised when the defendant has committed a crime through the use of force to repel an imminent, unprovoked attack that would have caused him or her serious injury. Self-defense may also apply to the defense of others or of property.

Self-authenticating document—The Federal Rules of Evidence (Rule 902) create a category of self-authenticating documents. Such documents require no extrinsic evidence, such as witness testimony, as to their authenticity. They are deemed authentic on their face, or at first glance.

Sentence—The sanction imposed on a defendant upon conviction for a criminal offense.

Seventh Amendment—Constitutional amendment that provides for the right to a trial by jury in federal civil trials.

Silent hound exception—Rule 803(7) and 803(10) are known collectively as the silent hound exception. They are the mirror images of the business records and official records exceptions, respectively. Rule 803(7) says that the *absence* of records kept in accordance with the business records exception is admissible to prove the nonoccurrence or nonexistence of the matter. Similarly, rule 803(10) says that *absence* of records kept in accordance with the official records exception is admissible to prove the nonoccurrence or nonexistence of the matter.

Sixth Amendment—Constitutional amendment that provides certain rights associated with the criminal trial including (1) the right to a speedy trial, (2) the right to a public trial, (3) the right to a trial by an impartial jury, (4) the right to notice of the charges against oneself, (5) the right to representation by counsel, and (6) the right to confront the witnesses against oneself.

Specific question—A question that does not call for a narrative response.

Speedy trial—The idea that the defendant must be brought to trial without "unnecessary delay."

Spousal privilege—Privilege granted to a spouse to not give adverse testimony against a marital partner.

Standards of review—The three levels of review used by courts in cases where a citizen alleges an infringement on their constitutional rights. These levels include (1) strict scrutiny, (2) intermediate scrutiny or (3) rational basis review. The appropriate level of review depends on whether the right involved has been deemed "fundamental" or whether a suspect classification is involved.

Stare decisis—Latin term for "let the decision stand."

State secrets privilege—This privilege originally allowed the government to prevent the disclosure of military and diplomatic secrets.

Statement—A verbal assertion or a nonverbal act intended to be an assertion.

Statements made by a party opponent's co-conspirator—This hearsay exemption is frequently raised in criminal trials. However, two additional requirements must be satisfied for a co-conspirator's statement to be exempt from the hearsay rule. Not only must the statement be made by a co-conspirator, it also must be made: (1) during the conspiracy, and (2) in furtherance of the conspiracy

Statistics—The use of mathematics and probability for the purpose of drawing inferences.

Statute—A law enacted by the legislature or other government body.

Stipulations—Agreements between opposing attorneys about some important fact.

Strict scrutiny—A method of determining whether a state may abridge someone's fundamental rights; a higher standard of proof is required than with rational basis review, and the courts generally find in favor of the individual.

Subject matter jurisdiction—Authority conferred on a court to hear a particular type of case.

Subpoena—A court document requiring the presence of a particular witness.

Subpoena duces tecum—An official court document requiring that a witness bring certain documents or material to court.

Substantial capacity test—Test that defines insanity as lacking substantial capacity to either control his or her conduct or appreciate the wrongfulness of his or her conduct.

Substantive objection—Objections based on particular rules of evidence.

Supreme Court—The final arbiter of constitutional and legal matters.

Suspect classification—Classifications based on race or gender.

Sustained objection—An objection that is upheld by the court/judge.

Syndrome—A pattern of behavior or mental attitude exhibited by a particular person.

Tacit judicial notice—Form of judicial notice in which the judge does not provide any statement to the court that judicial notice is being taken regarding a certain fact.

Tenth Amendment—Constitutional amendment providing that the rights not delegated to the federal government by the Constitution are reserved for the states or individual citizens.

Testimonial evidence—Evidence that is relevant provided that four conditions are satisfied: (1) the witness accurately perceived the event he or she is testifying about, (2) the witness now correctly recalls that perception, (3) the witness now wishes to communicate that recollection accurately and honestly; and, (4) the witness has the verbal skills to effectively narrate the events he or she is testifying about.

Testimonial privilege—Privilege invoked when a witness is either shielded or barred from testifying.

Testimony—Oral or verbal description of a witness's present recollection of some past event or set of facts.

Then-existing mental, emotional, or physical condition exception—A statement of the declarant's then-existing state of mind is admissible to prove that state of mind regardless of whether the declarant is now available (rule 803[3]). In other words, statements that describe the declarant's mental, emotional, or physical condition at the time of the statement are admissible.

Third Amendment—Constitutional amendment that prohibits the quartering of soldiers in private homes against the wishes of the owner at any time.

Thirteenth Amendment—Constitutional amendment prohibiting slavery.

Total incorporation—Applying the entire Bill of Rights to the states.

Total incorporation plus—Applying the entire Bill of Rights as well as other unspecified rights to the states.

Transactional immunity—Extending immunity to matters discussed far beyond the scope of the questions asked.

Trial courts—Judicial bodies that conduct initial trials.

Trial de novo—An appeal for a new trial in the court of original jurisdiction requested by the losing party of a case.

True bill—An indictment or charge issued by a grand jury.

True man doctrine—A philosophy of self-defense which centers upon the notion that an at-risk individual is not required to retreat before defending her/himself.

Truth of the matter asserted—When a statement is "offered in evidence to prove the truth of the matter asserted," the in-court witness is "repeating" what another person said for the purpose of supporting his or her position.

Ultimate issue rule—A rule that prohibited experts from expressing opinions on final issues of which the judge or jury was charged with deciding.

Uniform Judicial Notice of Foreign Law Act—An act requiring that every court in a specific state give notice of the common law or statutes of every other jurisdiction in the United States.

Use immunity—Immunity in which anything the witness says on the stand cannot be used against him or her in a criminal proceeding.

Validity—A technique is valid if it actually measures what it purports to measure.

Venue—Geographic jurisdiction.

Verdict—A pronouncement of guilt or innocence.

Voir dire—A questioning process used with either jurors or expert witnesses.

Vulnerable declarants—Refers to those witnesses who would likely suffer severe harm or trauma from testifying.

Waiver—A privilege may be relinquished by its holder, expressly or by implication, intentionally or inadvertently. Failing to assert a privilege when the holder is able to do so constitutes a waiver of the privilege.

Witness—A person who has knowledge about the facts of a case.

Witness exclusion—At the request of a party the court shall order witnesses excluded so that they cannot hear the testimony of other witnesses, and may make the order of its own motion.

Witness sequestration—The process of separating witnesses while they are outside the courtroom. Sequestration is sometimes done to discourage witnesses from speaking to one another and unduly influencing one another's testimony.

Writ of certiorari—An order issued by the Supreme Court to a lower court to send the record of a case up to the Supreme Court.

Writing—Every means of recording on any tangible thing in any form of communication or representation.